Please return or renew by
latest date below

LOANS MAY BE RENEWED BY PHONE
648-5710

THE JOHN HARVARD LIBRARY

Bernard Bailyn
Editor-in-Chief

THE JOHN HARVARD LIBRARY

NEW TRAVELS IN THE UNITED STATES OF AMERICA

1788

By

J. P. BRISSOT DE WARVILLE

Translated by Mara Soceanu Vamos
and Durand Echeverria

Edited by Durand Echeverria

THE BELKNAP PRESS OF
HARVARD UNIVERSITY PRESS
Cambridge, Massachusetts
1964

E
164
B89
1964

CONTENTS

NEW TRAVELS IN THE UNITED STATES
OF AMERICA, 1788

CONTENTS

CONTENTS

INTRODUCTION

When in 1791 Brissot de Warville published his *Nouveau Voyage dans les Etats-Unis* he had already lived through two years of intense political activity as a prominent member of the Paris Commune and the publisher of the revolutionary newspaper, the *Patriote Français*. Ahead still lay his two culminating years of national leadership as the chief of the Girondin Party, to end in his dramatic fall from power in June 1793 and his death on the guillotine November 1 of the same year. It is therefore not surprising that this book, composed as it was in spare moments during the violence of the French Revolution, bears the sharp imprint of these years of stress. It is the account of the six-months trip Brissot had taken to the United States three years before, in 1788, but it is also a document pertinent to the history of European thought and of the French Revolution.

In the broadest frame of reference, this is a book concerned with the relationship between Europe and a European colony. There seems to be a law which dictates that unless colonies are territorially contiguous, the ties of political and economic union with the mother country tend either to break or gradually weaken as the colony matures, but that the sense of cultural community between the old and the new societies may persist and even strengthen. It is obvious that ex-colonies continue to need the sustenance of new ideas, new discoveries, and new artistic inspiration, but it is less easy to understand why the mother country, or, as in the case of Western Europe as a whole, the mother civilization, strives to keep her independent offspring within her own area of cultural relevance, with an instinct that one is tempted to call indeed "maternal."

This "cultural maternalism" was particularly evident in European attitudes toward the United States both before and after their independence. Not only England but the Continental nations as well from the first half of the eighteenth century became increasingly curious about the nature of American society and anxious to read into it meanings which would demonstrate a kind of transatlantic community of interests and prove the pertinence of American experiences to European problems. This tendency was most marked in France; and, though there were those like Joseph de Maistre who wished to shrug off America as an irrelevant monstrosity, a succession of important writings, beginning with Voltaire's *Lettres philosophiques* and culminating in Tocqueville's *De la Démocratie en Amérique,* saw in America the image of Europe's best hope for the future—or, occasionally, the portent of Western degeneration.

It is in this literary tradition that Brissot's *New Travels* forms a significant chapter. This is of course a book about the United States, but it is essentially a European book, deeply concerned with European problems and interested in America because America is seen as an integral and peculiarly significant part of Western European society.

The word *New* in the title has important connotations, for Brissot meant more than that this was to be merely another addition to the stock of French books on the United States which had been accumulating since 1776. What he meant was that to the new France of the Revolution the American experiment now had a new meaning. The first reports of American revolt against British "tyranny" had, as the Count de Ségur wrote, "electrified everyone." The verb, with its Franklinian overtones, was peculiarly apt, and from 1776 to about 1790 a powerful current of pro-Americanism, which expressed itself in what has been called the American Dream, electrified all classes of the French nation. This phenomenon is easily explained. As France approached the crisis of revolution the antimonarchical opposition, both democratic and aristocratic, found in America a most convenient and persuasive proving ground to demonstrate the practicality of all the doctrines and reforms it was preaching.

But after the actual achievement of a republican, libertarian, and democratic revolution in France the American example quickly lost its polemic value, and the political success of the United States began to appear not only irrelevant but even possibly embarrassing.

It was precisely this reaction which Brissot wished to counter. His argument was that after having inspired France to revolt against monarchical absolutism and aristocratic corporatism, the United States now had even more valuable lessons to give in the organization of the modern, liberal, and democratic state. In his Preface he wrote, "A book of travels will undoubtedly seem at first glance quite irrelevant to the problems France faces today." But, he insisted, this was not true. The United States had taken on a new significance, and therefore this was to be a new—that is, a different—kind of *Travels*. It was not to be another eulogy of the brave *insurgens américains* in revolt against despotism. "We too have won our liberty," he wrote. "We have, therefore, no need to learn from Americans how to attain this blessing. But we do have to learn from them the secret of preserving it." The lessons of the new American Constitution were as pertinent in 1791 as the lessons of Valley Forge and Saratoga had been in 1778.

Of course, these lessons were those which Brissot chose to read into the American example. This is an extremely tendentious, partisan, and ideological piece of writing. It is Brissotin propaganda produced in the heat of political conflict. "I should be the first to reproach myself for the time I have spent preparing these pages for publication," he said, "if I did not believe they will constitute a work not only useful but even necessary for the success of our revolution."

This account of America in 1788 is, therefore, far from a piece of objective reporting. We have called it a tendentious book. But tendentiousness has certain advantages. Tocqueville was also tendentious. If one can read Brissot with a critical and sympathetic mind one can learn much from him, about both the United States and France.

In order to appreciate Brissot's interpretation of the United States it is necessary not only to realize that he wrote the book for revolutionary purposes and in the midst of a revolution, but also that when he landed in Boston on July 24, 1788, he arrived equipped with a full set of preconceptions which were fairly typical of the liberals of his generation, but to which his personality gave peculiar and individual patterns and qualities.

Jacques Pierre Brissot,[1] born in Chartres in 1754, was a member of the lower bourgeoisie (his father was a prosperous restaurant keeper), and though his political activities kept him from making much money, he absorbed from his class heritage a natural respect for material wealth and the virtues of capitalism. After a conventional classical education, which did not prevent him from discovering at an early age the *Philosophes,* he began the study of law, and in 1774 he went to Paris to serve as a clerk in a law office. But

[1] In his youth Brissot added to his surname the aristocratic appelation "de Warville," an anglicized form of Ouarville, a little village in which his father owned some property, and he was so called throughout nearly all of his life, though by 1791 he was finding the particle politically embarrassing.

he soon grew dissatisfied with this profession and drifted into the career of journalist and professional writer which he was to follow until the Revolution.

It was inevitable that Brissot should become interested in the United States at the start of his literary activities. Franklin had arrived in Paris in December 1776 and had quickly become a popular and well-known figure in Paris. The newspapers were full of news of the American Revolution, and everyone was talking about the brave Americans and their fight for liberty. Brissot's *Testament politique de l'Angleterre* (1778), a satirical attack on the British cabinet, was his first work in support of the American cause. Its success gained him the position of editor of the French edition of the *Courrier de l'Europe,* which gave fuller coverage to American news than any Continental newspaper of the time. After the war Brissot's interest in the United States continued. The "real purpose" of his ten-volume *Bibliothèque philosophique du législateur* (1782–1785), he later wrote, "was to make generally known the principles of Liberty as practiced in England and America," [2] and his *Philadelphien à Genève* (1783) identified the *Représentants,* the popular party in Geneva which had attempted a democratic revolt in 1782, with the Americans as champions of the principle of popular sovereignty. But until 1784 his interest in the United States remained secondary; his attention was directed mainly toward the problem of earning a living and his energy was absorbed by his unsuccessful efforts to establish in England his *Lycée de Londres,* an ambitious project which was to comprise a "philosophic club" of artists and writers, an athenaeum for public lectures, and a monthly publication, the *Journal du Lycée de Londres.*

In May 1784 he returned to Paris to attempt to raise funds for his hard-pressed *Lycée* and was imprisoned for two months in the Bastille on a *lettre de cachet* issued on false evidence supplied by a personal enemy, the libelist Théveneau de Morande. This experience had a radical effect on Brissot. He emerged from prison deeply embittered not only against his personal enemies, who, he believed, had brought about his imprisonment and the failure of his *Lycée,* but also against the government and the whole social system which had lent itself to their machinations. It was at that moment that Brissot became a zealous reformer, a revolutionary, and a fanatical Americanist. From an easy-going and undirected

---

[2] *Mémoires,* ed. C. Perroud (Paris, n.d.), I, 226–227.

though industrious literary hack he turned into a combative, aggressive politician.

In 1785 he began to consider seriously the idea of emigrating to the United States with his wife, whom he had married in 1782. The immediate stimulus of this idea seems to have been Saint John de Crèvecoeur, the author of the *Letters from an American Farmer,* who was then in Paris on leave of absence from his post as French consul in New York. Brissot felt for him an immediate and extreme admiration. "He seemed to me the true man of nature," he later wrote. "I loved his simplicity, his preference for solitude, his contempt for academic vanity, his hatred of vice. I conceived the most complete devotion for him and was with him constantly." [3] This intense admiration was paralleled by an idealization of the land which Crèvecoeur had depicted in such idyllic terms in his *Letters.* "I told him of my plan to settle in America. I was weary of the despotism under which France suffered. As a writer, I hated to grovel at the feet of the idols of the day, and yet I could manage to live only by practicing such subservience. I would far rather, I told him, live in America, even if I had to labor at some humble trade . . . My fondest hope was to raise my children in a land far removed from the eye of tyranny, and I would give everything to be able to do so." [4]

In this sudden enthusiasm for Crèvecoeur's libertarian Arcadia the influence of Rousseau played a large part. Brissot had started to read Rousseau even before he left Chartres, and when he came to Paris he was strongly tempted to seek out this great man, as he later wrote, "whose philosophic life I admired and whose misfortune I pitied. Not daring to offer myself as his friend, I should have gladly been his nurse . . . I worshipped him." [5] He reread the *Confessions* six times and in a self-portrait which he entitled "Portrait de Phédor" he complacently traced resemblances and parallels between himself and Rousseau.

For Brissot, as for many of his generation, Rousseau embodied total concern for the moral regeneration of man through what Brissot called "the innate sentiments . . . natural benevolence." [6] Yet the tragedy, which both Brissot and Rousseau suffered, was that this "inclination of the heart" [7] made the individual cruelly

[3] *Mémoires,* II, 49.
[4] *Mémoires,* II, 49.
[5] *Mémoires,* I, 147, 252.
[6] *Mémoires,* I, 18.
[7] *Mémoires,* I, 18.

vulnerable to the hatred and intrigues which infected society. There were two alternate and contradictory solutions between which both Rousseau and Brissot vacillated: to reform society, to make it safe for the Man of Sentiment; or to withdraw into the solitude of the self and the peace of nature. "Rousseau," Brissot wrote, "loved to travel alone, on foot. He feared conversations; they stole from him the sweet joy he found in gazing upon a beautiful sky or a meadow of flowers. Phédor [i.e., Brissot] too would have loved to walk alone . . . [He] has found few friends who could share his secret inclinations or his mute sentiments." [8] Yet there was also the Rousseau who wrote the *Social Contract,* and the Brissot who attempted to turn the *Social Contract* into political reality.

The peculiar appeal of Crèvecoeur's vision of America, not only to Brissot but to his generation, was that here was a land which seemed miraculously to offer the reconciliation of the two alternatives: a free and egalitarian society in which modern man was regenerated, and at the same time the bucolic retreat of the *Nouvelle Héloïse.*[9]

To the influence of Rousseau and Crèvecoeur was added Brissot's interest in Quakerism and the antislavery movement. The legend of the "Good Quaker" as a symbol of religious toleration, virtue, and pacifism had been commonplace in French literature ever since Voltaire had written in his *Lettres philosophiques* (1734) of the "golden age" which William Penn had recreated in Philadelphia. Brissot's private enthusiasm seems to have started during his two years in England from 1782 to 1784, when he was attempting to establish his *Lycée.* He became acquainted with a number of Quakers, notably a Miss Capper, a childhood friend of his wife, and in 1784 he published in the *Journal du Lycée de Londres* a eulogistic "general description of the private conduct and public morals of the Quakers." (See Letter 33.)

Then in 1786 the Marquis de Chastellux published the first complete edition of his *Voyages dans l'Amérique Septentrionale,*

[8] *Mémoires,* I, 22.

[9] The Rousseauan quality of Crèvecoeur's *Letters,* or rather of Crèvecoeur's own French translation of them, *Lettres d'un cultivateur américain* (Paris, 1784 and 1787), was no accident, for the French versions were rewritten under the influence of Mme d'Houdetot, with whom Rousseau had been in love at Montmorency, and who coached Crèvecoeur in transforming his earthy and realistic English version into a Rousseauistic idyll which was as false and "literary" as it was well suited to the public taste. On this curious case of literary transformation, see Howard G. Rice's excellent study, *Le Cultivateur américain* (Paris, 1933), pp. 75ff.

written while he had been serving with Rochambeau's troops in the United States. Brissot immediately attacked Chastellux in a book which revealed how deeply he had already committed himself to the concept of the American Dream. This was his violent, controversial, and highly successful *Examen critique des Voyages . . . de M. le marquis de Chatellux* (London, 1786). Chastellux, though certainly no democrat, had expressed great admiration for the leaders of the American Revolution, particularly for Washington and Jefferson, and had given an intelligent and sympathetic picture of American life. Nevertheless, like most of Rochambeau's officers and indeed like most of their American allies, he had been irked by Quaker neutralism and had permitted himself several satirical pages on American Quakers, calling them "smooth-tongued, mealy-mouthed, jesuitical, and . . . indifferent to the public good." [10]

Brissot answered in the white heat of anger. He interpreted these passages as a personal attack on his friend Crèvecoeur, who had given in his *Letters* an idealized portrayal of the American Quakers, and he devoted the major portion of the *Examen* to an apology of Quakerism in general and of the American Quakers in particular. But he also made two other interesting accusations against Chastellux. In the first place, Chastellux had spoken in belittling terms of Negroes and abolitionists, and Brissot's twenty pages of refutation of these aspersions were an indication of his developing interest in the antislavery movement. Brissot's most significant accusation, however, was that Chastellux had "decried Man and the People." [11] By this he meant not merely that Chastellux had been guilty of aristocratic prejudice and snobbery, but that he had implicitly denied the principle of the natural and universal equality of all men, the principle that men, if free, are capable of equal dignity and equal development of their moral and intellectual faculties. "I believe," he wrote, "that the nature of the government determines three quarters of man's nature. I believe that man progresses as he has more liberty and that he degenerates as he has less. I believe that an ignorant, barbaric slave born on the banks of the Bosphorus would be an enlightened republican were he born in Philadelphia . . . There is no more difference between the nature of modern man and that of ancient man than there is between the nature of a Negro and that of a white man

[10] Chastellux, *Voyages* (Paris, 1786), I, 235–243.
[11] *Examen*, p. 4.

INTRODUCTION

. . . The dignity of man consists in his liberty, in his equality before the law, in his independence, in his subjection only to those laws to which he has given his consent, in the control he exercises over those to whom he has entrusted political authority. Lastly, the dignity of man consists in the perfect development of his moral and intellectual faculties, in the effort he makes to discover truth and to bring about the reign of truth." [12]

In 1788 Brissot again felt compelled to spring to Crèvecoeur's defense, this time against the *Recherches historiques et politiques sur les Etats-Unis* (Paris, 1788), written by the Italo-American Filippo Mazzei with the aid and encouragement of Jefferson. Mazzei's main purpose had been to clean up what John Adams had called the "Augean Stables" of French misconceptions of America, for which Mazzei held Crèvecoeur in good part responsible. "I ought to warn the readers of *Lettres d'un cultivateur américain*," he had written, "to be careful not to imagine that the manners and customs described in that book are general in America . . . I have been very much surprised to learn that many people have conceived the most chimerical notions from the reading of this book . . . My intention is not to discourage Europeans who would become American citizens, but only to save them from regretting too late that they have done so." [13] But Brissot was a man of total, passionate commitments, and he could not accept even so reasonable a qualification of the American Dream. He repeated the words with which he had greeted Crèvecoeur's work in 1784: "These *Letters* . . . will perhaps inspire or reawaken in blasé souls of Europeans the taste for virtue and for the simple life . . . Energetic souls will find in them something more. They will see here a country, a government, where the desires of their hearts have been realized, a land which speaks to them in their own language. The happiness for which they have longed does in truth exist." [14]

It was during a trip he made to England in the winter of 1787–1788 that Brissot became a militant abolitionist. Probably through his connections with English Quakers, he was introduced to the committee organized in 1787 under the presidency of Granville Sharp for the suppression of the slave trade. Although he did not,

[12] *Examen*, pp. 104–110.
[13] *Recherches historiques*, IV, 90–100.
[14] *Réponse à une critique des Lettres d'un cultivateur américain* . . . (n.p., 1788), pp. 2–3.

apparently, meet Wilberforce, perhaps the best known of English abolitionists, he conceived a tremendous admiration for Sharp and Thomas Clarkson, another member of the committee, and for their ideas. He returned to Paris fired with enthusiasm for this new cause, and on February 19, 1788, he held a meeting to organize a similar antislavery group in France, the *Société des Amis des Noirs*. A Swiss banker named Etienne Clavière, whom Brissot had met in Geneva in 1782, was elected president, and among the other members were Mirabeau, Lafayette, and Condorcet. Under Brissot's leadership the Society was to become an important political force during the Revolution and the pressure it exerted contributed eventually to the abolition of slavery in Santo Domingo and the other French colonies.

Abolitionism was only one of Brissot's lines of political action in the years between his imprisonment and his departure for the United States. In the fall of 1786 he became secretary to the Chancellor of the Duke of Orleans, the future Philippe Egalité. The political household of a Prince of the Blood may seem to have been a strange place for a democrat, but it must be remembered that at the time there existed no effective means for democratic political action, and that since about 1771 the partisans of the Third Estate had been making it their common practice to seek their real objectives by allying themselves either with the aristocracy against the Crown, or with the Crown against the aristocracy. The House of Orleans had long sought to further its ambitions by aligning itself against the Throne; Brissot hoped to use it as a weapon against the aristocracy as well. In August 1787 he wrote to the Chancellor, the Marquis Du Crest, a remarkable memorandum proposing the organization of a political party headed by the Duke of Orleans, which would seek broad popular support by championing the cause of the people and would offer a platform of democratic control of taxation and constitutional reform. This party was to begin its operations by infiltrating the aristocratic Parlements with secret cells and thus use the *Noblesse de Robe* to break the power of the Ministry. But once this first stage had been achieved, the party would rid itself of its aristocratic allies and establish its support on its true base, the people. This was genuine revolutionary conspiracy.[15]

All these activities and influences—Crèvecoeur, Rousseau, Quakerism, abolitionism, Brissot's efforts to find an avenue for effec-

[15] Brissot, *Correspondance et papiers*, ed. C. Perroud (Paris, n.d.), pp. 149–160.

tive political action, and, of course, the general current of Americanism which was strong in Paris—all converged and directed Brissot's thinking toward the United States.

To these factors was to be added the incentive of personal gain. As we have seen, by 1785 Brissot was thinking seriously of emigrating to America, and in April 1786 he started to draft a letter (which he apparently never sent) to Calonne, the minister of finance, asking for a diplomatic appointment to the United States.[16] He realized, however, that this plan had small chance of success, and in the same year he began to consider forming a group which might be willing to subsidize a voyage to America.[17]

From this idea came the organization in January 1787 of the *Société Gallo-Américaine* with the collaboration of Crèvecoeur, Clavière, and Nicolas Bergasse, a Parisian lawyer. The ostensible purpose of the society was to advance the welfare of the two countries by promoting mutual understanding and exchange of information, and in particular by encouraging the growth of Franco-American trade. No doubt Brissot and his friends were sincerely interested in these objectives, but it is also clear that they intended the society to be a center for discussion and possibly for action, and they expected that it would be concerned with questions other than Franco-American relations. In July 1787 Brissot wrote the future revolutionary Roland, "Freedom of thought is the basis and object of this Society, and that is why I belong to it." [18]

Even before the Society's first meeting, Brissot and Clavière had started to write a book on Franco-American commercial relations, *De la France et des Etats-Unis*, which was published in March 1787. Like the *Société Gallo-Américaine*, this work had an avowed immediate objective and a broader unavowed purpose. In his *Mémoires* Brissot later wrote, "I proposed to make known the commercial and political relations which France could establish with the United States, and I also hoped that the picture I drew of the future prosperity of America would induce my compatriots to imitate their conduct and regain at last their own liberty." [19]

It is important to note that Brissot links liberty and economic advantage; this is a key to Brissot's developing concept of Americanism, a doctrine of the trinity of liberty, virtue, and a good

[16] *Correspondance et papiers,* pp. 90–92.
[17] *Correspondance et papiers,* pp. 92–93.
[18] *Correspondance et papiers,* p. 143.
[19] *Mémoires,* II, 52.

profit margin. He and Clavière argued that the American Revolution offered two great advantages to France: first, its "salutary influence on the progress of human knowledge and on the reform of social prejudices"; and, second, "the immense opportunities for trade which that revolution offers to the French." [20] Better information and the implementation of sound policies would open France's ports to a commerce with the United States which would not only produce handsome profits but would also "accelerate that revolution in behalf of the people which is being prepared in the cabinets of Europe" [21]—a reference perhaps to his own activities at the moment in the Chancellery of the Duke of Orleans. This same formula is repeated throughout the *Travels:* Reforms in French economic policy toward the United States would produce bigger profits for French businessmen and would at the same time serve to make the French people more aware of the advantages of the American political system and so speed up constitutional revision in France.

Indeed it was the profit motive and not political idealism which finally made possible Brissot's trip to the United States. In the spring of 1788 his friend Clavière entered into an agreement with two bankers, Pierre Stadinski and Théophile de Cazenove, to speculate in the American domestic debt. They needed someone to go to the United States to negotiate with the American financiers William Duer and Andrew Craigie, with whom they proposed to deal and whose representative, Daniel Parker, was already in Paris. Brissot was their obvious choice, and they drew up a contract to pay him 10,000 livres for his expenses, in return for which he was to obtain information on the amount and current price of American government securities and on a number of other related matters.[22] Parker gave him the necessary letter of introduction to Craigie in Boston.[23] In addition to the basic mission, Clavière also charged Brissot with investigating possibilities of investment in American public lands for resale to Europeans either as long-term investments or for the purpose of establishing an organized settlement of French emigrants. The latter idea was apparently suggested by Duer and Craigie, who were already planning their Scioto venture, an ill-fated attempt to establish such a

[20] *De la France et des Etats-Unis* (London, 1787), pp. xxx, xxxiii.
[21] *De la France et des Etats-Unis,* p. xxxii.
[22] *Correspondance et papiers,* pp. 179–181.
[23] E. Ellery, *Brissot de Warville* (Boston, 1915), pp. 433–434.

colony in Ohio. Clavière also requested information on a wide variety of other aspects of American life, and his queries are printed in the form of six letters preceding Brissot's narrative. The *Travels* were written in the form of a series of letters addressed to Clavière, and although Brissot devoted much space to his own special interests, particularly Quakers and the Negro problem, the work was ostensibly composed to answer Clavière's questions.

In addition to being charged with obtaining information for his backers Brissot sailed with two other purposes. The first was the political one of observing "a society of men who had just achieved victory in their struggle for liberty"; the other was the serious intention of locating a suitable place in which he might settle with his family.[24] His brother-in-law, François Dupont, who since 1783 had been planning to emigrate to the United States,[25] gave up his business in Poland to join Brissot, but he did not arrive in the United States until January 1789, when Brissot was already on his way back to France. He stayed on, however, purchased a farm near Philadelphia which Brissot had inspected, and was later joined in 1791 by his sister Nancy. The seriousness of Brissot's intention to settle permanently in the United States is further attested by a questionnaire which he drew up before leaving and to which he obtained replies from an unidentified American in Paris, asking about such matters as the cost of passage for his family and what household goods to bring.[26]

After a number of delays Brissot finally sailed from Le Havre on the ship *Cato* and landed fifty-one days later in Boston on July 24. Having called on Craigie and inspected Boston and Cambridge, he departed by stagecoach on August 6 and arrived in New York August 9. His journey, described in the *Travels*, took him through Worcester, Springfield, Hartford, Middletown, New Haven, Stratford, and New Rochelle. After two weeks in New York, during which he attended a meeting of the New York Manumission Society,[27] Brissot continued by way of Newark, Trenton, and Bristol

[24] In his "Projet de défense devant le Tribunal Révolutionnaire" (October 1793) Brissot wrote, "Indignant against the despotism under which France suffered, I traveled, in 1788, to the United States of America, to learn there how to carry out in my own country a similar revolution, or else to settle there with my family if I had to abandon my hopes for such a revolution." *Mémoires*, II, 275.

[25] *Correspondance et papiers*, p. 53.

[26] *Correspondance et papiers*, pp. 184–186.

[27] Aug. 21, 1788. Minutes of the New York Manumission Society, New-York Historical Society.

to Philadelphia, where he arrived August 26. For three weeks he busily inspected the city's institutions and made trips into the surrounding area. Then about the middle of September he returned by coach to Boston, from where he made on October 2–4 an excursion to Salem, Newbury, and Portsmouth. On October 12 he took the stage to Providence, where he boarded a packet, intending to sail directly to New York; bad weather, however, forced the ship to put in to Newport for six days, until the eighteenth. Finally on October 20 Brissot reached New York, where he met Craigie and Duer and signed a contract in the name of his backers to form an association to buy up both the American debt to the French Crown and also portions of the domestic debt.[28] Early in November he was again in Philadelphia, but he left on the fifteenth to go by way of Wilmington to Mount Vernon to visit Washington for three days, carrying a letter of introduction from Lafayette. Brissot had intended to visit the Shenandoah Valley, which he believed might be a suitable location for his future American home, but when he reached Alexandria he learned the news of the summoning of the Estates-General in France. Abandoning all his plans, he hastened back to New York, whence he sailed December 3. After a rough passage of forty-one days he landed in Falmouth and, after passing through London, was back in Paris by the end of January 1789.

Brissot admits candidly in his Preface the imperfections of the *Travels* as literature, and he pleads as his excuse haste and the necessity of getting his ideas before the public while they were still politically timely. Yet it cannot be said all Brissot's literary faults could have been corrected by polish. Perhaps his greatest weakness was that he was not a truly original thinker. He picked up ideas everywhere, from men as well as from books—Locke, Montesquieu, Rousseau, Helvétius, Voltaire, Franklin, Linguet, Clavière, Crèvecoeur, the English abolitionists, the American Quakers, and even Laurence Sterne—and he stored up all he had read and heard in his prodigious memory, bringing everything together into a sort of loose system. But he never was able to fuse all he had amassed into truly original concepts. He was a collector of ideas and information, but not a discriminating one. He poured everything into his writings, the trivial and the profound, the significant and the incidental. His logic was often loose and confused. Also, it must be granted that he did not have the gift of expression. He had all of Rousseau's sentiment, but none of his sense of style;

[28] *Correspondance et papiers*, pp. 208–212.

all of Voltaire's indignation, but none of his irony. He was without either humor or poetry. Yet he was one of the great publicists of his age, for he possessed one great gift, that of total commitment to his subject. He was the prototype of the *écrivain engagé*. Brissot was a man of sudden, intense enthusiasms, of passionate loyalties. When he wrote with the fire in him—as he did when composing his *Examen critique de Chatellux*, the work of which he was justly most proud—he achieved true eloquence.

This is not the place for a description of his complete ideology, but we may briefly consider the principal ideas expressed in the *Travels*.

At the basis of his thought seems to have been his belief in the universal equality of all men; therefore his opposition to Negro slavery was the keystone of his entire political philosophy. He repeatedly insisted, as he had earlier in the *Examen critique,* that Negroes had just as great moral and intellectual capacities as their white masters, and he demonstrated his thesis by examples of Negro prodigies he had encountered in America. If this equality of potential existed between whites and Negroes, it existed *a fortiori* among men of different nations of the world and among men of different social groups within a nation. Here he was deriving his ideas directly from Helvétius, and he impatiently rejected both climatic determinism and Voltaire's polygenesis, the doctrine of inherent inferiority of the nonwhite races.

If all men everywhere had the same physical, moral, and intellectual potential, then the actual differences among social groups, as for instance between the Negroes and whites in America, must be due to social institutions. If Negroes had a higher death rate this was not because they were a physically inferior race, but because they had a lower standard of living and inferior medical care and because their moral and intellectual energy had been drained by the effects of social discrimination. If slaves were guilty of crimes, the true culprit was not the slave but the institution of slavery, and Brissot offered the striking suggestion that masters should be legally responsible for the crimes of their chattels.

It is easy to smile at Brissot's total disregard of any distinction between material and moral values. But he lived before the Romantic disavowal of capitalism, and he firmly believed that a man's morality was a function of his economic condition. He saw nothing incongruous in the fact that a pauper or a slave should be a criminal or that a wealthy Quaker merchant should be a man of virtue. Similarly, physical health was a function of morality and economic well-being. But these three desiderata were in turn functions of a just and free society. In other words—and here Brissot paralleled Condorcet exactly—all men everywhere in all times were capable of moral, physical, and intellectual perfection. The key to progress was liberty and equality and the key to liberty was moral regeneration. Mankind advanced by a series of parallel offensives. Every step forward to greater liberty and equality supported flanking moral, economic, and intellectual gains, and every gain on these latter fronts in turn made possible greater liberty and equality.

Brissot found in the United States ample documentation for his thesis. In Rhode Island the economic depression and the degeneration of public morals which he witnessed were, he said, the result of a faulty constitution which permitted the exploitation of the people by unprincipled financial adventurers who had tricked the people into a depreciated paper currency. Correct the political abuses, and prosperity and virtue would return. But if liberty and good government had been defeated in a few places, in America as a whole they were marching forward triumphantly. "How grand the idea of liberty appears! . . . Liberty need but command, and forests are cleared, mountains are leveled, and rich farms arise to provide havens for numberless generations." In a passage which strikingly anticipated Tocqueville he pointed out the shocking contrast between the prosperity of the free states and the economic stagnation of the slave states (p. 237). Equally sharp was the contrast he saw between the dynamic growth of the free American West and the stunted economy in the fertile but enslaved Spanish colony of Louisiana. "O Liberty! Liberty! How great is your power! Out of your womb is born industry, which brings the dead to life." And this very power of liberty to produce economic vitality meant that the free nations would conquer the slave nations. "It would be easy to prove mathematically that the American War cost the English four times as much as it did the Americans . . . Love of liberty has resources unknown to despotism."

Buffon, De Pauw, Raynal, and others had evolved a theory of American degeneration, which asserted that the New World was an environment which because of its peculiar climate was an inferior human habitat; in it men, unless they could find means to change this climate, must inevitably degenerate physically, morally, and intellectually. Brissot, believing in the omnipotence of social institutions, rejected this geographic pessimism. Men's physical well-being, and consequently their moral and intellectual well-being, depended upon government alone.

Wherever property is concentrated in the hands of a few and where employment is precarious, dependent, and uncertain, human life is briefer. It is shortened by worries and cares, which, even more effectively than actual want, cut off the very source of life. Wherever government is arbitrary, where tyranny, descending and subdividing itself at each rank of society, stops only at the members of the very lowest classes, to crush them all, there the life of the common people must be shorter. For such people are slaves, and a miserable slave, forever trodden under the feet of his masters, enjoys neither the material well-being, nor the regularity of existence, nor the inner contentment that are necessary for the sustenance of the principle of life (p. 284).

Like a good sociologist, Brissot supported his theory with life expectancy tables.

It has been said that eighteenth-century liberalism was the gospel of bourgeois capitalism. We shall not argue the case, but it is certainly true that for Brissot "thrift and attention to business . . . [were the two sources from which] all private and civic virtues flow." He believed there was no more absurd *non sequitur* possible than to belittle the virtue of the Quakers on the grounds that they were successful businessmen. "A man who is by principle thrifty and businesslike is not afraid . . . of having a large family. If he has many children, he loves them and he sees ways of planning for their future. Such a man is neither a gambler nor a profligate. He is a good husband, for, putting his whole happiness in his family life, he is forced to be good in order to be loved, and he can be happy only by making those around him happy." The argument may not stand up well to careful analysis, but the bourgeois ideal was seldom better stated.

Chastellux had accused the Quakers of an overdose of the acquisitive instinct, but to Brissot the building up of capital was no crime. "Acquisitiveness consists in accumulating a lot of money, in saving it, in keeping a constant eye on one's business, in missing no possible speculation or opportunity. This acquisitiveness is considered a crime, particularly by nobles, who, concerned only with the problem of dissipating wealth and always hungry for the gold they pretend to despise, seek to dishonor those whose business is to accumulate money in order to put it to profitable use." This was the capitalist morality which taught that it was a virtue to increase working capital, and a crime to dip into it. The Quakers were blameless because they used their amassed wealth soberly and did not waste it either to buy political power or in excess expenditures—what Brissot and his century called *luxe*. It was this bourgeois morality which made possible the industrial and colonial expansion of Europe in the nineteenth century.

One may well wonder what was the place of the arts and literature in such a scheme of values. The answer is that they had no place. This was by no means an exceptional position in the eighteenth century. Even Chastellux in his *De la félicité* (1772), reviewing those activities of man which might be conducive to human felicity, had rejected both the "agreeable arts"—painting, sculpture, and architecture—and "frivolous talents like poetry and music." These belonged, he said, to the infancy of mankind, and the example of the Greeks proved that artistic perfection could be accompanied by the worst sort of moral corruption and tyranny.[29] The key to human happiness, Chastellux asserted, lay in free government, economic prosperity, adequate leisure, and the protection of private property. Brissot's answer was the same: moral, social, and economic values must take precedence over aesthetic and intellectual ones. In Boston he met a watchmaker who had invented an orrery, or planetarium, but despaired of finding financial backing, and who in his bitterness said, "This country is too poor. It cannot encourage the arts." In rebuttal, Brissot pointed out that patronage of the arts and sciences was possible only in a society in which wealth was unequally distributed and in which the rich had excess capital to give to "the encouragement of the frivolous and agreeable arts." The happier and more virtuous nation was the one in which wealth was equitably distributed and was devoted only to socially productive purposes like homes, bridges, ships, and street lighting, which, alone, he said, promote true felicity. "The ability to give encouragement to the agreeable arts is a symptom of national calamity." The Quakers did not waste their time "on entertainment, science, or literature." Instead they devoted themselves to business. They were simple, sincere, open, honest, and if they were not witty and urbane like the French aristocrats, they were human, they had common sense, and their hearts were true.

Such ideas are shocking to the modern ear, especially because they are expressed without hypocritical qualifications. But it is

[29] *De la félicité* (Amsterdam, 1772), I, 31.

difficult to say that they are un-American. The eighteenth century was fundamentally anti-intellectual, antiaesthetic, moralistic, pragmatic, capitalistic, reformist, and progressionistic, and Brissot was a most suitable exponent of the final ideology of his age on the eve of the French Revolution. For all his enthusiasm and prejudices, what Brissot saw in America was not a mirage but an accurate prophecy of a future that his century most ardently desired.

Brissot's *Travels* appeared just at the moment that France was beginning to turn its back on the ideology of the *Philosophes,* to commit what Professor Baldensperger called *le désaveu des lumières.* So in the final reckoning, this turned out to be in ideology and spirit much more an American book than a French one. There are of course many errors in these hastily noted observations on American life in 1788—on its towns and countrysides, its people, its institutions, its political, economic, and social problems. There is much that is not original. But for good or ill, Brissot caught the spirit of the United States on the eve of its reconstitution as a federal republic.

A NOTE ON THE TEXT

The *Nouveau Voyage* was published in French in two editions in 1791.[30] Joel Barlow, the American poet, who was in Paris in 1791 and who knew Brissot, recognizing the interest of the work for English and American readers, made a translation which was published in London in 1792 and was immediately republished in pirated editions in New York and Dublin in the same year, and in Boston in 1797. In addition, the original publisher in London brought out a second "corrected" edition in 1794, of which there were two reprints.[31] There were also five German publications, four in 1792 and the fifth in 1796, one in Dutch published in

[30] These two editions have identical title pages but are set in different type and have different pagination. Of the "Large-Type" edition there are two different printings. The present translation is made from the first printing (distinguished by the pagination error 33 for 53 in volume I); in the second printing pages 1–80 of volume I have been reset.

[31] Barlow tried to avoid American pirating of his translation by sending a copy of his manuscript to a friend in the United States for submission to an American publisher, but he was anticipated by the New York edition, copied from the first London edition. This second unpublished "American" version of Barlow's translation is in the library of the Connecticut Historical Society in Hartford.

Amsterdam in 1794, and one in Swedish published in Stockholm in 1797.[32]

Although Brissot sent copies of the French edition to his friends in America (including one inscribed "For the Library and University of Cambridge [Harvard]," from which this new translation has been made), the work was known to English and American readers mainly through Barlow's translation. This was unfortunate, for it was a most unfaithful and incomplete rendering and contained only about fifty-five per cent of the original text. The excisions, made throughout the length of the book, ranged in length from single words to entire chapters. In some cases long passages were rewritten or summarized, and in others paragraphs were telescoped. The result would not have been disastrous had Barlow attempted to give a fair condensation of the original, but the omissions were often, apparently, merely the result of haste, fatigue, carelessness, or simply an unwillingness to wrestle with a difficult problem in translation. Worse still, Barlow felt it his duty as translator to improve upon his author, to correct his errors, and to delete most of the passages which were too sharply critical of the United States. The result was that in Barlow's translation the book approached an unremitting eulogy of all things American, whereas actually Brissot, for all his admiration, did not hesitate to underline heavily the problems the United States faced and the mistakes that had been made by Americans. Consequently a new English edition of the *Travels* demands a new translation.

The French and also several of the English editions included an extra volume containing Brissot and Clavière's *De la France et des Etats-Unis*. While this study formed for the eighteenth-century editor a suitable companion volume to the *Travels*, it is a separate and distinct work and is therefore not included in the present publication. In all other respects this translation is a complete rendering of the French text. All editorial additions, both within the text and in the form of footnotes, appear within brackets. Misspellings of proper names, minor inaccuracies in quotations and clearly false references in footnotes have been corrected, but these are the only changes introduced.

[32] All these editions are listed in either Sabin, *Bibliotheca Americana* or Ellery, *Brissot de Warville*, p. 479, except *Neue Reise durch die Vereinigten Staaten von Nordamerika*. In *Magazin von Merkwürdigen Neuen Reisebeschreibungen* . . . (Berlin, 1792), VII, 1–292.

INTRODUCTION

In conclusion, we thank Mr. Thomas R. Adams and his staff of the John Carter Brown Library for their most active and willing assistance, and particularly Mrs. Elaine Remley Perachio, Research Assistant of Pembroke College, for her unflagging and accurate labors. Needless to say, the errors that remain are ours.

New Travels in the
United States of America
1788

NOUVEAU VOYAGE

DANS

LES ÉTATS-UNIS

DE

L'AMÉRIQUE SEPTENTRIONALE,

FAIT EN 1788;

Par J. P. BRISSOT (WARVILLE),
Citoyen François.

On peut conquérir la liberté, sans mœurs ;
on ne peut la conserver, sans mœurs.

*Nemo illic vitia ridet, nec corrumpere, nec
corrumpi sœculum vocatur....... Plusquam
ibi boni mores valent quam alibi bonæ leges.*
TACITE.

TOME PREMIER.

A PARIS,

Chez BUISSON, Imprimeur et Libraire, rue
Haute-Feuille, N°. 20.

AVRIL 1791.

*The original title page, from the copy given by J. P. Brissot to the
Harvard College Library.*

J. P. BRISSOT,

Born the 14th of Jan.y 1754.

Deputy of the Department of Paris

in the first Legislature.

Suffered by the Guillotine.

on the 31.st of October 1793.

Published Sept.r 1.st 1794 by J.S. Jordan N366. Fleet Street.

Frontispiece of the Second Edition, Corrected, London, 1794. Courtesy the John Carter Brown Library, Brown University.

PREFACE

A book of travels will undoubtedly seem at first glance quite irrelevant to the problems France faces today. I should be the first to reproach myself for the time I have spent preparing these pages for publication if I did not believe they will constitute a work not only useful but even necessary for the success of our Revolution. The purpose of my voyage was not to study ancient works of art or to discover exotic flora, but to observe a society of men who had just achieved victory in their struggle for liberty. No longer can we French consider as foreigners or strangers any free people.

We too have won our liberty. We have, therefore, no need to learn from Americans how to attain this blessing; but we do have to learn from them the secret of preserving it. This secret, I maintain, lies mainly in the moral principles and practices of the nation. Americans possess this secret, but I find to my sorrow not only that we have not yet learned it, but that we are not even firmly convinced of the absolute necessity of moral principles for the maintenance of liberty. The point is crucial; on it depends the success of the Revolution. It therefore deserves careful examination.

What is liberty? It is the most perfect state of society. It is the condition in which man is subject only to the laws he has himself made; in which he must perfect the use of his reason so that these laws which he makes may be good laws; and in which in order to execute these laws he must fully employ all the powers of this same reason. Coercion is dishonorable to free men and is virtually nonexistent in a true state of freedom. If it becomes necessary then liberty has started to disappear.

Moral principles are simply the application of reason to human action, and by the force of these principles the law is executed. In a free nation, reason and moral principles are to the execution of the law what chains and whips and gallows are in a slave nation. Destroy morals and common reason, and you must replace them with the chains and whips, or else society is transformed into a state of war and collapses into a tragic anarchy ending finally in the dissolution of the state.

Without moral principles there can be no liberty. Without moral principles a man cannot love his own liberty and he destroys the liberty of other men. For if a man abandons himself to luxury,

3

to ostentation, to reckless gambling, or to wild extravagance, he necessarily opens his soul to corruption. To satisfy his desires he must traffic in his popularity and talents and deliver the people over to the forces of despotism, which are ever lying in wait to cast the nation once more into chains.

But, it is objected, a man can love liberty and yet be immoral. No, I reply, it is not liberty that he loves, but a new tyranny. The immoral man overthrows despotism only in order to be a despot himself, to satisfy his pride or his other passions.

Certain immoral men differentiate public morality from private virtue. A false and chimerical distinction, invented by vice for its own security! No doubt a man may be virtuous in his private life without practicing public morality; he may be a good father without being an energetic champion of liberty. But he who is without private virtue can never truly possess public morality. In this respect the two are inseparable, for their origin is the same— *reason*. A man without private virtue is a profligate, a spendthrift, a gambler, an unfaithful husband, an unnatural father. Now what sort of public morality can we expect from a man with such vices? Shall we believe that in his home he outrages reason but respects it beyond his own doorsill in his dealings with his fellow citizens? Can reason, unable to check his excesses in his private life, control them in his public life? A man who does not respect reason under the eyes of his penates never sincerely respects it anywhere. In an immoral man a public respect for reason and the laws is no more than fear or hypocrisy. The moment he is safe from the police power of the state his fear vanishes and his vice reappears. Moreover, the hypocritical pretense of public morality by an immoral man is both an additional scandal and a dangerous deception; the standards of public morality are undermined by the scandal, and the deception is a pitfall into which liberty falls and is destroyed.

Indeed what faith can we put in these men who see revolutions only as rungs on the ladder to wealth? How can we trust men who publicly pay reverence to moral principles only in order to delude the people, and who delude the people only to rob and enslave them? Can we believe these men who, with a beguiling rhetoric paid for in gold, hypocritically preach the abolition of special privilege while they are secretly sacrificing all that is most sacred on the altar of their own self-interest? What trust can we put in men whose private conduct is a continuous outrage to moral principle and an insult to liberty? Is not liberty either the exercise of reason or else a mere empty word? What faith can we have in men whose conduct is a scandalous denial of the very doctrines they preach—men, to use the words of Juvenal,

Qui Curios simulant, et Bacchanalia vivunt.[1]

Happy the people who are disgusted by such hypocrisy, who have the courage to dismiss, to stigmatize, and to ostracize these two-faced men whose words seem to belong to the sweet reign of liberty but whose diseased souls long only for the despotic corruption of a Tiberius! Happy the people who, well aware that liberty is preserved not by eloquence but by the constant practice of virtue, despise and fear oratory when it is not the expression of a moral life. Such a people, by the stern voice of public opinion, force men of genius to be men of virtue. They banish corruption from their midst, they strengthen the foundations of liberty, and they prepare for themselves a long and prosperous future.

But what of a rash, unthinking people, totally lacking in foresight, who are swept along by the eloquence of an orator who flatters their passions, and who are so dazzled by his talents that they are willing to forgive his vices? What of a people who do not protest at the sight of an Alcibiades parading in his mantle of purple silk, giving sumptuous banquets, sleeping on the bosom of his harlot Nemea, or stealing from a husband the joy of his home? [2] What if the splendor of his wealth, the grace of his person, the sweet sounds of his words, and his reputation for bravery reconcile them to his crimes? What if they pay him the homage which is properly due only to talent wedded to virtue, and lavish on him adoration, power, and honors? Such a people give in their mad

---

[1] [Who pretend to the virtues of the Curii but live like bacchantes. *Sat.* II, 3.]

[2] Plutarch tells us [in his life of Alcibiades] that the sumptuous games and public shows which Alcibiades organized for the city of Athens, his munificence to the people, the glory of his ancestors, the grace of his person, the force of his eloquence, his strength of body, and his great courage prevailed upon the Athenians to endure patiently his excesses, to indulge many things to him, and to give the softest names to his faults, attributing them to youth and good nature. When the painter Aristophon painted the harlot Nemea holding Alcibiades lying on her bosom all the people rushed to see the picture and delighted in it. But all these things greatly displeased the older and wiser citizens, to whom they seemed certain signs of Alcibiades' ambition to be a tyrant and to violate all the laws and customs of his city. One day as he was leaving an assembly, well satisfied with having obtained all he had asked for and pleased with all the honors the people were paying him, Timon the misanthrope walked up to him and, holding out his hand in a friendly way, said, "Go on boldly, my son, and increase in credit with the people, for thou wilt one day bring them calamities enough." Timon's prophecy was fulfilled.

infatuation the measure of their own weakness, folly, imbecility, and corruption. They cut their own throats, and the hour is not far off when they will be sold by their Alcibiades and his favorites to the Great King and his satraps.

Is this a fanciful picture I am drawing? Or could it be our own? I shudder at the resemblance. Great God! Can we have achieved the most inconceivable, the most unexpected of revolutions merely to snatch out of obscurity a few schemers, a few mediocrities, a few ambitious men to whom nothing is sacred, whose very words are not golden and whose souls are things of filth? These infamous men! They try to excuse their weakness, their venality, and their eternal compromises with despotism by saying, "This nation is still too corrupt to be given complete freedom." Yet they themselves stand as examples of the very corruption they deprecate! And meanwhile they are shackling new chains on the people, as if chains could enlighten and uplift men!

O Providence! To what fate have you destined France? The French are a good people, but easily swayed and credulous, enthusiastic but easily deceived. How often have they in their infatuation applauded traitors in disguise preaching the basest perfidy!

Such folly is either the symptom of a kind of national senility foreshadowing the imminent collapse of the country, or else it is the behavior of a childish race, of a people who are still acting instinctively and are not yet mature enough for liberty. For a free man is by definition a rational man. When he gives praise it is the expression of rational conviction, and if he ever does feel admiration, it is a measured admiration. He does not cheapen his tributes by wasting them on dishonorable men. A people degraded enough to commit such follies will soon be rejoicing in the golden chains that bind them. This was what the English did when they dragged in the mire the Parliament to which they owed their liberty and showered flowers on the infamous Monk,[3] who was selling them to a new tyrant.

I have seen at first hand these men by whom the people are so easily infatuated. How few true patriots did I count among them! How few men did I see who sincerely loved the people and who were constantly devoted to the welfare and progress of the nation,

---

[3] George Monk (1608–1670), later Duke of Albemarle, commanding officer in the armies of the Commonwealth, who played a leading role in the restoration of Charles II.

how few who always ignored their own self-interest! Such true friends, such true brothers of the people you will not find haunting those infamous dens where we see the representatives of the nation gambling with the blood of citizens. You will not find them among those vile courtiers who have changed masks but not changed character, nor among those one-day patriots, who extol the Declaration of the Rights of Man while gravely considering the choice of a new cabriolet or a fashionable waistcoat. Such frivolous men have never risen to the elevated levels of meditative thought which make the love of humanity and the exercise of reason a constant need and a daily duty. Simple needs and tastes may indeed be the only sure signs and guarantees of patriotism. A man with few wants is not forced to sell himself; but the citizen who has a mania for ostentation, gambling, and thoughtless extravagance is a man constantly driven to expedients, is the property of the first person who offers to buy him, and everything about him stinks of corruption.

Would you then prove to me your patriotism? Let me enter into your home. What! I find your antechamber full of insolent lackeys who stare at me contemptuously because I am like Curius, *incomptis Curius capillis*.[4] They call you My Lord and still give you the vain titles that liberty scorns. You accept all this, and you call yourself a patriot! I go on to another room. What luxury on every side! I see gilded paneling and magnificent vases on your mantelpieces; I walk across the most luxurious carpets; I find on your table the most expensive wines and the most delicate dishes; all around hover a crowd of servants, whom you treat with arrogance. No, you are not a patriot. The most intense sort of pride reigns in your heart, pride in your birth, pride in your wealth, pride in your ability. A man with this triple pride does not believe in equality. You lie to your conscience when you prostitute the word patriot. And where does all this wealth come from? You were not rich before. From the people? They are still poor. Who can say that this gold was not the price of their blood? Who can say that at this very moment when I am speaking with you there is not a secret pact between you and the Court? Who can swear that you have not said to the Court, "Give me what power you have left, and I shall bring the people back to your feet, I shall harness them again to your chariot, and I shall silence the tongues and pens of those independent men who defy your authority. To enslave a nation you do not always need a Bastille."

---

[4] [Curius with his hair unkempt. Horace, *Odes* I, xii, 41.]

7

I do not know whether all the spectacles which daily meet our eyes will convince us of the impossibility, or at least of the prodigious difficulty, of combining public incorruptibility with personal depravity. But I am convinced that it is easy and will one day be necessary, if we wish to preserve our Constitution, to demonstrate this axiom: *Without private virtue there can be no public morality, no civic spirit, and no liberty.*

But how can we create private virtue and public morality in a people who are just emerging from a mire of servitude and ignorance which has been accumulating for twelve centuries?

We have a host of means at our disposal: laws, precepts, good examples, education, increasing the number of men of principle, encouraging rural life, the division of estates, and respect for the crafts.

Is it not obvious, for example, that there is a natural connection between private virtue and rural life, and consequently that we can improve the morals of the nation by encouraging a movement of the people from the cities to the country, and by discouraging migrations from the country to the cities? If Americans have such high moral standards and practices, it is because nine tenths of them live on farms scattered across the land. I do not say that we should enact direct laws which will force people into the country or limit the size of cities; for any prohibition or restriction is an absurd and ineffective injustice. If you would bring about right action, make it to the people's interest to act rightly. If you would repopulate the rural areas, make it to the interest of the country people to stay there. Wise laws and a proper allocation of taxes can produce these results indirectly. Laws which will tend to bring about the breaking up of estates and to divide wealth more equally among the citizens will likewise contribute to the restoration of private virtue and public morality. For poverty cannot but be indifferent to the common weal, and its wants often define the limits of its virtue.

Would you propagate public spirit in all of France, in every department and every village? Then promote the diffusion of enlightenment and the sale of cheap books and newspapers. How quickly would the Revolution be consolidated if the government had the wisdom to allow all newspapers to be posted free of charge. You have already heard that three or four millions spent this way will prevent a host of disturbances either favored or committed by ignorance. The redress of the damage and harm these disorders occasion will cost much more than three or four millions. Moreover, the dissemination of information would accelerate a great many useful enterprises and thus cause a general increase in prosperity.

I can also cite the example of another law which would infallibly contribute to the improvement of public spirit and morals, namely, short periods of tenure for all public offices and the prohibition of immediate re-election. Under such a system the legislature would pour every two years into the provinces three or four hundred good patriots who during their stay in Paris had been educated in the spirit of the Revolution and who had been penetrated by the enlightenment, the fierce energy, and the patriotism which burn so brightly in this city. The deputies would be required to return to their departments and to their humble homes, and to live there. Moreover, by this rotation of public offices we would educate many men in the science of politics. The welfare of the state, better understood, would become thus successively the affair of *all*. In this way we might repair the fault of which the representative system is accused, namely, that of making government the business of *a few*.

I cannot discuss here all the means which might be used, but it would be a great aid to the Revolution if we could discover and indicate those which may serve to instill good morals and public spirit in the people.

I do not wish, however, to abandon this interesting subject without making one very important reflection. Neither political nor individual liberty can long exist without personal independence. Now no man can be independent unless he owns property or has an honorable profession or trade which protects him from want and keeps him from being dependent on others.

I have already said that the reason that Americans are and will long remain a free people is that nine tenths of them are farmers. When we suppose a future population of America of two hundred million men, we must remember that all of them could be landowners. A landowner depends only on his harvest, and his harvest depends upon the heavens, which can never fail him completely. If the rains ruin his wheat his cattle will grow fat in his meadows and his fields will yield large crops of potatoes.[5]

[5] The potato is a food admirably suited to the man who seeks liberty and knows how to be free. It grows everywhere and is both easily raised and easily prepared as food. The more such chores can be eliminated, the less is the need for money

We are not in that happy position. If we divided all the fifty million acres of productive land in France, we should have but two acres per person. Can a man subsist on two acres of land?

The nature of things requires many French citizens to live in cities. Commerce, the trades, and various sorts of industry must provide a living for the inhabitants. For we must now count little on income from public office. Such salaries compensate a man for his efforts but they do not enrich him or give any assurance for his future needs. A man who expects to live on what he earns in public office will always be the slave of either the people or of various powerful persons. Every man, then, who wishes to be truly free, if he does not own property, must practice some art or craft.

At this word "craft" patriots still tremble. We are beginning to respect merchants, but in spite of all the preaching of equality we do not honestly feel that we are on a level with craftsmen. We have not yet freed ourselves of the prejudice which considers the crafts as inferior to banking or commerce. This is the bourgeois aristocratic spirit, and it will be most difficult to root out.[6]

Would you have the crafts honored and respected? Educate those who practice them. Choose among them those who seem the best educated, place them in positions of public trust, and give them advancement. Do not be too proud to confer on them places of honor in the assemblies.

I regret that the National Assembly has not yet set such a holy example, that it has not crowned the genius of agriculture by electing as its president the good farmer Gérard,[7] and that no members of the Assembly who are merchants or who practice any of the practical arts have as yet enjoyed this honor. Why this exclusion? It is very fine to write in the Declaration of Rights that

---

and work to satisfy private wants, and the greater the time that can be devoted to public service.

[6] Though I hesitate to say so, this aristocratic spirit appears even in officials elected by the people. How contemptuously do they look the manual worker over from head to foot! How brutally do many of our National Guards treat the poor wretches they arrest! With what insolence do they carry out their orders! Look at most of our public officials. They are as haughty in the exercise of their duties now as they were obsequious before the *Assemblées Primaires* [the Revolutionary assemblies of the people which nominated the *Electeurs*]. A true patriot, as I have said elsewhere, is always the same, neither servile when he is seeking election nor arrogant in the performance of his duties.

[7] [Michel Gérard (1737–1815), a Breton farmer elected to the Third Estate in 1789. He arrived in Paris wearing his native Breton dress, and his picturesque appearance and geniality quickly won him great popularity and the nickname Le Père Gérard.]

all men are equal, but we must also practice this equality, we must engrave it on our hearts, impregnate our entire beings with it, and consecrate it by all our actions. It was the duty of the National Assembly to set this great example. Perhaps by so doing it would have also forced the executive power to respect the principle of equality. Do we find the executive going down into the craftsman class for simple but well-educated men of modest means who have never been courtiers to be its agents and envoys?

Our democrats at Court do indeed praise with affected enthusiasm Franklin, Adams, etc. Indeed they mention, in a stupidly surprised sort of way, that one was a printer and the other a schoolmaster. But do they go into our workshops to look for capable men? No.

But of what importance now is the conduct of a ministry whose detestable principles will make it essentially antipopular and consequently vicious? [8] It will never be virtuous, but only wear a mask of virtue. It would be madness to try to reform it; the only wise course is to find independently-minded adversaries to oppose it. And we must remember that the secret of an independent mind is in this maxim: "Have few needs, and practice a secure and steady trade to provide the money to meet those you have."

But, it will be objected, property or a trade cannot take care of a man's every need. A craftsman may fall sick. Yes, and this is the reason why we must increase the number of life insurance companies and all the other ingenious institutions so common in England which permit an artisan or a worker, by putting aside a certain sum each week, to live without fear of illness or of leaving his children penniless. In this way insurance companies serve to make possible for all men personal independence, thrift, and a moral life. They serve to eliminate that degrading sense of dependence which makes so bitter the bread of charity. The worker who is helped by these institutions can always hold up his head, for he is being supported by his own savings, by the product of his own labor. He need bow to no man. The craftsman takes pride in a trade which assures him his independence. He feels no envy toward men in high places, for he knows that he too can attain such honor if he proves himself worthy. He worships no man, no matter who he is, for he respects himself too much to be a worshiper of men. He admires men not because they are in positions

[8] [I.e., the ministry of Louis XVI in office in April 1791, which included Montmorin, Du Port, Duportail, and Bertrand de Moleville.]

of power but because they have deserved well of their country. Honors do not dazzle him. In the sixteenth century the leaders of the Dutch revolution sat on the grass and ate herring and onions as they received in proud simplicity the envoys of the haughty Spaniard. Those were men who felt their own dignity, who knew the nobility of a free man and his superiority over all the slaves of royalty.

Quem neque pauperies, neque mors, neque vincula terrent.[9]

Oh, when shall we hold ourselves in such high esteem? When shall all our citizens look with mere contempt on all those idols before whom they used to prostitute their superstitious adoration? When shall we finally have a great body of civic spirit?

I have no fears for the new generation. The pure souls of our young people breathe only the air of liberty, and they have not yet been tainted by the foul breath of personal interest. A truly national education will create men who will surpass the Greeks and the Romans. But what of that older generation whose backs have been so long bent under the chains of servitude and who have been trained to revere rank? [10] Who will straighten their shoulders once more? Who will free them of their former selves? *Education.* And the best way to educate the people is by multiplying those popular clubs in which those who have so unjustly been classified as "passive citizens" [ineligible to vote] may come and instruct themselves by reading works on the principles of the Constitution and on the current political situation. There it will be possible to display continuously to the eyes of the people the great examples offered by ancient and modern history. There selections from this present work could serve to teach our fellow citizens the means by which liberty can be preserved.

Frenchmen, if you would learn what these means are, study the Americans of today. Open this book. Here you will see, on the one hand, to how high a level of prosperity liberty can raise human industry, how much it can improve men and dispose them

[9] [Whom neither poverty nor death nor chains frighten. Horace, *Satires* II, 7, 84.]
[10]   Qui stultus honores
        Saepe dat indignis, et famae servit ineptus,
        Qui stupet in titulis et imaginibus.
                        Horace [*Sat.* I, 6, 15.]
[The fatuous mob, which often bestows office on the worthless, stupidly caters to reputation, and stands awestruck before ancestral inscriptions and busts.]

PREFACE

to universal brotherhood. On the other hand, you will learn what are the means by which liberty is maintained. The permanence of liberty depends on good moral principles and practices. This is a truth which is revealed at every step as one observes the present state of America.

You will learn in these *Travels* of the prodigious effects of liberty on morals, on human industry, and on the improvement of mankind. You will find that those grim Presbyterians who once raised gallows for those who did not think as they did and who imposed enormous fines on those who were impious enough to walk about or travel on Sunday now accept and fraternize with men of all sects and reject those odious superstitions which, in order to adore the Supreme Being, used to martyrize a part of the human race. You will find that all Americans, in whose minds British envy at one time sowed the most absurd prejudices against other nations, now renounce these errors, unite themselves to all peoples, reject any idea of war, and dream only of creating a universal confederation. You will find here the Free American who now knows no boundaries but those of the universe and no constraints or prohibitive restrictions but the laws made by his own representatives. You will see him undertaking every sort of enterprise, cutting fertile furrows in the soil of ancient forests, sailing over unknown seas, opening new routes, creating new markets, establishing in his own land valuable new industries which once were the exclusive prerogatives of England, and by all these many activities turning the balance of trade in his favor. You will find him meticulously faithful in honoring his word, though his enemies may everywhere proclaim his bankruptcy. You will see him under the auspices of liberty improving his abilities, cultivating his virtues, and reforming his government, using only the voice of reason to convince his opponents and elicit the support of his brothers. You will see him multiplying on every hand the number of benevolent institutions and patriotic societies. Above all, you will find that he never separates public morality from private virtue. This is the reassuring picture which these *Travels* offer to the friends of liberty.

The other side of this picture is not less reassuring. If liberty is a sure guarantee of a high level of material prosperity and if it instills virtues in men by perfecting their abilities, it is no less true that these same virtues become in their turn the strongest

1 3

support of liberty. A perfectly moral people would have no need of government, and the law would require no special powers for its execution.

This is why liberty in America is safely carried to so great a degree that it almost approaches the liberty of the state of nature. This is why the government has so little force and is often virtually nonexistent. The ignorant conclude that this must be a state of anarchy. Enlightened men who have observed at first hand the effects of such a political order are convinced of its excellence, for in spite of the weakness of the government society flourishes. This is because the prosperity of any society always increases in direct proportion to the degree of liberty it enjoys, and liberty exists in reverse proportion to the extent of governmental powers. The power of the government can increase only at the expense of liberty.

Can a people without government be happy? Yes, if we can suppose a people all of whom are virtuous. This is not a utopian dream. Do you wish a striking example? Look at the American Quakers. Although many in number and scattered throughout Pennsylvania, they existed for more than a century without any municipal government, without a police force, and without coercive laws for the administration of their almshouses and their state. How could this have been done? Read the description of their way of life and you will find the answer.

Coercive laws and liberty cannot exist together. A free people detest any form of repression. But then, if coercive means are not used, who will execute the laws? Reason and the force of moral principles. Take these away, and you must either employ the arm of violence or else fall into anarchy. If then a people would abolish the shameful device of coercion they must exercise their reason so that it may teach them the necessity of constant respect for the law.

The habitual practice of reason produces in America a large number of what are called "principled men." The term suffices to indicate their character. They are a type so rare in France that we do not even have a word for them. Some day we too shall have, I do not doubt, our own "principled men," but for the present I see only unstable, excitable persons who do good by impulse and in fits of enthusiasm, never as a result of reflection. Now there can be no permanent revolution unless reflection plans each stage and ponders every principle.

PREFACE

It is among these principled men that you find the true heroes of humanity, Howard,[11] Fothergill,[12] Penn, Franklin, Washington, Sidney, Ludlow.[13]

Show me a man of such temper, whose needs are limited, who lives simply, who has no secret passion, whose only ambition is to serve his country, a man who, as Montaigne said, "has super-celestial ideas without having subterranean morals,"[14] a man, in short, who is guided in all things by reflection. That man is the man of the people.

In short, my fellow citizens, if you would be forever free, if you would forever have freedom of choice and freedom of thought, if you would always limit the executive power within narrow limits [15] and diminish the number of your laws (*in pessima republica plurimae leges*),[16] then *establish good moral principles and practices*. Morals and customs can take the place of laws completely and even make them unnecessary. Laws take the place of morals and customs only incompletely and inadequately.

Would you increase the population, that basic resource of every nation? Would you improve the well-being of each individual citizen and promote industry, agriculture, and every activity that can contribute to the general prosperity of the nation? Then *establish good moral principles and practices*.

This is the double effect of morals and liberty in the United States, whose form of government still frightens timid and prejudiced men. The descriptions of American life to be found in these *Travels* will vindicate republicanism, which evil men wittingly calumniate and fools cannot comprehend, but which they will someday learn to understand. What can give better proof of the worth of a political system than its results? Arguments may deceive, but experience never does.[17] If liberty by its power does

[11] [John Howard (1726–1790), English philanthropist and prison reformer.]

[12] [Samuel Fothergill, leader of the London Quakers in the eighteenth century and an ardent abolitionist.]

[13] [Edmund Ludlow (1617–1692), regicide.]

[14] [*Essais*, III, xiii, "De l'Expérience."]

[15] This is one of the principles of republicanism, to restrict the power of the executive and to reduce the need of such power by forcing men to be virtuous. It is this noble objective that is being travestied until it seems almost criminal. Those who wish to give great power to the executive slander the people, the Revolution, and the Constitution.

[16] [The more corrupt the state, the more numerous the laws. Tacitus, *Historia* III.]

[17] Some excellent arguments on this subject are to be found in the forceful work

in fact produce high moral principles and practices and if it does contribute to the enlightenment of mankind, why should free men continue to be violently opposed to the form of government which is based on still greater liberty and which produces still greater prosperity? In short, why should they fight against republicanism?

I have thought it most useful and most necessary to demonstrate the truth of these principles by forceful examples. This is why I am publishing these *Travels*. Examples are always more convincing than precepts. There is something dramatic about morality in action, and the French still love drama. This is my first purpose. It is national, or rather universal in nature. For if it is clearly proved that liberty improves morals, and that morals in their turn create and maintain liberty, then is it not obvious that opposition to the extension of liberty is abominable since it is defeating progress, prosperity, and the union of the human race?

My second purpose in publishing these *Travels* is also national. I wished to depict for my fellow citizens a people with whom they should establish close ties of every sort. The moral relationships which should draw the French to the Americans are developed in the first two volumes; the third deals more specially with commercial relations. This third volume was previously published by M. Clavière and myself in 1787.[18] Since this edition is now out of print I thought it my duty to republish it with corrections. Everything in this earlier work still is and will long continue to be useful to French readers. The principles, facts, and figures which it contains are still unknown to French merchants, but this lack of information cannot endure any longer. For when liberty is solidly established it is impossible that a people should not strive to improve their industry and trade. This third volume points out to the French extremely profitable opportunities for trade, which will improve rather than diminish with the passage of time.

A fourth volume is needed to complete this work, one on po-

---

just published by the famous [Thomas] Paine, entitled *The Rights of Man.* Read especially the "Miscellaneous Chapter."

[18] This work [*De la France et des Etats-Unis*] has been translated into English and published in London and in the United States. The editors of the *Monthly Review* (January 1788), though influenced by English prejudices, have paid tribute to its principles. It has also been made available to everyone in the United States by the publication of selections in the newspapers. For newspapers are the channels through which information is circulated in America, and that is why the public there is generally well informed. [*De la France et des Etats-Unis* is not included in this edition. See Introduction.]

PREFACE

litical relations between France and America and on the present confederation of the United States. I have the materials at hand but lack the time to put them in order. A comparative study of the governments of France and the United States would require a great many comparisons of various sorts and much careful thought. Time has already judged one constitution, and the other has just been born.[19] Perhaps it is also true that public opinion needs a calmer climate, fewer prejudices, and less ignorance before it can arrive at a sane judgment of the American Constitution. There are some truths that one must not risk uttering when a casual word or a misunderstood phrase can cause them to be discredited or denied.

We must wait until the people are mature enough to be able to judge things objectively and not be misled by polysyllabic magic words which seem to conceal some great significance but in reality merely cover up a complex of errors which the laziness of the human mind accepts because it is afraid to think about them. But we must prepare the people for this maturity, which is not far off; and these *Travels* will hasten its coming by demonstrating truthfully the advantages of the only form of government which deserves any confidence.

If I had kept to the spirit of the old literature and had cared about what used to be called pride in literary reputation, I should have wasted several years in polishing this work. But I believed that these pages which are so necessary at the present moment would be useless and belated in a few years. We have come to the time when men of letters must think first of all of being useful; when, lest they be overwhelmed by the forces of reaction, they must make haste to propagate the truths that the people can stand; when, consequently, they must be concerned more with facts than with words; and when refinement of style and coloring would be no more than petty vanity and literary aristocracy. Montesquieu if he were alive today would blush to spend twenty years composing epigrams on laws. He would write for the people, because the Revolution can be maintained only by the people, and by an enlightened people. Today he would write simply and as his heart dictated, and he would not twist and torture his ideas to make them sound brilliant.

[19] If the art of drawing general conclusions were widely understood, who would not see that all political evils are derived from one single source, and that there is only one way to correct them?

NEW TRAVELS IN THE UNITED STATES

After having explained the purposes which caused me to take up my pen, I must now give an account of the sources from which I have drawn and the rules which I set up to govern my observations.

Provided with letters of recommendation from men who enjoy the highest respect in America, I received everywhere the sort of hospitable welcome that is owed to a brother, to a friend who travels only for the good of mankind. I cannot say why it was that I immediately felt at home with the most important figures in the United States. After a few hours of conversation it was as though I had been born in their midst, as though I were one of them. Is it not perhaps true that this is a mutual effect produced when two virtuous and right-minded men meet? The good and upright, though they may be meeting for the first time, have been in communication with one another all their lives, and they are immediately at ease in one another's presence.

The work which M. Clavière and I had published, *De la France et des Etats-Unis,* was already known in America. Scholars and statesmen made special efforts to provide me with all the memoirs and data that I could desire. It is to their zealous courtesy that I owe the information with which I was able to compensate for the rapidity of my travels and the brevity of my stay. I have paid to them in the pages of this work the acknowledgments which are their due. My tributes will not be suspect; I have proved that I am chary of bestowing praise and commend only from the heart. No, never shall I dishonor my pen by praising any man, however powerful he may be, whom I hate or who deserves the hatred of the people.[20]

He who would travel with profit should first study men; second, books; and third, places.

First, men: You must meet men of all classes, of all sections of the country, of all ages, and under all kinds of conditions. They must trust you, regard you as a friend, have no interest in misleading you, and always feel "at home" with you, to use the English expression.

I read in the newspapers that the ambassadors of Tipou Sultan

[20] It troubles me to praise any powerful man, even one who is virtuous; I am afraid lest my motives be poisoned. It has been said that if we would do good we must not be so scrupulous, that we should even praise useful evils. I cannot see what good can come from a base action. Are we to believe that a vicious man will be deceived by our own corruption? In any case, the good that is done by such traffic is an evil. A bad principle, a bad example. This note is timely, for there are those who believe we should praise vice when vice is sometimes useful.

[Tippo Sahib] [21] were feted everywhere. They were dragged to balls, to the theater, to factories, to arsenals, to palaces, to army camps. I do not know whether when they returned home after six months of such entertainment they thought they knew France. If they did, they were wrong, for all they had seen was the surface brilliance. It is not by the surface that one can judge the strength of a nation. The ambassador must escape from the confines of his dignity; he must climb up into garrets; he must travel alone across the countryside; he must go into stables to see the horses and into barns to inspect the quality of the grain.[22]

Everything is misrepresented to deceive the important visitor. A prince pays a visit to the Hôtel des Invalides and he is offered some of the soup and meat to taste. Are we to imagine that the governor of the Invalides was stupid enough not to have given his cook special orders that day? The only valid observations are those made unexpectedly of everyday occurrences.

A traveler before departing should inform himself about the country he is going to visit by reading books and talking with people. Thus he will have *facts;* he will be able to compare what he sees with what he has been told.

He must have a plan for making his observations. If he wishes nothing to escape him he must get used to noting things rapidly and in such a way as not to miss anything.[23] Especially he must force himself to put down in his journal every evening what he has seen, writing out the conversations he has had, the facts he has learned, the observations he has made, and the general truths he has perceived. The traveler's rule must be:

Nulla dies abeat quin linea ducta supersit.[24]

He must never let himself fall behind in his journal, for the observations pile up in his mind, the labor of writing them all down leads to negligence, and omissions encourage laziness.

---

[21] [(1749–1799), the last Nabob of Mysore, a friend of the French in India and an enemy of the English.]

[22] This is the way Mr. Jefferson traveled in France and Italy. He had only one servant with him. He observed everything with his own eyes. I am sure few journals would be as judiciously written and as useful as that which this philosopher wrote on his travels; but his modesty has kept all his observations buried in his notebooks.

[23] M. Clavière and I made such a plan, which I have included at the beginning of the first volume. Like the letters which accompany it, it may prove useful to other travelers who are less hurried than I was and less pressed by imperious circumstances.

[24] [Let no day go by without leaving a line drawn. Pliny, *Natural History* xxxv.]

The art of asking useful questions is a necessary one to the traveler who would enlighten himself and his readers. To it he must join a certain critical skill so that he can assay the credibility of the person he is questioning, which is an art more difficult than may be supposed. For how can he know whether what he is being told is the truth? He must compare it with either facts or the testimony of other witnesses. But neither of these may be available, and so he can be guided only by what he knows of the person's character. If his informant is an honest man with good judgment and no interest in misleading the observer, then he can be trusted. But how can one be sure that it is not to his advantage to deceive? The traveler must then question other men about him, learn the story of his life, his character, his circumstances, what party he belongs to, whether he is a member of the one in power or whether he is in the opposition. Questions of this sort about a third person are always very delicate and the answers almost always have an equivocal, disingenuous, and hesitating quality which does nothing to dispel the traveler's doubts.

Men in public life would perhaps be the best to consult, since they are supposedly intelligent, well informed, and experienced, if they ever came to be candid, straightforward, and communicative as well, the maxims of traditional politics notwithstanding. Surely if such a revolution in human affairs is to come to pass, it will be under republican governments, in America. For indeed why would there be any need for secrecy and reserve? Such is not yet, however, the case. Whether it be because of respect for the precepts of traditional politics, or contact with European ministries, or an English habit which has not yet been extirpated, it is in any case true that you will often find in America this disheartening reserve.

At the same time I must here pay homage to several well-known leaders of the American republics who feel that the greatness of their country lies not in the petty subterfuges which conceal incompetence in order to escape censure, but rather in the excellence of the forces by which the government operates. They revealed to me frankly all that petty politicians elsewhere try to keep wrapped in impenetrable mystery.

The choice of persons from whom to obtain information about a country is rather difficult. Natives are often too prejudiced in favor of their native land, and foreigners are too prejudiced against it. Here, I met such bias in almost all foreigners. The American

PREFACE

Revolution confounds and bewilders them. They cannot accustom themselves to the idea of a "sovereign" people, of a president, or "elective king," who shakes hands with a workingman, has no guards at his door, travels about on foot, etc. The foreign consuls are the ones who most relentlessly decry the American Constitution, and, I say with sorrow, I found in some of our own consuls this same animosity. When I landed in America they told me that the United States was on the brink of ruin. According to them, government had ceased to exist, the Constitution was detestable, Americans were not trustworthy, the public debt would never be paid, and nowhere in the country was there any honesty or justice.

As a friend of liberty I could not help being revolted by these calumnies against the American government. I countered them with rational arguments. My adversaries, who cast in my face the length of their experience and the brevity of my own, must now understand that the lens of reason gives a clearer image than the murky glass of governmental bureaucracy. Almost all these men were intelligent and well informed, but almost all had been trained in the lower echelons of the French administration, and they had all the prejudices of that organization. In their eyes a republic was a monstrosity, a minister was an idol whom they revered with superstitious awe, the people were to them only a flock of sheep to be governed with strict severity, etc. These were the favorite maxims of the men raised in the school of traditional politics. It is obvious that, used as they were to judging governments from this point of view, our consuls inevitably found the American system detestable.[25] If you asked them for facts they did not give you any significant ones. I did indeed hear of some minor examples of injustices, but when they recounted them they forgot the countless atrocious iniquities of which our own despotic governments are guilty every day.

A man who lives off the depredations of despotism is always a bad judge of a free country; he feels instinctively that he would have no place under such a system and he is frightened by the prospect of his own nonentity.[26]

[25] I must say that of the French consuls, M. Crèvecoeur [French consul in New York in 1788] was the only one whom I did not hear voice these antirepublican sentiments. M. [Philippe] Létombe [French consul in Boston] also seemed to judge Americans from a somewhat less monarchical point of view than did his colleagues.

[26] The following incident will give an idea of the insolence with which the agents of the former despotism used to judge and treat the heads of honorable republics.

I found in French travelers the same prejudices as I did in our consuls, and I was not surprised. Most Frenchmen who travel abroad or emigrate know nothing and are untrained in the art of observing. Excessively presumptuous admirers of their own manners and customs, they are impelled to ridicule those of other peoples. This gives them a double pleasure; it satisfies their pride and it humiliates others.

The more a Frenchman finds the customs of the country he is visiting different from his own the more he ridicules them. This I found true of those of my compatriots, for example, whom I questioned about Philadelphia. American men, they said, were grave and serious, and the women staid. They found no frivolous females, no free and easy married women, no cafés, no public walks. These French found everything in Philadelphia execrable because they could not strut along a boulevard or chatter in a café or seduce pretty women with their important airs and fashionable curls. They were almost scandalized to discover that no one admired them and that nobody spoke French, and they were shattered to discover they could not speak English with equal facility. They were so much less effective when their wit could not scintillate!

When men so trivial and superficial presume to disparage Americans it is only themselves that they are judging. A sober, serious, and reflective people can be well observed and appreciated only by someone of like character.

This sort of fatuity was characteristic of the French in the past. They saw everything superficially, believed everything lightly, satirized everything frivolously, and in everything they said sought only to be brilliantly witty. We must hope that the Revolution will correct these detestable traits.

Indeed the Revolution must change completely the character of the French and make of them men in every sense of the word, or else they will not long preserve their liberty. Liberty which does not improve men is soon supplanted by a new form of servi-

I once heard M. De Moustier, formerly ambassador to America, boast of having told the President of the United States in his own home that he was nothing but a tavern keeper. And the American governments were kind enough not to demand his recall! This action alone is enough to make obvious the horror that this man felt for the present revolution. He openly proclaimed himself its enemy while he was in the United States. He declaimed violently against its leaders. These facts are publicly known. I reported them to M. Montmorin [Minister of Foreign Affairs], who, nevertheless, gave him the ambassadorship to Berlin, no doubt to reward him for his antirevolutionary activities.

PREFACE

tude. It is a remedy which is ineffective in a thoroughly paralyzed body; it causes a few violent convulsions, which are followed by an even more complete lethargy.

But if the French raise their moral standards and become more enlightened they will go far. For the essence of reason and of enlightened liberty is endless progress and the universal triumph of truth over error and of principle over prejudice. They will gradually free themselves of the political misconceptions which still mar the fine constitution they have created. They will imitate the Americans as much as geographical and political circumstances permit. They will imitate them, and by so doing they will achieve only a still greater happiness, for the general good does not lie in absurdities and contradictions and cannot be born of complexities and conflicts of power. There is only one real power, and only by continually restoring power to its true source do we make it a beneficial and salutary force. The further it is removed from this source the more dangerous it becomes. In short, *the less the government is active and powerful, the more society is active, powerful, and happy.* This is the truth demonstrated by the United States today.

These *Travels* prove the second part of this political axiom. They bear witness to the activity, power, happiness, and general progress achieved by Americans. They prove that Americans are called to be the foremost people in the world, but not to be the terror of the world.

On what foundation does this high destiny rest? On three principles:

1. All power is elective in the United States.
2. Legislative power is frequently rotated.
3. The executive power, which is also elective and revocable, has little strength.[27]

[27] The last point deserves some attention in the present circumstances. The President of the United States is elected just as are the presidents or governors of the individual states. In America the idea of "hereditary capacity" transmitted from generation to generation seems inconceivable. Americans shrug their shoulders at this European nonsense, and during the last sixteen years they have experienced none of those troubles in changing presidents that the ignorant in Europe fear. This sort of election is just as peaceful as those held to choose representatives. Men who cannot meet rational arguments invent phantoms to combat. Not enough attention is given to the effects of the progress of reason and of the people's *instinct for analogy.* As soon as the people are used to the idea of electing a body of representatives every other election presents no difficulties.

In countries where the chiefs of state are hereditary it is this very same use of reason by the educated and this same instinct for analogy among the uneducated

23

It will be easy for me someday to derive from these three principles all the good results I observed in America. For the present I have confined myself merely to describing these results, for I wish to leave to my readers the task of reasoning from these results to the principles which are their causes, and then of reasoning logically back from these principles to their application in France.[28]

I have not even given all the facts; I had too little time either to write them all down or to draw myself from them all the possible conclusions. I am surprised that I have been able to complete so lengthy a work in the midst of all the varied occupations with which I am simultaneously overwhelmed, and with the *entire* re-

which inspires a perpetual distrust of the executive power. To decree a hereditary monarchy is to decree the existence in the people of an eternal distrust of the head of the executive power. Indeed it would be against nature for the people to trust an individual who claims to enjoy a supernatural superiority, who does possess *de facto* such a superiority, and who is independent of the people. Sincere and open confidence can exist only in governments in which the executive power is elective, for then the governor is always dependent upon the governed.

As soon as we understand the truth that public confidence is impossible in a hereditary monarchy while it is a necessary consequence of a fully elective form of government, then it is immediately clear why there are perpetual conflicts between the people and the government in any hereditary monarchy; why recourse to violence is frequent; why the treason and crimes of ministers go unpunished; why liberty is violated; why there is a constant alternation of despotism and anarchy; and, finally, why such states enjoy only a factitious or partial sort of prosperity often stained with blood, while under representative governments, in which the people have by their right of suffrage the power to censure all the members of the government, there exists a unity of interest which engenders a real, general, and peaceful prosperity.

English publicists have greatly exaggerated the powers granted to the President of the United States; they have compared him to the King of England, just as they have compared the American Senate to the House of Lords. This is a double error. The President of the United States is elected, while the King of England holds hereditary power. The former holds office for only four years, and the latter for life. Likewise the Senate is elected for a fixed term of office, while seats in the House of Lords are hereditary and are held for life.

It is important to note that the President of the United States can sign no treaties, nominate no ambassadors, and make no appointment to office without the consent of the Senate; that the Senate is elective; that the President is responsible; that he can be charged, tried, suspended from office, and sentenced to punishment; that neither the public welfare nor reason suffer any injury from the existence of this responsibility; that the positions of the President and his cabinet officers have not fallen vacant because they are hedged in by so many restrictions; and, finally, that they are all filled by men of recognized merit. A people who have the power of electing the members of their government do not choose, as chance is wont to do, imbeciles for governors, or rascals and petty tyrants for ministers as kings are wont to do.

[28] I know all the arguments which can be advanced against such application, but I know also that there are none which cannot be easily refuted.

sponsibility for a newspaper founded with the sole intent of restoring in public opinion this powerful revolutionary instrument.[29] This latter duty keeps me constantly busy watching a thousand enemies, repelling endless attacks, and defending just principles. How much time has been taken by my civil and political duties, by so many special pamphlets, by the obligation to attend meetings of clubs where the truth is being made ready, and by the duty I have assumed of defending Negroes and colored persons! If I mention all these facts it is only to prove some claim to my readers' indulgence. The basic purpose of my life gives me an even better right to their forbearance. *Consilium futuri ex praeterito venit,* says Seneca. "The past must guide the future." [30] A far greater future must be opened for us. It was therefore my duty to hasten to make known to France the nation whose success can guide our steps.

N.B. Some of my readers will be surprised to find in the first volume my name given as *Brissot de Warville.* Lest they be shocked, I should explain that the printing of the first volume was begun before June 19, 1790. I have retained the *Warville* within parentheses and without the particle *de* on the title pages for the benefit of my American readers, who know me only by that name and for whom these *Travels* are also written.[31]

Paris, April 21, 1791.

[29] [*Le Patriote Français,* which Brissot had founded in July 1789.]

[30] [*Moral Epistles* LXXXIII, 2.]

[31] [The title pages of both volumes of the French edition, which were printed in April 1791, carry his name as "J. P. Brissot (Warville), Citoyen Français." However the letters from Clavière (I, 1–45), which he says went to press early in 1790, when the particle had not yet become suspect, are addressed to "M. Brissot de Warville." Such were the vicissitudes of literature during the Revolution.]

TABLE OF CURRENCIES OF THE UNITED STATES, COMPARED WITH
THOSE OF EUROPE

European Currencies	Massachusetts New Hampshire Rhode Island Connecticut Virgina			New York North Carolina			Pennsylvania New Jersey Maryland Delaware			South Carolina Georgia		
	£	s.	d.	£	s.	d.	£	s.	d.	£	s.	d.
French écu of 6 livres		6	8		8	9		8	4		5	5
English guinea	1	8		1	17	4	1	15		1	1	9
Old louis d'or of 5.6 grains	1	7		1	16	4	1	14	6	1	1	5
Spanish dollar or piaster. Worth 5 livres 5 sous in 1788; 5 livres 8 sous in 1791		6			8			7	6		4	8
In all the states, one pound equals 20 shillings, one shilling equals 12 pence.												
The shilling is worth	About 16 French sous			About 13 French sous			About 14 French sous			About 22 French sous.		

The accounts of Congress are kept in dollars and cents, the cent being about one hundredth of a dollar, or a little more than a sou. The dollar is the standard coin, to which all the state currencies are compared. The variations in the state currencies, which cause great confusion in accounts, have led Congress to decree a uniform and general currency based on the decimal system. It is as yet being used only in the accounts of Congress.

Gold is rare in the United States; it keeps flowing out to foreign countries in payments of debts and purchases. Silver is more common, and one sees many dollars and French écus of six livres. There are also American gold pieces. These are coins made from the clippings of guineas. People make the assumption that the weight of the guineas is above titre and so they diminish it by clipping, in order, they say, to save the trouble of weighing the coins. From these clippings they make the gold pieces. This is a contemptible business which does not even achieve its ostensible purpose. For who can answer to me that you are honest, and that some other Jew will not come after you and clip off some more gold? So I must still weigh every coin. The government has also struck some gold coins bearing the arms of Congress and worth about two guineas, but you see few of them.

In general, payments are made in guineas, six-livre écus, English shillings and half shillings, and in copper, which is a mixture of a great variety of coins. Louis d'or are also used, but only the old kind, and they are accepted at the rates indicated in the table above. The new louis d'or are always weighed, and as their weight varies they lose or gain accordingly on the exchange. There are some which weigh eight to ten grains less than the old ones, and others four to six grains less. This is an enormous difference. I know this from my own experience in Philadelphia. On 8 louis I lost 12 s. 6 d., the shilling being worth 14 sous. A grain of gold is valued at 4 sous.

The large variety of coins in the United States is an occasion for much dishonesty and gives great inconvenience to travelers. It would be easy to reduce everything to dollars instead of to pounds, which vary in value.

From the signing of the Peace Treaty to the present there has been an extremely heavy exportation of specie from the United States. A very well informed merchant assured me that every English packet takes out of the country £30,000 sterling, in addition to what goes out on merchant ships. He has calculated from the most reliable figures that since the peace more than $10,000,000 has been exported through the port of New York.

TABLE OF WEIGHTS AND MEASURES OF THE UNITED STATES

The weights and measures used in the United States are the same as those of England.

An American acre of land contains 38,284 [French] square feet.

The common French arpent is 32,400 [French square feet]. Therefore 11 American acres equal 13 arpents.

The common American mile is 5,000 English feet.

The common French league is 13,705 [French] feet.

The American foot equals only 135 French *lignes*.

The French foot equals 144 *lignes*.

The American bushel, the usual measure for wheat, weighs about 60 [French] pounds. It takes 4⅘ American bushels to make a French *setier*.

The American pound weighs less than the French pound. The exact proportion is as follows:

100 American commercial pounds equal 91⅞ commercial Amsterdam pounds.

100 French commercial pounds equal 99⅛ commercial Amsterdam pounds.

The gallon, the measure for liquids, equals 4 Paris pints.

From M. Clavière to M. Brissot de Warville

PLAN FOR THE STUDY OF THE POLITICAL, CIVIL, MILITARY, AND LEGISLATIVE SYSTEMS OF THE FREE AMERICANS.[1]

May 18, 1788

The voyage you are about to undertake, my dear friend, will probably constitute the most interesting period of your intellectual life. You are going to travel to that part of the world where it is possible, with a minimum of obstacles, to observe and compare in the most striking way all the essential and interesting aspects of human life. If you are armed with a little courage, a great deal of patience, and a lot of *sang-froid,* if you are constantly on guard against your own mental and physical habits, if you can learn to forget completely your cherished opinions, if you will abnegate your vanity, and if you can train yourself always to form judgments slowly and carefully, then you will find in that country an opportunity to draw from the first-hand testimony of facts conclusions about the conditions under which man, the child of the earth, can hope to achieve his greatest and most lasting happiness in both private and public life.

In America it is possible, in but a few years and without running grave risks, to view a great variety of scenes; for there you can find a territory where the soil has been already exploited by the migrations of a large and active population yet which is not far removed from a wilderness untouched by the hand of man. It is a land where time, nature, and the inertia and weight of matter have been the only actors on stage.

[1] [Because the word *Américain* was used loosely in France in the eighteenth century to refer both to American Indians and to European colonists in any part of the New World, French admirers of the United States felt the need for a distinctive new term to designate the citizens of the new republic. At the second meeting of the Société Gallo-Américaine in January 1787 Brissot moved the adoption of the name *Américain libre.* Both he and Clavière use this term and also its derivative *L'Amérique libre* in their writings as proper nouns, and we have translated them *Free Americans* and *Free America.*]

Between these two extremes, various intermediary stages of development can undoubtedly be found, and no doubt it will be when you visit these various settlements that your sense and sensibility will best agree in choosing the most suitable way of life for us.

But what will be the limit of men's needs when nothing controls the activity of their minds, when nothing stops the prodigious variety of the new ideas they produce? Is it in truth in the land of liberty that we must hope to find a way to enjoy life on this earth? Is it there that man will be so satisfied with the relationship between himself and the state that he can no longer desire any change in his government, at least for many centuries? We do not know enough about ancient history to answer this question, nor can we find the answer in the study of modern times.

The present state of Free America will perhaps allow us to see what hopes for the future are justified. But who can be an impartial judge, who can free himself from the influence of his own age, of his own temperament and education, or of circumstances? Who can avoid looking at new places through the spectacles of his own tastes and habits? Who can muzzle his own imagination and suppress feelings which may excite his fancy? I hope, my dear friend, that you may have the strength required to achieve all this, and you must do everything in your power to gain such strength by constantly keeping in mind the goal of your enterprise. Since it is your purpose to enlighten men and to make level their road to happiness, you above all others must beware of being deceived by appearances and of forming false conjectures.

Consequently, when you are studying the famous American constitutions in the very land of their birth, beware of exaggerating both the shortcomings of Europe and the virtues of America, which you will be comparing and contrasting. In all your observations, your first objective should be to find out if it cannot be said, "Essentially, it's just like home; the difference is so small it's not worth the trip." I believe this is the best way to avoid errors. It is also important to be fully aware of the effects of going from one place to another and to keep them constantly in mind. Voltaire has said, "Our native land is where the heart is fixed." [2]

It is your purpose to study "the effects of liberty on the development of man, society, and government." When conducting this study, may you never lose the impartiality, self-control, and cau-

[2] [*La patrie est aux lieux où l'âme est enchaînée—Mahomet*, I, ii, 22.]

tion that such an analysis requires, so that you may bring back to your friends reports which will neither mislead them nor strain their credulity.

It does not seem likely to me that you will find in America new motives for a reasonable European to love liberty more than he already does. But you will earn our gratitude if you describe what liberty is in America, both in deed and in thought, and what forms it is likely to take over a period of time under the pressure of the unavoidable vicissitudes which mar the happiness of mankind.

Men are quarrelsome beings and everywhere they are made alike; everywhere they have the same passions. But the issues which divide them can be, from one state to another, either more or less likely to disturb the general harmony and individual happiness. For example, there is little to be feared from diversity of opinion in religious matters where universal tolerance prevails.

When political institutions force authority to submit to clearly delineated forms of government and when at the same time these institutions have the support of public opinion, then political dissension must be less of a danger. This is why, my friend, it is important that we know about the American political situation. Give us, in particular, your estimate of the effects, both present and future, of the considerable differences between the constitutions of the several states: whether these differences will cause any major difficulty; whether they may not some day become a threat to the Union; whether this diversity may not impede the administration of justice in interstate matters, in normal commercial activities, and in cases under federal jurisdiction; whether or not there may be, now or in the future, disturbances in any of the states caused by attempts either to create uniformity between state governments or to preserve existing differences; whether there is already jealousy between the states; and whether such jealousy may not arise in the future as a result of these differences. Such rivalries deprive Switzerland of many of the advantages it could have enjoyed, and they have destroyed Holland and will prevent its rebirth. If they are to be unknown in America or are not likely to become serious, explain to us why this is and will continue to be so. You are aware that the conclusions you reach on this question alone may very well influence us either to remain where we are or else to select certain states in preference to others.

America has one advantage which Europe cannot offer, namely the possibility of settling in those parts of certain states which are still wilderness and thus of escaping the annoyances of domestic politics. But can such a move be made with all the security one might wish? Please try to let us have the most reliable information available on the Indians inhabiting all the areas of that vast continent, their numbers, customs, way of life, and the more or less inevitable causes which lead to a permanent state of war between them and the Americans. This will not be the least interesting part of your account. You know, of course, that the mere idea of Indians terrifies many good people. Incidentally, if you have the time, do not forget to gather all the available information on the ancient history of America.

Observe how much may still remain of that military spirit which the Americans needed to possess, and what prejudices they have on this matter. Are there among them men who might cherish dreams of military leadership? Are levies of troops likely? Is there any sign in the people of a latent inclination for the military life, which, when seconded by a natural liking for a life of idleness, might lead men to prefer to be soldiers rather than farmers or workers? For it is this unfortunate state of mind which in other countries makes it possible to raise great armies. Tell us about the Society of the Cincinnati, which is a real cause for concern to political philosophers.[3]

King Solomon said that there is nothing new under the sun, and this must be true. But do we know enough about all the political revolutions of the past to survey their complete cycle? Nowhere in history do we find the account of a revolution similar to that of the United States or of a government like theirs. You may, therefore, foresee in the future either continuations of present tendencies or new developments which will be more or less unlike anything we can learn from history.

You must try also to find out if America is likely to become involved in foreign wars, and whether or not those Europeans are right who claim that the United States will someday try to conquer new territories. Personally, I do not believe it. It is my belief, rather, that the example set by their revolution will be contagious, especially if their federal system succeeds in maintaining unity and peace among all the confederated states. If they achieve this goal,

[3] [This organization of French and American officer veterans of the American Revolution was believed by a number of observers in both France and the United States to be dangerously aristocratic in its principles and influence.]

they will have created the masterpiece of political systems. Therefore your thinking must concentrate on this point.

Finally, tell us whether in crossing the ocean the emigrants who are now settled in the United States have brought with them the mania for regimentation. You will undoubtedly find in America people who have been so impressed by the disorders caused by the Revolution that they are terrified of the slightest political action and wish there to be a law or a rule for everything. You will no doubt also find others who cherish the ideal of great individual freedom, who think that no matter how few laws and regulations there may actually be there are still too many.

Which of these opinions predominates in the United States? When one thinks how attractive and useful private enterprise must be there, one may hope that the government will remain simple for a long time. But we are told that the number of lawyers is disproportionately large, that their influence is frightening, and that the civil code is a rich source of troubles and lawsuits, as it is in England. Give us information on this question. We have often seen that civil legislation can vitiate the benefits of the best political institutions. The relationship between civil legislation and individual happiness is comparable to that between two married people—they can kill each other with pin pricks. Civil legislation can be just as deadly in the same way to society. Is such a danger present in America?

The assumption on which European governments are based is that man is depraved, unruly, and evil, and the fear which the possession of wealth inspires in the rich produces the idea that the poor can be controlled only by chains. Is this European axiom also believed in Free America?

NATURE OF THE SOIL, AGRICULTURAL PRODUCTS, IMMIGRATION, ETC.

May 20, 1788

After having told us everything about the political aspects of life in America, and especially about those on which internal and external peace and individual security depend, you must investigate the productivity of the land, which has so great an influence on the various ways of life of the inhabitants.

It would seem logical that all the large land areas of the world are equally fertile. It is, however, possible that the soil of America may be much more productive and contain proportionately many more natural resources. Give us an idea of the opportunities with which nature has endowed America and the incentives it offers to human intelligence. It will be much more worthwhile to give us full details on features which are merely indicated on maps than to dwell on scenes of interest only to painters, poets, or amateurs of English gardens.

We have presumed to advise the Free Americans to be farmers and to leave to Europeans manufacturing activities which could draw men away from agriculture.[1] It will undoubtedly interest you to find out how they feel about this. Their opinions on this question will probably depend on the availability of means of transportation. If, as seems likely, Free America can in a very short time and without burdensome expense be covered with a network of canals (provided, of course, that enough of the population realize the advantages so that steps can be taken soon to build them), then no doubt the energy of the people will be concentrated primarily on agriculture and on the production of raw materials. It is thought in Europe that production depends on consumption and that a decline in consumption leads to unemployment; that is why it is believed that cities and factories are necessary. But there is considerable confusion in this theory, which your study of a new society developing in the protection of liberty will help you to clarify. Perhaps you will find proof that men cease

[1] See *De la France et des Etats-Unis* [London, 1787], *passim*.

to be afraid of overproducing if they are not forced to exchange their products for money in order to pay taxes, interest, etc. I am inclined to think that they are not afraid that their excess production will be lost. If this is, however, the greatest fear, and if there are at hand inexpensive means of transportation which the producer can use, that is, if he, or one of his family, can without risk load his produce on a boat on which he can live, take it to another place and barter it, then mankind loves moving about too much to let the fear of surpluses prevent production. When a farmer produces in this way, with no other concern except that of spending his time growing more than he can consume, then I believe the product will attract or seek out the consumer. So I feel that for the farmer to exploit his land fully, it is not necessary that he be assured in advance of what he will do with his grain. Expenses are the great problem in all enterprises, but you will undoubtedly find in Free America conditions such that these expenses are not an encumbrance and that the theory of consumption and production is quite different from what is supposed in Europe. Try to keep in mind, my friend, that on this point we need many more details, comparisons, facts, figures, and proofs than are usually gathered by travelers, and also that this aspect of political economy is still in its infancy because of the difficulties, the abstractions, the cumbersome details, and the discouraging obstacles which prevent its progress in Europe.

It is on the basis of the information on these matters which you provide that your friends will form their decisions. Hitherto so many mishaps, misfortunes, and misunderstandings have afflicted emigrants, even though they were prudent, well-educated men of good character, that people are afraid to follow in their steps if their situation in Europe is at all tolerable. Witness, for instance, what the Genevans endured rather than go to Ireland.[2] Consequently, my friend, if you wish to provide information useful to those who are forced to escape from European tyranny or from the presumptuous ignorance and fumbling leadership of those who decide the fate of nations, if you wish to help those who are seeking for their children a position in life and a secure and honorable livelihood, then study the story of the emigrants. How could some immigrants have starved to death in regions where there is such vigorous vegetation? Can it be that among the nat-

---

[2] [A reference to the democratic *Représentants,* many of whom, including Clavière, were forced to flee Geneva after the suppression of the Revolution of 1782.]

ural products of the land there are none fit for food? Make an effort to explain the reasons for the disasters which have befallen travelers and to judge well their illusions. When you are at the places where settlers have landed determine carefully the precautions which are necessary to save future immigrants from painful regrets and incurable bitterness for having left Europe.

You will have fewer chances of making mistakes if you look at things from the point of view of your friends and acquaintances. Start with those with whose wealth, habits, tastes, needs, and energy you are familiar; then go down the scale gradually, all the way to the worthy fellow who though healthy and vigorous owns nothing but the clothes on his back and the stick in his hand. Tell each one what he should expect when, having reached his decision, whatever it may be, and taken certain precautions, he chooses to leave Europe and go to Free America.

Finally, my friend, whether you are observing private life or political life, and whether you are reporting on ways of making money or on opportunities for honest labor in the service of society, add to your remarks judicious evaluations of opportunities in Europe and compare them with what Free America has to offer.

PLAN FOR A COLONY TO BE ESTABLISHED IN AMERICA [1]

May 21, 1788

When one thinks of the American Revolution and the circumstances which have prevented it from creating a perfect society, when one examines the information which is now available for the creation of more perfect republics on lands assigned by Congress for the establishment of new states, and when one considers the many circumstances which will favor the organization of these new states and protect them in their infancy, then one is led in spite of oneself to form plans which, though they may seem fantastic at first sight, appear nevertheless upon further reflection to be extremely attractive. Such plans can be rejected only with regret and only because of the difficulty in having them adopted by a large enough number of people to bring them to successful realization.

Why should it be impossible, if one were given a certain piece of territory with clearly defined boundaries, to prepare it to receive a republic, just as one might prepare a home for one's friends? Why could it not be divided in advance into districts to be occupied one after the other?

Penn saw the need to plan in advance the development of his colony on the territory it was to occupy; we now have many more resources at our disposal than he had, and it should be possible to make and carry out plans similar to his with greater success. Instead of being threatened, as his settlement was, by Indians, one could now count on the support of the adjoining states.

Above all, I believe that once land were made available, one could with our greater experience today write laws for the republic to occupy it which would be far more conducive to the peace and happiness of the inhabitants than any past or present political constitution.

Up to now, chance or contingency have molded political institu-

---

[1] In order to understand this letter, the reader should remember that it was written at a time when despotism was forcing the best citizens to seek asylum abroad. No one knew then that the reign of liberty was so near at hand.

tions. Everywhere, new laws dictated by reason have had to be reconciled with old absurdities, enlightenment with ignorance, good sense with prejudice, wise institutions with barbaric ones; hence the chaos which has been an eternal source of insecurity, conflicts, and disorder.

Suppose that wise and enlightened men planned the organization of a society before it actually had a single member, foresaw as far as possible all aspects of its future development, set up institutions which would promote public and private virtue, and mapped out the economic growth of the state on the basis of the nature of the area. Must we say that such men would be mere utopians?

I think not. In fact, I believe that today the desire for profits, men's eagerness to try new things, and enlightened philosophy would all join hands to attempt such an undertaking, which until the American Revolution would have encountered too many difficulties to be considered practicable.

Therefore, my friend, put your stay in America to good use and find out if there still exists among the territories at the disposal of Congress an easily accessible region where the land is suitable for agriculture and where the first settlers would not encounter too many hardships.

The area should be such that it would permit the establishment of numerous means of transportation, both on land and by water, and that it would be easy and inexpensive to make a topographic map sufficiently detailed and exact to permit drawing all the necessary boundaries in advance. The map should indicate various points of elevation relative to a given point so as to allow in advance the determination of the practicality of building canals. The surveyors should have sufficient zeal, training, exactitude, and reliability to be able to observe in the course of their work the existence of needed building materials.

Methods of surveying have been much improved. I have seen a topographic map of the whole of Ireland which was completed in no more than four years and on which are marked the smallest rivulets, hillocks, and swamps. I am told that in America there are surveyors capable of doing equally well.

Such masterpieces of cartography are undoubtedly costly, but expensive projects such as this can be carried out by a large association, and there would be many and varied reasons for the formation of a society to promote such a project. Moreover, the surveyors could be promised, besides a suitable fee, a percentage of the land sales, which would be an additional incentive and would at the same time ensure honest work.

It would be necessary to find out on what conditions Congress would consider selling such an area and if it would agree to an arrangement whereby payment would be made in installments as the settlers took possession of the land.

The geography of the area chosen should be such that it would be possible to select a central and generally accessible location where a large establishment for the reception of settlers could be easily built. Here their needs would be supplied and they would find protection against the initial hardships and disasters which have brought upon most newly founded colonies misery, hunger, and despair.

Once one had a clear idea of the nature of the land, its geography, its connections with the surrounding areas, and the conditions of purchase, if everything were satisfactory one could then turn one's attention to writing the constitution and laws suitable to the new republic and to the local conditions. Work on these points should be advanced as far as possible, so that every settler leaving to become a member of the new republic would know before his departure the laws under which he would live. Thus he would have accepted them by contract with a full knowledge of the facts.

Advance planning should be so complete that each new arrival would know where he was to go, what he was to do, and how he was to set about either achieving his private purposes if he had bought land, or fulfilling his obligations if he had signed an agreement to work for wages.

Plots of land would not be sold haphazardly or according to the whims of the settlers, but a uniform procedure would be followed so that the population would advance and spread in the manner most advantageous for the development of the region. This progressive development would be planned in such a way that the settlers could help, protect, and encourage one another as much as possible.

Expenditures for government, religious worship, and education would be covered by the income from a part of the land set aside for this purpose in each district. In order to avoid any errors in estimating the amounts needed for these purposes, and to safeguard the landowners from unexpected demands from the government, the church, or anyone in a position of authority, the estimates of these expenses would be made at the maximum rate known in Europe.

These reserved lands would be public domain, and I think that they ought to be the first to be developed. They should perhaps be adjacent to the principal lines of transportation of every sort in order to link their exploitation to the maintenance of land and water routes.

It would perhaps be wise to establish a system which would ensure that there would never be any shortage of laborers for the building of roads and canals and for the cultivation of those public lands whose products would support these workers and other public servants. Under this system there would always be work available to new immigrants and thus it would be possible to receive all able-bodied men, even though they did not have the financial means to acquire land immediately, provided their character and morals were such that they deserved to be admitted into the new republic.

These details will suffice to keep fresh in your mind the principles of the project which we have often discussed. If you get from Congress the assurance of obtaining what is in its power to grant, and if all that is left is to find the company to carry out the undertaking, then I think that this can be done in Europe without difficulty.

This company would offer for sale lands whose value would rise as the demand increased, and it would work to render them desirable by making preparations for the colonists, and especially by taking precautions to protect the settlers from the more serious hardships they would be likely to encounter in the beginning. I therefore think that this project would be tempting enough to whet the appetites of persons seeking a good profit, and that enough buyers of shares would appear to provide several millions for the enterprise.

In order to arouse even more the interest of prospective investors, the shares would be divided into very small lots, and necessary measures would be planned to assure the shareholders of an administration worthy of respect and confidence which would prevent any diversion or misuse of income, and would see to the exact execution of all decisions in order to ensure the success of the enterprise and to fulfill the expectations of the settlers.

A systematic prospectus would inform the public of the nature of the enterprise, without appealing to emotions or making exaggerated predictions or unrealistic promises.

The purpose of the enterprise would be to establish in an area acquired by purchase a republic organized according to the lessons taught by experience and according to common sense and reason, and conformable to the principles of fraternity and equality which ought to unite all men.

The basic procedure whereby this project would be executed would be to buy lands which could be resold at prices low enough to attract settlers and yet high enough to reimburse the shareholders for their investments and give them an attractive profit as well. No claims or promises would be made which would not be warranted by the nature of the enterprise and by judicious estimates. For instance, it would be pointed out that the difference between the original value of the uncleared land acquired for the formation of a settlement and the value of the same land after the settlement had been established and there was a large population would bring the shareholders a tremendous profit on their initial investment. This profit would be all the larger in proportion to the original investment because it would be agreed with Congress to purchase all the land at a single fixed price, no matter what value the land not yet taken up by the company might have attained through the growth of the settlements and the clearing of land.

This, of course, assumes, as I have already said, that payments to Congress, with the exception of a certain initial payment upon taking possession of the land actually bought, would be made only gradually as each plot was sold to a settler. This is an essential condition without which the enterprise would require a much larger capital investment than one could hope to raise.

Thus the capital of the company would have to cover the following: (1) an initial payment to Congress; (2) the expense of a survey of the area and the running of boundaries; (3) the cost of the initial public works, of establishments where the settlers would be received upon arrival, and of the necessary precautions to protect the new arrivals from accidents that might discourage them.

Undoubtedly these three items would require a large sum of money, but the increasing value of the remaining land to be bought and sold, for which the company would make payment only when there would be settlers ready to buy, would ensure the investors a tremendous profit.

Besides, as disbursements would not be made rapidly, careful handling of the initial capital provided by the investors would make possible many savings.

These would be the attractions to investors interested only in profits. Other considerations presented in the prospectus would induce many friends of humanity, philosophers, and what one might call interested people to become shareholders.

This, I believe, is enough, my friend, to bring to your mind all the ideas on this project that I have, and many more. Give what I have written your careful consideration. As at first sight the project seems romantic, find a way to save it from such an accusation and discuss it with reasonable and well-informed men, particularly with those who will zealously support noble enterprises undertaken for the benefit and consolation of humanity.

My age forbids me the hope of participating in this great undertaking. It has, I believe, no precedent in past ages; it would serve greatly future generations and would be one of the finest possible results of the American Revolution. Are these not reasons enough to animate the noble ambitions of those endowed with sufficient youth, health, and courage to be undeterred by the difficulties and unafraid of the inevitable delays which will have to be endured in order to succeed?

[SITES FOR FRENCH SETTLEMENTS]

May 21, 1788

The Utopia described in my preceding letter may be only a dream, and you will probably find that, inevitably, the new American states are destined to grow gradually out of unorganized groups of settlers formed by the successive addition of families or individuals, without following any predetermined general plan and without thought of the laws which might be most suitable when the settlements have grown and are ready to become republics in the confederation. It seems that all political systems are doomed to mold themselves according to the already existing models of other states, as either the majority or some bold and trusted leader may decide.

If, then, our project will have to be abandoned, where are you to find a location for a settlement for the friends whom we nevertheless wish to bring together in America? Will you investigate the growth of population and settlements in Kentucky, about which so many wonders are told? But think how insecure our settlement would be if we ourselves had to do the preparatory work, build the houses, etc. Some of the group would have to be the pioneers, and in this case, when would the others join them? How many accidents could frustrate our plans!

When our group of emigrants is formed in Europe, the association must be self-sufficient and all its members must depart together and not become separated. Consequently, we shall have to choose an area where there is a good-sized town in which we can live until houses are built on the land we have chosen for our settlement. This consideration seems to rule out Kentucky, for no sufficiently large town is close enough to the land we would purchase. The members of our community who would undertake to lay the groundwork for the settlement would be too far from their families and would be separated from them for too long a time.

Investigate, my friend, the ways of meeting these various objections and of finding from the very beginning a solution likely to promise more happiness and satisfaction than suffering and misery. This study will demand a great deal of work. Remember that in order to persuade the sort of people we need to join us we must find an area where both farming and trade are possible. We must be near a navigable river which communicates with the sea and close to a port where ships and sailors can be found. In short, those of us who are used to business, trade, and manufacturing must not be faced with the absolute necessity of giving up our occupations and thus becoming bored and unhappy. You know that a man does not feel tired when he is walking beside a horse or a carriage which he knows he can use should he need to.

It is too bad that Pittsburgh is not a larger and more populous city and that Virginia is separated from the new states by wilderness.

There is no need for me to discuss these problems with you in great detail, for you know us well. I shall merely recommend that you pay attention to the climate and that you try to find a pleasant site which has clear skies, a temperature like that of Paris, no mosquitoes, and fertile soil. These are the indispensable conditions.

Moreover, the many observations which you plan to make for the information of the public will enlighten us on an infinite number of points which I should list here were they not included in your principal purpose.

When you study the tastes and habits of Americans, do not overlook music in respect to its effects on the faculties of the mind. The taste for music is becoming widespread in Europe and is being made one of the important parts of our education. Is this likewise true of America? I feel that a gift for music furthers no talents except the other equally frivolous ones to which it is related. An interest in music prompts one to study it constantly and to keep seeking greater perfection. What is the good to mankind of pursuing an art which is so foreign to the useful sciences and which takes up the time best suited to study? I should also like to know if the people in America demand theatrical performances.

Finally, as we are not as yet beggarly Scotsmen, think how you can best answer the questions you will hear from our wives, our children, and ourselves about what we are to do if we arrive in a large group in some American city. Being unable to send advance agents, we shall worry about disembarking in a place where we shall know no one.

[OPPORTUNITIES FOR INVESTMENTS IN LAND]

May 22, 1788

Having communicated to you my views on general matters, I now must discuss the easier, more concrete, and more definite benefits you can derive from your trip. I refer to possible advantageous purchases of land or of government stock.

Three types of people may wish to buy land in the United States: those who intend to till the land themselves, those who plan to have others farm their land, and those who consider the land an investment whose value will increase with the growth of population and the further extension of settlements in the United States.

The first two groups can make their choices themselves. The general observations on Free America which you will publish upon your return will supply the necessary information to such emigrants. It is up to those who plan to dwell on the land which supports them to choose their own homes, for they will have to find in them not only their sustenance but also their happiness— too important an objective to be entrusted to anyone but themselves.

The case is entirely different for mere speculators. Some will wish to buy land in order to resell it at a profit as quickly as possible. Others, having longer views and being uncertain of conditions in Europe, may find it very prudent and wise to make long-range property investments in a country where the value of almost all land is likely to increase within less than a century as a result of the population growth.

Many farsighted heads of families deposit their money in banks and leave it on deposit for the use of their descendants. The same providence would be exercised by many more were it not for the fear of unexpected changes and accidents. Now it seems to me that this prudent foresight would be best served by investing the money destined for the use of one's descendants in the still unsettled areas of the United States.

The information you will gather on this matter will be infinitely

45

useful. Some lands because of their location are not likely to be cleared for cultivation for a more or less long period of time; others, closer to the main routes of transportation, will be more profitable to clear. There are some which will someday become very valuable because of the forests they contain, for though the trees are worthless and a nuisance during one phase of population growth, they become very valuable when the population has increased. Perhaps there is now such a forested area, conveniently situated for transportation near a large river, that ought to be purchased by speculators merely with a view to future demands for timber, which may not be far off.

Knowledge of local conditions is important for those wishing to speculate on the eventual value of land, and such investors will undoubtedly be grateful to anyone who provides them with a systematic topographical description permitting them to estimate the probable growth of population and to foresee the various future relationships between certain sections of the country.

Is it possible to obtain absolutely sure title to land? Are there sure means of establishing claims to property which has been unoccupied for a long time? Does one not run the risk of finding when one is ready to take possession of the land either that it is occupied by someone else or that one has bought someone else's property?

The American Farmer, in a dialogue between a settler and a land jobber, gives some indication of the need for caution. "The settler," he says, "is suspicious of the validity of the title and asks how old the deed is." [1] Inform us about all these matters, my friend, and tell us quite positively how one can abandon land one has acquired to the reign of wild animals and yet at any time in the future re-establish the original boundaries. It seems to me that a caretaker must be absolutely necessary to prevent others from taking possession of one's property.

You will be in America during the period which will decide Europe's confidence in the United States.[2] I have no doubt that the proposed confederation will be adopted, and then all clear-thinking people will see that Free America is well on the road to permanent prosperity. When this happens, many Europeans will undoubtedly give thought to the acquisition of land in the United

[1] [Saint John de Crèvecoeur, *Lettres d'un cultivateur américain*, Paris, 1787], I, 126.
[2] [Clavière refers to the pending ratification of the Constitution.]

States. We know of no other period when the speculative spirit was as widespread as it is now, or of any revolution in history similar to that achieved by Free America, or of any nation with as firm a foundation as that which the United States is to have. Therefore examples from the past cannot be brought as arguments against my assumptions regarding the spirit of the times. I should think that a person who had mastered all these facts about land values and who was able to supply answers to all the questions which might be raised by clear-thinking, farsighted, and cautious buyers would be able to persuade Europeans to purchase great quantities of land.

I do not think that the prospects for land speculation for large quick profits are equally attractive. However rapid may be the growth of population in the United States, it will not be fast enough to bring about within a short time a sudden rise in the value of a large area. Therefore I consider dubious any short-term land speculation. It could be successful only in the case of a few strips of land around the cities or in certain townships which are already actively developing. But a wise investment of this sort requires familiarity with local conditions and specialization in this business. One would have to have reliable friends who could either provide information or act as one's agents whenever there was an opportunity to buy up land that was about to rise in value.

I therefore think that speculators who are looking for quick profits should prefer national debt stocks. These will rise rapidly as soon as people believe that the American government is firmly established and as soon as there are concrete proofs of the government's intention to pay the national debt in full. It will be all the more advantageous to prefer these stocks since they can also be used to buy lands when the opportunity presents itself.

THE AMERICAN DEBT

You have told me, my friend, that the English have flooded America with tremendous amounts of counterfeit government stocks, a fact mentioned by Mr. S.[1] in his memoir, though he did not seem to attach great importance to it. If, however, the quantity of this counterfeit stock is indeed so large, then there is no need to seek elsewhere the reason for the great depreciation of the domestic debt in spite of the good will shown by the state governments and Congress. Only certificates of this type could have been counterfeited, and if there is any difficulty at all in securing their validation, it is easy to understand the disastrous effect on their value. Many holders of such stock must be afraid of validations and prefer to sell their paper on the market and get what they can. Hence the continual offers to sell, which must keep prices very low.

This sorry situation would come to an end if the states generally increased validations, for this facility would then permit many conditional transactions, which would be less onerous for sellers.

I even think that the states ought to order a general validation and a forced exchange for new issues, which would suddenly make valueless any old certificates not turned in. Perhaps, however, it is feared that too violent a reaction might follow the sudden complete invalidation of the counterfeit certificates. Or perhaps the states themselves are happy to permit the perpetuation of this situation, which will be advantageous to them if they intend to buy up their certificates.

A great deal of information needs to be gathered on this point, and it is only when you are in possession of the facts that you will know the real reason for the great depreciation of the American debt.

We are told that certificates on the domestic debt are in greater demand now that the adoption of the new constitution has become probable, but what proof do we have of the truth of this?

[1] [Probably William Seton, a New York merchant and financier associated with William Duer, Andrew Craigie, Clavière, and Brissot in their speculations. The memoir on the American debt is lost; it obviously was sent to Clavière and his financial partners before Brissot's departure from France.]

The Dutch and other prudent speculators will buy these certificates only when their legality is certified and provided they have guarantees that the papers are not counterfeit. But this, by itself, will be sufficient to induce sellers to raise their prices even though the certificates are still greatly depreciated in their own country, for the validation will be a very slow and difficult process and may result in reducing to a very small number the certificates acceptable to Dutch and other buyers. Here, then, are some very important points on which you ought to gather information. The greatest attention should be paid to the procedure the Treasury uses to validate and register certificates, for what would be the use of contracting for transactions whose execution would be very slow and very uncertain? Moreover, what guarantee is there that the bona fide certificates, once sold, will be actually delivered to the buyer? For if their validation is to take place only some time after their sale, the price of these certified stocks may be such that the sellers will no longer wish to part with them. They would have a convenient pretext to fail to make delivery, for they could merely say that the certificates they had contracted to sell had proved to be counterfeit. The good faith of American businessmen is already suspect, and indeed many Europeans would have no scruples about playing such a trick.

What is true of the certificates may also be true of the indents, for the lack of precautions against counterfeiting must have been the same in either case, and it seems that in spite of the resolutions passed by Congress the indents have not been redeemed with money. The English must have had the time to counterfeit them. A tremendous confusion may therefore exist both about the certificates on the domestic debt and about the indents.

One may seek the truth about these questions either as a speculator or as a historian. For the historian, who must trace the sequence of events back to their origins, the task will be long. The speculator, on the other hand, need only determine a reliable picture of the present state of affairs and find out what the value is of the paper he buys and whether any new depreciation is being considered. Only the policy of the American government can offer any guarantees on this latter question. Now what is this policy? Perhaps the Americans make a distinction between domestic and foreign credit and think that the latter can be maintained by faithful payments on the foreign debt while they disregard the former because of the chaotic state of the domestic debt.

Finally, Europeans will be interested in investing in the American domestic debt only if the interest can be collected in Europe. Now what are the prospects of such an arrangement? If the indents are not paid in cash and are above [below] par, the European investor can collect only an amount equal to their value in America, and consequently he will lose on his speculation.

Suppose your calculations ran as follows: If I buy for 50 livres certificates whose face value is 100 livres and which pay 6 per cent interest, my investment will bring in 12 per cent until such time as the certificates are redeemed. But if the interest is paid in indents which are worth less than their face value, the income will be decreased by the amount of this loss, so that the certificates which cost 50 livres may in fact bring in only 3 per cent on the invested principal.

In conclusion, the most essential point to clarify is the question of counterfeiting and its consequences. What view do the states and Congress take of it? Has internal politics thought of making capital of the situation? Are there any methods of validating the paper? If so, what are they? Are they slow or prompt? Do they exist in all the states? I cannot believe that the emission of all this paper was conducted in an orderly manner since it took place in a period of confusion and stress. Consequently, I cannot imagine how the validation can be successfully conducted, and since there is talk of counterfeit paper on a large scale, I am at a loss what to think of the domestic debt. You will have to exercise, my friend, all your sagacity and caution. You may find out the reason why no certificates have been delivered as yet to the Dutch, who contracted to buy them only on the condition that they would receive certificates of the domestic debt which had been registered by the Treasury.

It is obvious that the United States is in great financial difficulty generally. The resolutions passed by Congress are not being carried out, and the rate of interest on the domestic debt is such that it cannot be attributed merely to scarcity of cash, unless specie invested in commerce, agriculture, and the clearing of land yields a higher annual interest than 12, 15, 20, or 25 per cent, or even more, since some certificates representing an investment of 14 livres pay 6 livres interest. Apply your methodical mind to all these problems, my friend, and clarify them.

Here is another financial operation the study of which will be enlightening. Congress has contracted for the minting of 300 tons of copper coins on a 6 per cent loan repayable in 20 years. Examine this transaction, determine the intrinsic value of the copper, add to this the mintage, and calculate what percentage of the value of this coinage will be fictitious by comparing the actual cost of the coins with their monetary value. Then see what part of this fictitious value Congress has paid to the contractors, and from this make an evaluation of its credit. It must be very weak if Congress has retained only 13 per cent of the fictitious value. At least this is what I understand by the "premium" of 13 per cent to the profit of the United States.

Under what circumstances would an American enter into an agreement? Note that these difficulties we have mentioned may not affect an American if they are due only to the scarcity of cash, for the high value of specie will enable him to gain on one hand what he loses on the other. It would not be surprising if Americans advised you to invest in their domestic debt, since this operation would produce specie for them.

We have already noted in our book [2] that Americans must need cash because of the opening up of new land. You will undoubtedly find confirmation of our assumption, and you will probably discover that cash is greatly needed for an infinite number of undertakings such as the construction of large buildings and for other income-producing investments. You know, besides, that in America labor is extremely expensive, and if you can estimate the number of workers employed at one dollar a day, you will find that the amount of hard money which has to be in circulation for payments by employers to their workers is very large for states with large foreign obligations.

[2] [*De la France et des Etats-Unis.*]

PLAN OF INVESTIGATION TO BE FOLLOWED DURING MY TRAVELS IN AMERICA [1]

My main object is to *study the effects of liberty on the development of man, society, and government.*

This is to be the central purpose of all my investigations, and to achieve it I must note each evening in a journal everything of particular interest that I have observed in the course of the day.

In the composition of this journal the only order to be followed will be that of day-by-day entries.

As my observations are to fall into five or six major categories, I must have a notebook for each category in which I shall write down one after the other all the pertinent observations, facts, documents, and materials that chance may put in my way.

These categories will be the following:

THE FEDERAL GOVERNMENT

Gather all the available material on the old Congress [and] on the new, everything that has been published on the subject, and in particular *The Letters of Publius.*[2]

Note the main disadvantages of the old constitution, the advantages of the new one, the criticisms expressed of the latter, and the general attitude toward the Union.

Remarks by my friend M. Clavière. The most advantageous sort of political association is undoubtedly one formed of small states whose governments need not be too complex, united under a federal government whose duty it is to maintain peace among them, to safeguard the tranquility and security of all, and to represent the union with dignity abroad. Consequently, you must concentrate on observing existing conditions and circumstances in order to foresee the probable future of the present federal government of the United States.

[1] I thought I should publish this plan, which may prove useful to other travelers. The plan is mine; the remarks are by M. Clavière.
[2] [*The Federalist,* by Hamilton, Madison, and Jay.]

PLAN OF INVESTIGATION

THE STATE GOVERNMENTS

Politics: Study the constitution of the general assemblies, the senates, and the executives; the elections and the abuses for which they are criticized. Compare the results so far achieved by the various legislatures to find out which has the best constitution.

Remarks. What can be expected from the existence of different systems? What are the principal characteristics of each?

All nations have recognized the sovereignty of the people, but not all have respected it to an equal degree, and one cannot expect civil tranquility in a state where the people are powerless to regain their sovereignty except by sedition. Public order is also in jeopardy in any state where the voice of the people is not subject to the control of formal procedures. The various states should be studied in the light of these principles.

CIVIL LEGISLATION, CRIMINAL LAW, AND POLICE ORDINANCES

When studying these matters it is essential to concentrate on the facts. Comparisons with the facts in other countries of the world will be made after my return.

TRADE BETWEEN THE VARIOUS STATES AND THE INDIANS, CANADA, NOVA SCOTIA, THE BRITISH WEST INDIES, FRANCE, SPAIN, HOLLAND, THE NORTHERN STATES OF EUROPE, MEXICO, CHINA, THE INDIES, AND AFRICA

Note the main exports and imports, the number of ships employed, and the amount of money invested in this trade.

Remarks. Do not fail to determine the mediums of exchange used by Americans in dealing with the various countries and particularly with the Spanish colonies, which must be the principal source of silver and gold for the United States. Can the western part of North America be reached by land? Do Free Americans travel in the neighboring Spanish territories?

Is the monetary system simple, easy to understand, and invariable? Will the money maintain a fixed value so that in the course of time it will be possible to estimate price fluctuations by comparison with a constant standard? This will be possible only if a single metal is used as the standard in relation to which the value of every other metal is determined either as a commodity or as a token, like a letter of credit which has no intrinsic value but stands for a right to a certain sum of money. For instance, a copper sou is in effect a letter of credit on a certain amount of the metal adopted as a measure of value and never has an intrinsic value equal to that of the quantity of the standard metal which it represents.

BANKS

Remarks. Banks are an extremely important part of a state. The ratio between the amount of specie in their vaults and the amount of the notes they circulate is the criterion of their soundness. Those that have little or no specie yet circulate many notes are in a very precarious position and are a great danger.

It is essential to read carefully [Adam] Smith's history of the banks of Scotland, but only after having acquired a clear understanding of the true principles of banking in order to penetrate more easily Smith's obscure writing. It is very easy to go astray in studying these problems, which can never be simply enough expressed.

FEDERAL REVENUE OF THE STATES; THEIR SYSTEMS OF TAXATION AND TAX COLLECTION; EFFECTS OF TAXATION

Remarks. What is the prevailing tax system? If it is believed that taxes should be levied only on land values, is it understood that it is dangerous to discourage agriculture? Why have no public lands been reserved for the use of the states?

THE FEDERAL DEBT OF EACH STATE. PRIVATE DEBTS. THE FEDERAL EXPENSES OF EACH STATE. ACCOUNTING

Remarks. The debt has been reduced, and this reduction has been justified on the ground that tremendous profits were made on the sale of the various supplies which occasioned the debt. Reread on this topic the memoir of Mr. S.[3] and you will see that there was a point where this depreciation became unjustified.

There is interesting research to be done on this subject. Why

[3] [See note p. 48.]

were people making such large profits before a depreciation was suspected? It was because they ran a different kind of risk; they doubted they would be reimbursed because they doubted the success of the Revolution. But from this point of view, how can one justify the scale by which the debt was reduced, particularly in the case of creditors who had no interest in the Revolution?

Cash must have been very scarce; that is always an important cause of lack of credit. Those who were forced to borrow undoubtedly had to pay high interest rates, and this in turn led to soaring prices. Then have not certain reductions of the debt been unjust?

I repeat, it will be a very interesting story, if you can follow its development from the very beginning. It may perhaps lead to the conclusion that a fraudulent bankruptcy has been committed. If this is true, we should not fear to state the facts. Besides, even if we suppose extortion on the part of the creditor, repudiation by the debtor of part of his debt cannot be justified; the only excuse can be that of necessity.

According to the new *Encyclopédie*,[4] the irregularities which have caused the depreciation of the debt can be traced back to the period preceding the Revolution. Yet before the war, though there was paper money, not all the state currencies were depreciated, and there was no currency issued by Congress. But now all paper money without exception has been discredited. The unquestionable fact is that there has been a bankruptcy. Perhaps by a thorough investigation of all the facts relative to American finances conclusions may be drawn which will prevent the recurrence under similar circumstances of a similar shameful operation.

The *Encyclopédie* claims that foreigners are not suffering by the depreciation. Is this true?

It is very important to find out what the public expenses of the United States are likely to be in the future, and to determine as well as possible the sort of public spirit which animates Americans. How do they look upon loans? Sometimes loans are good, but it is a wise government that resists this recourse; for once one starts down this road there is no telling where it will lead. Government loans always mean capital withdrawn from the uses of industry, and the theory that money flows back to private enterprise is misleading. Besides, Americans must be averse to such loans because

[4] [Article "Etats-Unis," by J. N. Démeunier in the *Encyclopédie méthodique*, section *Economie politique et diplomatique*, II (1786), 345–433.]

of the difficulties they are now experiencing—unless, of course, they believe that they owe to these loans their liberty.

THE COUNTRY AROUND THE CITIES, FURTHER INLAND, AND NEAR
INDIAN TERRITORY. FARMING; CAPITAL INVESTMENT IN
AGRICULTURE; THE VARIOUS AGRICULTURAL PRODUCTS.
FACTORS WHICH ENCOURAGE OR DISCOURAGE THE
CLEARING OF NEW LAND. MONEY IN CIRCULATION
IN RURAL AREAS; RURAL MANUFACTURING

Remarks. It is said that quite close to New York the land is un-cultivated, that the city is surrounded by forests, and that although wood is cheap the inhabitants prefer to burn coal despite the higher cost. If this is true, then either commerce is so profitable in New York that agriculture is neglected, or the products brought from elsewhere are less expensive than those grown close to the city. If these reports are true, here are mysteries undreamed of in Europe which demand explanation. You must study the state of commerce and agriculture in America and determine why one may be pre-ferred to the other.

You may find that the origins of the immigrants are to a great extent responsible for their choices of profession. The English arrive intending to go into trade because they come supplied with a certain amount of money. The Scotch, Irish, Germans, and others, who have no money and are for the most part refugees from rural areas, turn to farming. When studying these questions, you must tell us what a supply of capital combined with industry and simple tastes can achieve in agriculture.

What is the real reason for the low prices for which one can purchase cleared land with standing buildings? There is no doubt an excess of production over consumption, in which case land must earn a very small income for those who plan to live on the sale of their products.

There has been much talk of the advantages of raising cattle.

Nations, like individuals, have their prejudices, tastes, and fancies. What are American attitudes toward manufacturing? Is there in the United States a predominant system of agriculture? Are there any special terms for agriculture on a small and on a large scale?

PLAN OF INVESTIGATION

MANNERS AND MORALS IN SEAPORTS, IN INLAND CITIES, AND IN THE COUNTRY

Remarks. I wonder whether you will find distinctly American manners and customs in your travels, or rather merely the practice of European ones? I do not mean, of course, those traits which, being universally human, are found everywhere in the world.

Tell us about private and public education. Do Americans waste the time of their children, as we do in Europe, on useless or unimportant studies? Try to become acquainted as much as possible with clergymen. Is paternal authority more respected in America than in Europe? Is the mild sort of education which Rousseau propagated practiced by Free Americans? Is there libertinism? I have heard reports that in this respect Philadelphia is no better than a European city.

What was the effect of the war on morals and customs, and what changes are to be expected in the future?

THE PRICES OF COMMODITIES OF PRIME AND OF SECONDARY NECESSITY IN VARIOUS PLACES

Remarks. Which foods are most plentiful? Do Americans store grain? Are they gluttons or moderate eaters? Do not forget to visit the markets wherever you go, for they offer an excellent opportunity to get an idea of the way the farmers live, what they grow, and how prosperous they are.

Do people drink spirituous liquors?

THE ALREADY EXISTING INEQUALITY OF WEALTH, ITS CAUSES, AND ITS PRESENT AND FUTURE EFFECTS

Remarks. In connection with this point, do not fail to tell us about customs relative to marriages, dowries, and wills, for these practices retard or accelerate the development of inequality.

MENDICITY. HOSPITALS. PRIVATE AND PUBLIC EDUCATION. COLLEGES. RELIGION, IN ITS POLITICAL ASPECTS; THE MANNER IN WHICH VARIOUS SECTS MANAGE TO EXIST SIDE BY SIDE. PUBLIC MANNERS AND MORALS. ATTITUDES OF THE INHABITANTS OF EACH STATE TO ONE ANOTHER, TO THEIR GOVERNMENT, AND TO THE CONFEDERATION

Remarks. It is claimed that American businessmen are sly and deceitful and very dishonest. It is possible that they have been corrupted by the violent circumstances through which they have lived, that the huge profits they have made have exacerbated their greed, and that in general probity has suffered greatly as a result of the operations to which the government itself was forced to resort in connection with the public debt. These are interesting questions to examine and eminently worth clarifying if at all possible.

DOMESTIC SERVANTS. SLAVERY, AND THE MEASURES BEING ADOPTED TO ABOLISH IT

Remarks. Is it true that the only servants available are Negroes? Their actual civil, political, and moral status and the freed Negroes' opinion of their own position are all philosophic subjects worth careful study.

Your observations may lead to conclusions on practical means of raising this unfortunate class to the level of other men.

OPPORTUNITIES FOR THE ACQUISITION OF LAND; HOW SUCH PURCHASES MAY BE MADE. CLEARING OF LAND. INITIAL INVESTMENTS NEEDED. PURCHASE OF GOVERNMENT STOCK. BUSINESS OPPORTUNITIES, ETC.

Remarks. Make inquiries about the brokers dealing in government stock, and in general investigate the sort of men in this business. Have brokers become necessary?

Also examine immigration into Free America since the peace, and find out from what countries the majority of immigrants come, how successful they are generally, etc.

Events in Kentucky, in the neighboring settlements, and in the Ohio Valley, and the story of the group of settlers who recently gathered in Pittsburgh and who have since left, are all likely to furnish you with interesting details especially important to future immigrants. What sort of a place is Pittsburgh?

The points listed above represent, I believe, the main considerations on which I must concentrate wherever I go.

I must gather the largest possible amount of written material and copy as many extracts as I can. I must collect pamphlets and books published in America which contain information on the United States.

I must also consult at every step of my journey the travelers who have written on every city I shall visit and on every topic I shall study, and add to their statements my own marginal comments.

Remarks. Are there no travelers who have explored the western regions of America and whose accounts are well regarded in America but are unknown to European readers? Is the number of writers increasing? What is the state of publishing and printing in the United States?

LE HAVRE

Havre de Grace, June 3, 1788

Here I am at last, my dear friend, within sight of the sea and of the ship which is to carry me away from my country. I leave without regrets, for under the ministerial depotism which is tearing asunder the nation, I foresee for the future nothing but fearful storms, slavery, or war. May the disasters which threaten this fair land spare the dear ones I leave behind!

I shall not describe to you the country or the cities through which I have passed on my way here. My thoughts were still too full of the heartrending spectacle I had left behind,[1] and my mind was besieged by too many worries and fears to be able to preserve its powers of observation. I was indifferent to all the scenes that unfolded before me, and the sight of a few cantons in Normandy which reminded me of England barely roused me from this intellectual paralysis.

The fields of Normandy, and especially those of the region of Caux, display a great variety of crops. The peasants' cottages, better built and with more windows than those of Picardy or Beauce, proclaim the affluence which prevails in this province. The peasants are well clad. You are familiar with the odd headdress worn by the women of Caux: that bonnet which rises up like a sugar loaf, that sort of vain finery which always disfigures simple nature, and that hair combed up in a tight mass and plastered with powder and grease. All this appears rather ridiculous, but one condones these ornaments and this extravagance when one thinks that if their husbands were poor like the peasants in other provinces they could not afford to pay for them. Norman peasants have the same look of contentment and independence which, you may recall, impressed us when we saw the peasants of Austrian Flanders.[2] They

---

[1] [A reference, added no doubt later and with a revolutionist's hindsight, to conditions in Paris a year before the storming of the Bastille.]

[2] The road from Mons to Antwerp offers a magnificent spectacle. The countryside is like a superb and immensely rich garden. The fields, the cottages of the peasants, their carts, their strong horses, the stout clothes they wear, their appearance, the look in their eyes—everything proclaims the prosperity of the people. I saw few young girls who did not look interesting and attractive. With what

have the same open, peaceful faces—an infallible sign of "the golden mean"—the same virtue and dignity. What is the cause of the material well-being peculiar to the country people of Normandy? Is it their nearness to the seacoast, their flourishing trade, the division of their farmland into small fields? I have been unable to determine the true cause. But undoubtedly if France is ever governed by a free constitution, none of its provinces will be better situated or better endowed with advantages necessary to achieve a high degree of prosperity.

Around Bolbec and Bottes, near Le Havre, there are some delightfully picturesque spots which would be well suited for a philosopher's hermitage or for the simple home of a small family content to find within itself the sources of its happiness.

I should avoid the area of Rouen, as I should avoid all large cities. Poverty and opulence dwell there side by side; you see a great number of dejected-looking men, clad entirely in rags, with sunken cheeks and emaciated bodies. Everything indicates that there are factories in this city, that is to say, one sees a horde of wretches who are starving to death so that a few individuals may bask in opulence.[3]

During the two days I have been in Le Havre I have seen only three or four merchants; this is too short a time and too few people to judge a city. The merchants complain a lot about the new trade treaty between France and England,[4] which they think at least premature, considering the fact that we lack a constitution and that English industry is superior to ours. They also complain that merchants were not consulted about it. I tried to console them by suggesting that the consequences of this treaty, together with other circumstances, will undoubtedly bring about a free constitution which, by breaking the chains shackling French industry and trade, will allow us to make up our present losses, and that a few bank-

---

pleasure did I see young women nursing their babies on the threshold of these neat cottages while the older children played on the grass around them! This is what I pray for: a little house in a fertile land, near a river, in the midst of a people who are still virtuous and who enjoy a certain degree of liberty. This part of Flanders greatly resembles England; the houses in particular (with the exception of the doors which do not have the two small columns) look as clean and neat as English houses.

[3] Not all manufacturing offers this picture. Conditions depend on the diversity of the products and on the freedom of the country. See *De la France et des Etats-Unis* [by Brissot and Etienne Clavière (London, 1787)], and what I shall say in later letters.

[4] [Signed September 28, 1786.]

ruptcies and temporary financial embarrassment will not be too large a price to pay for liberty. As to the failure of the ministry to consult the merchants, I explained that this was the result as much of the merchants' servile fear and lack of public spirit as it was of the principles of unlimited monarchical government. This form of government admits to the ministry only shortsighted, presumptuous, and dishonest intriguers, and this kind of minister is not given to consulting others.

Le Havre is, after Nantes and Bordeaux, the principal center of the slave trade. Many in this city owe their fortunes to this infamous traffic, which, far from diminishing, is increasing. A recently arrived piece of information will even further inflame the avidity of the gamblers who play this "lottery." The news is that a slave ship with a cargo of Negroes, upon arrival in Santo Domingo, sold them for 2,300 livres apiece, colonial money.[5] Its owners are counting on a very handsome profit.

There is a great demand for Negroes in the colonies. I inquired the reason and was told that it was the increased demand for our colonial products, such as sugar, coffee, and particularly cotton. These goods now sell at higher prices than in former years. By his profits the planter is able to increase the number of his Negroes and to pay a higher price for them. I asked the reason for the rapid rise in the European demand for sugar, coffee, and cotton, and I was told that there is an increased consumption of cotton goods, and also of sugar and coffee. Does this mean that wealth is increasing everywhere? It would appear so, if you travel through England. But our French countryside, despite its great fertility, does not give the same impression.

The owners of the slave ships believe, however, that without the considerable subsidies granted by the government the trade could not be maintained very long, for the English sell their Negroes cheaper than do the French. Their highest price is from 1,100 to 1,200 livres a head.

I gathered some of this information from an American captain who knows well the East [West?] Indies and Africa. He assured me that Negroes are generally better fed and treated more kindly on French ships than on English ones. This is perhaps the reason that the French cannot compete with the English, who feed their Negroes worse and spend less money on them.[6]

[5] Note that at our African factories each Negro costs an average of 300 livres.
[6] The real reasons are the greater expenses and higher pay of the French captains

NEW TRAVELS IN THE UNITED STATES

I discussed with the merchants mentioned above the societies which are being formed in America, England, and even in France for the abolition of this evil trade.[7] They knew nothing of the existence of these societies, and they view their efforts merely as the expression of a blind and extremely dangerous sort of fanaticism. Filled with inveterate prejudices and not having read any of the profound discussions which this philosophical and political revolution in the cause of humanity has aroused in England, they keep repeating that sugar can be grown only by the use of Negroes —enslaved Negroes. Whites, they say, cannot be employed because of the extreme heat, and no work can be got out of Negroes except by brandishing a whip. To this and to a dozen other arguments that I have heard a hundred times elsewhere, I objected with the conclusive counterarguments with which you are familiar.[8] I pointed out the example of the East Indies, but I did not convert anyone. Self-interest still speaks too loudly and is too unenlightened.

One of these merchants, to whom I extolled the method of emancipation practiced by the Spanish and its favorable influence on the intelligence and on the moral qualities of the Negro population, told me that the Negroes in the Spanish islands have not developed any greater skill than they have elsewhere, and that the plantations of sugar cane are no better there than in our own colonies. I had the opportunity to check this statement when I consulted a reliable American who had been in Havana several times. He assured me that almost all the commission merchants there were free Negroes, that they displayed the greatest industry both in farming and in trade, and that he had often seen Negroes who were capable of superintending the loading of cargo for a whole ship.

and crews. The English captain eats salt meat when at sea and remains a captain all his life. The French captain, on the other hand, demands luxury and expensive comforts, and he wants to make his fortune in three voyages. See M. Pétion de Villeneuve's interesting *Discours sur la traite des Noirs* [Paris:] Au Bureau du Patriote Français, Place du Théâtre Italien, 1790.

[7] [The Pennsylvania Society for Promoting the Abolition of Slavery (1787); in New York, The Society for Promoting the Manumission of Slaves (1785); in London, The Society for the Abolition of the Slave Trade (1787); and in Paris, Brissot's own Société des Amis des Noirs (1788).]

[8] They can be found in the excellent *Essay on the Impolicy of the African Slave Trade* [London, 1788] by [Thomas] Clarkson and in the very sensible and reasonable work of Dr. [Benjamin Sigismond] Frossard, *La Cause de l'humanité, etc.* [*La Cause des esclaves nègres et des habitans de la Guinée, portée au tribunal de la justice, de la religion et de la politique*] (Paris: Gattey [1788]).

These French merchants confirmed a fact that the [antislavery] society of London has denounced, namely, that the English are trading in slaves under the names of French firms [9] and are taking advantage of the high subsidies paid by the French government.[10]

I talked to them about the free settlement established in Sierra Leone for the raising of sugar cane by free workers in an attempt to develop this type of agriculture and to extend the reign of civilization in Africa.[11] They replied that this establishment would not last long, that English and French traders viewed it with displeasure, and that a half-English half-French shipowner had declared he was going to resort to arms in order to destroy this budding colony.[12]

My conversations with these merchants gave me the impression that they are governed more by prejudice than by inhumanity and that if one could make available to them a new, more lucrative kind of trade it would not be difficult to persuade them to abandon the traffic in these unhappy Africans. We must therefore continue to write and to publish, and we must never weary of spreading our message.

In the port of this city I saw one of the packets intended for service between France and the United States of America and afterwards employed in the very useless and very expensive "royal" service to our islands, a system which was adopted only to favor, at public expense, some of the creatures of the ministry then in office. This ship, the *Maréchal de Castries*, was built in America and is said to be an excellent sailer. Here, then, is the best answer to all the fables repeated in the offices of the Ministry of the Navy at Versailles against the quality of American timber and American shipbuilding.

This packet service seems now to be doomed. Two months have passed since the departure of the last ship, and there are no orders

[9] See M. Pétion de Villeneuve's *Discours sur la traite des Noirs*, p. 45.
[10] The subsidies amount to almost half the original price of the Negroes. *Ibid.*
[11] [Established by Dr. Henry Smeathman in 1787 on St. George's (Kra) Bay.]
[12] His prediction has come true, and this infernal, greed-inspired project has succeeded. But this greed will be defeated in its turn, for the free settlement is to be started again with much greater support. Two new societies of *whites* are being formed in London to go to Africa to colonize and to civilize the Negroes. See the judicious pamphlet [by François Lanthenas] entitled *M. Lamiral réfuté par lui-même* [, *ou Réponse aux opinions de cet auteur sur l'abolition de la traite des Noirs* (Paris:] Au Bureau du Patriote François [1790]). [Brissot is referring to the St. George's Company, organized in 1789 by Granville Sharp and others, and the Sierra Leone Company, 1791, of which Henry Thornton was chairman and Sharp president.]

for another to sail.[13] It seems, indeed, that no more will be sent. Thus will disappear the only means whereby we could maintain communication with Free America and which would have permitted us to gather someday the fruits of the expensive assistance we have given that country.

Undoubtedly the principles of this undertaking were poorly conceived. This enterprise should have been organized with an eye to the problems and the possibilities presented by the newly established relations between France and the United States. Simple but comfortable ships should have been built, and they should have been constructed in American shipyards, since the cost there would have been half what it is here. Special inducements, such as regularity of service, should have been offered to merchants to persuade them to make use of these ships. The vessels should not have been overmanned with crews drawn from the Royal Navy, that is to say, by overpaid, insolent, wasteful, and careless sailors. Moreover, this undertaking should not have been entrusted to the supervision of Parisian bankers, who, being too far removed from the scene, could neither see the mismanagement nor correct it. All these follies, particularly the attempt to make a fancy show where simplicity was called for and the entrusting of the supervision to men who did not have the slightest interest in the enterprise, have resulted in an expense of close to two millions in a single year. The consequence is that the ministry wishes to abolish, "for the sake of economy," a useful but poorly conceived undertaking. Undoubtedly, economy should be preached, but while the abolition of the packet service to the French West Indies is very reasonable and prudent, it is unwise and absurd to suspend the service with Free America, for it deprives us of the only means of communication with its inhabitants. The number of merchant ships leaving our ports for both the United States and our [West Indian] islands is less than 700 or 800 a year. Moreover, this interruption of communications with us may force the Americans to form closer ties with the English, who dispatch packets as well as merchant ships to American shores.[14]

[13] The Ministry was so negligent at the time that the mail destined for Free America which was scheduled to leave in May 1788 remained in the office four or five months, together with what came in later. I do not even know whether it was ever sent. This negligence caused great damage in America to the reputation of France, and it ruined the opinion the Americans had of French principles and government. It was all the more unforgivable because the *Cato*, on which I sailed, as well as other ships, offered to carry the mail but was refused.

[14] Concerning these packets and those that have been recently established, see one of my following letters. [Letter 43, n16.]

LE HAVRE

Farewell, my friend. The wind is fair and we are about to embark. I am consumed with impatience; all I see afflicts and disturbs me. Everything, even talk of action and of patriotic motives, alarms me and seems suspect. Such is the disastrous influence of arbitrary government; it severs all ties, it diminishes the trust of men in one another, it invites suspicion, and consequently it condemns freedom-loving men of sensibility to self-imposed isolation, or to unhappiness, or to the constant fear of compromising themselves. This is the picture of the martyrdom I have endured since the cruel year of 1784.[15] For the last six months especially I have never had an easy mind except when I managed to lose myself in diversion; I have not seen a new face without becoming suspicious. This situation was too great a strain. In a few hours my heart will be at ease; my soul will shed its anxiety. What happiness I shall enjoy when I breathe the air of liberty!

[15] [Brissot's imprisonment in the Bastille.]

THE COMMERCE OF LE HAVRE

A well-informed man who has studied the commerce of this city and who also has reliable accounts from other sources has had the kindness to communicate to me the information in his possession, which I hasten to pass on, knowing that these details will be of interest to you.

The commerce of Le Havre has four branches: trade with the colonies, the slave trade, and the offshore and inshore coastwise trade.

Trade with the colonies has doubled here since the Peace of 1762 and the export to foreign countries of colonial goods has almost tripled, as is attested by the customs receipts, which are more than twice as large as they were before. If the present plans for enlarging the port of Le Havre are carried out, this city will no doubt become one of the most flourishing commercial centers in the world.

Each year, 120 ships are fitted out here for trade with the West Indies. Of these, 30 are of 350 to 430 tons, and the rest of 150 to 240 tons. No other port ships out richer cargoes; the value of goods exported is estimated, on the average, from 300,000 to 350,-000 livres. These shipments include foodstuffs such as salt beef, butter, lard, salmon, dried codfish, unsmoked and red herring, olive oil, wine, brandy and flour, as well as all kinds of manufactured products such as silks, haberdashery, linens, hardware, silverware, jewelry, beaver hats, gold and silver braid, furniture, mirrors, novelties, wearing apparel, laces, watches, iron pots, woodwork, wagons and carriages, barrel staves and hoops, wickerwork, roofing tiles, bricks, flooring tile from Caen, earthenware from Rouen and Le Havre, tallow, candles, etc.

Before the Peace of 1762, not more than three or four ships were needed for the Guinea trade, but the double subsidy granted since then to the slavers has increased the number to thirty.

The cargoes for Guinea are usually made up of India cloth, linen from Rouen, silks, piping from Beauvais, brandy, cider, gin (generally manufactured in Holland), muskets,[1] pistols, sabers (usually

[1] These muskets, destined for the slave trade, are manufactured in Liége. In

from Liége), knives, glass beads, iron bars, hardware (from Germany), haberdashery, silverware, jewelry, stone bottles, coral, cowrie shells, copper, tin, lead, gunpowder, cloth of Carcassonne, and cloaks made of this latter material.

The blue Guinea cloth from Rouen was for a long time in great demand for this trade. The following facts demonstrate how important it is, if commerce is to prosper, to strive to supply consistently good merchandise; nations are not for long the dupes of swindlers. A manufacturer from Rouen found a process whereby he could imitate the blue Guinea cloth, both striped and checkered, made in India and also the fast colors produced in that country. His product was welcomed and found a ready market on the Guinea Coast, and so great a demand for it developed in Guinea that when a ship arrived from Europe the natives would ask for Guinea cloth from Rouen. This material was so beautiful that it came to be preferred to that from India. Since then, however, it has been slowly falling into disrepute. This decline is to be attributed to different causes. It may be that the manufacturers have been economizing on the indigo or on the quality of the cloth, or else that they cannot compete with a similar cloth made in Holland, or perhaps that they no longer find it profitable to cheat by passing for Indian Guinea cloth goods manufactured elsewhere. In any case, Rouen Guinea cloth is now exported only in small quantities and is in fact regarded with suspicion on the Guinea Coast. In an attempt to cheat the Africans, the merchants pack into the barrels of this Guinea cloth layers of pepper and other spices, hoping thus to create the impression that these goods come from India, since Indian cloth generally has an inimitable spicy Indian smell.

I am ashamed for my country when I report these miserable frauds. What can one think of merchants who build their hopes

---

1787, when I visited one of the factories, I met a merchant from Bordeaux whose name I shall not divulge, in order to spare his honor. The manufacturer showed him some muskets priced at six livres apiece, and others at six livres ten sous. I asked what was the reason for the difference in price. He told me that even if he were offered the crown of France he would not fire one of the first sort, but that he would gladly fire one of the others because they had been tested. It was a pure gamble whether or not a man firing the first ones would be killed or wounded. I expressed my horror at the atrocity of trading in such guns, and I begged the Bordeaux merchant to choose the second kind. "My friend," he told me, "if a merchant obeyed such fine humanitarian sentiments he would die in the poorhouse. I am going to order one thousand of the rifles priced six livres, and I shall make a clear saving of 500 livres."—And people who reason thus dare call themselves human beings! They value a man's mutilation or life at *ten sous!*

on such fragile and immoral foundations? Why do they not realize that their tricks are obvious to their foreign competitors, who are as clever as they and who will expose these ruses to the public? Can one easily regain the confidence of the buyers of a country when one has deserved to lose it? Good faith, and good faith alone, is the soul of commerce and industry, and no commercial or industrial enterprise can last without it for long. This truth will appear more evident as time goes by and as enlightenment spreads. Then merchants will become honest once again, and they will see that honesty is the only true road to wealth.

The French use Spanish dollars in the Guinea trade, particularly for buying Negroes. It is important to distinguish between the purchase of Negroes and the direct slave trade. The slave trade proper is conducted directly with the Africans on the French slave coast, which stretches from Fort Saint Louis to the fort on the island of Gorée and covers all the adjacent inland territory, including Cayor, Sin, Sallum, Les Oualos, and Les Poules.[2] This trade furnishes each year approximately 2,200 Negroes brought in either by the Moors, who have stolen them, or by the princes, who have had them stolen. All the trade goods mentioned above are used for barter in this slave trade. It is this source which furnishes Negroes at the cheapest price.

The other Negroes, whose enslavement is improperly attributed to the French slave trade, are actually supplied by foreigners. These Negroes are purchased for dollars at English or Portuguese trading stations and even at ports as distant as Saint Eustatius. We are forced to conclude that the profits of this infamous traffic actually go to foreigners, for of the approximately 20,000 slaves that French merchants bring to our colonies, about 18,000 are supplied by foreign slave traders. Assuming that these Negroes cost 400 livres a-piece, it is evident that they cause a deficit in our balance of trade of 7,200,000 livres every year. Add to this sum the cost of the 10,-000 Negroes smuggled by foreigners into our West Indian colonies and it will be evident that this absurd method of recruiting men in Africa for the cultivation of our islands costs France every year more than 20 million livres, which go into the pockets of foreigners.

[2] [Cayor, Sin (or Bursin), and Sallum (also spelled Salum or Saloum) were regions between the Senegal and Gambia Rivers. Les Poules is probably the Gallinas or Moa River, farther south and near the present boundary of Liberia, at the mouth of which was an important slave trading center. Les Oualos is unidentified.]

The return cargoes brought back by the ships that go to the Guinea Coast and thence to the West Indies are refined sugar, green coffee, cotton, indigo, cocoa, ginger, rawhides, dyewood, marquetry, preserves, liquors, syrups, and rum.

Part of these products are reshipped abroad. France keeps for its own consumption all the cotton, part of the sugar from Santo Domingo, and part of the coffee from Martinique; the rest of the sugar, coffee, and indigo from Santo Domingo and from the other islands is exported abroad, either by land or sea. Ships from Holland and the Hanse towns carry this cargo. The merchandise shipped by land is smuggled into Switzerland, Germany, Lorraine, and Austrian Flanders.

The offshore coasting trade with Spain, Portugal, Italy, Russia, etc., employs a large number of ships, but not all of them belong to Le Havre; most are owned by merchants of Saint-Valéry-sur-Somme, Dieppe, Caen, and Rouen. These ships carry highly valuable cargoes of merchandise from factories all over France, notably goods manufactured in Lyons, Paris, Rouen, Amiens, Abbeville, Saint-Quentin, etc.

French ships returning from Spain or from Portugal carry the products and manufactured goods of these countries: wines, brandy, fruit, soda, wool, and merchandise from the East and West Indies and from the American colonies of these two kingdoms, such as Guatemalan indigo, cochineal, hides, dyewood, coins, gold and silver ingots, etc.

From Italy French ships import olive oil, lemons, oranges, drugs, sulphur, and Levantine goods. Le Havre serves as the warehouse for the distribution of all these products to Paris, Picardy, upper and lower Normandy, Champagne, etc.

French ships do not carry colonial goods to foreign ports. This export trade is in the hands of merchants from Holland, Hamburg, Danzig, Sweden, and Denmark, because their freight rates are low and because their ships are operated economically. These foreign ships carry return cargoes from their own countries of wood, hemp, pitch, tar, material for Guinea cloth, etc.

From November to March the trade with Marseilles is usually by ships from Saint-Malo and Granville, which carry to that port the dried codfish they have caught. They have an advantage over all other ships because they are willing to charge moderate freight rates rather than return in ballast.

For the last few years two or three medium-sized ships have

been carrying raw sugar to Fiume and Trieste, where refineries have been established by the emperor.

Because of Le Havre's restricted location there has not been room for the construction of factories and refineries within the city, but some potteries have been built on the outskirts. The earthenware they produce is beautiful and is exported to the colonies. The workshops in the suburbs manufacture all the heavy hardware and the iron agricultural tools required by the colonies. This is a good business, and the manufacturers have made tremendous profits. In the same suburb a successful sugar refinery was established some time ago. Lastly, there is near Le Havre a brickyard which supplies the whole province with building bricks and even exports some to the colonies.

The inshore coasting trade consists of two branches: one, counting a dozen ships, carries merchandise in both directions between Le Havre and Bayonne, Bordeaux, Nantes, La Rochelle, Saint-Malo, and Dunkirk; the second consists of very small craft sailing from Le Havre to various ports in the province of Normandy, such as Rouen, Caen, Dieppe, Saint-Valéry-en-Caux, and Honfleur. They carry back and forth essential commodities.

Having surveyed these various branches of our French shipping out of Le Havre, it is necessary to consider foreign shipping entering this port. I shall neglect no detail, for these facts will indicate what imports we can obtain cheaper from the United States. This trade is carried on mainly by the English, Dutch, Swedes, Danes, the Hanse towns, by a few Prussians, Swiss, and Portuguese, and occasionally by Spaniards from Bilbao.

England, Scotland, Ireland. England employs between 90 and 110 sixty-ton ships to export to Le Havre pigs of lead and tin, dyestuffs, wheat, and flour; and 15 to 20 ships carrying coal, grindstones, and vitriol. The return cargoes consist of wines, brandies, batistes, linens, ladies' wear, plaster, ribbons, and silk stockings; the colliers carry coffee and sugar to Holland and to the Hanse towns.

Fifteen to twenty Scottish ships supply tobacco to the farmers-general; five or six small craft bring in salt salmon in barrels and always return with wines and brandies, although formerly they also used to carry sugar, linens, etc.

The Irish carry on a more extensive and steady trade in salt beef, lard, pickled tongues, butter, tallow, candles, and salmon for the colonial and Guinea trades, and also in rawhides, ox horns, ox and cow hair, and finished goatskins. Their return cargoes consist of wines, brandies, tea, Rouen linen, Beauvais batistes, Cambrai linen, barrel hoops, etc.

Holland. Formerly the Dutch used to carry to Le Havre merchandise from everywhere in Europe—from the north, as well as from Italy and Spain—but this coastwise trade has ceased since the French have increased the harbor dues and charges on coastwise shipping levied on foreign ships going from the French Mediterranean ports to French Atlantic ports. This is a minor loss to the Dutch, for it means only a reduction of fifteen to twenty voyages. They are content to export to France only their country's own products, and their ships even enter French ports in ballast to take on our sugar, coffee, and manufactured goods. They also supply us with spices, drugs, Guinea cloth of all kinds for the African trade, etc.

The Dutch have suffered large losses since the neighboring nations have become more aware of their own self-interest. No more than twenty years ago they still were the peddlers for all of Europe. From St. Petersburg and from Stockholm letters would come to Amsterdam asking for the delivery of a coach or of new fashions from Paris, and in fact Sweden wrote asking for salt. Today we ship these goods ourselves, but it is still true that the Dutch are well ahead of us in international trade.

Sweden. Sweden has eight to ten 200-ton ships carrying iron bars, steel, brass wire, alum, pitch, tar, and fir planks. They sail to Bordeaux for wines and to Brouage for salt, sugar, coffee, cotton, a few textiles from Rouen, Lyons, and Tours, wines from Burgundy and Champagne, fruit, etc.

Denmark. Forty-five to fifty 140- to 160-ton ships bring in goods similar to those carried by the Swedes, with, in addition, salt mackerel in barrels, oars, tar, pitch, and fish oil. They return empty or with cargoes similar to those carried by the Swedes, but with the difference that Denmark imports more textiles because it is a richer country and because there is a greater demand for articles of fashion than there is in Stockholm.

Hamburg, Danzig, Bremen, Lübeck. Hamburg does a large trade. Its ships bring to Le Havre alum rock, pitch, hemp, copper, furs, sheet iron, iron bars, wool, yellow wax, fir planks, dimity from Haarlem, linen, trade goods for the Guinea trade, azurite, lead pigs, and white and black iron in casks. They carry away three quarters of the American goods in cargoes of sugar, coffee, and indigo.

Ships from Danzig bring fir planks (known as sheathing and used in the construction of ship decks),[3] some masts and spars, and large quantities of wheat, and take on cargoes of sugar and coffee from the colonies.

The three or four ships from Bremen and Lübeck transport the same merchandise as do the ones from Danzig. Bremen ships load, in addition, raw sugar for refineries.

The Prussians rarely enter Le Havre and when they do their cargoes are similar to those of the ships from the Hanse towns.

Russia. The Russian trade is a more interesting topic, but the Russians frequent our ports very little, which is a great loss to commerce. Perhaps they will be encouraged to cross the seas, with which they are becoming as familiar as we are, and to come more often to our ports now that the amount of the charge assessed against foreign ships at the port of first entry is deducted from the harbor dues. They bring tar, pitch, masts and spars, fir planks, horsehair, sailcloth, pelts and fine furs, iron bars, hemp, tallow, isinglass, and yellow wax. They carry away many of the products manufactured in Lyons, Paris, and Rouen, such as silverware, jewelry, fine furniture, and carriages.

Portugal. Few Portuguese ships visit our ports, and in the last nine years only two have been seen in Le Havre, either because of the harbor dues to which they are subject or because French ships which trade with Portugal charge cheaper rates. Portuguese products are imported into France on our own ships, and we carry to Portugal products of Lyons and Rouen, furniture, jewelry, and haberdashery.

Very few Spanish ships come to Le Havre and they bring almost nothing but wool from Bilbao, returning in ballast. Those that do take on cargoes carry to Cadiz and Barcelona goods manufactured in Amiens, Nogent-le-Rotrou, Elbeuf, Louviers, Le Mans, Abbeville, Lille, Reims, Saint-Quentin, and Sedan, namely, cotton cloth, plush, panne, callemande[?], moquette, Utrecht velvet, barracan, camlet, coarse muslin, wax, and candles.

---

[3] [Brissot: "qu'on nomme bois de bordage, pour faire les ponts des navires." Brissot seems to be in error here. *Bois de bordage* is properly translated "sheathing," the covering for a ship's bottom and sides, but fir sheathing would hardly be used for deck planking.]

THE VOYAGE TO AMERICA

Boston, July 25, 1788

Here we are at last in the land of freedom, after having wandered over the ocean for fifty-one days. Refuge of liberty, I greet you! Would that you were closer to Europe! Then many friends of liberty would no longer weep there in vain.

On the evening of June 3 I embarked on the ship *Cato,* of American construction but sailing under Dutch owners, bound for Boston.[1] Captain Stevens has the reputation of being a skillful navigator; he is, besides, a likeable man, straightforward and generous. Five or six passengers who had been waiting in vain to embark on a royal packet took advantage of the chance to sail with us.

You surely do not expect to receive from me, my friend, those long descriptions which used to be written by old-fashioned travelers. I aim to write the truth; I shall therefore be very simple and very brief.

Scarcely had I come on board when I suffered the fate shared by almost all people who sail for the first time, even though I had crossed the Channel several times. My indisposition lasted thirty-six hours. I ate nothing, and I drank nothing, staying in bed and leaving to nature the responsibility for my recovery. The result was what I had foreseen. Two days later I resumed my usual existence, or rather, I conformed to the one I found established on board. A breakfast of tea, coffee, or chocolate; for dinner, meat, vegetables, wine, and beer, no coffee, and only rarely spirits; tea at five o'clock; for supper, eggs and rice. Such was our life.

I know, my friend, that you enjoy reading the details of travel; the following about our meals may be useful if you ever make a long voyage. Why do not French ships derive greater profit from the experience of the English and Americans with this diet? We

[1] The Dutch companies which trade with Free America have given up using Dutch ships, which, being much heavier than American ships, take more time for the crossing. I have learned since that the *Cato,* which later made a voyage to Marseilles, was sold to a French company there. This sale of American-built ships is a branch of commerce which will some day grow and become very profitable to Americans.

should not lose so many sailors each year as we do because of this cruel lack of concern.

American ships have, on the whole, good and plentiful provisions. Their salt beef is almost as good as the kind the Irish make. We had potatoes right up to the moment we landed in Boston. This fact will surprise you, no doubt, for it is generally believed in France that as soon as spring comes, potatoes sprout and turn bad. These potatoes had been dug in Holland. The lemons, of which the captain carried two boxes, were most welcome for lemonade and punch, of which Americans are very fond. We also put to good use the onions he had on board. Americans of the northern states refuse to eat them and grow them only for sale to Southerners and to the West Indies. Every night we were served onion soup. I discovered that it facilitates digestion and prevents that stale taste one has in one's mouth in the morning.

Our sailors were equally well fed. For dinner they had salt beef or pork or stockfish and potatoes; for breakfast and supper, tea, coffee, hardtack, butter, and cheese; sometimes they were given brandy or rum, and they constantly drank a kind of sour small beer, to which our captain attributed their good health.

These sailors were very religious, as were the American sailors with whom I have traveled since.

It is a great disadvantage to sail from Le Havre for America, for one is forced to beat to windward beyond the Isle of Wight, which often causes a great loss of time. It took us more than four days to get clear of the Channel. The sea was very calm until we entered the Atlantic, when it became rough. The heavy roll of the ship, which I had never experienced before, made me seasick again, but a strict diet soon brought recovery. A stout heart, exercise, distractions, no indiscretions at the table, these are the most efficacious remedies for this strange illness whose real cause has not yet been found and which produces such varied symptoms.

On June 15 we met an English vessel which was returning from the whale fisheries off the coast of Brazil. She had been out of London eleven months. The catch had been poor,[2] not more than ten

[2] This misfortune, which often befalls English whalers, will undoubtedly discourage them. They will never be able to compete with Americans, who are favored by every circumstance and who will for a long time sell whale oil and fish cheaper than Europeans can. The wise Mr. [Adam] Smith noted this truth long ago when he said that whaling languishes in Great Britain despite government subsidies. According to some sources (whose figures I cannot guarantee) these subsidies are so excessive that they pay for the major part of the raw product. See [Adam] Smith,

tons of oil, which, at 50 louis per ton, amounted to 12,000 livres. After deduction of the expenses, half of this goes to the shipowner, and the other half to the crew, composed of the captain and thirteen men. The ship had little food left, so we gave them some. They took our letters to Europe. How comforting are such meetings in the midst of the terrifying solitude of the ocean!

After we parted from this ship we ran into heavy weather. I was cruelly laid low again with seasickness. I stayed in bed two days and followed the same diet. I was very thirsty; but as I had taken a dislike to tea, hot lemonade was all I drank. Luckily, I had no headache, though my head felt weak. I did not have the strength to read or even less to take an interest in serious ideas. This collapse of the mind, resulting from the exhaustion of the body, is unbearable. It is at such moments that one regrets having embarked so lightly and that one promises oneself never again to expose oneself to the cruel effects of the sea. These promises are, however, quickly forgotten when good health returns in the wake of good weather. I experienced all this as I slowly regained my strength and vitality. Thanks to a lot of exercise, the functioning of my stomach, which had been interrupted during my indisposition, returned to normal.

From June 15 to 26 we made small progress, encountering either head winds or calms during all this period. There was nothing to do but wait patiently. I spent the time reading, meditating, and giving a thousand thoughts to the plans I was to carry out. Knowing well that I could not succeed in my projects unless I spoke and wrote English fluently, I resolved to devote several hours a day to studying the structure of the language, using as my texts works by good authors, and to acquiring a good pronunciation by talking to the Americans aboard ship. Soon I noticed that I was making progress.

To kill time, which passed slowly for the others, I did what I used to do in the Bastille: I divided my time among several different occupations, reading French books, studying English, meditations, etc. Thus I learned something and was not bored.

The work of Blair on rhetoric and languages fell into my

An Inquiry into the Nature and Causes of the Wealth of Nations, book IV, chapter 8 [5?].

It seems that the English plan to open up new whaling grounds in the Pacific off the northwest coast of North America, near Nootka Sound. The oil they have extracted from whales already taken in these waters is said to be much better than that from other whale fisheries.

hands.[3] It is held in high regard by the English. Upon studying the text with care I noticed that Blair's style is very close to that of our French writers; I concluded that the task I had set myself of becoming proficient in English would be less difficult than I had imagined.

An idea then occurred to me, one which I must not forget because I can develop it some day. Undoubtedly one of the great obstacles to understanding among nations and to their becoming united in one family is the diversity of languages. Men ought to use words only in order to achieve mutual understanding, since understanding leads to esteem and love. Consequently nations which wish to draw closer together and whose languages are not entirely unrelated, instead of tending to multiply the words and idioms that are different, should, on the contrary, adopt each other's terms and phraseology. This would render much easier the study of their languages. Seen from this point of view, those who insist, as certain writers do, on preserving what they call the genius of a language are enemies of humanity and of peace.

I carried this idea further, and I said to myself: Americans must detest the English; they will try, if they can, to erase every trace of their origin. But since their language will always betray them, they must introduce innovations into their language as they have in their constitution; and the same principle must guide them, namely, a philanthropic one. America must be the haven of all men; Americans must maintain sympathetic communication with all the inhabitants of the earth; they must try to make themselves understood by all men, to draw closer to all nations and particularly to those with whom they communicate most, such as the French. What, then, would stop them from adopting turns of phrase peculiar to the French language? Why would they make fun, as the English do, of Frenchmen who introduce gallicisms into their English? There is a double advantage to be derived from this method of universal naturalization that I propose: Americans will be drawn closer to other nations and will be drawn farther away from the English. They will create a language of their own; there will exist an American language.

Another idea, of a different nature, also struck me forcibly, namely the *unnaturalness* of life at sea. Considering this question from all points of view, I thought that man is not made for life at sea, even though he has shown great genius in subduing this ele-

[3] [Hugh Blair, *Lectures on Rhetoric and Belles Lettres* (London, 1783).]

ment. At sea he lives alone, separated from his wife and children. The result is that he ceases to feel for his wife that tenderness which is kept alive by domestic life; he cannot bring up his children; he cannot be cherished by them. All alone, what can a woman do? Left alone for months at a time, is it surprising if she falls into debauchery? If she stays faithful, she is unhappy, for she is always devoured by anxiety. Life at sea is a lottery; you can win and lose a great deal at it. It is a kind of life that leads a man to throw his money away; it makes habits of orderliness and economy impossible. If a man has made a lot of money, he squanders it; if he has lost his money he robs and steals. The seaman is accustomed to issuing imperious commands when he is at sea, and he carries this habit into his family and into his social life. Used to dangers and to the most extreme exertions, he loses his sense of compassion; the sufferings of others arouse no feelings in his soul. Highly spiced foods and strong liquor tend to sour still more his character and to inflame his blood. And finally, filth, unavoidable on ships, is another thing characteristic of life at sea incompatible with a domestic existence, and hence incompatible with happiness.

The conclusion to be drawn from these observations is that a republic, a state which seeks to maintain internal peace and which sets morality above all else, should not encourage seafaring, or at least should discourage very long voyages to foreign countries; the coastwise trade is not so unfavorable to home life because it gives seamen longer intervals to be spent in the bosoms of their families. For this reason one sees a great difference between the coasting sailors and those who sail to distant ports; the former are less given to liquor, less hardened, and more religious.

From June 26 to July 5 we had constantly either calms or unfavorable winds. The wind was almost always from the southwest and even from the west. This is the wind that generally prevails in these parts, especially at this season. The captain told me that such winds are less common in March and April, when it is possible to make the crossing in from thirty to thirty-six days.

We met with many ships, and this comforted us. We asked them all for their estimated positions, but we rarely found agreement among their calculations.

Three quarters of these ships were English. You could tell by the sourness or scorn of their replies that they had not yet forgiven the Americans for winning the Revolution. Among these vessels there was one belonging to the East India Company returning from Bengal. The first question the captain asked us was about Mr. [Warren] Hastings' trial. He asked us if we had any English newspapers and we answered that we did. He then asked us somewhat insolently to send them over to him by our ship's boat. We replied, even more insolently, that if he wanted them he could send over his own ship's boat. He got the point, and sent his mate with a piece of nankeen for the captain. I am reporting this incident because it is typical of the English. They really believe they are the rulers of the waves, an idea which will slowly be erased by the enlightenment and the universal brotherhood of man, for which the English, by reason of their constitution, should already be prepared.

A whaler from Dunkirk, which we next met, was more polite. The captain was a Quaker from Nantucket, but all the crew were French.[4] Their voyage had been successful and they had killed eighteen whales.

Whaling ships carry two boats always ready to be lowered. This is an extremely good practice, and I have always been surprised that it is not followed on other ships. A person can easily fall overboard and be drowned, for it takes more than a quarter of an hour to clear a boat lashed down on deck and get it over the side.

We saw a large number of those enormous fish which provide so rich a branch of American commerce. We saw even more porpoises, which are remarkably swift and agile in their movements, and also dolphins, so striking in the variety of their colors. We harpooned one, which we found very good eating.

From July 3 to 7 we sailed on various courses between 51° and 66° longitude and 42° to 44° latitude, almost constantly in fog and rain. We heard thunder only once.

We passed fairly close to Sable Island, the terror of mariners, where so many ships have been and still are wrecked every year. It rises only slightly above sea level, and as it is almost always enveloped in fog it is very difficult to sight. This island is inhabited only by one family and by wild horses placed there by the English government for the succor of castaways on this barren spot. English ships, and especially ships of other European nationalities, are wrecked here more frequently than American

[4] [A colony of Nantucket whalers, headed by William and Benjamin Rotch, was established at Dunkirk in 1787 under the auspices of the French government, with the purpose of creating a French whaling industry.]

vessels, which know the island well and keep clear. The English government maintains a lighthouse.

When we were close to St. George's Bank we met an American fishing boat returning from Newfoundland, which gave us several fresh codfish. These were a great treat, for except for some chickens we were completely out of fresh meat and we were tired of salt beef and salt pork. All I was eating was salad made of potatoes. In exchange, the captain gave the good fisherman beef and pork. This barter pleased me greatly, for it reminded me of the primitive age, with which we associate ideas of greater virtue and happiness. It was the second voyage of this ship to the banks off Newfoundland. It was bringing in 450 quintals of cod estimated at 20 to 24 pounds a quintal. It had a crew of nine men and it had spent seven weeks on the Banks. The captain was planning, as is usual, to return for a third voyage. Marblehead, near Boston, is the principal port of these fishermen, who, as you see, make a good deal of money. Quite often they return within fifteen or twenty days from the Banks to Boston. It seems, therefore, that fishermen from the south of France or from Spain would gain greatly if they sailed directly back to their own countries to sell their fish; it would not take any more time, and they would earn more, since they could bring in fresh cod, which is much better than salt cod and brings a higher price. This would be a good way to gain a competitive advantage over the English, who supply most of the markets of Spain; [5] at the same time they would provide better, fresher, and cheaper fish.

I must not forget a strange incident which occurred during my voyage. I was going to America to escape from European tyranny. It so happened that the ship on which I traveled had a crew partly composed of Dutch sailors, all partisans of the stadholder. The captain, as a good American, sided with the Patriots, so in our conversations we made a good many sarcastic remarks about the stadholder and his worthy partisans. Our jokes irked a German who worshiped the stadholder and who became seriously in-

[5] The author [Jean François Bourgoing] of the *Nouveau Voyage en Espagne* [. . .(Paris, 1789)] estimates at 3 million dollars the value of the cod furnished each year by England to Spain. This is an error. This figure may represent the total amount of foreign cod consumed by Spain, but it is not supplied by England alone. See Smith, the passage cited above, and Lord Sheffield's [John Holroyd] *Observations [on the Commerce of the American States with Europe and the West Indies . . .(London, 1783)].*

censed when we blasphemed (as he called it) his idol. He had to smoke two or three pipes before he could get over his anger. I noticed that this German, who had so tender a feeling for despotism and who, like most of his countrymen, smoked incessantly, never was seasick.

He was not the most original character we had on board. Among the passengers there was a young Indian of the Oneida tribe, whom you may have met at M. De Lafayette's. That good French-American had brought him to France to give him an education which would enable him to civilize his fellow tribesmen. The attempt had failed, either because of lack of aptitude in the young man or for some other reasons. This Indian was, however, well built and very nimble. He danced well, played the flute rather poorly, and spoke both French and English fluently. But he could not produce a single idea. He was a great child, without a thought for tomorrow. After three years in Paris he had not lost this typically Indian character. I should not wish to conclude, however, from this fact that Indians cannot be educated and civilized. Before drawing any such conclusion, it would be necessary to study more cases than we have so far.[6]

We arrived in Boston on July 24 after a fifty-one-day crossing, but our landing was not without some danger. Giving in to the impatience of his passengers, the captain entered the bay in spite of a heavy fog and kept sailing all night. At four o'clock in the morning, not being certain of his position and believing he was close to the lighthouse, he fired several cannon shots, but to no effect. At about eight o'clock in the morning, in a very thick fog, we found we were within pistol range of a rocky reef. Luckily the wind was light and we came about very quickly. A few more seconds and the ship would have been on the rocks. But we still had no better idea of our position. A fishing boat appeared, and we invited the fisherman to come aboard. At first he refused obstinately, saying he did not know where he was and that he did not want to be responsible for the loss of our ship. This sort of

[6] When this Indian arrived in Boston he caused as much surprise as he had in Paris, for Indians are never seen there. They have been gone from Massachusetts for so long that people have forgotten what one looks like. Consequently this Oneida was well entertained everywhere, even by the governor. He was lucky again in New York, where the governor was about to leave to conclude a treaty about some lands with the Oneidas. He received the young Indian very well and had him accompany him. But as soon as the Indian arrived and saw his former fellow tribesmen, the taste for the savage state came back. He sold all his belongings, spent the money on spirits, married a squaw, and forgot all about Europe.

talk was not very reassuring. Finally, however, he agreed to pilot us. But in spite of his familiarity with the local waters we found we were once more among rocks and islands, which we could not make out in the fog. Again heaven came to our rescue; the fog vanished and with a favorable wind we reached Boston Harbor sailing up the narrowest channel. The city, built in the form of an amphitheater, presents a very pleasant appearance. The port was full of ships from almost all the countries of Europe. And we did not have to endure (as we would have had to do in all the countries from which these ships came) the vexations—even more humiliating than tiresome—usually inflicted by customs officers.

BOSTON

Boston, July 30, 1788

How joyfully, my dear friend, did I leap ashore to tread this land of liberty! I was weary of the sea, and the sight of woods and towns—even of men—was wonderfully restful to my eyes, tired by the empty desert of the ocean. A refugee from despotism, I was at last to have the happiness of witnessing freedom, of seeing a people whom nature, education, and tradition had endowed with that equality of rights which is everywhere else considered a chimerical dream. With what pleasure did I look upon this city, the first one to shake off the English yoke, the city which had for so long resisted all the seductions and threats of Britain and had endured all the horrors of civil war! What a delight it was to wander along that long street whose simple wooden houses face Boston's magnificent harbor, and to stroll past the shops which displayed for sale all the products of the continent I had just left! [1] How I enjoyed watching the shopkeepers, the workmen, and the seamen at their various tasks! This was not the noisy, distracting bustle of Paris; the people did not have the tense, harried look of the French, that intense preoccupation with pleasure, nor did they display the towering pride of the English. They had instead the simple and kindly but dignified look of men who are conscious of their liberty and to whom all other men are merely brothers and equals. Everything on this street seemed to say that here was a city still in its infancy, but one which even in its infancy was enjoying a great prosperity. I felt as though I were in Salentum, of which Fénelon's sensitive pen has left us such an entrancing picture. But the prosperity of this new Salentum was not the work of a single man, of a king or of a minister; it was the creation of Liberty, mother of industry. Under her protection all the achievements of men are rapid, noble, and enduring. Prosperity brought about by a king or a minister is as ephemeral as the royal reign or a minister's tenure. Boston is barely reviving from the horrors

---

[1] [Brissot was probably referring to the long street which ran along the waterfront, starting as Lynn Street and becoming successively Ship Street, Fish Street, and finally Ann Street as it entered Market Square.]

of civil war, but its commerce is flourishing; it is not yet a century old, but its arts, manufactures, products, and learning offer the opportunity for innumerable curious and interesting observations. I shall write down for you those I made during my first stay after my arrival and during a second visit.

The manners and customs of Boston are not quite like those described in the *Letters from an American Farmer,* that work so full of sensibility.[2] You will no longer find that intransigent Presbyterianism which condemned all pleasure, even that of a walk, which forbade traveling on Sunday, and which persecuted those who opposed its doctrines. Bostonians now combine with their simplicity French politeness and that delicacy of manners which renders virtue all the more amiable. They are courteous to foreigners and obliging to their friends; they are tender husbands, loving—almost adoring—fathers, and kind masters. Music, which their preachers formerly proscribed as a diabolical art, is now beginning to form part of their education. In certain wealthy homes you now hear pianofortes. This art, it is true, is still only in its infancy, but the young girls who are learning to play are so sweet, so kind, and so modest that the pleasure they give you is far greater than any that proud proficiency could offer. God grant that the women of Boston never imitate French women in their mania for technical perfection! It is attained only at the price of the homely virtues.

Girls here enjoy the same freedom that they have in England and that they used to have in Geneva when that city was a republic and moral standards were respected. This freedom they do not abuse. Their sensitive and open hearts need not fear the deceits practiced by the roués of the Old World, and seductions are very rare. A girl believes an oath pronounced by love, and her young man keeps his word or else is forever disgraced. You see girls go off for a drive in the country with their sweethearts in a chaise, and their innocent pleasures are never beclouded with insulting suspicions.

When they become mothers, the women of Boston grow reserved, but they are just as natural, kind, and sociable as in their youth. Entirely devoted to their households, they care about nothing but making their husbands happy and about bringing up their

[2] [By Saint John de Crèvecoeur, London, 1782. The two French versions, *Lettres d'un cultivateur américain,* translated, revised, and augmented by the author, to which Brissot is here referring, were published in Paris in 1784 and 1787.]

children well. In cases of adultery the law provides heavy penalties such as the pillory or imprisonment. But these punishments are seldom inflicted, for almost all marriages here are happy, and, being happy, are pure.[3]

Neatness and cleanliness without extravagance are the visible signs of this moral purity, and these qualities are to be seen everywhere in Boston, in the dress of the people, in their houses, and in their churches. Nothing is more agreeable than the sight of a congregation gathered in a meetinghouse on a Sunday.[4] The men are dressed in good cloth coats and the women and children in calicoes and chintzes, without any of those baubles and gewgaws which our French women add out of boredom, whim, or just bad taste. No powder or pomatum ever sully the hair of youths or children, but I am unhappy to say one does see them on the heads of some men, for the art of the hairdresser has, alas, already crossed the seas.

I shall never recall without emotion the pleasure I felt one day when I heard a sermon by the Reverend Mr. Clarke,[5] successor to the famous Doctor Cooper,[6] to whom every good Frenchman and

[3] Toward the end of 1788 an unfortunate event caused a scandal in Boston. A young lady committed suicide; she was pregnant. Rumor pointed an accusing finger at her brother-in-law, a married man, who, it was said, had cruelly driven her to this desperate act. This affair attracted great public attention; letters concerning the scandal were written and published and families were divided by the controversy. The brother-in-law was vindicated, however, by two respected men, Mr. John Adams and Mr. Bowdoin, who thoroughly investigated the case. This mystery is best forgotten. But the pain which this event caused to almost all the citizens of this city proves how pure morals are here. [This scandal involved the Apthorp and Morton families. Frances Theodora (Fanny) Apthorp fell in love with Perez Morton, husband of her sister, the poetess Sarah Wentworth Morton, had an illicit affair with him, gave birth secretly to a female child late in 1787, and subsequently resumed relations with her lover. Eventually the affair became known. Morton attempted to disclaim responsibility, and James Apthorp, enraged at both his daughter and son-in-law, insisted on a sort of family trial in which the guilty parties would confront each other. Finally Fanny, depressed by her lover's rejection and ridden by feelings of fear and guilt, committed suicide August 28, 1788. In order to allay the public scandal and make peace between the two families, John Adams and James Bowdoin, friends of both the Mortons and the Apthorps, were appointed as mediators. The outcome of their deliberations, printed in the *Massachusetts Centinel*, October 8, 1788, was that Morton was acquitted of blame, peace and harmony between the two families was proclaimed, and Fanny's suicide was implied to be the action of an unsound mind. See E. Pendleton and M. Ellis, *Philenia: The Life and Works of Sarah Wentworth Morton* (Orono [Maine], 1931), pp. 32–35.]

[4] In America, a church is merely a meeting place where brothers come together to clasp hands and to think and pray together.

[5] [John Clarke (1755–1798), pastor of the First Church of Boston, 1778–1798.]

[6] [Samuel Cooper (1725–1783), pastor of the Brattle Square Church, a strong supporter of the Revolution and a warm friend of the French.]

every lover of liberty owes a debt of gratitude for the affection he bore the French and the zeal with which he preached and defended American independence.[7] Mr. Clarke's rather large congregation displayed the same look of well-being which I have mentioned, that air of serious meditation produced by a tradition of solemnity in the presence of the Almighty, that reverent decorum which is equally removed from superstitious, groveling idolatry and from the impudent, wanton airs of those Europeans who go to church as they would to a theater.

Spectatum veniunt; veniunt spectentur ut ipsae.[8]

To crown my happiness, I saw none of those livid, ragged wretches that one sees in Europe, who, soliciting our compassion at the foot of the altar, seem to bear witness against Providence, against our inhumanity, and against the chaos of our society. Sermon, prayer, ritual—everything had the same simplicity. The sermon was instinct with the highest moral thoughts and the congregation listened to it with attention.

This kind of superior moral tone characterizes almost all the sermons of all the sects on this continent. Rarely do the ministers speak of dogma; tolerance, born with American independence, has banished dogmatic preaching, which always leads to disputes and quarrels. Only the preaching of virtue, which is the same for all sects, is accepted as being suitable in a great society of brothers.

This tolerance is most striking in Boston, in this very city which once witnessed such bloody persecutions, in particular those suffered by the Quakers. Now there are Friends—indeed, in very small number—in this place where several of their predecessors paid with their lives for their perseverance in their religious opinions. Just Heaven! How is it possible that men who sincerely believed in God could have been barbarous enough to put to death a woman, the intrepid Dyer,[9] because she thee'd and thou'd God and men, because she did not believe in priests, and because she tried to follow the Gospel literally?[10] But let us draw a curtain

[7] See the eulogy of this minister in Chastellux's *Voyages* [*dans l'Amérique Septentrionale*, Paris, 1786], II, 216. Mr. Clarke delivered a eulogy on this worthy pastor which must have drawn many a tear from his listeners.

[8] [They come to see, and they come also that they may be seen. Ovid, *Ars Amatoria* I, 99.]

[9] [Mrs. Mary Dyer, together with Marmaduke Stephenson and William Robinson, was tried and convicted in 1659. The two men were executed. Mrs. Dyer was reprieved but eventually hanged in Boston on June 1, 1660.]

[10] See [John Tomkin's] *Piety Promoted, in a Collection of Dying Sayings of Many*

over these scenes of horror; they will undoubtedly never again defile this new continent destined by Heaven to be the haven of liberty and humanity. Today in Boston everyone worships God in his own way; Anabaptists, Methodists, Quakers, and even Catholics, all freely profess their opinions. There is as yet no Catholic chapel, but one will soon be built by a Protestant minister recently converted to Catholicism. The Reverend Dr. Thayer, son of a Bostonian, has been traveling in France and in Italy. He says that the life and miracles of the blessed Labre, who for the love of God let himself be devoured by vermin, made him see the light, which he intends to preach in America.[11] He has sent ahead to Boston chasubles, chalices, and all the other articles of Catholic ritual. His mission, which twenty years ago would have incited persecution, now merely excites curiosity. The Puritans may make fun in the newspapers of the converted minister and of the "miracle" of his conversion, but they will certainly not persecute him.[12]

The ministers of the various sects live in such harmony that they substitute for each other when private business detains any one of them from his pulpit.

This indifference to religious disputes is the result of a war

---

of the People Called Quakers . . . (London: Mary Hinde, 1784), in which it is recounted that Parnell, one of these Quakers, used to argue with some Puritans. One of these, furious at being put to silence, struck him with a great staff saying: "There, take that for Christ Jesus's Sake." To which he returned this answer: "Friend, I do receive it for Jesus Christ His Sake." He was arrested and thrown into prison, visits from his friends were forbidden, and he was forced to lie on the stones which in wet seasons would run down with water. Then they put him into a hole in the wall scarcely large enough to hold a man, and he was starved and cruelly treated. He endured everything patiently and died crying, "Here I die innocently. Now I must go."

[11] [John Thayer (1755-1815), born in Boston, a graduate of Yale in 1779 and a Congregational minister, traveled in Europe after the American Revolution. He was in Rome at the time of the death of the beggar-saint Benedict Joseph Labre (1748-1783), and the miracles reportedly wrought through intercession of "The Holy Tramp" resulted in his conversion to Catholicism in 1783. Thayer was ordained a priest in Paris in 1789 and returned in 1790 to Boston, where he was given the charge of the newly organized congregation of the Church of the Holy Cross on School Street. See Thayer's *An Account of the Conversion of the Reverend Mr. John Thayer* . . . (London, 1787).]

[12] This prediction has come true. Since the time when these lines were written Mr. Thayer has held mass in Boston with the greatest pomp. Protestants went to watch as though it were a theatrical performance; they found the ceremony entertaining. Curiosity was so great that the tax collector assessed a tax, and people had to have tickets to go to mass just as if it were a play—a good enough business in a country where there are no theaters.

during which Americans came into contact with men from many countries and, as a consequence, broke loose from their old habits and prejudices. When they saw that other men with religious opinions different from their own could none the less be virtuous, they understood that it was possible to be a good man whether one believed or not in transubstantiation or in the divinity of Christ. So they concluded that they should tolerate one another, and that this was the kind of worship most agreeable to God.

Before these ideas had become widespread, another essential principle was generally accepted, namely, the necessity of simplifying divine worship as much as possible, of freeing it from all the superstitious ceremonies which formerly gave it the appearance of idolatry, and particularly of refraining from paying their ministers salaries which would permit them to live in luxury and idleness. In a word, they believed in the need to restore evangelical simplicity. In this they have succeeded.

In the country, land is set aside for the support of the church, but in Boston the ministers are supported entirely by the collections made each Sunday and by the rents paid for pews. This is an excellent practice which induces the ministers to be learned and to fulfill conscientiously their functions, for those whose sermons are most popular are in the greatest demand and have the largest incomes; [13] in contrast, in France ignorant and corrupt priests are just as sure as learned and virtuous ones of their emoluments. Another consequence of this practice is that the unbeliever is not assessed. Is it not tyranny to force men to pay for the support of a religion they have rejected?

Bostonians have become so philosophical on the subject of religion that they have recently appointed a man as minister even though he had been refused regular ordination. The members of the sect to which he belonged installed him in their church and

[13] The truth of this statement struck me in Boston and in those parts of the United States that I have had the opportunity to visit. Almost all of the ministers are men of ability, or at least of learning. Despite their precarious pay Boston ministers still manage not only to live decently but even to marry and to raise fairly large families. This fact confirms the judicious opinion published by M. Clavière concerning how easy it would be for priests to be married even though their salaries were moderate. Here fathers who desire their daughters to have educated and virtuous husbands wish them to marry ministers. The same thing will happen in France when priests marry. They have therefore no need to fear marriage on their modest salaries. See ["Lettre de M. Clavière . . . sur les objections faites contre le mariage des prêtres,"] *Courrier de Provence*, No. 151 [VIII (June 2–5, 1790), 420–424].

empowered him to teach and to preach; and he does teach and preach with considerable skill, for the people rarely make a mistake in their choices.

This canonical ordination, unprecedented except in the primitive church, has been censured by those who still believe in the tradition of the apostolic succession. But Bostonians are so close to believing that every man can be his own priest that the apostolic doctrine has not found very strong advocates. Ministers in America will soon be in the position which M. D'Alembert assigned to the pastors of Geneva.[14]

Since the old Puritan austerity is slowly disappearing, one is not surprised to see card games introduced among these good Presbyterians. Men and women filled with evangelical fervor and those who endure religious persecution are never bored; for their minds feed continually on their hatred and their misfortunes. But when life is peaceful and easy there are moments of leisure, and for a people who have no theaters, card games are a natural way to fill such moments. This is particularly true in a country such as this, where men do not spend their time courting women, where they read few books, and where they are even less interested in learning and the sciences. This taste for cards is certainly very unfortunate in a republican state; it is a habit which stultifies the mind. Fortunately, there is no heavy gambling, and you never see heads of families risking their entire fortunes at the card table.

There are several clubs in Boston. M. Chastellux mentions a private club which meets once a week and to which he was invited.[15] I went there several times and was always delighted with the members' politeness to foreigners and with the learning they displayed in their conversations. There are only sixteen members and one can be admitted only by a unanimous vote. Each member may bring one guest. Meetings are held at the home of each member in turn. Clubs no longer meet in taverns, and this is a blessing, for people drink less, drinks are cheaper, and less money is spent.[16] The need to save cash, which was felt at the end of the

[14] [D'Alembert in his controversial article "Genève" in the *Encyclopédie* had written, "Religion in Geneva is reduced almost to the adoration of one God, at least among all those classes above the level of the common people. Respect for Jesus Christ and for the Scripture are perhaps the only things which distinguish the Christianity of Geneva from pure deism." *Encyclopédie ou Dictionnaire Raisonné* (Paris, 1757), VIII, 578.]

[15] [*Voyages,*] II, 219.

[16] Madeira wine costs approximately four Boston shillings a bottle if you buy it in a shop, but six in a tavern.

war, probably led to this change in custom, to the benefit of public morals.

There are no coffeehouses in this city, or in New York or Philadelphia either. There is, however, a single establishment known by this name which serves as a meeting place and exchange for merchants.

One of the principal pleasures of the inhabitants of these cities consists in parties in the country with one's family or a few friends. The favorite drink, especially after dinner, is tea. In this, as in their whole way of life, Bostonians and Americans in general greatly resemble the English. Punch, hot or cold, is drunk before dinner. Excellent beef or mutton, fish, and vegetables of all sorts, as well as Madeira or Spanish wines, and Bordeaux in the summer, are to be found on their bountifully served tables. Spruce beer and the excellent local cider precede the wine. English porter used to be served exclusively, but it has now been replaced by an excellent porter brewed near Philadelphia, which is so similar to the English that even British palates have been deceived. It is a great advantage for America not to have to pay extra to English brewers for their product.[17] This country will soon be self-sufficient in another product when the making of cheese has been perfected. I have tasted some delicious cheeses which can compete with English Cheshire and French Roquefort. Excellent cheeses are made at Weymouth, a small island belonging to the respected former Governor Bowdoin.[18] He used to raise a great many cattle on the island, but during the last war they were all destroyed or stolen by the English. He is now beginning to replace his losses. Soon his Weymouth cheese will become a profitable local industry and will displace the English product, to which rich men are still attached by habit, despite the enormous duties placed on it by the state.

After forcing the English to surrender control of the country, Americans now want to rival them in all fields, and this competitive spirit is visible everywhere. A Mr. Break [19] and several

[17] Before the war English porter cost only one Boston shilling a bottle. Its sale has been prohibited, but you can still buy it. It is smuggled in (with no great difficulty) and sells for two shillings a bottle.

[18] [Barlow in his translation amended this sentence as follows: "This may with truth be said of that made on a farm on Elizabeth Island, belonging to the respectable Governor Bowdoin." (London, 1794), I, 58. James Bowdoin (1726–1790) was governor of Massachusetts 1785–1787 and first president of the American Academy of Arts and Sciences.]

[19] [Probably Samuel Breck (b. 1747), an important Boston merchant and a member of the legislature for seven years.]

other private investors have built in Boston a superb glass factory —a most useful industry in a country rich enough for good liquors to be within the reach of all citizens and consequently for glass containers to be a necessity, and where window glass is used in an astonishing abundance, even in country houses. A German was supervising the erection of Mr. Break's useful glassworks, built in the form of a rotunda, and his knowledge of chemistry had led to the discovery of a sand which makes better bottles than Europe can provide.

It is this spirit of competition which has opened up for Bostonians so many avenues of foreign trade and is sending them out into the most remote regions of the globe. Two ships have already completed voyages to the East Indies with great success. They carried salt beef,[20] lumber, and other cargo to the Cape of Good Hope and to Ile Bourbon,[21] which they exchanged for dollars and coffee.

Would you care to hear a story illustrating this circular trade? One of their ships returned with 300 barrels of coffee which cost 6 s. per pound; it sold 150 barrels in America and carried 150 to Gothenburg, where it loaded tea, which was sold in Constantinople. Note that these were seas and ports hitherto unknown to Americans. Formerly they sailed only in certain narrowly restricted regions.

Nil mortalibus arduum est;
Audax Japeti genus.

(Nothing is impossible to mortals,
To the daring race of Japetus.) [22]

If these lines can apply to any people, surely they apply to Free Americans. No danger, no distance, no obstacle stops them. What have they to fear? All nations are their brothers; they wish to be at peace with all men.

The first voyages made to Canton filled the people of Boston with such enthusiasm that to commemorate the achievement they

[20] This product has been greatly improved in Boston, and it is hoped it will soon be equal in quality to Irish salt beef. The experiments conducted so far promise success. Boston salt beef has been shipped to Bordeaux, thence to the East Indies, then to the Antilles, and finally back to Boston, and after all this travel it was still in good condition. This salt beef has been tried in Marseilles and in other French ports and it is beginning to be well thought of. Being much less expensive than Irish beef, it will no doubt be preferred.

[21] [Réunion Island.]

[22] [Horace, *Odes* I, 3: 37, 27. The lines are not consecutive in the original.]

struck a medal in honor of the two captains who made the trips.[23]

It is this spirit of competition which has so increased the number of fine ropewalks in this city and has improved their product; it has likewise created factories for spinning hemp and flax,[24] which provide a good occupation for young people without forcing them to work in crowded groups to the ruin of their health and their morals, and which supply a particularly suitable occupation for women left idle by the long voyages of their seafaring husbands or by other accidents.

To the same spirit of competition and enterprise are due the saltworks now being built,[25] the factories producing wallpaper and nails, the papermills, of which there are many in the state, especially in Watertown, and the distilleries making the cheap rum previously used in the Guinea trade. Much less rum has been consumed since the suppression of this traffic and since the Quakers and the Methodists have begun to preach so fervently to the country people against the use of spirits. As a result distilleries are becoming fewer around Boston. Humanity will be the better for this; and what small loss American industry may suffer by the disappearance of these poison factories will be soon repaired.

At the present moment the American people are afflicted by two ills: the wave of emigration to the West, of which I shall speak later, and the growth of manufacturing. Massachusetts is trying to rival Connecticut and Pennsylvania in its industrial growth, and there has been organized, as in the latter state, a society for the encouragement of manufacturing and industry.[26]

Usually such societies are formed by merchants, farmers, and leading government figures in the state. Each member contributes his knowledge and a modest sum of money. Wit or intellect are not in great demand in these groups, which instead stress practical benefits and whose members are trying to be useful.

[23] [The first Massachusetts ship to visit the Far East was Captain Ebenezer West's *Grand Turk* of Salem, which returned May 22, 1787, a year before Brissot's arrival in Boston.]

[24] I was told that the flax mill in Boston employs 150 people, both women and children, of whom some work at home and some in the plant.

[25] At Yarmouth, not far from Cape Cod, there is a saltworks where salt is produced by the simple process of evaporation and where machines replace manpower. An expansion is planned which will make it possible to undersell European salt. The product I saw was excellent in taste and appearance. It is difficult, however, to believe that it will soon be as cheap as French or Portuguese salt.

[26] [The society was organized in 1786 under the leadership of Governor Bowdoin and in 1788, the year of Brissot's visit, it published a circular announcing its purpose to encourage industry and promote local manufacturing.]

If there is a monument which testifies to the great and rapid development of the industry of the inhabitants of this state, it is without a doubt the three bridges which have been erected in a short time over the broad Charles, Malden, and Essex rivers.[27]

Boston has the glory of having given America its first college, its first university. The building where students and teachers meet is located on a superb plain four miles from Boston, in a place called Cambridge. The foundation of this useful institution dates back to 1636.[28] No effort of the imagination could conceive of a more suitable location to combine all the essential conditions for a seat of higher education. The university is sufficiently remote from Boston for the students to be protected from the hurly-burly and temptations of worldly life and for them to be able to devote themselves to the tranquil meditation that is possible only in solitude. It is also far enough away to prevent the large numbers of foreigners and the sort of licentiousness which exists in this commercial city, even in a land of freedom, from influencing the morals and way of life of the students.

On the other hand, Cambridge is surrounded by delightful country houses used by Boston merchants for vacations, and here the students can find pleasant company and agreeable conversation. Another advantage is that news from Europe reaches Cambridge practically as soon as it reaches Boston. The air is infinitely pure; the environs are charming and offer a vast space for the exercise of the young men.

The university consists of several buildings very well laid out. Since the students, who come from all parts of the United States, are already rather numerous and since their numbers increase daily, additional construction will be necessary.

Inside the buildings, two striking things draw one's attention, the library and the philosophy chamber. A fire almost completely destroyed the library.[29] The loss had to be repaired, and thanks

[27] The Charlestown Bridge is 1,684 feet long and 30 feet wide; the opening for the passage of vessels also measures 30 feet. The bridge is opened by a most ingenious machine which is moved so easily that two ten-year-old boys can operate it. The Essex River Bridge is even simpler. The Charlestown Bridge is very well lighted at night.

[28] At that time the General Assembly contributed approximately £6,000, to which was later added a large donation by Mr. Harvard of Charlestown, whose name the college bears. The state still contributes toward the maintenance of the college the income from the ferry which used to link Boston and Charlestown before the present bridge was built.

[29] This misfortune occurred on the night of January 24, 1764. About 5,000 volumes were lost. The library now has 12,000 to 13,000 volumes.

to the kindness of a great many generous Englishmen and Americans the disaster is beginning to be forgotten. The heart of a Frenchman beats faster to find Racine, Montesquieu, and the Encyclopedia in a place where a century and a half ago the Indians smoked their calumets.

The course of study is almost the same as at Oxford University. It is impossible that the recent revolution will not bring about a great reform. Free men must quickly cast off their prejudices and realize that they must be, above all else, men and citizens, and that the study of dead languages and of tedious philosophies and theologies should occupy few hours of their lives, which can be more usefully devoted to studies more suitable to the great family of mankind.[30]

This revolution in the course of studies is all the more likely to take place since Boston possesses an academy composed of worthy scholars versed in all the sciences, who, being free of certain religious prejudices, will undoubtedly soon lay out the surest and shortest road which education must follow in order to form philosophers and good citizens.[31]

The president of this academy in Cambridge is Mr. Bowdoin, a man of universal knowledge, who combines profound erudition with administrative talents and with the soundest political principles.[32] This respected man is the descendant of one of those Frenchmen who were forced by religious persecution to emigrate during the last century. Mr. Bowdoin's actions both before and during the war and his views on liberty have gained him so much respect from his fellow citizens that they have elected him to a number of honorable offices, including those of Governor of the State of Massachusetts and delegate to Congress. Never has he betrayed the trust of the people, and he has always remained above suspicion even though a general outcry arose against his son-in-law, Mr. Temple, both during and after the war. Mr. Temple incurred the citizens' wrath first by the deviousness of his conduct during the war and later by his open allegiance to the English,

[30] One might almost say that in Boston too many years of study—eight or nine—are required before allowing young men to practice medicine. It is, however, a good idea to require that those who are preparing for this profession pass the different examinations now required.

[31] [The American Academy of Arts and Sciences, founded in 1780.]

[32] Mr. Bowdoin has written several memoirs on physics and astronomy which can be found in the first volume of the *Transactions* [*Memoirs*] of the Boston Academy. He has also written anonymously, because of his modesty, a number of works on the theory of commerce and on politics.

who rewarded him by appointing him consul general in America. The people, however, never confused the separate identities of Mr. Bowdoin the father-in-law and Mr. Bowdoin the citizen, and his wife, his only comfort during that unhappy war, shares with him the public's respect. Mr. Bowdoin was governor during one of the state's most difficult crises and he acquitted himself skillfully and successfully, in spite of the strength of the opposition party. But we shall write about these events at greater length when we discuss the strange insurrection which disturbed Massachusetts for several months.[33]

To return to the university at Cambridge. Mr. Bowdoin is ably seconded by other members of the Academy and by the learned professors who direct the studies, among whom the most outstanding are Mr. Willard, Dr. Wigglesworth and Dr. Dexter, the latter a professor of physics, chemistry, and medicine and a man who combines modesty with great erudition.[34] He told me, to my great satisfaction, that he was reproducing the experiments conducted by our French chemists. He was using the excellent work by my own respected teacher, Dr. Fourcroy,[35] which taught him the rapid strides that this science has lately made in Europe.

In a free country everything ought to bear the stamp of patriotism; and indeed patriotism, which was so happily displayed in the foundation, endowment, and encouragement of this university, is again evidenced each year in a solemn celebration honoring learning held on the third Wednesday in July on the Cambridge plain. This celebration, which takes place in all American colleges, but on different days, is called Commencement. It resembles somewhat the exercises and distribution of prizes in our own colleges. It is a day of joy for Boston; almost all the inhabitants and all the government officials assemble on the lovely Cambridge plain. The most distinguished among the students display their talents before the public and are awarded prizes. These

[33] [Shays' Rebellion.]

[34] [Joseph Willard (1738–1804), president of Harvard, 1781–1804. Edward Wigglesworth (1732–1794), Hollis Professor of Divinity, 1765–1791, and acting president in 1780. Aaron Dexter (d. 1829), Professor of Chemistry and Materia Medica, 1783–1816.]

[35] [Antoine Fourcroy (1755–1809), a well-known chemist famous for the popular public course he gave, became in 1784 professor at the Jardin du Roi in Paris and in 1785 was elected to the Académie des Sciences. He later played an active role in the French Revolution and was president of the Club des Jacobins. Brissot attended Fourcroy's course in 1780 and under his influence became greatly interested in chemistry.]

academic exercises, which are principally on patriotic subjects, terminate in an open-air party where unrestrained gaiety and the most touching brotherhood reign supreme.

It has been noted that in countries where commerce predominates, learning never reaches a very high level. This could be applied to Boston. The university at Cambridge undoubtedly has scholars worthy of esteem, but interest in learning is not widespread among Bostonians. Trade occupies all their thoughts, turns their heads, and absorbs all their speculations. Consequently there are few writers and few great works. The expenses of publication of the first volume of the *Memoirs* of the Academy of this city have not yet been covered by subscriptions, though it is two years since it appeared.

The history of the recent trouble in Massachusetts was published not long ago.[36] It is a very well written book, of which I shall speak later. Its author found it somewhat difficult to cover his printing expenses. Likewise, the valuable history of New Hampshire by Belknap has never been published in its entirety for lack of financial support.[37]

For the same reason, poets must be even scarcer in America than other writers. I have, however, been told of an original, though indolent, poet by the name of Allen.[38] He is not the same man as the author of *The Oracles of Reason,* a work which has caused a great sensation here.[39] His poems are said to be full of

[36] [George R. Minot, *The History of the Insurrections in Massachusetts in the Year MDCCLXXXVI and the Rebellion Consequent Thereon* (Worcester: Isaiah Thomas, 1788).]

[37] [Jeremy Belknap, *The History of New Hampshire. Volume I, Comprehending the Events of One Complete Century from the Discovery of the River Piscataqua* (Philadelphia: R. Aitken, 1784). Volume II was published in 1791 and Volume III in 1792.]

[38] [James Allen (1739–1808).]

[39] [Ethan Allen's *Reason, the Only Oracle of Man . . .* (Bennington, 1784), which Brissot here refers to as *Les Oracles de la Raison.* Saint John de Crèvecoeur, author of the *Letters from an American Farmer* and close friend of Brissot, met Allen while serving as French consul in New York and took a copy of the book when he returned to Paris in 1785. He wrote Allen, "I will show your book to my friends and carefully transmit you their observations thereon." In March 1786 Allen replied to Crèvecoeur and asked him to lay the work (which he referred to as "the Oracles of Reason") "before the royal academy of arts and sciences at Paris . . . I am . . . sensible that my reputation as a reasoner (even in America) will depend on the reception that the work may meet with in the learned cities of Paris and London." (*Records of the Governor and Council of the State of Vermont*, Montpelier, 1875, III, 383–392.) Apparently Crèvecoeur did bring about the translation and publication of Allen's freethinking book in 1786 under the title *Théologie d'Allen, ou les Oracles de la raison* (See *Biographie nouvelle des contemporains*, Paris, 1820,

passion and power, especially a manuscript poem on the famous Battle of Bunker Hill. But he refuses to have it printed. He has La Fontaine's indifference to fame and money.

Though the number of newspapers is quite considerable it is only recently that a magazine was started here, while Philadelphia, for instance, has two excellent magazines, the *American Museum* and the *Columbian Magazine,* which proves that learning is more highly regarded in that city. A large number of newspapers indicates great commercial activity and a public taste for politics and news, while the number and the quality of political and literary magazines are an indication of the cultivation of learning.[40]

You may infer from these details that the arts and sciences, with the exception of those that pertain to navigation, are not greatly encouraged. The story of Mr. Pope's orrery proves it. Mr. Pope is a very ingenious craftsman and clockmaker.[41] The machine he has constructed to explain the movements of the heavenly bodies is astonishing, particularly when one considers that he had no help from Europe and very few books to which to refer. He owes everything to himself. He is, like the painter Trumbull, a child of nature and of meditation. He spent ten years of his life perfecting this orrery. He tried to establish a modest fund to compensate himself for his labors, but it was never subscribed to in full.

This discouraged craftsman told me one day that he was going to Europe to sell his machine and to build others like it. "This country," he added, "is too poor. It cannot encourage the arts." I was struck by these words, "This country is too poor." I thought that if they were uttered in Europe they might suggest a false idea of America, for the idea of poverty conjures up an image of rags and hunger, and yet no country is further removed from such a sad state of affairs than is America.

When wealth is concentrated in the hands of a few individuals, the rich possess a great superfluity, and this superfluity they can

---

I, 119), but no existing copy of this translation is known. Evidently Brissot was acquainted with the translation since he referred to it under the French title.]

[40] Fleet's *Almanack* for the state of Massachusetts, published in Boston, is excellent; it contains all the political, civil, commercial, and literary information a citizen or a foreigner could wish. It is similar to the *London Kalender* and superior to our *Almanach Royal.* It is not surprising to find such a book in an old country, but that there should be such a book in a new one, and that it should be in demand, is proof of the interest that everyone takes in public affairs.

[41] [Both Robert Pope and Joseph Pope were active watchmakers in Boston in 1788.]

spend on their pleasures just as they can use it to further the progress of the frivolous and agreeable arts. But when wealth is more or less equally distributed among all the people, there is little excess money and consequently there are few means for the encouragement of agreeable inventions. Now, of the two countries, which is rich, and which is poor? According to European views, and in the sense that Mr. Pope understood the word "poor," the country first described is the rich one. But surely in the light of reason it is neither the richer nor the happier of the two. Consequently, the ability to give encouragement to the agreeable arts is a symptom of national calamity.

Let us not condemn the Bostonians; they think of the useful before acquiring the agreeable. They do not possess magnificent monuments,[42] but they have pretty and comfortable churches and good houses; they have superb bridges and excellent ships; their streets are illuminated at night, while there are many ancient cities in Europe which have not yet thought of preventing the grave dangers of darkness.

Besides the societies for the encouragement of agriculture and manufacturing, Bostonians have founded still another by the name of the Humane Society.[43] Its purpose is to revive drowned people, or rather to prevent deaths caused by ignorance. This society, modeled on that of London, which in turn is copied from the one in Paris, knows and practices all the methods used in Europe. It has rendered important services, for you may well imagine that in a seaport accidents occur very frequently. This society has about 153 members, who contribute toward its expenses. It awards prizes to those who have saved the lives of persons in danger of drowning or who have quickly alerted the society in such cases. It has constructed buildings on the three most dangerous points on the coast, where help is given to the shipwrecked.

The Medical Society is no less useful than the Humane Society.[44] It conducts correspondence with all villages and towns to learn of outbreaks of disease, to study the symptoms, to find the best remedies, and to alert the citizens.

Another valuable establishment is the Almshouse. It is intended

[42] I did see, however, in a church a monument in honor of an Englishman named Vassal, who sided with the republicans in 1640, lost his fortune, and went to Massachusetts, where he did a great deal of good.
[43] [Founded in 1787.]
[44] [The Massachusetts Medical Society was incorporated November 1, 1781.]

for those who are unable to make a living either because of illness or old age. I was told that it cares for 150 persons—women, children, and old people.

The Workhouse, or house of correction, is not, you may be sure, so well populated. It is natural that in a young country, in an active port where provisions are very cheap, in short, in a city where virtue prevails, the number of thieves and rogues must be very small. This kind of vermin thrives on poverty and unemployment; here there is no poverty and the supply of work is greater than the supply of workers.

A great many people are employed in fishing and in the many related industries, and even more in commercial enterprises. Despite former losses, despite the obstacles erected by English rivalry, and despite all the lies spread by English newspapers, there is so much prosperity that the rate of exchange with Great Britain and France is at par, while in New York, I am told, the exchange upon London is at a five per cent discount, and there is no exchange at all with France.

To prove to you how many new branches of trade have been opened up by the enterprising citizens of Massachusetts since the signature of the peace treaty, I might include here tables of the exports of this industrious state, but I refer you to the general tabulation of data on American trade which I shall present later.[45]

One of the professions which, unfortunately, is quite lucrative in this state is that of the law. There are still preserved here the costly forms of English legal procedure, forms which common sense and a taste for orderly methods will undoubtedly eliminate, but which at present make lawyers necessary. American lawyers have also adopted from their English forefathers the habit of demanding very high fees. But this is not the only harm that lawyers cause this state; they also worm their way into the houses of the legislature and into the administration, which they infiltrate with their vexing disputatiousness.

Employment in government offices and in the legislature is in great demand—in the cities because the pay, which is quite considerable, brings in cash; in the country because in addition it lends prestige. People complain that this pay is much higher than it was under the English government. They do not realize that the English government and its creatures managed to compensate themselves for their inadequate pay by abuses which have now

[45] [Letters 43 and 44.]

been abolished. The governor of Massachusetts receives £1,100.[46] The governor of New Hampshire, not even £200. The latter state does not spend more than £2,000 for its entire civil list.

In spite of the abuses to which the law is subject, the people of Massachusetts complain very little about their lawyers. Those whom I have met such as Messrs. Sumner, Vendell [Wendell], Lloys [Lowell?], and Sullivan [47] seem to enjoy excellent reputations as men of integrity.[48]

Their behavior was especially honorable at the time of the enactment of the Tender Act.[49] This act authorized debtors lawfully to pay their creditors in depreciated paper currency. The judges used all possible means to circumvent this dishonorable law which, it was believed, circumstances had made necessary. Their enlightened philanthropy is also in part responsible for the law of March 26, 1788, which punishes by a fine any person who either imports or exports slaves, or who is connected with this infamous traffic. Lastly, they contributed greatly to the success of the Revolution by their writings, by their speeches, by taking the lead in Congress, and by serving on diplomatic missions.

To recall the memorable days of the Revolution is to bring to mind one of the most renowned members of the American bar, the famous [John] Adams, who from a humble schoolmaster rose to the highest honors and whose name is as respected in Europe as it is in his own country, which he has served so well during the difficult ambassadorial missions with which he has been entrusted.[50]

[46] This is approximately 22,000 French livres for the chief executive of the state of Massachusetts, which has over 500,000 inhabitants and covers a great expanse of territory.

[47] [Increase Sumner (1746–1799), governor of Massachusetts, 1797–1800. John Wendell (1731–1808), a prominent real estate lawyer and conveyancer. John Lowell (1743–1802), member of the General Court of Massachusetts and of the Continental Congress. James Sullivan (1744–1808), justice of the Supreme Court of Massachusetts and elected governor in 1807.]

[48] One incident will show how untouched by corruption are this country's legislative assemblies. The sheriff of a county, I do not recall which one, by the name of Mr. Greenleaf, was accused of a crime, prosecuted before the legislature, convicted, discharged from office, and punished, despite the fact that he was a very close relative of the present governor.

[49] [Brissot is presumably referring to the new Massachusetts Tender Act of November 1786, which suspended for eight months the collection of debts in specie. Debtors could satisfy executions by offering real or personal property. By a series of extensions, the law remained in operation much longer than eight months, though creditors fought every renewal.]

[50] [Brissot had known John Adams in Europe, and in his *Mémoires* (I, 373) he mentions meeting Dr. Richard Price at Adams' house in London in January or February 1788.]

He has finally returned to his home, amidst the acclaim of his fellow citizens. I have seen him by his rustic penates at Braintree, where he is busy tending his farm, oblivious of the time when he struck down the pride of his king, who had put a price upon his head and who later was forced to receive him as the ambassador of a free country. He is like one of the generals or ambassadors of the golden ages of Rome and of Greece, an Epaminondas, a Cincinnatus, or a Fabius.[51]

It was impossible to meet Mr. Adams, who is so familiar with European constitutions, without discussing with him the one which seems to be being prepared in France. I do not know whether he does not have a high opinion of our character, or of our stability, or of our enlightenment; in any case, he does not believe that this new constitution can establish in our country a liberty comparable to that enjoyed by the English.[52] He does not even believe that we have the right under our old Estates-General to demand that no tax be imposed without the consent of the people. I had no difficulty in meeting his arguments, not only by citing the social contract, which cannot be invalidated by any passage of time or by any concession, but also by citing authorities on the French constitution.

At that time, forgetful of his books and of royal courts, Mr. Adams was devoting himself to his farm. When I expressed my surprise to see so few fields sown with feed crops, and especially not to see any alfalfa, which can be harvested three or four times a year and is such good fodder for cattle, he replied that he had indeed tried many times during the last twenty-five years to naturalize it, but without success. He attributed his failures to the periods of extreme cold common in these regions. Other difficulties prevent raising various other crops. For instance, there is a kind of tree, the locust, which is extremely useful in building ships and making furniture, but which it has been impossible to grow because at a certain age the trees are attacked by worms.

Mr. Adams complained that land around Boston was expensive and that it did not yield a profit proportionate to its value. Since the return amounted, in his estimate, to three per cent, he found it more profitable to invest in government stocks, which bring in six per cent.

[51] Since this letter was written, the United States of America have rewarded Mr. Adams for his labors and achievements by elevating him to the second highest office of the republic, that of vice-president of Congress [the United States].
[52] Events have proved how wrong he was.

This fact can be easily explained. Land yields a small return to owners who do not farm it themselves but instead have it farmed by others, for in this country labor is expensive and scarce. But the land produces well over six per cent for those who work it themselves.

I was astonished to learn that land is so expensive, particularly as I knew that so much was for sale because of the two kinds of emigration that are ruining this state. Beside the emigration to the West, I have been told that the region of Maine, to the north, is increasing in population at the expense of Massachusetts. Some even believe that the time is not far off when Maine, having become more thickly settled, will secede from Massachusetts and form a separate state.

This emigration from the state of Massachusetts is not caused by any lack of land available for clearing. Two thirds of Massachusetts is vainly crying for workers. And, except for Connecticut, this is the case in almost all the states. If you look at Evans' large map of New England,[53] you see an enormous stretch of land to the north of Massachusetts, between New Hampshire and the new state of Vermont. It is divided into numbered squares, and the sites of future towns even are indicated.[54] When will they be built? No one knows. There is even reason to believe that these vast territories may never be inhabited despite the incentive provided by the lotteries held every year to attract inhabitants.

I must return to Mr. Adams, who enjoyed on his farm the pure delights described by Horace in his beautiful ode *Beatus ille qui procul negotiis*. He is not the only man who distinguished himself in this great revolution and who has retired to the obscurity of country life. General Heath [55] is another worthy imitator of the Roman Cincinnatus, but he bears no love for the American Cincinnati; he thinks their eagle is a gewgaw fit only for children to play with.[56] Heath showed me a letter from the immortal Wash-

[53] [Brissot was probably referring to the "Map of the Middle British Colonies in No. America First Published by Mr. Lewis Evans of Philadelphia, in 1755," annexed to Thomas Pownall's *A Topographical Description of . . . Parts of North America* . . .(London, 1776).]

[54] I have noted with great pleasure that one of these towns [in Vermont] bears the name of Ludlow, the man who played such an important part in the English Revolution of 1640 and who, by his virtues and enlightenment, deserves so well to be called a republican. [Edmund Ludlow, the regicide.]

[55] [Major General William Heath (1737–1814) after the Revolution spent the rest of his life on his farm in Roxbury.]

[56] [See note p. 32. The Society of the Cincinnati had as its emblem a gold figure of an eagle suspended from a deep-blue ribbon edged with white, symbolic of the French-American alliance.]

ington, whom he loves as a father and reveres as an angel, and he said, "Here is a letter which, to my mind, is worth more than all the fine ribbons and all the eagles in the world." It was a letter in which Washington complimented him on a mission he had successfully concluded. With what joy did this worthy man show me over all the parts of his farm! How happy he seemed to live there! He is a true farmer. His house is not, it is true, as simple as that of Cato which, according to Plutarch, was neither plastered nor painted. Heath's house is decorated with a simple wallpaper. The glass of cider which he offered me with a friendly smile seemed to me far better than the most exquisite wine. I remembered the words of Curius, that the man who can be content with such a dinner has no need of gold. When men have this simplicity they are worthy of liberty, and they are sure to enjoy it a long time.

This simplicity is characteristic of almost all the men in the state of Massachusetts who played a great part in the Revolution. Such are Mr. Samuel Adams and Mr. Hancock, the present governor. If ever a man sincerely worshiped republicanism, that man is Samuel Adams. No one ever combined more virtues to lend weight to his opinions. He has all the republican virtues almost to a fault: complete honesty, simplicity, modesty,[57] and above all, sternness; he will make no concession to abuse of power; he fears as much the despotism of the virtuous and talented as he does the despotism of the vicious. Though he loved and respected Washington, he voted in favor of removing him from his command after a certain time. He remembered that Caesar succeeded in overturning the republic only by having his command of the army prolonged. Events have proved that Caesar's example did not apply to Washington, but for that we must thank a miracle, and the welfare of a nation must never be risked on faith in a miracle.

Samuel Adams is one of the strongest supporters of Governor Hancock's party in this state. You are familiar with the prodigious sacrifices Hancock made during the Revolution and you know how courageously he declared his position in the early days of the insurrection. The same patriotic spirit still inspires him. His char-

[57] When I compare our modern legislators with their air of importance, always afraid that they are not making enough noise or that they are not being highly enough appreciated, with these modest republicans, I confess that I fear for the success of our revolution. A vainglorious man has always seemed to me a close neighbor to a slave.

acter is a mixture of great generosity and lofty ambition. He possesses the virtues and the talents of the popularist; that is to say, without any effort he makes himself every man's friend and equal. I supped at his home in the company of a hatter who seemed to be an intimate friend.[58] Mr. Hancock is amiable and polite when he wishes to be, but he is accused of not always having this wish. At such times, he develops a miraculous case of gout which protects him against all visitors and bars the door of his house. Mr. Hancock is not as highly educated as his rival, Mr. Bowdoin, and seems even to scorn learning. Bowdoin is more esteemed by men of education; Hancock is more loved by the people.

Among the followers of the governor I also remarked two most estimable men, the Jarvis brothers. One is comptroller general of the state; the other is a doctor and a member of the legislature.[59] The former is calm and deliberate in studying a problem and his judgments are profound; the latter is quick to penetrate to the heart of a matter, handles ideas with dexterity, and expresses himself in a lively style. They have one trait in common, their simplicity, that great virtue of republicans, a virtue which is inborn in Americans but which we French are obliged to acquire!

I shall not linger over the description of all the personalities worthy of esteem that I have met in this pleasant city, for there would be no end to this gallery of portraits. On the whole, I have met everywhere that hospitality, that affability, and that cordiality toward the French which M. Chastellux has praised so highly. I have in particular found these qualities in Mr. Break [Breck?], in Mr. Russell, in Mr. Gore, and in Mr. Barrett, and in many others.[60]

All these friendly people have kept me busy, but I have found time, as you can imagine, to take a few trips into the area around Boston. The surrounding countryside of well-tilled fields is delightful, with extremely handsome and well-situated houses. Among the hills surrounding the city one can see Bunker Hill. This name brings undoubtedly to your mind the memory of one of the first martyrs of American liberty, Warren. I owed hom-

[58] [The copy of the *Nouveau Voyage* presented to Harvard College by Brissot bears a handwritten notation that this hatter was a Mr. Balch.]

[59] Dr. Jarvis received three votes during the last elections [in the legislature] for one of the two senate seats. [Dr. Charles Jarvis, a well-known Boston physician, was a delegate to the Massachusetts Convention of 1788.]

[60] [Thomas Russell (1740–1796), a leading Boston merchant and a delegate to the Massachusetts Convention of 1788. Christopher Gore (1758–1827), a lawyer and governor of Massachusetts, 1809–1810. Samuel Barrett (1726–1800), a graduate of Harvard College.]

age to his noble spirit and I hastened to pay it. Bunker Hill is reached by the superb bridge which I mentioned above. It crosses the river to Charlestown, which appears to be not so much a separate town as a part of Boston. Charlestown was entirely burned by the English during the attack on Bunker Hill, but it has been now almost completely rebuilt with pretty wooden houses. Here you may see the store of Mr. Gorham, formerly president of Congress.[61]

Bunker Hill, which dominates the city, is one of the most astonishing monuments to American valor. It is impossible to conceive how seven or eight hundred badly armed and weary men who had hastily dug a few miserable trenches and who had little or no experience in the use of arms could resist so long the attack of thousands of English soldiers, fresh, well disciplined, and attacking in rank after rank. But so vigorous was the American resistance that the English, before they became masters of the hill, lost more than 1,200 men, killed or wounded. Moreover, we must remember that the English had two frigates which, crossing their fire over Charlestown, prevented the arrival of American reinforcements. Yet it is highly probable that the English would have been forced to withdraw had the Americans not run out of ammunition.

No lover of liberty can look upon this scene, where there still remain traces of the fortifications, without shedding a tear in memory of Warren, and without sharing the love of liberty by which he was inspired.

Such feelings as these are reawakened by the sight of the moving and expressive painting of the death of this hero, painted by Mr. Trumbull, whose talents may someday equal those of the most famous masters.

I must finish this long—too long—letter. How many more things do I still have to write you of! The constitution of this state, its public debt, its taxes, etc. But I shall include them in the general description I shall give of all the states.

The number of taxpayers in this state is estimated at upwards of 100,000. There are more than 200,000 acres of arable land, 340,000 acres of pasturage, and more than two million acres still uncleared. Boston's merchant marine amounts to more than 60,000 tons.

[61] [Nathaniel Gorham (1738–1796), Member of the Continental Congress and delegate to the Federal Convention of 1787.]

JOURNEY FROM
BOSTON TO NEW YORK

August 9, 1788

The distance between Boston and New York is about 260 miles.[1] Several persons have joined together to establish a kind of public stage suitable for the regular conveyance of passengers from one city to the other. Between Boston and New York travelers must change coaches several times. In summer the trip lasts four days, but it is necessary to make the departures at four o'clock in the morning, for the coaches travel sixty to sixty-six miles a day. Passengers pay threepence (Massachusetts currency)[2] per mile, and also threepence per mile for luggage in excess of the first fourteen pounds, which are carried free.

We set out from Boston at four o'clock in the morning in a coach suspended from springs, seating six passengers. First we passed through the pretty town of Cambridge, which I have already mentioned. The country appeared well cultivated as far as Weston, where we had lunch; thence we went to Worcester, an attractive and well-populated town forty-eight miles from Boston, where we dined. The printer Isaiah Thomas has made Worcester famous throughout America.[3] He publishes most of the works which appear here, and his editions, it must be said, are accurately and carefully printed. Thomas is the Didot[4] of the United States.

The inn, where we had a good American dinner,[5] is a charming, prettily furnished wooden building. It is kept by Mr. Pease, one of the owners of the Boston stages. He deserves praise for his hard work and industry, but it is to be hoped that he will modify his present method of changing the relays of his horses. They become

[1] English miles.

[2] See the table of American currencies [p. 26] following the Preface. The Massachusetts penny is worth about seven French *liards*. The shilling is worth about sixteen French sous. Six shillings eight pence are equal to our *écu* of six livres.

[3] [Isaiah Thomas (1749–1831), one of the leading publishers of the day, founder of the *Massachusetts Spy* and of the American Antiquarian Society.]

[4] [A famous family of French printer-publishers.]

[5] If I sometimes mention our meals, it is not to give the recollections of a gourmand, but in order to show the customs of the country and to give the prices of food, which have been so much exaggerated by M. Chastellux.

exhausted by the long distances between stops and by the rough roads, and are soon ruined by this hard usage. The result, obviously, is that the journey lasts longer and travelers are delayed. He has adopted an infallible method for killing his horses: The coach is pulled by four horses; after fifteen miles, the two wheel horses are replaced; [6] the other two are merely rested, and, compelled to do another fifteen miles, they are necessarily forced by their new companions, who are fresh and full of vigor.[7]

Either travel between Boston and New York is still light, or else stagecoaches are not very profitable, for in order to complete the chain of stages to New York Mr. Pease has been forced to establish a line from Fairfield to New York. These conditions will continue as long as the interior of Massachusetts remains unsettled. The clearing of the land will bring the establishment of interior lines of transportation and good roads. For the time being, since the only cultivated land is near the coast, products going out of the state are exported by sea, and the roads are used only by those who prefer to travel by land.

We spent the first night at Spencer, a newly built village in the midst of the woods. There were still only three or four houses and the inn was but half finished, but everything that was completed had that look of cleanliness which delights because it indicates a material comfort, an excellence of morals, and a refinement such as we should not dream of finding in one of our French villages. The rooms were clean, the beds comfortable, the sheets white, and the supper passable. We had cider, tea, and punch—all for one and a half or two shillings a person. There were four of us.

Now, my friend, compare this state of affairs with what you have experienced a hundred times in our French inns: hideous, dirty rooms, beds infested with bedbugs—those insects which Sterne calls the rightful inhabitants of hostelries, if, as he says, long possession does indeed establish a right—badly washed sheets giving off a fetid odor, shoddy blankets, wine almost always watered, and everything at its weight in gold; greedy servants who give service in proportion to the hopes inspired by one's carriage, sub-

---

[6] I asked the coachman how much he paid for the keep of the two horses which he left in the care of the owner of a house situated in the middle of the woods. He told me that he paid one dollar a week for both, or about seven shillings a day for each.

[7] I observed the effects of this bad practice during a second trip to Boston, two months later. The horses, which, during my first trip, were vigorous and well fleshed, now seemed to me worn out and nearly ruined.

servient to the rich, insolent to those they suspect of not being too well off—such are the eternal torments of travelers in France. Add to this the fear of being robbed and the precautions that must be taken each night to safeguard one's possessions. In contrast, in all the United States you travel without fear and unarmed,[8] and you sleep peacefully in the middle of the woods, in an open room or in a house with unlocked doors. Now I let you be the judge as to which country deserves to be called civilized and which one displays more signs of general felicity.

Cleanliness, as you know, my friend, is a sign of property, of material well-being, of good order, and consequently of happiness. That is why you find it everywhere among Americans, even in the smallest things. Have you observed in the country in France the place where men and women go to satisfy their needs? It is usually a hole dug in a garden out-of-doors; both one's sense of decency and one's sense of smell are offended. Have you observed this same place in the houses of our refined Parisians, even in the homes of our great lords, who think that luxury can replace cleanliness? I still shudder at the thought of those disgusting habits. Well, compare them with the ways of Americans, even of those who live in the wilderness. There is not a single house, even one isolated in the woods, where you will not find in the middle or in a corner of the garden, thirty or forty yards away from the house, a very clean and often even attractive structure specifically designed for this purpose. In all of them there is a lower seat for the children— a mark of parental solicitude which shows how much care is paid here to the smallest details of education. Our delicate readers will smile deprecatingly at this paragraph. But you, my friend, are a philosopher, and you will recall that statesman who judged whether a government was good or whether the people were wretched by the excrements he saw infecting the streets.

We left Spencer at four o'clock in the morning; another coach, a different proprietor. It was a vehicle without springs, a kind of wagon, and the owner himself drove. At the first jolt, a Frenchman who was traveling with me began to curse the coach, the driver, and the country. "Let us wait," said I, "before we pass judgment. Every custom must have a reason, even among bar-

---

[8] I traveled with a Frenchman who, thinking there were great dangers in a wild country, had provided himself with pistols. The good Americans smiled at his fears and advised him to lock the pistols up in his trunk. He had the good sense to believe them.

barians, let alone among a civilized people. There is, no doubt, a reason why a wagon is preferred to a coach with springs." I was not wrong. After we had bumped over rocks for thirty miles, we were convinced that a coach with springs would have very soon upset and been smashed to pieces.[9] I admired the skill of our driver, and even that of the horses, which held back perfectly on the steepest downhill grades. When I saw the height of the first hill we descended, I expected the driver to put on the brakes, but he did not do so, and I have never seen this done in America. Once again, every custom has its reason, and here the reason seemed to me obvious. The steepest hills, like the one called Horseneck, which I shall describe later, are studded with rocks and covered with stones which check the descent of the coach and make braking unnecessary.

In regard to the road from Boston to New York, and in general all the highways between the various states, we must remember that almost all have been built since the Peace of 1783. The English ministry, mistrusting the various states, took care to make communication between them difficult, and consequently it neglected the building and maintenance of the roads. This infernal policy was carried even further; the ministry implanted jealousy and fomented discord among the states, fanned their reciprocal prejudices and encouraged enmity by the means of deprecatory names and nicknames—for instance that of "Yankee," given to the New Englanders.

So the rocky, stone-covered road between Boston and New York must be judged with leniency, for it was started only a few years ago. And it is actually surprising that with so much work demanded of the inhabitants of Massachusetts, and with all the shortage of manpower and money, they have managed in so short a time to build the road at all. For sixty or eighty miles it passes between rocks which must have presented incredible difficulties. I was told that a very rich citizen has offered to improve it and make it smooth and passable for the entire distance, that is, to make it into what in England is called a turnpike road, for $50,000, or 250,000 livres. This seems to me a small sum for the work involved. I have no doubt, however, that someday this project or another will be executed. The nature of the soil—everywhere sand, gravel, or rock—will favor the undertaking.

[9] I had proof of this during a second trip I took, when a carriage which was following us broke down.

JOURNEY TO NEW YORK

Travelers are amply compensated for the hardships of this road by the variety of romantic sites, the beauty of the views encountered at every turn, and the constant contrast between wild nature and the art with which man struggles against her. These large ponds lost in the midst of the woods; these rivulets which water meadows recently torn from the wilderness; these pretty houses scattered in the depths of the forests and swarming with happy, healthy, well-clad children; these fields covered with stumps left to time to destroy, hiding among stalks of Indian corn; these enormous heaps of half-rotten trees blown down by the wind and with smoke-blackened branches; these oaks which still preserve the image of their ancient vigor but which, girdled at the base, raise to heaven only dry and naked branches which the first gust of wind will bring to the ground—all these objects, so new to a European, impress and absorb his attention and plunge him into a pleasant reverie. The denseness of the forests and the prodigious height and girth of the trees remind him of the time when this country had no other inhabitants but the Indians. This ancient tree no doubt has seen some of them; they filled these forests. Now, there is not a single Indian left—they have made room for another race. Now the farmer no longer fears their vengeance; his musket, which he used to carry when he worked the fields, now hangs in his house. Alone in the midst of these vast forests, with no other companions but his wife and children, he sleeps and works in peace; he is happy. If happiness is to exist anywhere, it must be in these solitudes where man's pride, without the goad of any ambition, can conceive no vast designs. His happiness depends on himself alone and on what surrounds him.

Such were the thoughts that occupied me during the greater part of the trip. They were supplanted at times by others of a very different kind, inspired by the sight of the houses one encounters every two miles or so, solitary and surrounded by the silent forests of Massachusetts. Their neat and tidy appearance gave every one of them a sort of beauty. Like English houses, they all had two stories, often with attics, and all had an abundance of windows. Within we found papered walls and tea and coffee on the table. The girls, true daughters of nature, wore calico dresses. What enchanted me above all was the fact that the faces of the people bore the imprint of honesty, frankness, and decency, virtues which accompany material well-being. Almost all these houses were inhabited by men who were at the same time farmers, artisans, and merchants. One was a shoemaker; another, a tanner; and another had a store that sold goods from Europe and the Indies. The country stores are always separate from the homes. This division is proof of a love of order and of respect for the home and for women, for by this arrangement persons who seek the services of the worker come in contact only with him.

The stores are well stocked with all sorts of merchandise, especially in the rural regions. You find hats, ironware, nails, liquors, etc. Such a variety is particularly necessary in new settlements, and it is to be hoped that these general retail stores will not disappear and be replaced by special shops. If this happened it would indicate that the towns were growing and that there were enough customers to keep each trade and profession fully occupied. This would be bad, for a retail trade, which is indeed most desirable when it is conducted along with farming and when it does not keep the farmer from his fields, becomes dangerous when those who practice it live exclusively on this income and give up farming. Greed for profits leads them to dishonesty, profits make them chase after new pleasures, and idleness induces dangerous tastes. In a word, moral standards deteriorate and new vices exert a bad influence on the general morality of rural life. In a country where so much land still awaits cultivation one must beware of weakening men's love of the soil.

It is believed that less than one third of Massachusetts is now cleared land. Because of the emigration I mentioned above, it is difficult to foresee when the state will be completely brought into cultivation. Though all the land is not yet cleared, it is at least parceled, and the owners are careful to enclose their properties, and even their woods, with fences. These fences are of different sorts and the type of construction indicates how well the region has been settled. Some are made of branches, and these are the least durable. Others are made of whole trees laid one upon another. A third kind consists of four pieces of timber, each about twelve feet long, resting upon one another and forming an angle at their extremities. A fourth type is made up of carefully hewn timbers fitted into mortises. The fences which enclose the gardens are like those seen in the country in England. Another kind is made of stones piled up one or two feet high; these are the most sturdy and the least expensive and are seen especially in Massachusetts.

JOURNEY TO NEW YORK

The price of a piece of land is indicated by the quality of the fence that encloses it. If the land is valuable, the owner tries to protect it better, not from men but from animals. And although the land may not yet be producing, the owner safeguards it with an investment which may be sterile for the time being but which will eventually repay him. If we judge the value of property by the sturdiness of the fences, it appears that land in Pennsylvania, for instance, is worth more than land in Massachusetts.

To get back to my trip: From Spencer to Brookfield, where we stopped for lunch, there are approximately forty-five miles of good road.

As you may know, my friend, in the interior of America the word "town" designates a territory of eight or ten miles over which are scattered 50, 100, or 200 houses. This division into towns is necessary to permit the people, who are spread over a vast area, to come together for elections. Otherwise the inhabitants would go sometimes to one town meeting and sometimes to another, and this would lead to great confusion. Besides, it would be impossible to determine the population of each township, and population must be considered as the only true basis for the division of the state. Thus the precise establishment of boundaries must be a necessary consequence of a free constitution. No people have given this point as much attention as have Americans.

Brookfield is situated on a picturesque site. While waiting for lunch I read the gazette and the newspapers, which are brought by the stagecoaches which pass through. These coaches are the means of distributing along the roads all that the coastal cities produce.

Lunch consisted of tea, coffee, grilled and roasted meat, etc., and cost each traveler ten pence, Massachusetts currency.

The road between Brookfield and Wilbraham Plains runs all the way through rocks and woods. We stopped at a house which stands almost alone in the forest, where we changed coaches. A small light carriage, well suspended and drawn by only two horses, appeared and took the place of our heavy wagon. Unfortunately there were five of us, and I could not see how we could all fit into this Parisian sort of carriage. We demanded another. The driver answered that there was no other, that we would be very comfortable, and that we would travel fast with two horses. We had to submit. So we were piled in; the driver took off like lightning, and after two or three hundred yards he turned and asked us with a derisive laugh if he had not been right. Indeed, the road was smooth and level, though it still ran through the woods. In less than an hour and a quarter he drove us to Springfield, which is ten miles away. We found this road truly enchanting, and I felt as though I were traveling along the beautiful avenue around the Palais Royal which now exists only in our memories.[10]

I inquired why the driver insisted on driving such a cramped carriage, and he explained the reason. Many travelers coming from New York stop in New Haven and other towns in Connecticut. He calculated that if he kept a coach with four horses, it would often not be filled, it would cost him more, and he would make less money. This fellow was one of the liveliest, the most alert, the most industrious men I have ever seen, and at the same time he was patient. In the course of the two trips I made through this part of Massachusetts I heard travelers speak to him very harshly; he either did not reply at all, or else he gave reasonable answers. Most of the drivers I have met in America behave in the same way under similar circumstances; in Europe the least of these insults would have given rise to a bloody quarrel. This fact proves to me that in a free country reason extends her empire over all classes.

Springfield, where we dined, is an almost European town; that is to say, the houses are built very close together. On a hill that overlooks this town are arsenals for storing gunpowder, munitions, and arms, belonging to the state of Massachusetts. These are the arsenals that the rebel Shays attempted to capture [11] and which were successfully defended by General Shepard.[12]

After dinner we left for Hartford. We crossed on a ferry the river that flows by Springfield.

[10] [The famous *allée*, planted with elms and lime trees and ornamented with fountains and statues, which bordered three sides of the Palais Royal and which was one of the most popular promenades in Paris in the eighteenth century.]

[11] When I made my second trip through this region a trial arising from this insurrection was being held in the court which meets in Springfield. A citizen had started proceedings against one of the rebels who had wounded him while he was taking part in the attack on the insurgents, and he was suing for damages. The General Court, it was true, had granted amnesty to all the rebels, but the wounded man claimed that the amnesty did not apply to his case and his rights. I have not been able to learn what the court's decision was. When I entered the courtroom for a moment, one of the judges, Mr. Sumner, whose name I have already mentioned, very kindly offered me a seat on a bench usually reserved, I believe, for the lawyers. Being unable to stay, I refused this kind offer, which is a courtesy judges usually extend to foreigners.

[12] [William Shepard (1737–1817) was appointed in 1786 major general of the militia for Hampshire County. In that capacity he found himself responsible for the defense of the Federal Arsenal and for the protection of the Federal Court at the time of Shays' Rebellion.]

The construction of the ferries used on the various rivers in America is not always the same. Those in Pennsylvania are, in general, wide boats which can easily carry a coach and four horses. They are usually propelled by oars, sometimes by sails. On the Stamford [Housatonic] River, the ferry is a round-bottomed boat which can carry only one coach. To transport the vehicle, the horses are unhitched, the coach is rolled onto two planks laid across the boat, and the wheels are blocked with stones, thus giving the coach equilibrium; but the slightest gust of wind or some other accident can easily upset it into the river. The men and the horses cross in another boat. I have no doubt that this inconvenient ferry, which causes loss of much time, endangers the coaches, and requires the use of two boats and four men, will soon be replaced by a simpler, safer, and less expensive craft. I asked why this sort of boat was being used and was told that there used to be a flat-bottomed ferry, but it had capsized during a windstorm, causing the loss of several lives. The state Assembly ordered that henceforth the ferry would be round-bottomed. Unfortunately the new boat was not constructed large enough to accommodate coaches. I have been assured that it is planned to propose at the next session a law permitting a more convenient ferry. On the Merrimack River in New Hampshire I saw a different method of transporting carriages. They are brought aboard over the stern; the shafts are in the boat but the wheels drag in the water.

When you see the inconveniences of these ferries, you realize the usefulness of bridges. Passage is less expensive; no time is lost; you can cross in any weather and in any season; and you are not forced to get out and be exposed to the rain, cold, or heat of the sun. For I must also point out that prudent passengers get out of the coach when they cross on a ferry, and they are wise; in case of an accident there is a better chance to escape if you are outside the coach.

On the road from Boston to New York one has to take four or five ferries. Passengers must pay a fee even though the coach's toll is paid. The owners of the stagecoaches ought to spare their passengers this irritation, particularly since travelers are always ready to suspect that they are being cheated and are prone to start arguments. Everything ought to be done which can facilitate travel and transportation.

I have passed twice through Hartford and both times at night, so I cannot give an exact description of the town. It seemed to me to be a fairly large place. It is a "rural" town, for the majority of its inhabitants are farmers. This latter fact accounts for the general appearance of prosperity. For the pleasures of society, Hartford is considered one of the most agreeable towns in Connecticut. It is the home of one of the most respected men in the United States, Colonel Wadsworth.[13] He enjoys a considerable fortune,[14] which he owes entirely to his own labors and industry. He is perfectly versed in the arts of agriculture, in animal husbandry, and in the East India trade. During the last war he rendered the greatest services to the American and French armies, and he is generally liked and respected and has many fine qualities and virtues, the greatest of which is a singular modesty. His manner is frank, his countenance open, and his speech simple. You cannot help liking him as soon as you meet him, and you like him even more when you come to know him well. I give here the impression he made on me.

In praising this respected American, M. Chastellux made an error that I must correct. He said that Colonel Wadsworth made several voyages to the coast of Guinea.[15] It is incredible that this writer should have persisted in printing this statement as a fact after Colonel Wadsworth had requested him to delete it. "To maintain," the colonel said to me, "that I have traded on the Guinea Coast is to suggest that I was engaged in the slave trade. I have always felt the greatest abhorrence for that infamous traffic. I asked M. Chastellux," he added, "to delete from the French editions of his *Travels* this statement as well as other errors which I had noticed in the American edition of his work. I cannot understand why he did not correct anything."

In the countryside around Hartford one sees well-tilled lands, beautiful and elegant houses, and large meadows filled with herds of cattle of enormous bulk, which furnish meat to the markets of New York and even of Philadelphia. The sheep resemble ours, but they are not, as in France, watched by shepherds and tormented by dogs. You see sows of prodigious size, each surrounded by a large litter of pigs, wearing around their necks triangular pieces of wood designed to keep them from getting through the fences and into the fields of crops. The farmers keep large numbers of turkeys and geese and raise big crops of potatoes and other

---

[13] [Jeremiah Wadsworth (1743–1804), Commissary General of the American Revolutionary Army.]

[14] His wealth is estimated at between 60 and 80 thousand pounds sterling.

[15] *Voyages dans l'Amérique Septentrionale* [Paris, 1786], I, 25.

vegetables. All the various sorts of farm produce are both cheap and of excellent quality. The only thing lacking in this universal abundance is fruit, for the orchards are not given as much attention as the other crops. Peaches are plentiful, but they are detestable. Apples are grown for cider, which is exported in great quantity.

Once you have described Hartford you have described the area around Middletown and New Haven, and Connecticut in general. Here nature and art display all their treasures; it is indeed the paradise of the United States. M. Crèvecoeur, who has been so often accused of exaggeration in his description of these parts, has actually not done them sufficient justice. Read again his charming description, which will supply what it would be useless for me to repeat here.[16]

This state owes all its advantages to its geographical situation. It is a fertile plain enclosed between two mountain ranges which make difficult communication by land with the neighboring states and hence provide security and protection. It is watered by the superb Connecticut River, which flows into the sea and provides a safe and easy passage to navigation throughout its length. Agriculture being the basis of the state's prosperity, wealth is more equally distributed; there is more equality, less poverty, more simplicity, more virtue, more of what constitutes republicanism.

Connecticut gives the impression of being one continuous town. As soon as we left Hartford we entered Wethersfield, which is no less beautiful. It extends for a long distance along the road and is filled with well-built houses. I was told that it is the birthplace of the famous Silas Deane, one of the prime movers of the American Revolution.[17] Having risen from schoolmaster in this town to the rank of envoy from Congress to Europe, he has now been accused of betraying the glorious cause of his country. Is the charge true or false? It is difficult to decide. But this American has for a long time been living in misery in London, and it is a proof of American generosity and virtue that his best friends and benefactors are still former American Whigs.[18]

In Wethersfield I was shown the house of a shoemaker who a few years ago killed his wife, his child, and himself. He was found stretched over their bodies. This man had suffered losses which he

[16] [See Crèvecoeur, *Lettres d'un cultivateur américain* (Paris, 1787), II, 68–71.]

[17] [Silas Deane (1737–1789), sent to France in 1776 as the first representative of the United Colonies.]

[18] He has since died in poverty.

thought he could not make good. Having resolved to take his own life and being unwilling to leave his wife and child in poverty, he made them share his death. This example of suicide is unique in this region, for prosperity reigns here, and it could only have been the act of a man of somber and melancholic temperament.

During my stay in America I heard of another suicide, in Boston, committed by a young lady whom unfortunate circumstances had forced to choose between dishonor and death.[19] The impression that this event made on every mind and the talk it caused proved to me how little people here are accustomed to these painful accidents, which almost always are an indictment more against the organization of society than against the sanity of the victims.

Wethersfield is remarkable for its immense fields of onions, which are exported in prodigious quantities to the East Indies, and for its elegant meetinghouse. They say that every Sunday an enchanting spectacle is offered by the numerous pretty girls who gather here and by the pleasant music with which the divine service is interspersed.

New Haven yields nothing to Wethersfield as far as the fair sex is concerned. At the balls that take place during the winter, despite Puritan strictness,[20] it is not a rare sight to see a hundred charming girls with those bright, rosy cheeks which you seldom see farther south and dressed with elegant simplicity. In Connecticut the physical beauty of the people is as striking as is the size of the population. In whatever tavern you enter you will find cleanliness, decency, and dignity. The tables are often served by a modest, pretty girl, or by an amiable matron whose attractive features, untouched by age, still retain their youthful freshness, or by a man who carries himself with that dignity which equality inspires and who has none of the base subservience that most of our innkeepers display.

On the road you often meet some of these fair Connecticut girls, either driving a chaise or on horseback, galloping boldly all alone, wearing an elegant hat and a white apron over a dress of printed calico. These are ways and customs which prove not only how mature these girls are (since in spite of their youth they are trusted unaccompanied) but also how safe the roads are, and which demon-

[19] [Fanny Apthorp. See note p. 86.]

[20] Those who have traveled or lived in Connecticut before the Revolution find that a great change in manners has taken place. There is much more sociability and gaiety, but people are still afraid to travel on Sundays.

strate the general moral innocence of these people. You also meet girls venturing to travel alone and without an escort in the public stages. But I am wrong to say "venturing," for who could offend them? Here they are under the protection of public morals and of their own simple virtue. It is their consciousness of their own innocence which renders them so outgoing and friendly; a stranger may take their hand, press it, and laugh with them, and they take no offense.

Further evidence of the prosperity of Connecticut is provided by the number of new houses being built; you see very, very few in need of repair. Evidence lies also in the number of rural factories, which are rising on every hand and of which I shall speak later.

There is, however, in this state much land for sale. What is the reason? One of the main ones is the emigration to the West. The desire to better one's lot has poisoned the contentment of even the inhabitants of Connecticut. Perhaps this urge to emigrate arises in them from the hope that they will escape taxes, which, though low and in fact almost nonexistent in comparison with European taxes, seem to them very heavy. Perhaps it is due to the fact that land is expensive—that is, expensive in comparison with the price of new land. It should not appear surprising that, with the population growing so rapidly, many people are emigrating from a region where they already feel overcrowded.

It is in Connecticut that I met, during my second trip, several families coming from New Hampshire who were traveling at a brisk pace to Kentucky. The vanguard consisted of two young women on horseback and a young man who accompanied them; the women, fresh-complexioned, full of vitality, and modestly dressed, were going on ahead to prepare the lodgings for the night. An hour later the main body of the army appeared, consisting of two wagons full of children who were playing on mattresses, surrounded by household utensils. An old woman was watching over them. Beside the wagons walked young women and older children. "Where are you going?" I asked them. "To the Ohio," they replied gaily. We wished them in all sincerity a successful trip. They had to travel 1,100 miles to reach their destination.

One feels that in a country like the United States everything must foster the desire to emigrate. The emigrants are sure everywhere to find brothers, friends who speak their language and admire their courage. They are sure in the region where they are going to find men who will welcome and help them. Moreover, provisions are cheap all along the road. They need fear neither searches by customs officers, nor tolls, nor taxes, nor persecution by the constabulary, nor thieves, nor assassins. Here man is free as the air he breathes. The desire to emigrate is augmented by repeated accounts in all the papers of departing families and of the low cost of food in the Western Territory. Men are everywhere like sheep. They say: "So-and-so has succeeded. Why shouldn't I? I am nobody here; I will be somebody in Ohio. Here I work hard; there I shall work less." We asked these good people why they were emigrating. "Oh," they said, "it is so cold in New Hampshire; we can't feed our cattle through the winter." They were right about the cold, but they were wrong about the rest. There will be fodder for the cattle when people take the trouble to raise it by sowing more fields to hay and by raising bigger crops of beetroot.[21] But Americans will not take all this trouble.

To get back to my trip. Before arriving in Middletown, where we had lunch, we stopped on the mountain which overlooks this town and the immense valley in which it lies. This is one of the most beautiful and magnificent views that I have had the opportunity to admire in America. I could not get my fill of the variety of scenes which lay before my eyes. Middletown resembles Hartford: broad streets lined on both sides with trees; pretty houses.

We changed horses and coach at Durham, and after having admired a host of picturesque spots we arrived for dinner in New Haven. Its university enjoys a great renown on this continent, its port is very active, and the social life, they say, is infinitely agreeable. New Haven has produced a famous poet, [John] Trumbull, author of the immortal poem *M'Fingal,* which rivals if it does not surpass in its keen humor the famous *Hudibras.*[22] Colonel Humphreys, one of whose poems much admired in America has been translated by M. Chastellux, was also born in this city.[23] The president of the college is a respected scholar, Mr. Stiles.[24]

---

[21] For instance, in a garden in New Hampshire I saw beets which weighed eight to ten pounds.

[22] [John Trumbull (1750–1831), leader of the "Hartford Wits" in the 1780's and 1790's, published his comic epic *M'Fingal,* a satire of the British soldiery, in 1782. Actually he was born in Watertown.]

[23] [David Humphreys (1752–1818), another of the "Hartford Wits," published in 1780 *A Poem, Addressed to the Armies of the United States of America,* which the Marquis de Chastellux republished with a facing French translation in Paris in 1786, under the title *Discours en vers addressé aux officiers et aux soldats des différentes armées américaines.* So far as is known, this was the first American poetry published in France. Humphreys was born in Derby, outside of New Haven.]

[24] [Ezra Stiles (1727–1795) had been elected president of Yale in 1777.]

We had to leave this charming town in order to reach Fairfield, where we planned to spend the night. We crossed the river on the inconvenient Stratford ferry, which I have already mentioned. Then we were assailed by a violent storm, from which we were fairly well protected by a double curtain of leather attached on the outside of the coach. The driver refused to stop and, although drenched by the rain, continued on in the pitch-black night. I was astonished that Heaven preserved us from an accident.

We spent the night at Fairfield, a town rendered famous by its sufferings during the recent revolution. It endured the full fury of the English, who burned it. The scars left by their infernal rage can still be seen. Most of the houses have been rebuilt, but those who knew the town before the war say that it was much finer then and that it was noted for its prosperous, even opulent, appearance. I was shown the home of the richest citizen, where important visitors and distinguished travelers were received, and where the infamous Tryon,[25] who led that expedition of cannibals, had been entertained several times. Impervious to any sense of gratitude, honor, or humanity, he treated the mistress of this house, who had received him as a friend, with the utmost cruelty, and, after giving her his word that he would respect her home, he ordered it set on fire.

The agreeable part of our journey ended at Fairfield. For thirty-three miles from this town to Rye we had to fight our way over rocks and precipices. I did not know which to admire more, the driver's daring or his skill. I cannot conceive how he succeeded twenty times in preventing the carriage from being shattered, or how his horses could check the coach when going down the veritable stairways of rocks. The word "stairways" is no exaggeration. One of these, known as Horseneck, is nothing but a steep slope of boulders; if the horses slipped, the coach would tumble 200 or 300 feet down into the valley below.[26]

This terrifying precipice was the scene of an intrepid action performed by the most daring general America has produced, General [Israel] Putnam. To understand his feat, you must visualize the terrain. Imagine a plateau at one end of which there is a church which overlooks a valley almost directly below. To permit people to reach the church on foot from the valley, about one hundred stone steps had been built on the steepest part of the slope. But

[25] [William Tryon (1729–1788), major general in the British army, who conducted a series of raids from New York upon Connecticut during the Revolution.]
[26] [In West Greenwich, Connecticut.]

horses and carriages, in order to reach the plateau from the valley, had to follow a long spiral road which encircled the mountain. Governor Tryon, at the head of 1,500 men, was in hot pursuit of Putnam, who had with him about a hundred horse, and surprised him near Horseneck. When Putnam reached the edge of the plateau he saw that if he followed the road the English would inevitably capture him. Resolved to escape or perish, he immediately made his decision; he hurled himself and his mount down the stone stairway. Whether by luck or because American horses are used to these mountains, he reached the valley below without accident. Needless to say, the English did not dare imitate this feat of daring; they took the long, winding road, and Putnam escaped.

Americans still tell with awe of his intrepidity in killing a she-wolf of monstrous size which had been terrorizing all of Connecticut and which had taken refuge in an impenetrable cavern. He had the courage to have himself lowered into the cave on the end of a rope tied around his body, with a torch in one hand and a gun in the other. He was lucky enough to kill this ferocious beast at the very moment when she was springing at him.[27]

I cannot mention Putnam, who is so famous in American annals, without being tempted to relate some of his adventures, little known in Europe, which will give you a high opinion of his intrepidity, for intrepidity is the distinguishing mark of this famous hero.

He possessed not only the intrepidity but also the vigorous laconism of a Spartan. One day in his camp [28] a certain Palmer, a Tory and a lieutenant in the new levies, was arrested as a spy. Governor Tryon, who was in command of these levies, asked his release on the ground that he was an English officer and pointed out to Putnam what a criminal act it would be to hang an officer commissioned by His Majesty and what a terrible vengeance Putnam ran the risk of incurring. Putnam answered him in these words:

SIR,

   NATHAN PALMER, a lieutenant in your king's service, was taken in my camp as a *Spy*—he was tried as a *Spy*—he was condemned as a *Spy*—and you may rest assured, Sir, he shall be hanged as a *Spy*.
         I have the honor to be, etc.,
                  ISRAEL PUTNAM

P.S. Afternoon. He is hanged.

[27] [The scene of this fabulous exploit is near Pomfret, Connecticut.]
[28] [At Peekskill, New York.]

But the intrepid feat which surpassed all others occurred when he dared to take a boat over the terrifying Hudson River Falls. It was during the famous war of 1756, when Putnam was fighting the French and their Indian allies. He happened to be with a boat and five men on the eastern bank of the river, near the falls. The men he had on the other side of the river signaled to him that a considerable body of Indians were advancing to encircle him and that he had not a moment to lose. He faced three choices: to stand his ground, fight, and be sacrificed; to attempt to cross the river to the other side and expose himself to being shot; or else to take the chance of riding the boat over the falls, with the almost complete certainty of being engulfed. These were the alternatives. He did not hesitate; he leaped into the boat. And it was lucky that he did, for one of his companions who had stepped a little distance away was the victim of the Indians' savagery before he had time to rejoin him. The Indians arrived in time to open fire on the boat before it could get away. But hardly had the craft been swept out of range by the speed of the current when death, which Putnam had just avoided, faced him again in a more terrible form. For a quarter of a mile, rocks whose tops pierced the waters, masses of submerged trees, sucking whirlpools, and swift rapids left him no hope of escape save by a miracle. Nevertheless, Putnam, trusting in the support of Providence, whose protection he had so often experienced, tranquilly took his place at the rudder and steered the boat with the greatest calm. With admiration, with terror, with astonishment, his companions saw him avoid with the greatest dexterity the rocks and threatening waves which seemed ready to engulf him at every moment. They saw him disappear behind a wave, then rise on its crest, threading his way along the only existing channel, until at last he reached the calm waters at the foot of the falls. No less astounded were the Indians, whom this miracle astonished almost as much as had the sight of the first Europeans to reach their shores. They believed Putnam was invulnerable, for he had succeeded in navigating a violent torrent on which none of them had ever ventured without disaster. They believed they would outrage the Great Spirit if they made an attempt against the life of a man whom He so obviously protected.[29]

[29] These details are taken from Colonel David Humphreys' *Essay on the Life of Putnam,* printed in Hartford in 1788 and dedicated to the Society of the Cincinnati [*An Essay on the Life of the Honorable Major-General Israel Putnam: Addressed to the Society of the Cincinnati, in Connecticut* (Hartford, 1788)]. This work con-

You will, no doubt, forgive this digression on a man dear to the American people, who still have the privilege of his presence among them. Now, back to my trip.

Horseneck plateau holds recompense in store for the weary lover of scenery and nature, to whom it offers a vast and most magnificent view. Here nature displays her beauties and her horrors. In the midst of these fearsome sights you still discover houses and human shapes; but they do not have the prosperous, happy appearance they have in Connecticut. At Horseneck itself, however, we had a fairly good dinner; good meat, good vegetables, and, above all, good people and a large family, which surprised me. But these Americans are increasing everywhere.

After leaving this place, we went on to New Rochelle, a colony founded in the last century by French emigrants, but which does not seem to have prospered. Perhaps this is because of the recent war, for the region suffered greatly from the proximity of the English, whose general headquarters were in New York. Perhaps it is because the soil is rocky, gravelly, and unfertile. Or, finally, it may be because of the religious quarrels which divided the inhabitants even during the first years of the settlement. The founders of the colony were unwise in their choice of this site for another reason. The sea often flows through these rocks and when it withdraws leaves a muddy deposit which gives off noisome emanations. This is no doubt what causes the fevers which sometimes decimate the inhabitants.[30]

This town, though almost deserted, will be forever famous because it gave birth to one of the outstanding men of the recent revolution, a republican remarkable for his firmness and *sang-*

tains other equally interesting anecdotes, and will probably some day be translated. [These stories are taken almost verbatim from Humphreys' *Essay* (which never was, in fact, translated into French), the source from which they have entered American legend. It is interesting to note, however, certain omissions and modifications of detail which illustrate Brissot's tendency to gild the American lily. For instance Humphreys says that Putnam had 150 (not "about a hundred") men, that during his descent of the rocky cliff at Horseneck one of the bullets fired went through his hat, and that Governor Tryon later gallantly sent him a complete set of clothes "by way of compensation." Similarly, in the adventure of the wolf, Humphreys gives the realistic detail (which apparently did not appeal to Brissot) that Putnam first tried to get his dog to enter the cave, and then his Negro man. Only after both had refused did he in anger go in himself.]

[30] During my second trip, in October, I saw many such unfortunate victims, shaken and devoured by fever and ague.

froid and a writer distinguished for his pure style and close reasoning,[31] Mr. [John] Jay, the present Secretary of State.[32]

The following story will give an idea of the firmness of this republican. During the preliminary discussions of the Peace of 1783, M. Vergennes, inspired by secret motives, tried to persuade the ambassadors of Congress to be satisfied with their fishing grounds and to give up the Western Territory, that is, the vast and fertile lands beyond the Alleghenies. Above all, Vergennes insisted that American independence should not be one of the bases of the peace treaty but merely that it should be conditional. To gain his objective, he had to persuade Jay and Adams. Mr. Jay flatly told M. Vergennes that he would rather lose his life than sign such a treaty; that Americans were fighting for their independence and that they would not lay down their arms until it was completely established; that the Court of France itself had recognized American independence and that a reversal would contradict its earlier actions. Jay had no difficulty in bringing Adams to his point of view, and M. Vergennes never succeeded in overcoming his firmness.

Let us wonder here at the strange concatenation of events in this world. The American minister who forced the French minister to yield, who imposed terms on the English minister, is the grandson of a French refugee who in the last century fled to New Rochelle. Thus the descendant of one of those men whom Louis XIV persecuted with idiotic relentlessness forced respect for his decisions in the very palace of that sovereign, a mere hundred years after the banishment of his grandfather.

Mr. Jay was equally adamant in his opposition to the arguments of the English minister, whom M. Vergennes had managed to win over. He proved that it would be to the interest of England herself if the Americans were independent rather than in a situation which would make them dependent on their ally. He convinced the English minister and won his case, for this argument persuaded the Council of Saint James. When Mr. Jay went to England on his

---

[31] Mr. Jay's talents shone most brightly at the New York State Convention, which debated whether to accept the new Federal Constitution. Governor Clinton, heading the Anti-Federalists, had a large majority, but he was unable to defeat either Mr. Jay's logic or the eloquence of Jay's colleague, Mr. Hamilton.

[32] Since this letter was written Mr. Jay has been appointed Chief Justice of the Supreme Court of the United States.

way back to America, Lord Shelburne wished to see him. Shelburne, accused by his people of having given more than he was asked for in the peace treaty he had signed, wished to know whether the Americans would have continued the war if he had persisted in not ceding to them the Western Territory. Mr. Jay replied that he believed that this would have been the case and that he would have recommended such a course. Thus the fate of America rested on a single man.

It is thirty-one miles from Rye to New York, along a good smooth road built on gravelly soil. One stops at one of the best inns I have found in America, kept by a Mrs. Aveland, where we had an excellent and inexpensive dinner. Two other still more precious attractions made us cherish the memory of this inn, namely the infinitely kind and gracious mistress of the house and her charming, beautiful, and refined daughter, who played the pianoforte very well.

Before reaching New York we passed through the places which the English had fortified so strongly during their occupation. You still see the various redoubts and fortifications they built, which bear witness to the madness of that fratricidal war.

JOURNEY FROM BOSTON
TO NEW YORK BY WAY
OF PROVIDENCE [1]

On October 12 I left Boston in a four-horse stage for Providence, forty-five miles away. We set out at half-past seven in the morning, and without straining his horses the owner of the coach got us to Providence by six in the evening. The trip cost me fifteen shillings, Massachusetts currency.

The road is in general good; the soil in these parts is gravel with occasional sand indicated by clumps of pine trees. The country bordering the road appeared to me to be neither fertile nor particularly well populated. I saw tumbled-down cabins and children dressed in rags, though they seemed rosy-cheeked and plump enough.

The silence which prevails on Sundays in all the towns of America was still reigning in Providence on Monday. There were signs everywhere of a business depression. Few ships were to be seen in the port. Two distilleries, however, were under construction, as if there were not already enough factories producing this poison in the United States. Either because of my own prejudice, or because it was an actual fact, I sensed everywhere the silence of death, the death of commercial activity, killed by the introduction of paper money.[2] I seemed to see on all faces that look commonly attributed to Jews, that stigma which is the mark of those who traffic in fraud or who live by cunning. I also seemed to see every-

[1] Although this trip was made at a date later than the time when the succeeding letters were written, I thought it best to insert it here because it serves to complement the description of my trip to New York by land, and the reader may with greater ease compare the two accounts if they are set side by side.

[2] [Brissot's description of the economic depression in Rhode Island, which he blamed on the depreciation of the state's paper currency, reflects the concern he felt in 1790 over French monetary policy and his opposition to the issuing of notes not instantly convertible into specie or backed by marketable real property. Brissot, who favored the *assignats*, was not opposed to paper money in principle; but the example of Rhode Island, which had been issuing paper money since 1710 with generally unhappy results and whose recent issue of 1786 had depreciated as much as Brissot says, was to him a salutary warning of the dangers of an unsound currency.]

where the imprint of the contempt which the other states feel for Rhode Island and of the inhabitants' awareness that they deserve this contempt.

Paper money was, at that time, at the lowest discredit. A silver dollar was worth ten paper dollars. I inquired about the price of provisions: butter was six to seven sous a pound; beef, mutton, etc., two to three sous; oak wood, eight to ten livres a cord. As you may well imagine, two prices were quoted for each commodity, and the form of payment was stipulated.

I left Providence on Tuesday at eleven o'clock in the morning on the New York packet. We had wasted all day Monday because the captain had not finished loading. This dependence on the whims or avarice of the captain is not the least of the inconveniences of this sort of travel.

One can also go from Providence to Newport by land, but I preferred the packet. We arrived at half-past six in the evening after having fought for two hours against a contrary wind. Only thirty miles separate the two cities. Land was always in sight but I never noticed anything picturesque or interesting—merely sandy beaches, a few houses and trees, and unfertile land.

In the United States, the state of Rhode Island is considered to have the best harbors. Indeed, Newport seems destined by nature to be an important port. The bottom gives good anchorage and the harbor can accommodate the largest ships.

Newport played a fairly important part in the last war, and it was at that time a flourishing city. The successive occupations by American, English,[3] and French armies brought in a great deal of money. Since the peace treaty, however, everything has changed.[4] It is now an empty place, peopled only by groups of men who spend the whole day idling with folded arms on street corners. Most of the houses are in disrepair; the shops are miserably stocked and offer for sale only coarse cloth, packets of matches, baskets of apples, and other cheap goods. Grass is growing in the public square in front of the State House; the streets are badly paved and muddy; rags hang from windows; and tatters cover the hideous women, the emaciated children, and the pale, thin men, whose sunken eyes and shifty looks put the observer ill at ease.

[3] The English destroyed all the fruit trees as well as the other trees; they enjoyed devastating everything.

[4] This town owed part of its prosperity to the slave trade, which used to be very profitable and which *is now extinct*.

Everything speaks of poverty, the triumph of dishonesty, and the effects of bad government.

I visited the market. Great God! What a difference from those of Boston or Philadelphia! A few chunks of second-grade meat awaited nonexistent buyers. I asked the reason for this of an American who was very well informed about local conditions. He told me that most of the people lived on fish they caught themselves and on potatoes and a few other vegetables, scant pickings from their own gardens. Few ate meat. Farmers no longer sent beef or mutton to the market. Paper money, or rather dishonesty, was the main reason for this poverty. Newport resembled a graveyard where living skeletons fought over a few blades of grass. It reminded me of Volney's description of Egypt, which looked to him like a city whose inhabitants and houses had been devastated by plague and fire.[5]

You yourself, my friend, will be able to picture it exactly if you recall the impression that the sight of Liège made on us.[6] Remember those swarms of importunate beggars which we kept meeting along the road; that irregular conglomeration of Gothic houses, smoky, decayed, and empty-windowed, with half their roofs missing. Remember the faces of the people standing in doorways, barely human, their yellow skin showing through under a layer of coal dust; hordes of tattered children; rags hanging all over the bridges and houses. In short, remember Liège, that repair of hunger, vice, and impudence, the inevitable products of general poverty, and you will have a picture of Newport. And yet both these cities are well located for trade and are surrounded by fertile land. But in Liège the products of the country serve to satisfy the whims of some fifty ecclesiastical sluggards, who, justified by antiquated religious superstitions, wallow in their pleasures, surrounded by poor wretches starving to death.[7] In Newport the people, deceived by two or three knaves, have themselves brought about their own misfortunes and destroyed the blessings nature had lavished upon them. They have themselves sanctioned fraud and thereby have made themselves odious to all their neighbors

[5] [Constantin Chasseboeuf, Comte de Volney, *Voyage en Syrie et en Egypte pendant les années 1783, 1784 et 1785*, Paris, 1787.]

[6] [Brissot had visited Liège in September 1787 with Clavière and the Marquis Du Crest, Chancellor of the Duke of Orleans.]

[7] When I wrote these lines I was far from foreseeing the revolution in Liège. Liberty is now unfurling her flags over the city. May Heaven grant her total victory! [The Revolution of Brabant lasted from 1787 to 1790.]

and banished from their midst business and commerce; they have thus destroyed the channels which were outlets for their products and through which money flowed back, money which by its abundance once made this state so prosperous.

Now, my friend, reread M. de Crèvecoeur's glowing description of this city and of this state.[8] It was not exaggerated; all the Americans to whom I have spoken praise Rhode Island's former splendor and natural advantages for agriculture, for trade, for industry, and in fact for all the blessings of life. "Je n'ai fait que passer, il n'était déjà plus." [9]

Two miles from Newport I saw the ruins of a magnificent house which had belonged to a Quaker and which had been destroyed by fire. Large sections of it had withstood the flames; the garden still existed and despite its neglected state it revealed not only the fertility of the soil but all the care, work, and money the owner had given it. Here was a depiction in miniature of the whole state. Paper money has wrought the same devastation that the fire brought to the Quaker's house. It has stifled commerce, industry, and employment. Nothing is sold and no work is done, for fear that payment will be made in this discredited currency. Only retail trade remains, but it languishes, for it is conducted only in hard cash. The merchant circumvents the law by delivering his merchandise only for cash; but the worker, who is paid only after his task is finished, refuses employment because he is afraid he will be paid in paper money.

I noticed that even merchandise sold for cash was more expensive and greatly inferior to that offered for sale in Massachusetts. This was to be expected; in an area where the people are poor and where fraudulent business practices are the rule, retailers demand high profits in return for the risks they run, and wholesalers in the other states send in shoddy merchandise, for they assume that people with little money and no ethics care less about the quality of the cloth they buy.

The history of paper money in Rhode Island shows how easily shrewd, evil men can deceive an ignorant populace. Two citizens of this state, who enjoyed an excellent public reputation, purchased during the last war a large amount of land.[10] After the

[8] [*Lettres d'un cultivateur américain* (Paris, 1787), II, 52–59.]
[9] [I merely passed, and, lo, he was not. Racine, *Esther,* III, ix.]
[10] [Probably John Innis Clark (1745–1808) and Joseph Nightingale (1747–1797), Providence merchants and speculators.]

peace treaty, profits decreased, and so did their ability to pay for these lands. Since they did not wish to lose them, they conceived the idea of petitioning for the passage of a law to introduce paper money. As they were very influential among the people, and, consequently, in the legislative assembly, they succeeded in having the law passed. Then they obtained from the government a large amount of this paper currency, giving their title to the land as security. By a similar stratagem they bought a large number of cattle in the country villages, payed for them with paper, and then shipped them to the West Indies, where they were paid in sugar and molasses, which they then gave in payment, at exorbitant prices, to their creditors. Other notorious frauds were frequent in Rhode Island during that period. Lawsuits followed one another, in the course of which scraps of paper were offered in payment for the most sacred obligations.

Merchants used paper to pay debts contracted in trade with the other states; but out-of-state merchants were not allowed to pay the citizens of Rhode Island in the same currency. For when some citizens of Massachusetts who owed money in Rhode Island bought some of this paper and tried to use it to pay their debts, the swindlers who governed Rhode Island realized that if such reprisals were tolerated their maneuver would be turned to the profit of their neighbors. So they passed a law which forbade citizens of other states to pay inhabitants of Rhode Island in paper money. What was the result of this legalized fraud? A universal outcry of indignation against Rhode Island, and imports from other states ceased. Wood had formerly been brought into Rhode Island from the other eastern states; this trade now ceased. Trading even among the citizens of the state came to a halt. Distrust took hold of all minds; since fraud was the general rule, everybody practiced it and everybody feared it, and honest people stopped doing business. Such were the causes of the empty streets and the poverty that I observed. Money did not circulate, and all business was dead. Even the swindlers themselves who had instigated the law seemed to be demanding that it be repealed, so that they could enjoy with security the benefits of their fraudulence.

There were other reasons for the disaster besides paper money, or rather paper money had other effects which increased the public calamity. There were no public schools, no dissemination of public information through newspapers, and almost no public worship. Ministers did not receive salaries on which they could live, or else they were paid in paper money. Indeed, how can there be public worship when public trust is banished? How can one think about educational institutions when morality is trampled under foot? And when there is no morality among men, what becomes of the virtue of women? What becomes of patriotism? Can one even speak of patriotism in Rhode Island? The idea of patriotism presupposes the existence of fraternity, of a common interest; deception and fraud transform a society into a mass of men at war with one another.

Moreover the people had too much influence over the government and the magistrates. The members of the assembly were elected every six months, and this frequent rotation forced the candidates to be continually trying to please the people. Similarly judges were elected every year and the people often chose ignorant or vicious men who rendered the most absurd and unjust verdicts. These judges, being dependent either upon the people or upon those who controlled the people, were forced, if they wished to continue in office, to try to please; consequently justice was either venal or biased. The result was that the people felt the greatest contempt for the judges, and they had no respect at all for the law, which they defied. There was no sense of subordination, no sign of respect for authority; the vilest wretches often insulted the officers of the law. Attorneys vilified judges in gross terms and with impunity.

I could not conceive how under these circumstances a person could live in peace in Newport; for there was no restraint, no religion, no morality, no law, no respect for magistrates, no militia.

Once when fire broke out in a house I went to watch the people's behavior. They rushed and ran about, and amidst the disorder children jumped with joy. Nevertheless the people turned to with a will, the pumps arrived, and although there was no semblance of order, they managed to put the fire out. I noted with pleasure their eagerness and zeal and was consoled by this spectacle; I saw that not all virtue had been stifled in the citizens of this state.

Rhode Island will not flourish again until the circulation of paper money is stopped and the government is reformed. The magistrates must be free of dependence upon the people, and the members of the assembly must not be elected so frequently. It is inconceivable that all the honest people suffering under the present anarchy and the many Quakers, who form the solid basis of this state's population, have not yet joined forces to bring about these reforms.[11]

I have no doubt that if the reforms are not effected promptly the population of the state will decline. The majority of the settlers in Muskingum, near the Ohio, came from Rhode Island under the leadership of Colonel Varnum.[12] Many more families are also now preparing to emigrate. Almost all the honest people, disgusted with the anarchy into which the state has sunk, would leave Newport if they could find buyers for their property.

I also do not doubt that the example set by Rhode Island will be to many proof that a republican government leads to disaster. It would be wrong to draw such a conclusion. The example of this state proves only that there ought not to be too frequent rotation in the legislative body; that the executive power ought not to be unstable; and that it is just as dangerous to make magistrates too dependent on the people as it is to make them too independent. In short, the example of Rhode Island proves the case against *pure* democracy, but not against *representative* democracy. For representation for six months is tantamount to direct government by the people themselves; such representation is no more than a shadow that passes too quickly to be able to exist and to act in its own right. Therefore this example is not proof of the unwisdom of the system of more independent representation for longer periods, which constitutes true republican government and which is exemplified by the governments of the other states of the Union.

Yet in spite of the chaos in Rhode Island you hear no reports of thefts or murders, or even of beggars; for an American, even when poor, never stoops so low as to forswear all sense of equity or to renounce all shame, and this is another difference between Newport and Liége, which I described above. Americans do not beg and do not steal, and true American blood still flows in the veins of the people of Rhode Island. Moreover, men who live in the country do not suffer the same sort of poverty that city dwellers endure, and one does not find in them the same sort of dishonesty.

Condemned by unfavorable winds to spend six days in Newport,

[11] These reforms are not far off. The state of Rhode Island has just passed a resolution to adopt the new Federal Constitution. This fact proves that good principles are finally prevailing and that the corrupt practices that have been caused by special circumstances will disappear.

[12] [James Mitchell Varnum (1748–1789), a veteran of the Revolution, was a director of the Ohio Company and a U.S. Judge for the Northwest Territories.]

I should have died of boredom had I not been provided with books, pens, and ink. The inn where I stayed was full of travelers and seamen. Their conversation, which I took pleasure in listening to at first, eventually became very tiresome, and I was happy to get a small room where I could meditate and write without interruption.

I had time to think about the disadvantages of travel by sea and to become convinced that it is much better to take a stagecoach. The departure of the stage is certain, but winds are uncertain. On land, you are almost certain not to suffer illness, while at sea, particularly if the weather is bad, you can be very sick indeed. On land, you sleep at night in a good, or at worst in a mediocre, inn; at sea, you are often tossed about in a miserable cabin. On land, you have at least an equal chance of eating good or bad meals; at sea, you often get nothing but spoiled meat and a surly captain for company. Besides, it is most unpleasant to be day and night in the company of people whom you do not know, and to have difficulties changing one's linen, and in writing or reading. This mode of travel is particularly uncomfortable for women, and I shall never advise a woman to go to New York by sea; the journey by land, although rough and often unpleasant, offers fewer disadvantages. Packet boats are useful only if one is traveling with heavy baggage, or if one is a man and inured to inconveniences.

There is another serious disadvantage in sailing to New York from Newport; the packets cannot leave port if the wind is from the west or southwest, which frequently happens. Moreover, you cannot get under way in the afternoon or evening because thirty or forty miles offshore there are islands that can be dangerous in bad weather.

I saw in Newport a twenty-month-old Negro who repeated everything that was said to him, understood clearly what he heard, obeyed instructions, mimicked others, danced, etc. He showed signs of extraordinary intelligence. People amused themselves by getting him to perform spontaneously and especially by getting him to make funny faces. This seemed to me a cruel and thoughtless sort of diversion. It was an indication of the contempt in which Negroes are still held, a contempt which Americans, above all others, must renounce if they wish to be consistent. This feeling of contempt for Negroes makes children used to too much servility, and Americans must banish, even from their children's play, the image of servility.

In Newport I had the opportunity of hearing Dr. Murray, famous in America for his doctrine of universal salvation.[13] Because of this doctrine he has been excommunicated by all the other sects, so that at present he has no church and is an itinerant preacher. In Newport he preached in the room in which the court of justice meets. His audience was large. I was surprised to see pretty, well-dressed women wearing enormous, fashionable hats, for until then all the females I had seen had been hideous creatures clad in rags. The majority of the men present, however, were poorly dressed. The doctor began by asking his listeners not to be surprised by the strangeness of the place where they were assembled to worship the Eternal, for He, being present everywhere, could be worshiped anywhere. Then he addressed to Him a very long prayer, which everyone heard standing, which seemed to me very uncomfortable. I have never clearly understood why the reformers of the church, who have redressed so many abuses, have retained that of standing as an expression of respect.

After a few hymns the doctor started expounding his doctrine of salvation, purgatory, etc. He claimed that God loves everybody, and that He wishes to save everybody, or at least all those whose hearts are right. But when he reached the question of whether He would save those who do not believe in Christ, he became involved in distinctions which I could not follow, and it seemed to me he denied salvation to those who do not believe in the Bible. But to console these unbelievers, he promised them that they would not go to hell for eternity, but to purgatory.

What distinguished this doctor from other ministers was not only his doctrine but also his delivery. He made many gestures and spoke with theatrical inflections; his style was now trivial and comical, now bombastic and turgid; he sprinkled his theology with anecdotes which seemed to please the people. Moreover, he asked no money for his preaching, which perhaps pleased his listeners more.

I was detained in Newport by steady southwest winds until Satur-

---

[13] M. Chastellux tells in his *Travels*, in writing about Portsmouth, New Hampshire, of an individual called, I think, André, who was famous for his sermons on the same doctrine. I never heard the name of this André mentioned, and I am all the more inclined to believe that M. Chastellux was again mistaken because Murray was at that time a minister at Cape Ann and very well known in New Hampshire. See Chastellux, *Voyages* [Paris, 1786], II, 183. [John Murray (1741–1815), the founder of Universalism in America, settled in Gloucester in 1774, where he established a Universalist Society.]

day the eighteenth. At last toward midnight we set sail. The captain had refused to get under way sooner for fear of running on Block Island in the darkness. With the wind and tide pushing us swiftly along, we were making nine or ten knots and I thought we should reach New York the following night. I longed for our arrival, for the too rapid movement of the ship had made me seasick. But the captain refused to satisfy my impatience. He was afraid of a kind of whirlpool called Hell Gate, which is eight miles from New York, and so at eight o'clock in the evening he dropped the anchor. At six in the morning we got under way again, and we arrived at these terrible gates of hell. They are a kind of very narrow passage between the shores of New York and Long Island, obstructed by rocks which are covered at high tide. The currents of the whirlpool are scarcely perceptible at low water, but it is not surprising that vessels unfamiliar with the channel are wrecked if they attempt the passage at high tide. I was told of a forty-cannon English frigate which was lost here during the last war. You can see that these hellish gates are indeed an additional obstacle to navigation through this sound. On the other hand, it is quite usual during the summer months to cover the 200 miles in less than twenty hours when the tide and wind are favorable; but chances are always better sailing from New York than returning.

As you approach the city the coasts of New York and of Long Island draw together and offer a most pleasant sight, for they are adorned with pretty houses set in a truly rural landscape. Long Island is, as you know, famous for its farms.

The fare from Providence, food included, is six and a half dollars, or thirty-four livres, two sous and six deniers.

I must add a few words about the packet boats in this part of America and the facilities they offer.

Although, in my opinion, it is more convenient and often less expensive to go by land, I must praise the cleanliness and good order found on these ships. The one on which I sailed had a cabin with fourteen bunks arranged in two tiers, each with a little porthole. The cabin was well ventilated, so that you did not breathe that nauseating air which infects the Channel packets. It was well varnished. Two very comfortable recesses had been built on the stern as privies. The captain, two sailors, and a Negro cook made up the entire crew. The food was good, and my only complaint was about the delays and dawdling, which are of the nature of seamen.

RHODE ISLAND

Every one of the towns along this coast, New Haven, New London and the rest, has packets to New York like the one on which I sailed; all are equally clean and attractive and all offer the same comforts to the traveler. You may be sure that there is nothing like them in the Old World.

I arrived in New York just in time. A violent storm, which was to last for twenty-four hours, began two hours after my arrival. A European who goes through one of these terrible hurricanes for the first time thinks that the wooden house he is in will never withstand its fury.

NEW YORK

August 1788

I have reread, my dear friend, M. Crèvecoeur's description of this part of the United States, and having compared what he says with what I have seen, I can assure you that all the details of his picture are accurate.

Nothing is more magnificent than the situation of New York between the majestic East and North rivers. The latter separates the city from New Jersey and is so deep that ships of the line anchor in it. At this very moment I can see a 1,200-ton French ship intended for the East Indies trade which has come here to be refitted. This river has, however, two disadvantages, drifting ice in winter and the strong northwest winds. Ships can sail upstream with the help of the tide as far as Albany, 170 miles from New York.

Albany is on the Mohawk River, which flows into the North [Hudson] River. It is the principal city of that area, of which M. Crèvecoeur has given us such an attractive description. He makes the cold winter months there seem a season of delights, at least for those who love only the pleasures afforded by nature.

Albany will soon be surpassed in prosperity by a town recently established some distance from the Hudson River.[1] At this spot four years ago there was nothing but a farm; today there are about one hundred substantial houses, a town hall, and public fountains. The inhabitants own over fifty ships on which they export American products to the West Indies and even to Europe. Included in this total are two whalers. Consequently this new town, founded by Quakers, already enjoys a most flourishing trade. Its vessels do not spend the winter idly in port, as do those sailing out of Albany, but continue trading with the West Indies.

Poughkeepsie, on the same river, the city in which met the famous convention that adopted the new Federal Constitution, has doubled its population and the volume of its trade. The lack of interest of the citizens of Albany in foreign commerce may be attributed to the fertility of their lands. They devote themselves

[1] [Hudson, New York.]

138

entirely to agriculture and prefer not to brave the dangers of the sea for the sake of profits which they can easily make by farming their fertile fields.

The fertility of the soil and the quantity of good uncleared land are attracting many settlers to that area. New settlements are being established slowly, however, because the other states offer, if not equally good land, at least the advantage of a more temperate climate, for here the farmer has to endure long and extremely cold winters.

If this part of America becomes well populated, the North River will serve as an excellent route for the export of the products of the region. Navigable for over three hundred miles from its mouth, it communicates by the Mohawk River with Lakes Oneida and Ontario, and through these with Canada. Its waterfalls, especially the famous falls at Cohoes, can be someday bypassed with canals, which are so easy to build in a country endowed with a large supply of manpower and a great deal of money. Communication with Canada is also possible by the Hudson River through Lakes George and Champlain. This geographical situation will make New York a center for the fur trade of all the northern states, at least as long as this trade, which depends upon the existence of the Indian tribes and large expanses of unsettled land, continues to exist.

By the East River, the state of New York communicates with Long Island and with all the northern states. It provides excellent anchorages and deep-water moorings close to shore. Ships of the line can anchor near its wharves, where they are sheltered from the winds and the terrible storms which sometimes occur on these coasts.[2]

The East River presents only one danger to navigation but it is a terrible one, the whirlpool I have mentioned, the famous Hell Gate. M. Crèvecoeur did not give a full enough description and I think I should supplement it. It is the meeting of the two tides which forms the whirlpool called The Pot. Its powerful forces draw in and engulf any ships which because of the inexperience or imprudence of their pilots have failed to avoid its treacherous attraction. At certain tides the noise from this "Pot" sounds like boiling water in a huge cauldron. On the shore opposite this

[2] On August 19, 1784, New York suffered a fearful hurricane which uprooted trees, carried away roofs, blew down fences, and destroyed a large part of the Battery.

voracious funnel there is a reef called The Frying Pan. It was so named because of the horrible noise made by the breaking waves, like the sound of water dropped on a red-hot shovel or into boiling oil.[3] Vessels which have avoided the whirlpool are often caught up and shattered against this reef. Nor are these the only hazards. A third danger awaits ships which have had the luck to escape the first two. On a diagonal between the reefs a rock known as Hog's Back breaks the surface of the water. Incredible as it seems, in spite of all these many obstacles, vessels as large as ships of the line have dared these reefs. Among these was the *Experiment,* a fifty-gun ship whose captain, when pursued by some ships detached from D'Estaing's fleet then maintaining a blockade off Sandy Hook, had the daring to risk this passage which had previously been the scene of terrible disasters for vessels of such a size.

The advantageous location of New York is the reason for its extensive trade and for the fact that the English have always preferred it to other American ports. It is both the port of export for the products of Connecticut and New Jersey and also the center for the distribution to these states of all the products of Europe and the East Indies.

It is difficult to obtain figures on the exports and imports of this state. Colonel Lamb,[4] Collector of Customs, shrouds all his operations in the greatest mystery. This is a result of the Dutch influence, which is still dominant in this city. The Dutch are secretive about their business and their profits and live for their own interests. I have been able, however, to obtain some statements of accounts which you will find in my general table of the commerce of the United States.[5]

The English have a predilection for this city and its products, and consequently the port is always full of their ships. They even prefer its wheat. American merchants bring wheat from Virginia and sell it to the English as New York State wheat.

The presence of Congress and of the diplomatic corps and the influx of foreigners have greatly contributed to increase the corruption of the city by the evils of luxury. The citizens are far from complaining about this; they prefer the splendor of wealth and

[3] [Brissot's unfamiliarity with English obviously led him to invent this fanciful explanation of the name Frying Pan, or Pan, given to this reef.]

[4] [John Lamb (1735–1800), Revolutionary soldier, member of the New York legislature, and Collector of Customs for the port of New York.]

[5] [Letters 43 and 44.]

worldly pleasures to the simple life and the innocent delights it affords.

Smoking has not disappeared from this city with the other customs brought by its founders, the Dutch. People smoke mostly cigars imported from the Spanish West Indies. These are leaves of sweet-smelling tobacco six inches long, which are smoked without the aid of any instrument. This custom is revolting to a Frenchman; it may seem disagreeable to women, for it alters the purity of the breath; and the philosopher will condemn it because it is a superfluous need. Smoking does have, however, one advantage: it accustoms one to meditation and prevents loquacity. When one smoker asks another a question, he has to wait two minutes but he gets a well-considered answer. The cigar renders a man the same service as did the glass of water which the philosopher drank before replying whenever he was angry.

The great commercial activity in this city and the ease with which one may earn a living are resulting in a very rapid growth of population in this state. One can estimate the rate of increase by the speed with which losses have been replaced. In 1773 [sic] there were 148,124 whites; in 1786, the number was 219,996.[6]

The population of New York is increasing at the expense of the

POPULATION OF NEW YORK

Number of Inhabitants

	1756	1776	1786
Men			
Under 16	20,660	....	54,807
From 16 to 60	19,825	....	52,927
Over 60	2,767	....	4,731
Total	43,252		112,465
Women			
Under 16	18,984	....	51,766
16 and over	20,997	....	55,765
Women	39,981	....	107,531
Men	43,252	....	112,465
Total Whites	83,233	148,124	219,996
Slaves			
Men	7,564	....	9,521
Women	5,978	....	9,368
Total	13,542	19,883	18,889
Taxpaying Indians			12

other states. Forty-five Quaker families from around Burlington have recently emigrated to Montgomery County. A wealthy citizen of that county is giving them land on condition that, after seven years, they pay him each year sixpence sterling (twelve French sous) per acre. He even lends the settlers a pair of oxen for this period of time.

Quakers emigrate to rural areas, for the luxury which prevails in this city would be in disaccord with their simple way of life. There is, however, a fairly large group of Quakers here, who adhere closely to the traditions and strict morality of their sect.

If there is one city on the American continent which above all others displays English luxury, it is New York, where you can find all the English fashions. The women wear silk and gauze dresses, hats, and even elaborate hairdos. Carriages are rare, but the few that exist are elegant. The men dress more simply than the women, and they still disdain to wear frills, but they compensate for this simplicity when they sit down at table, where the most expensive wines make their appearance. Luxury is already breeding in this city a most dangerous class of men—bachelors. They are afraid to marry because it is so expensive to keep a wife.

As in England, tea is the main attraction at most of the entertainments in this city. It is to tea that a foreigner is invited, and tea that you go to drink in Mr. Cummings' pretty garden, the Florida Gardens of New York.[7] It is located on the North River and the view is delightful. But what a difference there is between this garden and those that serve for the entertainment of the English and the French! At Mr. Cummings' I saw some superb quinces, from which a preserve is made.

Fruits, though cultivated in this state with greater care than elsewhere in the nation, are still not as fine as the European products. I saw apple trees in September loaded with both fruit and flowers. I also saw peach trees bent with the weight of their fruit, but the peaches were very poor. Is their quality impaired because the trees bear so heavily or because of the extreme heat? The peaches often split and fail to ripen.

M. Crèvecoeur is right to praise the abundance and good quality of the products of New York—the vegetables, the meat, and espe-

---

[7] [The Florida Gardens, on the North River, named after the more famous Florida Gardens of London, were one of a number of such pleasure gardens in and about the city at which light refreshments were served and a variety of amusements were offered.]

cially the fish. It is difficult to find so many good things in one place. The milk, however, which is consumed in large quantities, has an unpleasant taste. I am told that this is caused by the garlic which grows in the fields, especially on Long Island. Food is more expensive in New York than in any of the other northern and central cities. Below is a list which will give you some idea of the prices.[8] Many products, particularly luxury items, are generally more expensive here than in Europe and in France. A hairdresser costs 20 shillings a month [9] or approximately 12 livres. Laundry costs 4 shillings, or 50 sous, for a dozen pieces. Etc.

I have heard Frenchmen complain of these excessive prices and accuse the people offering these services of cheating them. They fail to understand that where jobs are few they have a high value, and that where workers are few they are expensive. The hairdresser does not have as many customers as does his Parisian counterpart, so he makes them pay more. Since laundry is usually done in the home, a laundress washes only for foreigners; besides, she has to pay her help high wages, and soap, which is imported, is expensive.

Foreigners very often make this accusation that Americans cheat them. Before doing so they ought to define what cheap and expensive mean in business, and they should also cite precise facts. I have often heard this accusation, but few facts in support of it. Foreigners who, after having lived for a while in this country, have taxed Americans with guile and dishonesty have confessed to me that this accusation should be limited to the cities, and that in the country one does in truth find honest dealing. The majority of the

[8] The following are the average prices in French money:
Beef, 6 sous a pound. Milk, 8 sous a pint. Bohea tea, 40 sous a pound. Souchong tea, 12 livres. Green tea, 16 livres. The price of green tea has gone up greatly because its consumption has increased; in 1787 it cost only 12 livres. A loaf of bread weighing 2 pounds 5 ounces and made of fine flour, 6 to 7 sous. A good, ordinary beer, 3 sous a pint. Porter, from 12 to 15 livres a dozen bottles.

Laborers, masons, and carpenters get from 4 to 6 livres a day. American workers work well. Male servants earn from 25 to 30 livres a month and are well fed.

A cord of oak wood costs 24 livres in summer, 30 livres in winter. A cord is 8 English feet long, 4 feet high and 4 feet wide, and is divided into quarters. A quarter cord costs 6 livres 10 sous and is transported in a small, one-horse wagon fitted with four uprights, two of which are braced at the top with chains, the space between the four poles containing a quarter cord. The wood is taken off the boats which bring it and is measured in the presence of an inspector, who receives a penny per cord. Hickory is more expensive, almost double in price, but it is also much superior to oak, being more compact and heavier; it ignites more quickly, burns longer, gives more heat, and does not spark. A great deal of coal is also burned here.

[9] A shilling is a little more than 12 French sous.

persons who voiced these complaints were Frenchmen and they believed that Americans treated them more unfairly than they did the English. Even if this were really so, it would not surprise me. The Frenchmen I have met were forever exalting the services rendered by their nation to the Americans and forever criticizing the latter's tastes and customs, decrying their government, exaggerating the favors granted to Americans by the French government, and belittling the services rendered by Congress and the states to the French.

One of the greatest mistakes made by travelers is to judge the average cost of food in a country by the prices paid in an inn or boardinghouse. This is a false base. In a city, one should take the prices charged in the markets, that is, the prices paid by the working people and by the middle classes, which are about half those you pay at an inn or in a boardinghouse. This base would be false, however, if it were applied to the rural areas. In the country, foodstuffs which are very easy to grow and which are plentiful often sell for almost nothing; others, however, are high priced because of certain circumstances. For instance, fresh meat must necessarily be more expensive in a thinly settled region than in a town where because of the daily demand there are regular slaughterhouses. I feel I must make these observations in order to warn the reader against the estimates of food prices given by travelers.

There are still other circumstances which influence prices, such as, for instance, those which are the result of wartime conditions, of which M. Chastellux took no account when he exaggerated the high prices of American foodstuffs. In New York, food was much more expensive during the war. Since then prices have declined by almost half. Nevertheless, even at present, food prices are about the same as those in medium-sized European cities.

Most foreigners and members of Congress live in boardinghouses, where room and board cost four to six dollars (twenty-one to thirty-two livres) a week. French wine is extra. Lawyers' fees are higher proportionately and, as in England, are excessive, but doctors do not enjoy similar advantages. Since people are generally very healthy here, there is not much need for their services. Despite this fact, doctors are quite numerous.

I have spoken to a number of doctors and asked them what are the most common diseases. They tell me that the most frequent are bilious fevers and that the excessive cold and lack of proper care are responsible for the majority of illnesses. They add that there is little sickness here; the air is healthy despite the nearness of the sea and the city's insular position. The citizens are rather temperate; the well-to-do are not rich enough to indulge in the luxury and debauchery which in Europe kill off so many, and there are none who suffer from lack of food since fish and meat are very cheap.

Let those who doubt the prodigious effects of liberty on man and on his industry come to America! What miracles they will witness! While almost everywhere in Europe towns and villages are falling into ruin, here new buildings are rising on every hand. New York was partially destroyed by fire during the last war, but the traces of this terrible conflagration are disappearing. The activity which reigns on all sides announces the prosperity of the future. Everywhere streets are being widened and extended. Elegant buildings in the English style are replacing the gabled Dutch houses, of which there are some still left. The European observer views them with a certain pleasure, for they call to mind the origins of this colony, as do the manners and customs of the inhabitants, which are still marked by the traditions of the Netherlands.

I take a walk along the North River. What rapid changes in a few weeks! Two hundred feet of land have been reclaimed from the river by a very simple device. They construct a kind of box built up of very large logs laid one upon another at right angles with spaces between and fastened together by strong uprights. This floating dike is towed to the spot where it is to be located and where the water is often as much as forty feet deep. When it reaches its destination it is loaded with enormous rocks brought out on barges and is sunk. Then the space full of water behind the rocks is rapidly filled in.

On all sides houses are going up and streets are being laid out; everywhere I see workers filling land, excavating, building, laying pavements, erecting public pumps. At one and the same time they are erecting a building for Congress and are repairing the hospital, which was in such an abandoned and dilapidated condition that it could not receive a single patient. The administration of the hospital, formerly in the hands of the Quakers, had been taken from them because of hostility toward the sect. Now it has again been entrusted to them, and they immediately decided to repair the building. The work is proceeding rapidly. It is a large brick building, in an ideal location on the bank of the North River, and has every advantage: very healthful air, an abundant supply of water, vast grounds where the sick can take walks, and a magnificent view. It is both outside the city and conveniently nearby— far enough for the air from the hospital not to be dangerous, yet near enough for the sick to be transported there and for their people to be able to visit them.

It is likewise to the Quakers, to that sect which has been the victim of so much calumny (but of this I shall speak more fully later), that New York owes the good management of the workhouse under their supervision. It is also to their zeal that is due the establishment of a society for the abolition of slavery and of the slave trade.[10] As I shall devote to this important question a separate chapter, I shall not speak of it here.

A society with a much more resounding title, but one whose services are less real, was organized a short while back. Its object is the promotion of science and of all useful knowledge, but its members meet seldom and do no work. They have, however, 800 pounds in the bank, which remain idle. Its president is Governor Clinton, who is anything but a man of learning. This society is not likely to succeed here; the Dutch are no lovers of letters.[11]

But though this city does not abound in men of learning, at the moment the presence of Congress attracts the most celebrated persons from the various parts of the United States. I have seen, among others, Jay, whom I have already mentioned, Madison, Hamilton, King,[12] and Thornton.[13]

The name of Madison, famous in America, is also well known in Europe through the amply deserved tributes given him by his fellow countryman and friend, Mr. Jefferson. Although still young, he has rendered important services to Virginia, to the American confederation, and in general to the cause of liberty and humanity.

[10] [The Society for Promoting the Manumission of Slaves and Protecting Such as Have or May Be Liberated, organized in New York City in 1785. Brissot attended a meeting of the Society on August 21, presented a letter from the Société des Amis des Noirs proposing the establishment of "a fraternal Relation and mutual Correspondence" between the two groups, and on August 28 was elected an honorary member of the Society.—Minutes of the Society, New-York Historical Society.]

[11] [The Society for the Promotion of Useful Knowledge, organized in 1787.]

[12] [Rufus King (1755–1827), U.S. senator and minister to Great Britain.]

[13] [William Thornton (1761–1828), born on Tortola in the Virgin Islands, studied medicine in Scotland, came to the United States in 1786, and soon became an active proponent of the plan to resettle Negro slaves in Africa.]

He has contributed much, together with Mr. White,[14] to the reform of the civil and criminal codes of his state, and he distinguished himself particularly at the time that the conventions met to vote on the new Federal Constitution. For a long time Virginia hesitated to join the Union, but by his logic and his eloquence Mr. Madison persuaded the convention to favor acceptance.

This republican seems to be no more than thirty-three years old. When I saw him, he looked tired, perhaps as a result of the immense labors to which he had devoted himself recently. His expression was that of a stern censor; his conversation disclosed a man of learning; and his countenance was that of a person conscious of his talents and of his duties.

During the dinner to which he invited me there was much talk of North Carolina's refusal to accept the new Constitution. The majority voting against acceptance was one hundred. Mr. Madison did not believe that this rejection would carry any weight with Americans or that it would hamper the operations of the New Congress. I told him that, though it might not be fatal to Congress in America, in Europe it would be; that in Europe people would not take the trouble to try to appreciate the motives behind this rejection or to consider the small importance of North Carolina in the confederation; that this rejection would be construed as a seed or cause of discord, perhaps of a long-lasting disagreement likely to slow the operations of Congress; and that certainly this impression would prevent the revival of American credit abroad.

Mr. Madison attributed North Carolina's refusal to the strong support by the majority of the inhabitants of paper money and of the Tender Act [15] and to the influence of the party in power in that state, which probably derives financial benefits from the present currency system. He was greatly inclined to believe that North Carolina would not hold to its present position for long.

Mr. Hamilton is Mr. Madison's worthy rival as well as his collaborator. He looks thirty-eight or forty years old, is not tall, and has a resolute, frank, soldierly appearance. He was aide-de-camp to General Washington, who had the greatest confidence in him, a confidence he deserved. Since the war he has resumed the practice

---

[14] [Alexander White (1738–1804), Virginia lawyer and congressman. While a member of the state assembly he played an important part in advancing measures for religious liberty, for reform of the state court system, and for taxation reform.]

[15] [Requiring the acceptance of paper currency as legal tender.]

of law and has devoted himself mainly to public life. Elected to Congress, he has distinguished himself by his eloquence and by the soundness of his reasoning. Among the works which have come from his pen the most distinguished are a large number of letters inserted in *The Federalist,* of which I shall speak hereafter, and the *Letters from Phocion,* published in defense of the Loyalists. During the war Mr. Hamilton fought the Loyalists with success, but when peace came it was his opinion that they should not be driven to desperation by harsh persecution, and he was fortunate enough to win over to clemency his fellow citizens, who had been inspired by a justifiable resentment against the Loyalists because of the damage they had done. This young orator's moment of triumph came at the New York Convention. The antifederalist party was strong in New York City, and three quarters of the members of the convention when they left for Poughkeepsie were opposed to the new Constitution. Mr. Hamilton, joining his efforts to those of the celebrated Mr. Jay, succeeded in convincing even the most obstinate among them that the refusal of New York would have disastrous consequences for the state and for the Confederation. Consequently they voted in favor of the Constitution. The celebration in New York following the ratification was magnificent. The ship *Federalist,* which took part in the festivities, was renamed *Hamilton* in honor of this eloquent orator.

Hamilton married General Schuyler's daughter, a delightful woman who combines both the charms and attractions and the candor and simplicity typical of American womanhood.[16] At the dinner to which he invited me I met General Mifflin, known for his distinguished record during the last war.[17] He has the vivacity of a Frenchman, and is also extremely courteous.

Mr. King, whom I also saw at this dinner, is reputed to be the most eloquent man in the United States. What impressed me most about him was his modesty; he seemed completely unaware of his worth. Mr. Hamilton had the determined appearance of a republican; Mr. Madison, the thoughtful look of a wise statesman.

At this dinner, as at almost all the others I attended in America, they drank the health of M. Lafayette. Americans take pleasure in referring to him as one of their liberators, and they love him as

[16] [In 1780 Alexander Hamilton married General Philip Schuyler's second daughter, Elizabeth.]
[17] [Thomas Mifflin (1744–1800).]

their best friend. He deserves their affection and respect; they have no warmer supporter in France. His generosity toward them is unfailing and has been manifested on all public occasions, and even more in private ones, when his kindnesses have remained unknown. It is not perhaps to the honor of France or of the French who have visited America to point out that he is the only one who made a contribution for the benefit of the unfortunate victims of the Boston fire,[18] and the only Frenchman whose door is always open to all Americans.

Doctor Thornton, intimately connected with all the Americans I have just mentioned, is pursuing another career—that of helping humanity. Though by his dress he does not belong to the Society of Friends, he adheres to their principles and practices their moral code, particularly with respect to Negroes. He told me of his past and continuing efforts to accelerate realization of a great project he has conceived for their benefit. Convinced that there can be no sincere union between the whites and the Negroes, even should the latter accede to all political rights, he proposes to send them back and settle them in Africa. At first sight this plan seems terrifying; but upon examination, its necessity and advantages are quite apparent. I shall not discuss them here, for I shall take this matter up in my letter on the condition of Negroes in this country.[19]

Mr. Thornton, who by his vivacity and pleasant manners seems to belong to the French nation, was born in Antigua. His mother owns a plantation there, and it was there that, instead of growing callous like most other plantation owners, he acquired that humanity and compassion for Negroes which is such a source of torment to him. He told me that, had he been able to do so, he would have set his Negroes free, but since he could not, he treated them like human beings. Since his father likewise followed the same principles, there was no recruiting of Negroes on his plantation.

I cannot finish this letter without mentioning another American whose financial skill is well known here, namely Colonel Duer, Secretary of the Treasury.[20] It would be difficult to find a man who

[18] He gave 300 louis. [The Boston fire of 1787, which destroyed about a hundred buildings near Hollis Street.]

[19] [Letters 21–24 and 26.]

[20] [Colonel William Duer (1747–1799), Brissot's business associate, was appointed assistant secretary under Hamilton but resigned six months later.]

better combines a good head for figures, broad vision, and quick penetration in dealing with the most complicated problems. To these qualities, add goodness of heart. It is to his kindness and efforts that I am indebted for much valuable information on this country's finances, which I shall report in a subsequent letter.

I should also fail to repay a debt of gratitude if I did not mention here the kindness shown me by the President of Congress, Mr. Griffin.[21] He is a handsome, well-built Virginian, witty, soft-spoken, affable, and polite. At the first dinner to which I was invited I met seven or eight ladies, all wearing large hats, feathers, etc. It made me unhappy to notice that some of them were very vain and affected. One of them was giddy and vivacious; another one played the part of the woman of sensibility with much simpering and affectation. Two of them wore dresses which exposed much of their bosoms. I was scandalized by such indecency in republican women.

A President of Congress is far from being surrounded by the ceremony enjoyed by European monarchs—and so much the better. His position is not permanent—and again, so much the better. He never forgets that he has been a simple citizen, and that he will become one again. He does not give sumptuous dinners—once more, so much the better, for this means that he is surrounded by fewer parasites and has less opportunity to corrupt others.

I noticed that at this dinner many customs observed elsewhere were not followed: no tiresome introductions, none of those toasts that become so wearisome in a large company. After the ladies withdrew, little wine was drunk. These details are sufficient to give you an idea of the temperance practiced in this country. Temperance is the supreme virtue of republicans.

In concluding this letter I must add a word about the financial situation of the city and of the state of New York. The fact that it is easy for this state to tax its foreign trade, which is so flourishing, makes it possible to meet fully the expenses of government and to pay punctually the interest on the state debt and the state's share of the civil list of Congress. Revenues are believed to amount annually to £80,000, New York currency, that is, 41,000–42,000 louis d'or.

The expenses of the City and of the County of New York in

[21] [Cyrus Griffin (1748–1810), last president of the Continental Congress, from January 22, 1788, until its dissolution.]

1787 were one quarter [sic] of this sum, that is £10,100. An itemized list is given below: [22]

	£	s.	d.
Salaries	37	10	
Elections	62	12	
Pumps and wells	204	8	4
Roads and streets	734	2	1
Poorhouses	3,791	14	4
Bridewell, the House of Correction	899	11	4
Street lighting	1,439	19	
Night watchmen	1,931	2	
Prisoners	372	18	10
Repairs of public buildings	342	15	11
Wharves	25		
City of New York	137	19	
New York County	130	9	
	10,100	11	

The soundness of this city's [sic] finances and its promptness in paying the interest on its debt contribute greatly toward the stability of its paper money—for they do have paper money, in denominations even as low as one shilling, and this paper is received in the markets in payment of commodities at the same rate as coinage. But this paper loses eight per cent when you exchange it for silver, whether in order to travel or to make payments outside the state.

The Bank of the State of New York enjoys a good reputation in America; it is very capably administered. Its cashier or director is Mr. William Seton, the man to whom M. Crèvecoeur addressed his *Letters*. A good indication of his integrity is the fact that he was chosen for this important position in spite of his well-known loyalty to England. This bank receives deposits and makes payments without charge to the merchants and depositors who open accounts with it.

[22] [Brissot's figures actually should total £10,110 1 s. 10 d.]

JOURNEY FROM NEW YORK
TO PHILADELPHIA

I left New York on August 25, 1788, at six o'clock in the morning. I had reserved a seat on the "New Line of Stages to Philadelphia," [1] so called because it is not the same as the coach that takes you directly all the way from New York to Philadelphia; on this line you have to change seven or eight times.

To reach the stage I had to cross the North River in an open boat.[2] One lands at Paulus Hook,[3] where one finds the coach. The trip is two miles long and costs sixpence, New York currency.

The stage is a kind of open four-wheeled wagon with double curtains of leather and wool cloth which are let down against the rain or sun and raised whenever you wish to enjoy some fresh air and a view of the countryside. These stages have rather poor springs, but as the roads over which they travel are made of sand and gravel they are not uncomfortable. The horses are good and fairly fast. There are four benches which seat twelve people and under which there is room for light baggage. Trunks are fastened on the rear of the stage but there is not room for very many. These stages are the only means of transportation, and this is not a bad thing. There are no post horses; and this is not bad either. People who do not choose to take the stagecoach have one-horse carriages.

Let the French who have traveled in these stages compare them with those used in France—with those heavy coaches in which eight or ten persons suffocate; or with those cabriolets used around Paris, in which two people are wedged together and prevented from breathing by the presence of a filthy driver who torments his miserable jade; or with those *guinguettes* barely dragged along by two horses, in which the passenger sits at an angle in a cramped

[1] Two coaches of each line leave every day except Sunday from Philadelphia and from New York. One line takes one day to reach its destination, and the other one and a half days.

[2] Between New York and Philadelphia it is necessary to take a ferry four times, in addition to the passage by boat across the North River. There is no doubt that sooner or later bridges will, wherever possible, replace these ferries, which are often dangerous. I was close to death once on one of these ferries, while crossing the Hackensack River.

[3] [Just south of Jersey City.]

and awkward position, breathing poisoned air. What is more, these French carriages, which travel over the finest roads, do a league an hour. Oh! If Americans had such roads, with what speed they would travel! For despite the disadvantages of their present roads it takes only one day to cover the ninety-six miles (thirty-two leagues) between New York and Philadelphia. Thus, after no more than a century and a half of existence, and though thwarted by a thousand obstacles, Americans are already superior to nations which have been in existence for fifteen centuries.

In these stages you meet people of all walks of life, one after the other. A man who is going only fifteen miles yields his seat to another who is going farther; a mother with her daughter takes a ten-mile trip to dine with friends and will return home by another stage. Thus you make new acquaintances every minute. The frequency with which the stages run, the availability of seats even for short distances, and the low fixed prices (threepence per mile), all are reasons which encourage Americans to travel.

There is a special advantage of these stages: they maintain the idea of equality. A member of Congress sits side by side with the shoemaker who elected him and fraternizes with him; they talk together on familiar terms. No one puts on important airs as people do only too frequently in France, where it is fashionable to go posting about the country and where, for instance, a man of quality would blush to travel in a common vehicle like a stage, in which he might be thrown together with anybody. In France a person condemned to travel in a wretched *turgotine* [4] is humiliated by the sight of a private carriage. This inequality breeds envy, a taste for luxury, ostentation, avarice, and dishonesty. It is therefore fortunate for America that the nature of things here prevents the use of private carriages as marks of social distinction.

Moreover, the man of the people, that is, the craftsman or laborer, who finds himself in the same coach with a man of importance, keeps quiet; or if he does participate in the conversation he endeavors to rise to the level of the others, thus gaining, at least, some instruction. On the other hand, the man of importance is less proud and succeeds better in learning the spirit of the people.

It was in such a stagecoach that I crossed both the Jerseys. The son of Governor Livingston was among the passengers. [5] I should not have known it, so civil and simple was his bearing, if from

[4] [A public stagecoach in France of the time, named after Turgot.]
[5] [Henry B. Livingston, the son of Governor William Livingston.]

time to time the keepers of the inns where we stopped had not addressed him with respectful familiarity. I was told that the governor himself often uses these stages. You will have an idea of the character of this estimable man, who combines a life of writing, government and farming, when you learn that he takes pride in calling himself a New Jersey farmer.[6]

The convenience of these stages encourages women to use them. They often travel quite alone, unaccompanied by any person of their acquaintance; they need not fear suffering rudeness or hearing equivocal or licentious remarks directed at them by young men, as is only too often the case in French and even in English stagecoaches. This mingling of men and women can only serve to promote purity of morals and to prove that virtue is respected. If this were not so, American women would not travel alone. Men are more inclined to indulge in licentious thoughts and talk when women are not present.

Thus American stagecoaches are truly political vehicles. I can well imagine that our French fops would prefer a smooth-riding coupé, but this latter type of transportation is to be found where there are also Bastilles, in countries suffering from gross inequality and consequently from great poverty.

I have also heard Frenchmen complain about the custom of changing coaches so often in the United States, but this is a reasonable practice with definite advantages. The stage line is not run by one man alone but is maintained by several different private citizens who live in various towns along the route and who have made arrangements among themselves to supply horses and coaches. A citizen of New York drives the stage to Newark; a citizen of Newark goes on to Elizabethtown. Often it is the owner of the coach himself who drives, or else he has it driven by someone in his employ. In this way the owner makes sure that his horses are not overworked and that his coach is driven carefully, which would not always be the case if strangers were driving. The same horses and coach bring back returning travelers, an arrangement which makes it possible for the owners to ask very low fares. It cost me

---

[6] [A reference to *Observations on Government*, New York, 1787, written by John Stevens but erroneously attributed to William Livingston. This work was translated and published by Fabre d'Eglantine, Du Pont de Nemours, Condorcet, Gallois, and Mazzei under the title *Examen du gouvernement d'Angleterre comparé aux constitutions des Etats-Unis de l'Amérique, par un cultivateur de New-Jersey,* Paris, 1789.]

only 10 livres 10 sous to travel about 32 French leagues,[7] for which I would have had to pay 32 livres in France, not counting the small vexations I would have had inflicted upon me by the drivers, nuisances to which one is not subjected here.

It is true that you cannot take heavy baggage on these coaches, but this is not a disadvantage; travelers carry only what is essential, which amounts to a small package. They are thus obliged to travel simply and are not beset by a lot of cumbersome needs, as Europeans are; an American takes on a trip a comb, a razor, and a couple of shirts and cravats.

Part of the road from New York to Newark runs through marshes. I found this section truly astounding, and I was reminded of the indefatigable industry of the old Dutch settlers mentioned by M. Crèvecoeur. Built wholly of wood, with so much toil and perseverance, in the midst of water and on a shifting ground, this road proves what can be accomplished by the patience of men determined to conquer nature.

Although much of the extensive marshland in the two Jerseys has been drained, even more is still in its original state. The stagnant waters pollute the air, which has a perceptible noisome smell, breed mosquitoes, which are a cruel torment, and engender that epidemic fever I mentioned earlier which decimates the population in summer, and which is also known in Virginia and in the Southern states, particularly along the coast. The only way to escape it completely is by moving inland to the mountains, especially in the Eastern states.

I was told that the northern part of the Jerseys is free of fever and of mosquitoes. But this part is ravaged by an even worse scourge, a political one, namely, paper money. Paper money is still what Americans call "legal tender" in the Jerseys, which means that you are forced to accept it as legal payment in spite of the loss you incur.

I saw during this trip how many inconveniences and abuses result from this fictitious currency. A traveler who had bought some of this paper money in New York at a twenty-five per cent

[7] It is true that this low fare was temporary and the result of the competition between two private citizens who had each established a stagecoach line and who were trying to drive each other out of business, but the outcome of this competition was that the public received better service. In November 1788 the owners of the two stage lines agreed to raise the price from two to four dollars, that is, to twenty-one livres.

discount tried to pay his bill at an inn at the same rate, but the innkeeper demanded a discount of fifty per cent. I observed the innkeeper's face; he had the icy, shifty eyes of a cheat. I had the feeling that he knew all the tricks of dealing in this depreciated currency; he bought it cheap and resold it for twice as much in New York. This is an abominable traffic, for it is based on duplicity, and the speculator's profit must be made at the expense of the general good. Thus it both corrupts morals and is against the public interest. It makes the money-changer the enemy of all his fellow citizens. It makes a science of deceit and teaches a man to live not by honest and useful work but by dishonest and pernicious dealings.

The circulation of this paper has also resulted in a general lack of confidence. Silver is carefully hoarded and does not circulate. You can neither sell nor mortgage your land; in both cases, sellers and lenders are afraid of being paid in paper money which could continue to depreciate. Even friends do not dare trust one another, for examples of the most revolting perfidy have been known. The inevitable consequence is that patriotism dies out, clearing of land comes to a standstill everywhere, and trade falls into a decline. I was truly distressed by all of these evils. "How is it possible," I asked the son of the governor of New Jersey, who was traveling with me, "that so rich an area can have paper money? The Jerseys supply large quantities of products to the state of New York and to Philadelphia, from where there is a constant flow of money coming in. Why should a state which is a creditor and which receives payment in cash employ a resource fit only for an impoverished people who are unable to accumulate a supply of hard money? How is it that the members of your legislature have not thought of this? Why didn't they oppose the Tender Act?"

"The reason is simple," he replied. "At the end of the dreadful war we have been through most of our citizens were ruined and overwhelmed with debts. They saw in paper money an easier way of getting out of their indebtedness, and their influence was strong enough to force their representatives to pass this law."

"All right," said I, "but the evil exists now. It is obvious that the device is now working against its inventors, for those who have paid in paper money are themselves being paid in this same discredited currency. They see that it brings dishonor upon their state and that it is drying up the wellsprings of their trade and agriculture. Why then don't they use their influence to have the Tender Act repealed?"

"Strong interests oppose it," he answered, "the interests of the stockjobbers. They are prolonging this unfortunate game as long as they can in order to exploit more victims and increase their profits. Our only hope rests with the new Constitution, which will remove from the individual states the power to put paper money into circulation. But all decent people wish to see it dead, for then gold will reappear in abundance. That is what happened when Continental paper money disappeared."

The enemies of liberty induce from these facts that the people of a republic may at certain times will and enact an injustice if it is to their profit; this is a conclusion to which the partisans of monarchism eagerly subcribe. But this evil is a consequence not of republican government but of ignorance. For no injustice created by the majority of the people can fail sooner or later to affect this same majority; consequently, when the majority wills and orders an unjust law, they do so through ignorance; they do not see that they are cutting their own throats. For example, could one not say to the majority of the people of Jersey: "You are all debtors, you wish to pay your debts with scraps of paper and defraud your creditors. All right, but when this dishonest system is established, what will be the result? You will have to live. But you can live only by selling your cattle and your produce. You will be paid in paper money. If you wish to clear more land or enlarge your enterprises, you will need loans. But you will be able to borrow only paper money, that is to say, depreciated currency. Consequently you will find you are destroyed by the very weapon which destroyed your creditors. On the other hand, if you follow a different policy, repeal the Tender Act, and let things go their own way, then, credit being intact, commerce and agriculture will flourish, you will have more jobs, and therefore you will have more means of paying off your debts."

I do not know, but it seems to me that this argument should make an impression upon a practical and intelligent people. The ignorant will not like it; they enjoy the present and do not think of the future. They find it very convenient indeed to get rid of their debts with a scrap of paper; they do not see that the knife with which they cut the throats of their creditors today will cut their own throats tomorrow. The conclusion must be that this paper money can only have been the invention of blind cupidity.

The question which remains is whether such ignorant cupidity cannot be more easily enlightened in a republic than in a monarchy, and whether such errors, such dishonest dealings are more common under one form of government than under the other. Surely there is no room for debate on this point. The American people have answered the question by unanimously approving the article in the new Constitution which denies all states the right to circulate paper money.

From Newark we went on to dine in New Brunswick and to sleep at Trenton. The road between the last two towns is rather poor, especially after a rain; it seemed to me to be in bad condition and a difficult sort of road to maintain. We passed through Princeton. This part of the Jerseys is in a very good state of cultivation, and indeed M. Crèvecoeur's interesting description is not exaggerated. The houses in all the towns are well built, whether of wood, stone, or brick. These regions are famous in military annals and well enough known to dispense me from describing them.

On this road accommodations in inns are more expensive than in Connecticut or Massachusetts. In Trenton, on my way back, I paid for my dinner 3 s. 6 d., Pennsylvania money, that is, 50 sous. This will seem expensive for America, especially if you consider that one is served little wine in these inns and gets meals of local products. But, as I have already said, one should not judge the general cost of food by tavern prices.

We left Trenton at seven o'clock in the morning and crossed the Delaware on a ferry. This river, which separates the Jerseys from Pennsylvania, is a vast, superb stream navigable by large ships, but is closed by ice for two or three months in the year. In its waters ships are not attacked by those worms which in the southern rivers bore into and destroy vessels. Tidal currents from the ocean have built up sand dunes on the Jersey shore.

The view from the middle of the river is infinitely delightful. On your right you see mills and a factory erected by Mr. Morris; [8] on your left there are two charming little villages that overlook the water. The banks of the river are still very wild and are covered with a forest containing magnificent trees.[9] The few houses you

[8] [These were the large group of diversified mills erected by Robert Morris at Morrisville on some twenty-five acres he acquired during the Revolution.]

[9] During my second trip to Philadelphia I noticed that this forest was full of

see cannot compare in simple elegance with those of Massachusetts, but the inhabitants seem to be prosperous. I saw a woman come out of one of these log houses; she was tremendously fat and wore a pretty cotton dress.

We breakfasted at Bristol, a town across the river from Burlington. This is the place where the famous Penn first raised his tabernacles. But he was told that the river here did not furnish as good or safe anchorage as it did near the site already settled by the Swedes, where Philadelphia has since been built. He therefore decided to purchase this location from them, and he gave them in exchange other lands in the interior and abandoned Bristol.

We reached Philadelphia at two o'clock, after having crossed the Shamony [Neshaminy] River on a new bridge and after having passed through Frankfort on a very fine road which cut across well-cultivated fields and along which we saw elegant houses marking the approaches to a great city.

---

young trees. It would not be difficult to maintain the growth if the cattle could be kept out; but Americans are only interested in felling timber and give no thought to replanting forests, although in some places a scarcity of wood is already being felt.

JOURNEY TO BURLINGTON AND VISIT TO MR. TEMPLE FRANKLIN

August 27, 1788

I had been in Philadelphia scarcely a few hours when a personal matter called me to Burlington, on the Delaware River. It is a pretty little town, older than Philadelphia. Many of its citizens are Friends, or Quakers; it was formerly the place of their General Meeting.

From there I went to the country house of Mr. Temple Franklin, the grandson of the famous Franklin, who is as well known in France for his benevolence as he is for his learning and his talents.

Mr. Temple Franklin's house is five miles from Burlington, in the midst of a pine forest growing in sandy soil. It is a simple dwelling with a well-kept garden, and the view is gradually being extended as the trees are cleared. This American has a very good library. Here is a place which indeed seems to be designed to be the retreat of a philosopher.

I dined in the company of five or six Frenchmen. The conversation turned to this country and to the character of Americans, and the guests strongly criticized their lack of laws, their paper money, and their duplicity. I took their defense, or rather I asked that accusations be substantiated by *facts,* for I was determined not to accept individual opinions any longer.

"You want facts," said one of them, a man who had lived in America for three years. "I shall give you some. I say that this is a poor country. In Jersey, where we now are, there is no hard money; there is nothing but paper currency."

"Hard money is being hoarded," said Mr. Franklin. "Do you expect a man to be foolish enough to exchange it for a depreciated scrap of paper? Wait until the new laws have forced the withdrawal of paper money from circulation."

"But it is impossible to borrow money, even on the best securities."

"That is true," answered Mr. Franklin, "but it is because people are afraid they will be repaid in paper. These facts show not the scarcity of money but the prudence of men possessing capital and the influence of debtors on legislation."

They went on to another point. "Your laws are arbitrary and often unjust. For instance, there is a law which taxes the owner of a dog one dollar for a second dog, and the tax increases in proportion to the number of dogs a man keeps. So a farmer who needs dogs is deprived of their help."

"A farmer doesn't need dogs," said Mr. Franklin. "If he has any it is only for his pleasure, and if anything ought to be taxed surely it is pleasure. Dogs are a danger to sheep and instead of guarding them often kill them, even in this part of the country. I saw a dog kill one of my sheep, and I was one of the first to press for the passage of the law, because we were being infested with these dogs. To get rid of them, a tax was put on them, and it has had a good effect. The money from this tax is used to indemnify those whose sheep are killed by dogs."

My Frenchman returned to the attack. "But your taxes are so heavy!"

"You shall be the judge of that," replied Mr. Franklin. "I have an estate here of five to six hundred acres; my taxes last year amounted all in all to eight pounds in paper money, or six pounds in silver." [1] (At fourteen livres to the pound, this would amount to about eighty livres.)

Nothing could be more convincing than these replies. I should wager, however, that this Frenchman will forget them, and that when he returns to France he will go on repeating that in the Jerseys taxation is heavy, that the taxes on dogs are frightful, etc., etc.

Burlington is separated from Bristol only by the river. A certain amount of trade is conducted here, and there are some men of substantial wealth. The young people have the honest, healthy look which is characteristic of Quakers.

[1] I know a man near Trenton who owns a piece of property of 300 acres, of which 100 acres are cleared. His tax is about two or three pounds.

A VISIT TO A QUAKER FARM

August 28, 1788

When I returned from Burlington I went with Mr. Shoemaker,[1] who had accompanied me on my trip, to visit his father-in-law, Mr. Richardson, a farmer near Middletown,[2] twenty-two miles from Philadelphia.

Mr. Shoemaker is thirty years old. He was not raised as a Quaker, and he told me that in his youth he had been far from being a believer in Quaker principles and had led a life of pleasure, but that eventually growing weary of dissipation he had given thought to his conduct and had decided to change. He studied the Quakers' teachings and soon became a member of their society, even though his friends laughed at him for doing so. Later he married the daughter of a Quaker farmer, and it was to the latter's house that we were going. I was eager to see a true American farmer.

I confess I was charmed by the family as well as by the cleanliness and neatness of the house itself. There were three sons and seven daughters. Only one girl was married, though three others were of a marriageable age. They were modest but pretty and unaffected. Their dresses were very simple; on Sundays they wore fine cotton but the rest of the week the plainest sort of materials. These girls helped their mother with the household duties. Although plump, the mother was very busy and active. She held in her arms a pretty little baby girl, five or six months old, whom all the children caressed in turn. It was truly a patriarchal family. The father spent all his days at work in the fields. We talked about wheat, about the Society of Friends,[3] and about the French Society of Friends of the Negroes.[4] He showed me various books written by Friends.

In truth, I was never before so edified as I was in this house. It

---

[1] [Jacob Shoemaker, a Quaker merchant of Philadelphia, became a close friend of Brissot, and also of Brissot's brother- and sister-in-law, François and Nancy Dupont. After François's death he took Nancy into his home.]

[2] [About six miles northwest of Bristol, Pennsylvania, on Neshaminy Creek.]

[3] One must keep in mind that Quakers call themselves "Friends," and that they are called "Quakers" only by other sects.

[4] [The Société Française des Amis des Noirs, founded by Brissot in February 1788.]

was a haven of concord, of friendship, and of hospitality. As a friend of the son-in-law, I was cordially entertained; I was given a good bed, snow-white sheets, and a fine counterpane. The clothes-presses, the secretary, the chairs, and the tables were of well-polished, gleaming walnut. The garden near the house provided vegetables and fruit. There were ten horses in the stable. Last year's crop of corn, still on the cob, was piled high in a crib made of boards with spaces between so that the air could circulate. The barn was full of wheat, oats, etc. Cows supplied the family with delicious milk, from which were made excellent cheeses which were sold in town. Sheep furnished the wool from which was made the cloth worn by the master and his children. This cloth was woven partly at home and partly by a neighborhood weaver and then taken to a fulling mill nearby. All the linen was homemade.

All these chores kept the mother and daughters constantly busy while the boys were in the fields. I visited the whole property of this good farmer, which comprised an area of four to five hundred acres, part of which is on the banks of Shamony [Neshaminy] Creek and is still heavily wooded and not yet cleared. Mr. Shoe-maker showed me the spot where this worthy countryman planned to build a farmhouse for his eldest son. "You see," he said to me, "how well off he is. His father was a poor Scotsman who came to America, became a farmer, and through his industry and thrift amassed a sizeable fortune. All his children married, and this son, like his father, is very rich."

"But where does he sell his crops?"

"His grain he sells to a miller in the neighborhood; his vegetables, butter, and cheese are sent once a week to the nearby town."

I went to see this local miller. I recalled what M. Crèvecoeur said in praise of American mills. This one was indeed admirably clean and well organized. There were three millstones, one to grind fine flour for commercial sale, another for middling flour for local use, and a third to serve as a stand-by. For the production of the finest flour they use only French millstones, which are shipped from Bordeaux and Rouen. In these mills they have increased the number of gears and mechanical devices so as to save labor in operations such as hoisting the wheat, cleaning it, raising the flour to the place where it is to be spread, dropping it into the room where it is put into barrels, etc. The barrels are marked right in the mill with the name of the miller and with the quality of the flour. Flour for export is examined by inspectors at the port and is condemned if it is not up to market standards.

What a difference between these regulations and those we have in France! You will recall, my friend, that two or three years ago manufacturers of printed calico were required to have their cloth stamped, and often the official in charge of the stamping would not condescend to move from his office so that the manufacturer was forced to send the merchandise to him.

Next I saw the miller's house, where his wife and women from the neighborhood were making clothes for the children. Here, as in Massachusetts, most houses are separate from the mill or the workshop.

Millers in this state are also flour merchants. The one I saw in Middletown seemed to be competent in his trade and to be making a good living. Mills are a kind of property that yields a steady income.

I returned to Philadelphia by a very pleasant road. Hardly had I arrived when I began to feel violent pains in my stomach. My doctor attributed them to my imprudence in having eaten a dozen russet pears without drinking either wine or brandy. I was in great pain for two days. I vomited the water and tea I drank, and the rhubarb which I tried taking did not help me. The only thing that eased the suffering was a drink made of brandy, sugar, and water. There was one remedy which would have promptly relieved me, but no one uses it in America, and indeed people blush at the very sound of the word. This is an example of the sort of English prudery that one ought to get rid of. I learned from a Frenchman with whom I had dined in New York and who lived in the same inn with me that he too had suffered from the same stomach upset from having drunk water that was too cold. If I go into such details it is because they might be useful to Europeans who travel in this country.

A VISIT FROM THE GOOD
WARNER MIFFLIN

August 30, 1788

I was sick. Warner Mifflin came to see me. You know Warner Mifflin, having read the touching tribute to him in the *Letters from an American Farmer*.[1] It was he who first freed all his slaves; it was he who, without a passport, passed through the British lines and spoke to General Howe so firmly and with so much dignity; it was he who, unafraid of the Americans' hostility to Quakers, went to General Washington, again without a passport, running the risk of being taken for a spy, in order to explain and justify to him the Quakers' conduct; it was he again who, in the midst of all the horrors of war, acting impartially as a friend to the French, the English, and the Americans, gave generous help to all who were in suffering. This angel of peace and charity came to see me. "I am Warner Mifflin," he said. "I have read the book in which thou defendest the cause of the Friends, and in which thou preachest the principles of universal benevolence. I learned that thou wast here, and I have come to see thee. Besides, I love thy nation. I must admit I used to be greatly prejudiced against Frenchmen. Having been raised with English prejudices, I hated the French. But when I actually saw them, a secret voice told me that I must banish this prejudice from my heart, that I must come to know them and love them. I have therefore sought out their company, I have learned to know them, and it is with pleasure that I have found in them a kindness and a universal benevolence which I had not met among the English."

I shall not report our entire conversation or those I had later with this worthy Quaker, but they made a very deep impression on me. What humanity! What charity! It seems that his only pleasure, his very existence, is to love and serve mankind. He devotes himself entirely to the task of gathering all men into one family, and he does not despair of being able to do so. He told me of a society of Quakers established at Nîmes, and of Friends from Eng-

[1] [Warner Mifflin (1745–1798), a well-known Quaker pacifist and abolitionist, praised by Crèvecoeur.]

land and from America who visited them.[2] He considered such groups as instruments by which Quakerism would be spread throughout the world. I spoke of the obstacles to be overcome, of the corruption of our morals and the power of the clergy. "But, my friend," he answered, "is not the arm of the Almighty stronger than the arm of man? What were we when the Society was born in England? What was America thirteen years ago when Benezet [3] rose in protest against Negro slavery? Let us always do good, let us not fear obstacles, and the good will come to pass."

All this, my friend, was said without ostentation, without affectation. The words flowed straight from this good Quaker's heart. He said what he felt, what he had thought a hundred times; he was baring his heart, not displaying his wit. He demonstrated by his own example the prodigious effect of that inner spirit or voice of which the Quakers speak so much; he was inspired by it. His soul was depicted in the serenity of his countenance and in his pleasing gestures, for Quakers do gesticulate, notwithstanding the caricatures in which they are represented as being stiff and motionless.

Oh! Who could see and listen to a man so far above the common level of human nature without being forced to meditate on his own character, without blushing at his own weaknesses, and without making an effort to imitate him? What are the finest writings compared to so pure a life continuously devoted to the good of humanity? How small I felt as I gazed upon him! Yet men will calumniate the sect to which such a venerable man belongs! They will depict it as a hotbed of hypocrisy and duplicity! If such accusations were true, we should be forced to suppose that Mifflin is only pretending to love humanity, or that he is in collusion with hypocrites, or else that he is blind to their character. To act as though one loved humanity, to consent to sacrificing one's own interests, to being mocked and ridiculed, to dividing one's goods among the poor, to free one's Negroes—to do all these things hypocritically would indeed be a most foolish sort of hypocrisy. Hypocrisy calculates its own profits more astutely. On the other hand, if we assume that this man is sincere and honest, can we believe him to be in collusion with knaves? This would be an

[2] [In the village of Congeniés, near Nîmes in the Département du Gard. This small community, originally part of the Protestant Camisards in the Cévennes region, developed independently but late in the eighteenth century established connections with American and English Quakers.]

[3] Anthony Benezet (1713–1784), a French Huguenot who became a leading American Quaker abolitionist and writer.]

absurd contradiction. Finally, when we listen to this man, so full of good sense and sound judgment, reasoning so forcefully, can we believe that he has been all his life the dupe of a band of rascals, particularly if he has been a member of their most secret councils and one of their leaders? My friend, I repeat, the loyalty of an angel such as Warner Mifflin to the Quakers is the best possible defense for that society.

Warner Mifflin asked me to visit his intended wife, Miss Ameland, whom he was to marry in a few days. I met her. She is an angel entirely worthy of this respectable Quaker. What sweetness! What modesty! And at the same time, what a pleasant conversationalist! Miss Ameland once loved the world, wrote poems, composed music, and danced. But even though she is still young she has renounced all these amusements to embrace the life of an anchorite in the very midst of society. In spite of the jests of her friends she has persisted in her design, and together with her husband she will bring happiness to the people on her lands in the state of Delaware.

A QUAKER FUNERAL AND
A QUAKER MEETING

Sunday, August 31, 1788

I was taken by James Pemberton [1] to the burial of Thomas Holwell, one of the elders of the Society of Friends. I found a crowd of Friends gathered around the house of the deceased, silently waiting for his remains to be carried out. The body was in a walnut coffin without any covering or ornament, which was borne by four Friends and followed by several women, who, I was told, were his nearest relatives, and by his grandchildren. [2] Some of these women had covered their faces with handkerchiefs. All the friends of the deceased followed in silence, two by two. James Pemberton and myself were among them. I noticed that no place was specially reserved, that all, young and old alike, mingled together, but that everyone was equally grave and serious. We arrived at the cemetery, which is in the city but not surrounded by houses. I saw near some of the graves small pieces of black stone, markers on which, I was told, the names of the dead are carved. Most of the Friends regard these with disapproval; they say that a man should live in his friends' memory of his good deeds, not in vain inscriptions. The grave was six or seven feet deep as is the custom. The coffin was placed on one side, and on the other were some wooden chairs on which the three or four women that seemed most distressed sat down.

The Friends, having gathered around the coffin, spent five or six minutes in meditation. I studied all their faces; not a single one failed to express the gravity befitting this ceremony but none revealed any sign of suffering. After these few minutes, they lowered the coffin into the grave and covered it with earth. Then a man approached the grave, stuck his cane in the ground, hung

---

[1] [James Pemberton (1723–1809), a Quaker merchant and philanthropist, one of the founders of the Society for the Relief of Free Negroes (1775) and later of the Pennsylvania Society for Promoting the Abolition of Slavery.]

[2] None of the women wore black, for the Quakers consider childish this sign of grief. Congress, I have been told, has passed a law prohibiting the wearing of mourning. The Cincinnati wear black crape bands on their sleeves as a sign of mourning.

his hat upon it, and began to speak on the subject of this sad occasion. His whole body shook and his eyes rolled wildly.[3] Still unaccustomed to the Quakers' manner of speaking, I did not at first understand much of what he was saying, but after a while my ear became accustomed and I understood him better. His talk was on man's tribulations in this life, on the need to resort to God, etc. When he was done, a woman fell on her knees and said a very short prayer, the men took off their hats,[4] and then everyone left.

I was at first taken aback, I confess, by the preacher's shaking, for, taught as we are by our European philosophy to consider such behavior as charlatanry and as ridiculous, I had to make a great effort to overcome my prejudices. I did succeed, however; I recalled that innumerable times when excited by a topic or involved in an interesting discussion I had let myself become so carried away that I became blind and deaf to my surroundings and experienced a similar kind of trembling. I concluded that such shaking could be natural and was most likely to seize a man continuously occupied with meditations on the Eternal, on death, and on the future life. If any moving thoughts are capable of bringing on ecstasy, surely they must be those which concern our future life. It has been said that charlatans too fall into fits of ecstasy; this may be true, I do not know, but it seems to me that if a man is not truly inspired, and inspired by a great object, the fraud must soon become obvious.

After the burial I went to the Friends' Meeting. The deepest silence was observed for almost an hour. I was seated facing a bench raised above the others, which, I later learned, was reserved for the ministers or preachers; for the Quakers also have their ministers. They are ordained in the following manner: When a Friend has spoken a number of times and has shown aptitude and zeal, rather than talent, the committee of ministers and elders, which meets each week, recommends him to the Monthly Meeting or to the May Meeting, which, if it finds him suitable, appoints him as a minister. One of the Friends sitting on this bench rose, began to speak, said four words, stopped for a minute, said another four words, and delivered his whole talk in this manner. This style

[3] I have learned since that this Friend, a highly regarded preacher, was sick with consumption and had a very delicate constitution. The elders had pleaded with him to overcome his shaking, and he had replied that he had indeed tried, but without success.

[4] Although Quakers do not take off their hats when they enter their meeting-houses, they do regard this custom as a sign of respect to God.

must be quite common among Quaker preachers, for the next speaker also spoke with the same long pauses between his words.

I do not know whether my opinion is formed by what I have been accustomed to or by the dictates of reason, but this disjointed manner of speaking did not seem to me likely to create a great impression. The sense of the sentence being continually interrupted, either you have to guess it or you must wait for the meaning to emerge; and you either grow tired of guessing or bored with waiting.[5]

Let us not judge too hastily, however, and let us see what may have led the Quakers to adopt this style. Surely the manner of the ancient orators and of our own preachers is better suited to move listeners by the use of grand oratorical effects. They appeal in turn to the mind and to the imagination, to the passions and to the reason; they attempt to please their listeners in order to move them and to bring about their conversion; it is by the charm of their discourse that they seek to persuade. That is a sort of eloquence suited to blasé and world-weary listeners who wish to avoid the strain of thinking. But the Quakers are people of a different character; they are accustomed from their youth to meditation and contemplation and are used to searching within themselves for great truths; they are men of much thought and few words. Consequently they have no need of preachers who can utter resounding phrases and deliver long sermons; they despise elegance as a useless ornament, and lengthy orations seem to them to be out of proportion to the mind's powers of comprehension and ill suited to attain the purposes of the holy ministry. They believe the mind should not be burdened with too many truths at once if we wish these truths to take root, and that, the purpose of divine services being to convert, the preacher should seek to induce men to reflect rather than try to dazzle or amuse them.

[5] Seneca, speaking of the various manners of delivering a philosophical dissertation, makes the following wise remarks on this particular style: "Sic itaque habe, istam vim dicendi rapidam atque abundantem aptiorem esse circulanti quam agenti rem magnam ac seriam, docentique. Aeque stillare illum nolo quam currere. Nec extendat aures, nec obruat. Nam illa quoque exilitas et inopia minus intentum auditorem habet taedio interruptae tarditatis; facilius tamen insidit quod exspectatur, quam quod praetervolat." *Moral Epistles* XL. [And so you ought to consider that swift and copious style of speaking more suited to a charlatan than to one who is giving instruction on a great and serious matter. But I object as much to the dripping faucet as to the running torrent. One should neither weary the ear with waiting nor overwhelm it. For the overdeliberate and austere speaker also loses his audience by the boredom of his pauses and his slowness; nevertheless the listener grasps what is waited for more readily than that which flies past.]

The style of the Quaker preachers was new to me, and therefore I did not grasp many of the ideas expressed. I gathered that they preach a sound morality in the language of the Scriptures. But, I must admit, those who like the eloquence of our preachers should not attend Quaker meetings. *Non est hic panis omnium.*[6] But I reserve my final judgment until the time when I have heard a few more sermons.

I studied the faces of the men and women in the congregation. They looked grave and often sad. This, again, may be merely a prejudice on my part, but I should prefer people worshiping God to have a less gloomy look, to show more loving and lovable expressions, ones more likely to inspire them to love one another and to love religion. Such countenances would attract many young people who might be repelled by an excess of somber gravity. And indeed, if one has a clear conscience why pray to God with an unpleasant look on one's face?

The prayer with which the meeting ended was fervent; the minister who pronounced it fell to his knees. Then the men rose, taking off their hats, and everybody withdrew after shaking hands with his neighbor.

What a difference between the simplicity of this service and that of the Catholics! Religious reformation seems to have led step by step to greater simplicity of ceremony. You will find fewer and fewer forms as you go from Catholicism to Lutheranism, from Lutheranism to Presbyterianism, and from Presbyterianism to Quakerism and Methodism. It is in this way that man's reason always progresses toward perfection.

As I have considered the simplicity of Quaker worship and what to European eyes appears to be its atmosphere of lugubrious boredom, which, one would think, would repel young men and women (particularly when they see the greater gaiety, luxury, show, and glitter permitted by the other churches), I have often been astonished that this sect manages to survive and even to gain proselytes. In seeking an explanation, we may attribute this success to a number of causes: to the force of habit, which makes the soul pliant and adaptable even to the most disagreeable situation; to *esprit de corps,* which makes a group adhere, out of pride, to the principles to which it has subscribed and to defend them even when they are wrong—a feeling which is particularly powerful among the Quakers, who have carried further than any other sect

[6] [This is not food for everyone.]

the idea of equality, which has so great an appeal to the individual; to the bonds of family love and loyalty, which make each generation cling to the religion of their parents; and to self-interest, which may make a man fear that it will be to his disadvantage to abandon his fathers' religion. But the main reason for the Quakers' success is the reputation they have of leading a happy domestic life. Renouncing all worldly pleasures such as walking, the theater, or music, they devote themselves completely to their duties—to their wives, their children, and their business. So they are cherished by their wives, loved by their children, respected by all their brethren. Such is the picture which has often drawn to Quakerism men who had laughed at it in their youth. When the age of reflection arrives, men naturally turn their eyes to those who lead an exemplary life and adopt their doctrine and their practices.

The history of Quakerism will expose the fallacy of an argument often advanced by political philosophers, namely, that to maintain order in a mass of men it is necessary to have a form of worship which appeals to the senses, and that the more religious services resemble theatrical performances the greater will be their hold on the people. This theory has produced or justified plain chant, religious music, processions, ecclesiastical decoration, etc. Two or three hundred thousand Quakers have none of this mummery, yet theirs is an orderly society.

This striking fact has led me to another conclusion, the validity of which has also been hitherto contested, namely, that a nation of deists can exist.[7] A nation of deists which observes law and order will be the miracle of political religion. And why should it not exist when enlightenment will be more universal and has penetrated the lowest levels of the social order? What difference would there be between deists assembling to hear a talk on the immortality of the soul and to pray to God in a simpler language, and the Quakers, who do the same?

[7] Neither the English nor the Americans give to the word *deist* the same meaning as do the French. They consider a deist a sort of materialist. I am using the term here in the sense of a man who believes in God and in the immortality of the soul.

VISIT TO A BETTERING HOUSE [1]

Monday, September 1, 1788

I have just seen the charitable institution known as the Bettering House of Philadelphia. I went there accompanied by one of the directors, my friend Mr. Shoemaker, whom I have already mentioned.

It is located in the open country, in a part of Philadelphia already divided by regular streets but not yet built up. May God grant that these projected streets remain forever imaginary! If they should some day become lined with houses, it will be a misfortune for the charitable institutions, for Pennsylvania, for the whole of America.

The Bettering House consists of two large brick structures, one for men, the other for women, with a common courtyard separated into two parts. The institution fulfills various functions: it provides care for the poor, the sick, orphans, women in labor, and people with venereal diseases; and it also serves as a place of confinement for vagabonds, wrongdoers, and prostitutes.

There exists then, you will say, even in Philadelphia itself, this disgusting traffic in disease rather than in pleasure which has poisoned our own continent for so long! Yes, my friend, this leprosy afflicts two or three of the largest maritime cities of the New World. It was almost unknown before the Revolution, but the foreign armies stationed here naturalized it on this soil, and it is one more of the scourges for which Free America is indebted to us. But this trade is not carried on as scandalously as it is in Paris and London; it is restrained, restricted, held in contempt, and is almost unnoticeable. I ought to say, to the honor of Americans, that it is kept alive only by immigrants and European travelers, for the sanctity of marriage is still universally respected in America, and young men, finding it easy to marry while they are still young, are not tempted to dishonor and poison themselves in a house of prostitution.

To return to the institution which I was describing: There are

[1] It is called a "bettering house" because, unlike ordinary institutions of the sort, this one makes its inmates better.

special wards for each class of paupers and for each kind of sickness, and every ward has a male or female attendant.

The Bettering House used to be rich and well managed before the war; at that time its administrators were mostly Quakers. Changes were brought about by the war and by the introduction of paper currency. During the war the legislature resolved to allow in the administration only men who had taken the oath of allegiance to the republican government. Quakers were henceforth excluded, the management fell into not entirely clean hands, there was waste and misappropriation of funds, and paper money added to the difficulties. Some of the money owed to the institution was repaid in paper, which means that it was lost. About a year ago the legislative assembly, having received a report from the inspectors of charitable institutions on the abuses which had arisen in their management, concluded that the best way to effect a reform would be to entrust this asylum once more to the Quakers. Their decision met with public approval. Without any resentment for the affronts they had suffered during the war and mindful only of the good they could and should do, the Friends accepted the management of the Bettering House and proceeded to fulfill their duties as before with zeal and devotion. This change has produced the expected results, and slowly order is being re-established.

There are several appointed administrators who take turns inspecting the institution daily. Six physicians are attached to it and perform their services free of charge.

I have seen asylums for the poor and sick in France, both in Paris and in the provinces, but I know of only one, that in Besançon, which can stand comparison with the one in Philadelphia. Here every pauper and patient has his own well-furnished bed, but without curtains, as it should be. Each ward has windows on two sides letting in a great deal of light; light is one of the consolations of persons in confinement, and for this very reason tyrants are cruelly miserly with it. These windows also allow the rooms to be well aired. Most of them open on the surrounding fields, and since they are not very high above the ground and have no bars, it would be easy for prisoners to escape if they wished to, but the idea never enters their heads. This fact proves that even the prisoners are happy here and demonstrates how good the administration is.

The kitchens are clean and do not give forth those fetid and nauseating smells which emanate from the very best French kitchens. The dining rooms, on the ground floor, are equally clean and well aired; everywhere you find cleanliness, neatness, and good air. A rather large garden at the end of the courtyard supplies the necessary vegetables and herbs for the kitchen. I was surprised to see a great many foreign plants and shrubs. The vegetable garden is very well cultivated; many people work in it for pleasure. In the courtyard they raise a lot of pigs, for in America pork and beef are the main dishes throughout the year.

It is with difficulty that I describe to you the various sensations by which I was struck and which alternately delighted and saddened my soul as I walked through the different wards. However well such a place may be managed, it is to me always a painful spectacle. When I think what a consolation it would be for a sick man to be by himself, to be taken care of in his own home, by his wife, his children, and his friends, and to be consoled by them from time to time, I cannot help seeing these hospitals as vast sepulchers in which are gathered a crowd of individuals, strangers to one another, separated from all that they hold most dear, or perhaps with no one left to love. And what is a man without love? A fallen leaf drifting in a torrent, a corpse without desires, awaiting its imminent dissolution.

But then this thought yielded place to another. Since societies are condemned to have immense cities and since the inevitable products of these cities are vice and poverty, such institutions as this are beneficent asylums. Without them, what would become of most of these people who find their only refuge here? What would become of all these women, blind, deaf, and afflicted with all sorts of revolting maladies? They would be abandoned and soon die. Such were my thoughts when I entered the first ward. I saw some hideous faces. I do not know why a hideous woman is much more horrible than a hideous man. Perhaps it is by the contrast of memory. One is used to expecting in women grace and beauty; they seem fashioned for pleasure. But here horror replaces delight. Perhaps women's infirmities are in truth more disgusting, or perhaps the shrewish, grumbling disposition of most of these women added to my unpleasant impression.

Be that as it may, I saw in this hospital all that poverty and disease can produce. I saw women suffering on a bed of pain; others, whose pale faces, thin bodies, and pustules gave witness to their tragic incontinence; others who awaited with groans the moment when Heaven would deliver them of a burden which would dishonor them; others who held in their arms the fruit, not of a legal marriage, but of betrayed love. Poor innocent creatures born under an evil star! Why must man be predestined even from his birth to suffering? But let us thank God that there is at least one country where bastardy is no obstacle to happiness and to the rights of citizenship. I watched with pleasure as these poor mothers caressed their babies and drove the annoying flies away from their cheeks.

There were few children in the ward reserved for little orphans; they were all very healthy, and almost all were plump and looked happy and gay. Another director, whom we met there, was handing out pastries which he had bought on his way. So we see that the directors remember the patients under their care and, even when they are away from them, are concerned about their well-being! There exists then a land where the heart of a hospital director is not made of iron!

Both Negro men and women are mixed here with the whites and sleep in the same wards. This was an edifying sight to me and a balm for my heart. I noticed a Negro woman about thirty years old very actively spinning by her bed. Her eyes seemed to expect a word of consolation from the director. She received it, and when she did she looked as though she were in heaven. Had it been in my power to give her such joy, I should have been still happier, and I should have spoken more than a single word to her. Poor Negroes! How much we owe them for all the evil we have done to them, and for the evil we are still doing! And yet they love us!

The happiness of this Negress was not, however, equal to that which I saw shine on the face of a young blind girl who seemed to tremble with joy at the sound of the good director's voice. He asked how she was, and she answered him with delight. She was taking her tea, which was neatly set out on a small table beside her. Her tea! My friend, you are astonished at this luxury in a hospital. It is because there is humanity in this place and because here people are not crowded together to the point of suffocation. Tea is given to those whose conduct is satisfactory; those inmates who by their work manage to save some money can spend it on a few pleasures. But why tea? Why warm water? Why not instead a glass of wine? My friend, tea is a repast, and a complicated one; it represents a variety of pleasures, while a glass of wine is only a short-lived treat. The man of wealth likewise prefers delights which can be prolonged. I saw an old lady who was having her tea with butter and ham, and she claimed she did not feel well.

I myself believe that drinking hot water is bad for the health, and I wish there were a substitute for tea; but it is difficult to find one. And then too the force of habit is so strong, and breaking a habit is so painful, especially when the habit is so inexpensive! It is easy to calculate that the least expensive meal is certainly tea, particularly in a country where butter and sugar are infinitely less expensive than they are in Europe.[2] This fact will probably induce the management of this hospital to grant the privilege of tea to all the prisoners, as the doctors recommend. The tea they drink here is bohea tea, which is less likely to harm the nerves than green tea.

I noticed that women were much more numerous than men, and among the latter I did not see many with those hideous faces which are common in similar institutions in Paris, faces on which you see the imprint of crime, poverty, and insolence. They looked like decent, well-behaved men. Several asked the director to be set free, and their request was granted. I noted with pleasure that they spoke to him respectfully.

But what resources do they have when they leave this place? They have their hands, answered the director, and they may find useful occupations. What about the women? Their situation is less fortunate and that is the reason why the number of prostitutes increases. To combat this state of affairs, it has been suggested that the girls be employed in some productive occupation the income from which would be accumulated and given to them when they leave, or, if they preferred to stay on here and continue working, their earnings would be advantageously invested for them.

This plan will, I feel sure, be put into practice; the Quakers are ingenious and persevering in their efforts to better the lot of unfortunates. The author of this idea was my friend the director. He is beloved, respected, and constantly occupied with useful things—and yet he is only thirty years old! Is it astonishing that I praise a sect which produces such prodigies?

A small detail will show you what I mean. When we left the Bettering House, we drank a bottle of cider. Compare this frugal

[2] This is why in English villages even day laborers drink tea rather than beer. To be able to drink beer in a village one must make it oneself in some quantity and to do this one must buy a certain amount of draff. Since a day laborer cannot afford to spend the six livres at one time, he prefers a drink he can buy retail and which costs him only a few pence or a shilling.

repast with the sumptuous feasts given by the superintendents of the poor in London, those worthy inspectors who in order to reach a decision on repairs amounting to six pounds spend six guineas on a dinner. You will never find a Quaker guilty of such infamous theft from the poor, such betrayal of charity. Whether you be rich or poor, bless the Quakers; if you are rich because their honesty saves you taxes, if you are poor because their disinterested charity watches over you constantly.

The expenses of the Bettering House amount to about three shillings (Pennsylvania currency) per inmate a week, that is, six sous a day.[3] You know that in the Hospital of Paris, which is the most economically and most honestly administered, the daily expenditure per person is more than seventeen sous. And what a difference in the treatment given!

[3] A shilling is worth fourteen sous.

THE PENNSYLVANIA HOSPITAL
FOR THE INSANE

September 1, 1788

I have seen the hospital for the insane so justly celebrated by M. Crèvecoeur and which the humane M. Mazzei considers only a curiosity not worth visiting. The building is handsome, elegant, and well maintained. I was greatly pleased by the cleanliness everywhere, both in the wards and in the single rooms. In the library I was surprised to see Franklin's bust and I asked why it was there. I was told that this venerable man was one of the founders of the institution. The library does not contain many volumes, but they are well chosen; I noted with pleasure the presence among them of the fourth edition, in English, of the *Eléments d'histoire naturelle et de chimie,* by my young teacher and friend, M. Fourcroy.[1]

The ward on the first floor is for men, of whom there were five or six. The number of women in a similar ward on the second floor was no larger. These patients did not look miserable; they seemed to feel at home. I went downstairs from the first floor to see the so-called "lunatics," of whom there were about fifteen, about as many men as women. Each one is locked up in a cell where there is a bed, a table, and a large window with bars and shutters opening on a yard. There is also an opening in the door through which one can see these poor people. Between every two cells there is a stove set in the wall which keeps them warm in winter.

I was told that none of them were violent and that most of them suffered from religious melancholy or were women who had lost their reason because of a disappointment in love; one person had been driven mad by grief. I saw one inmate who seemed deep in meditation, a young and fairly pretty girl with gentle eyes, who reminded me of Sterne's Silvia [2] and who spoke to us in a touching, sad voice. The faithlessness of an English officer, whose name she still loved to pronounce, had reduced her to this pitiful state.

[1] [See note p. 96.]
[2] [Brissot was thinking of the mad Maria in *A Sentimental Journey,* whose dog was named Sylvio.]

These insane are treated with the greatest kindness. They are allowed to walk in the courtyard and are visited regularly twice a week by two doctors. One of them, Dr. Rush,[3] has invented a kind of swing which has been placed in the yard for their exercise.

What a difference between this humane method and the atrocious treatment to which we condemn the insane in France! There they are kept confined, and almost always they sink even deeper into madness. The Turks, on the other hand, we are told by the philanthropist Bernardin de Saint-Pierre, hold the insane in special respect. They press food upon them and show them all sorts of affection. The insane in Turkey have never been known to hurt anybody. Our lunatics, on the contrary, are dangerous because they are unhappy.[4]

The sight of these unfortunate people moved me even more deeply than that of the sick. The worst human misery, to my mind, is confinement, and I cannot conceive how a sick person can be cured in prison, for confinement itself is a protracted illness.[5] Exercise, walking, the sight of fields, the murmur of a brook, the song of birds seem to me, together with a vegetable diet, the best cure for the insane. It is true that such a treatment would require two or three attendants to each patient, who may of course have fits of violence.

Since it is impossible to adopt this method for a large number of patients, the hospital in Philadelphia has chosen its present system. Where attendants are scarce, locks and bolts are necessary. But why did they place the cells of these unfortunate people below the ground floor, where they are exposed to unwholesome humid-

[3] [Dr. Benjamin Rush (1745–1813), the well-known Philadelphia physician.]

[4] [Bernardin de Saint-Pierre,] *Etudes de la Nature* [Paris, 1784], III, 238.

[5] I am reminded of the huge prisons in France in which sick paupers are crowded together under the pretext of curing them. "When one of the lower class is sick," says the philosopher I have just quoted, "the only treatment he needs is some nourishing broth, and his family could make good use of the meat from which it is made . . . Hospitals for the poor have many other disadvantages. Diseases of a special sort are propagated there which are often more dangerous than those which the sick bring with them. The moral evils these hospitals engender are even worse. A well-informed person has told me that most of the criminals who end their days on the gallows are the products of these institutions." [*Etudes de la Nature*], III, 237. There are disadvantages to the present system of caring for sick indigents which deserve careful consideration. On these questions see the wise and judicious work of a doctor who joins to his professional knowledge and his experience working in hospitals the enlightenment of a philosopher and the love for liberty of a democrat. I refer to my worthy friend Dr. [Nicolas] Chambon [de Montaux], author of *Moyens de rendre les hopitaux plus utiles à la nation* (Paris, rue et hôtel Serpente [1787]).

ity? The humane and enlightened Dr. Rush told me that he had tried everything in his power to prevent this, but that he had failed. He explained that the hospital had been built at a time when it was believed unnecessary to take great pains with the insane. He also said that this arrangement had another disadvantage in that the violently insane lodged immediately beneath the sick ward caused disturbances which woke the other patients in the middle of the night, thus delaying their recovery. I noticed that none of these lunatics were naked or indecently dressed; this shows that Americans maintain, even in madness, their basic sense of propriety.[6] Some of these patients recover, however.

I could not avoid a bitter thought as I left: The most brilliant genius may finish his days in such a place! Had Swift not been rich, he would have dragged out his last days in a hospital for the insane! May you who have charge over these hospitals exercise your responsibility with all the mildness possible, for under your care may be a benefactor of humanity!

[6] There are some exceptions, but they are very rare.

BENJAMIN FRANKLIN[1]

Thank God he is still alive, this great man who has been for so many years America's mentor and who has so gloriously contributed to her independence. Death threatened his days, but now that his health has been restored our fears are allayed. I have just seen him and I have had the privilege of a conversation with him, sitting surrounded by the books which he still calls his best friends. The pains caused by his cruel illness, the stone, have not altered the serenity of his countenance or the calm of his conversation. If these attributes made such an impression on the Frenchmen who enjoyed his friendship in Paris, what would they think of Franklin here, where he no longer wears that sometimes chilling mask of reserve which his diplomatic position formerly forced upon him. Franklin surrounded by his family resembles one of those patriarchs he has described and whose language he has emulated so naturally. He is like one of those ancient philosophers who occasionally came down from their high spheres of genius to bring instruction to simple mortals and lend an indulgent ear to their foolish preoccupations.

I have met in America a great many enlightened statesmen and virtuous men, but none has possessed to such a high degree as Franklin the characteristics of the true philosopher. You know what these characteristics are, my friend: love of the human race to the extent that this love becomes the preoccupation of every waking moment; indefatigable zeal in the service of humanity; vast knowledge and understanding; simplicity of manners and purity of morals. Yet these traits alone would not establish a sufficiently clear line of distinction between him and other patriotic statesmen. Therefore one more of his characteristics must be listed; namely, that Franklin, in the very center of the broad stage where he played so brilliant a role, constantly has kept in view the far vaster stage of heaven and the future life. This view-

---

[1] In M. La Rochefoucauld's eulogy of this great man delivered to the Société de 1789 his name is constantly spelled Franklyn, which is an error. [This Eulogy by the Duke de La Rochefoucauld d'Anville was published in the *Journal de la Société de 1789,* June 19, 1790. Brissot was a member of the society.]

point is the only one that can give strength and detachment, enhance a man's stature on earth, and transform him into a true philosopher. Franklin's whole life has been devoted to the study and practice of philosophy. I should like to give you an outline of this life, based on information I have gathered here. As his biography has been greatly distorted, this sketch may serve to rectify some of the untrue anecdotes which are circulating in Europe.[2]

Born in Boston in 1706, Franklin was the fifteenth child of a former dyer who later established a soap factory. The father wished to raise this son for the latter trade, but the boy took an insurmountable dislike to it and preferred the life of a sailor. Instead, his father decided to place him as an apprentice with another of his sons, a printer and the publisher of a newspaper in Boston. Young Benjamin after working at the press used to deliver the papers to the subscribers. He displayed at this time three traits which gave the measure of his character and prefigured the man he would some day become.

He tested his talent by writing a few pieces, in disguised handwriting, which he addressed to his brother for publication. They were generally well received, but the brother, who acted more like a master than a relative, soon became jealous of Benjamin and caused him so much trouble that he was forced to leave and go to New York to seek his fortune.

Benjamin had read a treatise by Dr. Tryon on the Pythagorean diet, and, won over by Tryon's arguments, he abstained from eating meat for a long period of time. Only after having seen a codfish which he had caught in the open sea and in whose stomach he found several small fish, did he again become reconciled to eating meat. He decided that since fish ate one another, men might very well feed upon animals. The money he saved while on this Pythagorean diet he used to buy books, the first and constant passion of all his life.

It seems that young Franklin was early to detect the pretenses of the gloomy and austere Puritanism then predominant in Massachusetts. As his father delivered long prayers before meals and benedictions over every dish, Benjamin undertook to correct him in an amusing manner. One day, at the beginning of winter, when

---

[2] [The following biographical sketch is based upon the manuscript of the *Autobiography* (not published until 1798), which Franklin had left in Paris with his friend Le Veillard. La Rochefoucauld, Condorcet, and Vicq d'Azyr also used this source in composing their eulogies of Franklin.]

his father was salting down his provisions for the season, he said, "Father, you ought to say grace over this barrel of meat once and for all; it would be a great saving of time." This incident strikingly reveals Benjamin's character and the principle which was later to become the foundation of his politics.

Having left his father's house with almost no money, with no recommendations, and with no one to rely upon but himself, but none the less proud and independent, he met various mishaps which tested him but did not discourage him. Here was a poor working man, wandering in the streets of Philadelphia with a few shillings in his pocket, completely unknown, hungrily biting into a loaf of bread and carrying two more loafs under his arm, quenching his thirst with water from the Delaware River. Who could have recognized in such a figure one of the future legislators of America, a man who was to become the ornament of the New World, a leader of modern philosophy, and an honored ambassador to the richest, most powerful, and most enlightened country in the world? Who could have believed that France, indeed that all Europe would one day erect statues to the honor of this man who had no place to lay his head? I am reminded of the similar situation of Jean Jacques Rousseau: possessing a total fortune of six liards, exhausted and tormented by hunger, he hesitated between spending his small coin for a place to rest or for food. Having decided to buy a roll of bread, he lay down to sleep in the open air, but while abandoned thus by both nature and mankind he still enjoyed the former and despised the latter. The man from Lyons who sneered at Rousseau because he was badly dressed has died unknown, while altars are now erected to that ill-clad man whom he scorned. Such examples should console those men of genius whom fate has reduced to similar circumstances and who are forced to struggle against poverty. Adversity forms such men. If they but persevere the same reward awaits them.[3]

Benjamin Franklin's misfortunes did not end in Philadelphia, for Governor Keith deceived him with fine promises of future support which were never fulfilled and induced Franklin to embark

[3] M. La Rochefoucauld, in his eulogy of Franklin, in speaking of his subject's trip to Philadelphia says that the legislator of Pennsylvania [Penn], "although a fanatic," had loved liberty, and that consequently this state was better suited to receive the advantages of enlightenment. I do not understand how M. La Rochefoucauld came to apply the epithet "fanatic" to Penn. Fanaticism is defined by intolerance of opinion and zeal to persecute dissenters; Penn permitted all forms of religion and persecuted none.

for London, where he arrived with no financial means or recommendations. Fortunately he was self-reliant, and his outstanding skill as a printer soon brought him employment. By his frugality, his sober behavior, and his talent as a conversationalist, he won the respect and esteem of his fellow workers, and fifty years later he was still remembered in the printing shops of London.

A promise of employment by a Mr. Denham brought Franklin back to America in 1726. Fate had, however, more misfortunes in store for him, for his protector died and Franklin was forced once again to earn his living by working as a printer. His experience, plus some financial help, enabled him to start his own press and newspaper. His success dated from this period, and good fortune never abandoned him again for the rest of his life. He married a Miss Read, to whom he had long been attached and who well deserved his esteem. Sharing his economic views and his devotion to humanity, she was the model of a virtuous wife and a good citizen.

Now financially independent, Franklin could finally devote himself to his ideas for the general good. His newspaper was a regular medium by which he could instruct his fellow citizens; he gave it all his attention, and, as a result, it was in very great demand everywhere and may be considered to have contributed largely toward maintaining in Pennsylvania the excellent morals which still prevail today.

I own a copy of this gazette, partly composed by Franklin and printed in his shop.[4] It is a precious relic, a monument which I should like to put in a revered place to teach men to be ashamed of the prejudice which makes them scorn the useful and important

[4] The date is January 13, 1763. It contains, to begin with, a long list of undelivered letters waiting at the Philadelphia post office. This excellent practice has not yet occurred to anyone in an old country like France, where letters are simply kept for a while and then burned with a few formalities. No one has ever thought of informing the addressees by printing their names in the newspapers. Then there is an advertisement concerning a twenty-year-old girl, who, deported to the colonies for some crime, had run away. This reminds me of the ingenious criticism of the custom of deportation to the colonies which Franklin addressed to an English minister who had sent over a number of such criminals: Franklin offered to send him in return rattlesnakes to populate the king's gardens. I also find similar advertisements for runaway Negro slaves, or for the sale of slaves. At that time Franklin was not yet president of a society for the abolition of the slave trade. There also is an excellent article entitled "The Trinobantian," which exhorts the people to peace and attacks that philosophy, in great vogue at the time, according to which it was necessary to ruin the French in order to achieve prosperity. "Believe me, my fellow citizens," Franklin writes, "it is not the increase of French power that we must fear, but a relapse into our own vices and our own corruption." This piece indeed has the cachet of Benjamin Franklin.

profession of journalism. In a free nation, journalists are the people's best friends and their first teachers. When they combine talent with philosophy and patriotism, and when they use the press continually to spread truth, to dispel prejudice and hatred, and to unite the human race into one single family, then these philosopher-journalists become veritable pastors, missionaries, angels sent from Heaven for the happiness of mankind.[5] Let no one tell me, in an attempt to discredit this profession, of the evil use to which newspapers are put by the wicked in order to defend vice, despotism, and error. Are we to proscribe eloquence and the art of writing merely because some scoundrels happen to possess these gifts?

A work which contributed even more to spreading the practice of frugality, economy, and morality in America was *Poor Richard's Almanack,* with which you are familiar. It enjoyed great success in France, [6] but was even more popular in America, where Franklin published it for twenty-five years, selling over ten thousand copies yearly. In this work the greatest truths are expressed in a simple language comprehensible to everyone.

In 1736 Benjamin Franklin began his public career with his appointment as secretary of the Pennsylvania Assembly, a position he held for several years. Then in 1737 the English government entrusted him with the general administration of the post offices in North America. He made the postal system both a lucrative source of revenue and a useful service to the people, but most important, it served as a means to distribute widely his useful newspapers. From that time not a year passed without his having proposed and carried out some useful projects for the colonies. It is to him that Americans owe the establishment of fire insurance companies, so necessary in a country where houses are built of wood and where a fire can completely ruin a person. It is to be remembered, however, that in countries where fires are rare and do little damage such companies are disastrous.[7] It is to Franklin also that Philadelphia owes the establishment of its Philosophical Society, its library, its college, its hospital, etc.

---

[5] [Brissot was, of course, a journalist.]

[6] [Brissot is referring here not to the entire *Almanack* but to the famous "Way to Wealth," translated as "La Science du Bonhomme Richard," which enjoyed a phenomenal vogue in France from its first publication in the *Courrier de l'Europe* (March 28–May 30, 1777) until well into the nineteenth century.]

[7] [Brissot's comment is to be explained by the fact that in 1786 he had published

Franklin, convinced that before enlightenment can be diffused it must first be concentrated by bringing together enlightened men, has always been very eager to encourage everywhere the establishment of literary and political clubs. Here are the questions asked of a candidate for membership in one of the clubs which he founded: "Do you sincerely declare, that you love mankind in general of what profession or religion soever? Do you think any person ought to be harmed in his body, name, or goods, for mere speculative opinions, or his external way of worship? Do you love truth for truth's sake, and will you endeavor impartially to find and receive it yourself, and communicate it to others?" [8]

The spirit of the club is also recognizable in the questions asked at the meetings: "Have you lately heard of any citizen's thriving well, and by what means? Do you think of any thing at present, in which the Junto may be serviceable to mankind, to their country, to their friends, or to themselves? Hath any deserving stranger arrived in town since last meeting, that you have heard of? And what have you heard or observed of his character or merits? And whether, think you, it lies in the power of the Junto to oblige him, or encourage him as he deserves? Do you know of any deserving young beginner lately set up, whom it lies in the power of the Junto any way to encourage? Have you lately observed any defect in the laws of your country, of which it would be proper to move the legislature for an amendment? Or do you know of any beneficial law that is wanting? In what manner can the Junto, or any of them, assist you in any of your honorable designs?"

The time and work Franklin devoted to these literary and humane societies did not prevent him from fulfilling his public duties during these ten years, when he was a representative of the City of Philadelphia to the Assembly, nor did they keep him from his research and experiments in physics.

His work in this latter field is so well known that it is unnecessary to describe it to you. I shall merely point out one little-known fact, namely, that Franklin always concentrated on investigations which would procure the greatest advantages to all his fellow citi-

two lengthy pamphlets attacking a proposal to establish a fire insurance company in Paris.]

[8] [These and the following questions Brissot translated from Franklin's "Rules for a Club Established for Mutual Improvement" (The Junto), written in 1728. The English text here given is that found in *The Writings of Benjamin Franklin,* ed. A. H. Smyth (New York, 1907) II, 88–90.]

zens rather than on ones which would enhance his own fame. It is to this love of Franklin's for the people that we owe his invention of the lightning rod, his economical stove, his truly philosophical treatises on the means of preventing chimneys from smoking and on the advantages of copper roofs, the many paper mills in Pennsylvania he established or to whose establishment he contributed, etc.[9]

Since you are also well acquainted with his political career, I shall pass it over in silence, but I cannot omit mentioning his conduct during the war of 1756. At that time Benjamin Franklin enjoyed a great reputation in the English colonies. In 1754 he was appointed a member of the famous Albany Congress, whose object was to take all necessary measures to prevent a French invasion. He submitted an excellent Plan of Union, which was accepted by the Congress but rejected by the Colonial Office in London on the pretext that it was too democratic. It is most likely that had his plan been adopted the colonies would not have been exposed to the ravages of the horrible war which followed. During this war Franklin carried out several important missions such as the defense of Pennsylvania's northwestern border, the building of forts, the raising of troops, etc. Upon his return to Philadelphia he was placed in command of a regiment of militia. He entered into a struggle with the governor of the province in an attempt to force him to give his consent to a bill permitting the taxation of the Penn family. The Penns, owners of one third of Pennsylvania, refused to pay their share of the taxes of the province. Franklin was sent to London as a deputy, and he appeared before the Privy Council and was able to triumph over this powerful family. The skill and success of Benjamin Franklin in these negotiations foreshadowed the more important successes he was to achieve later as an envoy to France during the War of Independence.

Upon his final return to his country, he received all the honors he deserved for the important services he had rendered to Free America. His age and infirmities have finally compelled him to renounce the career of public service which he has followed so

[9] Dr. Franklin told me that he had established about eighteen paper mills. He made this statement with some emphasis because of what I and M. Clavière had written in *De la France et des Etats-Unis* about the paper produced in the United States. He seemed surprised that we did not know these facts. His grandson, Mr. Temple Franklin, is undoubtedly collecting all the useful letters he has published in American and English newspapers on various good and bad methods in the practical arts. This collection will be of great value.

gloriously. He lives in retirement with his family, in a large but simple house which he has built on the spot where sixty years before he landed and wandered homeless and friendless. He has established a printing press and a type foundry. After having been a printer he became an ambassador; now, after having been an ambassador, he has returned to his beloved presses, and he is teaching this valuable art to his grandson, Mr. Bache, whom he has placed at the head of an enterprise which will be infinitely useful. This is to be the publication of an edition, printed at the lowest possible price, of all the classical authors, that is to say, of those moral authors whose books ought to be in the hands of men who wish to become enlightened and to achieve happiness by promoting the happiness of others.

It is in the midst of these saintly occupations that this great man tranquilly awaits death. A man's views on death are the touchstone of his philosophy, and one can judge Franklin's philosophy by a letter he wrote thirty years ago upon the death of John Franklin, his brother, to Miss Hubbard, John's stepdaughter.[10]

My Dear Child,
    I condole with you. We have lost a most dear and valuable relation. But it is the will of God and nature, that these mortal bodies be laid aside, when the soul is to enter into real life. This is rather an embryo state, a preparation for living. A man is not completely born until he be dead. Why then should we grieve, that a new child is born among the immortals, a new member added to their happy society?

We are spirits. That bodies should be lent us, while they can afford us pleasure, assist us in acquiring knowledge, or doing good to our fellow creatures, is a kind and benevolent act of God. When they become unfit for these purposes, and afford us pain instead of pleasure, instead of an aid become an incumbrance, and answer none of the intentions for which they were given, it is equally kind and benevolent, that a way is provided by which we may get rid of them. Death is that way. We ourselves, in some cases, prudently choose a partial death. A mangled painful limb, which cannot be restored, we willingly cut off. He who plucks out a tooth, parts with it freely, since the pain goes with it; and he, who quits the whole body, parts at once with all pains and possibilities of pains and diseases it was liable to, or capable of making him suffer.

Our friend and we were invited abroad on a party of pleasure, which is to last for ever. His chair was first ready, and he is gone before us. We could not all conveniently start together; and why should you and I be grieved at this since we are soon to follow, and know where to find him?

[10] [It is highly probable that Brissot's translation of this letter was made from the publication in the *American Museum*, 7 (1790), 265, the text we give here. It varies only in minor details from the version in Smyth.]

This year Franklin has at last received the blessing of the death he awaited. I shall reprint here the thoughts which appeared in my *Patriote Français* of June 13, 1790, concerning both this event and the decree of the National Assembly on the occasion.

I must first remind you of the eulogy which M. Mirabeau the elder delivered:

Gentlemen:

Franklin is dead. That genius who liberated America and shed torrents of light over Europe has returned to the bosom of the Divinity.

The sage whom two continents claim as their own, whose name belongs to both the history of science and to the history of empires, held without question a lofty rank in the human race.

Long enough have political cabinets announced the death of those who were great only to their eulogists. Long enough has the etiquette of royal courts proclaimed hypocritical mourning. Nations ought to mourn only for their benefactors. The representatives of nations should recommend for honor none but the heroes of humanity.

Congress has proclaimed throughout all the states of the Confederation a period of two months of mourning for the death of Franklin. America, at this moment, is rendering this tribute of veneration to one of the fathers of her constitution.

Would it not be worthy of us, gentlemen, to join in this truly religious act, to participate in this homage offered before the eyes of the whole universe both to the rights of man and to the philosopher who has contributed most to spread these rights over the face of the earth? Antiquity would have raised altars to this mighty genius who, for the benefit of mortals, embracing both the heavens and earth in his thought, vanquished both the thunderbolt and the sword of tyranny. Enlightened and free Europe owes at least a testimony of remembrance and regret to one of the greatest men who ever served philosophy and liberty.

I propose that it be decreed that the National Assembly wear mourning for three days in memory of Benjamin Franklin.

The National Assembly acclaimed M. De Mirabeau's proposal and unanimously approved it.

The National Assembly by paying honor to the memory of Franklin will reflect glory upon itself. This tribute will give an indication of the immense difference between this Assembly and other political bodies. How many prejudices had to be overcome before France could lay her grief at the tomb of a man who, starting life as a journeyman printer and book peddler, raised himself to the rank of legislator and helped to place his country among the great powers of the earth! This sublime decree was voted by the Assembly without hesitation and with that enthusiasm which is inspired by the name of a great man, by a profound grief for his death, by the duty to honor his remains, and by the hope that this honor rendered to him may encourage others to lead virtuous and distinguished lives. May this Assembly, fully aware of the greatness of the homage which it has rendered to genius, virtue, and a pure love of liberty and humanity, never cheapen this tribute by giving this honor of national mourning to inferior and ambitious individuals who confuse talent with genius, muddled thinking with profound ideas, the desire to overthrow tyrants with love of humanity, and the homage of a fickle people with the approbation of enlightened and disinterested judgment.

The hope of such an honor may, no doubt, inspire a man of genius, an honorable man. But you who secretly aspire to a place beside Franklin, study his life and have the courage to imitate it. Franklin, indeed, had genius; but he also had virtues. He was simple, good, and above all modest. What talent can be of avail without modesty? When opposed, he did not display that unyielding pride which disdainfully rejects all the ideas of others. Instead, he listened.—Do you understand, reader? He listened. Why did he not leave us some of his ideas on the art of listening? He replied to the ideas of those with whom he was speaking, not to his own ideas. I saw him, eighteen months ago, patiently listening to some young men who, in their pride and frivolity, were intent on displaying before him a bit of superficial information. Although he knew how to value them, he did not humiliate them even by kindness, which always implies a certain condescension. Putting himself simply and sincerely at their level, he chatted with them without appearing to lecture. It is this easy sort of conversation alone which makes instruction attractive and digestible; the listener always closes his ears to the prepared lesson. Franklin had knowledge, but he wished it spread among the people; he was forever tortured by an awareness of the people's ignorance and by his duty to enlighten them. His constant consideration was how to lower the price of books in order to increase their distribution everywhere. In a word, genius, simplicity, kindness, tolerance, modesty, indefatigable love of work, affection for the people—these are the qualities that Franklin represents to me, and these are the qualities a man must combine if he aspires to a fame like Franklin's.

The smallest details about this great man deserve to be known. To repeat them is balm to a soul afflicted by the picture of human imperfections, and these anecdotes may induce those who are not too far removed from philosophy to imitate this great man.

Seneca in his Thirtieth Epistle speaks of a philosopher, Aufidius Bassus, struggling against old age and infirmity, who looked upon his own approaching death in the same spirit as he would have looked upon the death of a stranger. This was Franklin's very attitude in his last days, and with him, as with Aufidius, it was the product of the long and habitual practice of philosophic thinking and of the daily contemplation of death.

Three days before his death he asked that fresh sheets be put on his bed so that he could die, as he said, "in a decent manner." His daughter answered that she hoped she would see him get well and live many years more. "I hope not," he replied sincerely and firmly.

The excessive pains caused by the stone, which had tormented him for twelve months, made him long for the end.[11] During the intervals of peace afforded him by frequent doses of laudanum, he regained his usual gaiety, chatted with his friends and family, and devoted himself to public affairs and even matters dealing with private individuals, never letting escape an opportunity to do some good, and doing it with great pleasure. That was the way he was. He even enlivened his conversation with those *jeux d'esprit* and entertaining anecdotes which were the delight of all who heard him.

Sixteen days before his death he was seized with a feverish indisposition. He felt pains in the chest, attended with laborious breathing. The pains sometimes drew from him a groan of complaint, and his great fear was that he did not bear them as he ought. He acknowledged his grateful sense of the many blessings he had received from the Supreme Being, who had raised him, from small and low beginnings, to such high rank and consideration among men.

As his pain and difficulty of breathing entirely left him, his family flattered themselves with the hope of his recovery, but he himself no longer had any such expectations. He asked his friends to engrave on his tombstone an epitaph which he himself had

---

[11] [The following description of Franklin's last illness is a condensed translation of an account by Franklin's physician published in the *American Museum*, 7 (1790), 266.]

composed and in which he expressed his belief in a future life.[12] The true nature of his disease finally became apparent: it was an abscess of the lungs. It burst, but the weakened organs were no longer strong enough to expel the matter, his breathing became choked, he fell into a coma, and died on April 17.

The funeral of this great man included all the honors that a free nation owes to one of its liberators and to a benefactor of the human race. All the ships in port, including even the English, lowered their flags to half-mast. The governor, the Council, the Assembly, the judges, and all the political and learned associations followed the body to the grave. Never was such a large assemblage of citizens seen; more than 20,000 persons were present. Their seriousness, their silence, and the grief expressed by almost every face showed how greatly they mourned their loss.

At the reading of Franklin's will it was revealed that he had divided his considerable fortune between the public and his family.[13] He left legacies to the cities of Boston and Philadelphia, and to academies, universities, etc. These bequests bear the imprint of his character and of his economic principles, for he wished the capital to be used for the education of needy young men or as loans to citizens just starting out in business. The largest part of his fortune he left to his son William Franklin,[14] former governor of New Jersey, who has been such a constant supporter of the king, and to Richard Bache, his son-in-law, whose son manages the printing press recently established by Franklin. This young man, raised in his grandfather's principles, has just started a new gazette. He left to his other grandson, William Temple Franklin, his books and manuscripts and his memoirs, on which he worked with great care and which will be a precious monument for philosophers. We are assured that they will soon be published.

[12] Doctor Franklin's epitaph composed by himself forty years before his death: "The body of Benjamin Franklin, printer, (like the cover of an old book, its contents torn out, and stript of its lettering and gilding,) lies here, food for worms. Yet the work itself shall not be lost, for it will, as he believed, appear once more, in a new and more beautiful edition, corrected and amended by the Author."

[13] [The details of Franklin's will were probably taken from its publication in the *American Museum*, 7 (1790), 280–284.]

[14] I do not know whether this William Franklin is the same as the one who has just published an account of his travels in Bengal and Persia under the title *Observations Made on a Tour from Bengal to Persia* [Calcutta, 1788], dedicated to Lord Cornwallis. The English papers announcing this work say that the author is the son of Franklin and a supernumerary officer in the army in Bengal, and they praise his talents and his knowledge of Indian languages.

AN INVENTION FOR NAVIGATING AGAINST THE CURRENT— THOUGHTS ON THE CHARACTER OF AMERICANS AND ENGLISHMEN

Monday, September 1, 1788

I had breakfast with Samuel Ameland, one of the richest and most philanthropic of the Friends. A disciple of Anthony Benezet, of whom he speaks with enthusiasm, Ameland follows in his footsteps and is eager to participate in every deserving public cause and in every useful institution. This Friend loves the French and speaks their language. He treated me with the greatest cordiality, offering me his house, his horses, his carriage, and everything that belonged to him.

When I left him, I went to see a trial being conducted on the Delaware of a boat which was designed to ascend the river against the current. Its inventor, Mr. Fitch, has formed a company to back his enterprise. One of the shareholders and his most fervent supporter is Dr. Thornton, whom I have mentioned earlier. A Mr. Rumsey of Virginia has contended, however, that he and not Mr. Fitch is the inventor of this new type of boat, and their debate has occasioned a number of pieces in the public press.[1]

Regardless of this disagreement, the engine which I saw seemed to me well constructed and likely to achieve its intended purpose. It caused to move three large oars of considerable force, which made, I was told, twenty-six strokes per minute, although a rate of sixty had been promised.[2] I was also told that a steamboat capable

[1] Since writing this letter I have made some inquiries regarding Mr. Rumsey's invention and have met him personally in England. He is a man of genius, and I gather from his explanation that his invention, although based on the same principle as Mr. Fitch's, is quite different in execution. At the time I met him, in February 1789, Mr. Rumsey intended to build a ship which could cross the ocean to America in only fifteen days, without sails and propelled entirely by a steam engine. I am sorry to see that he has not yet realized this project, which if it were practicable and were actually carried out would perhaps bring about as great changes in commerce as did the discovery of the Cape of Good Hope.

[2] Various experiments have been conducted with this steamboat. Mr. Fitch once covered twenty miles in three hours, and with the tide can do eight miles an hour. This craftsman, a modest and estimable man, is constantly working to perfect his

of carrying from ten to twenty barrels of eighteen pounds each would cost only three to four hundred pounds to build and that it could be manned by two men, one at the tiller and the other feeding the fire, running the engine, etc.

I was sure that mechanically this invention would accomplish at least part of what is expected of it, but I doubted that it would ever be commercially useful; for despite the assurances given by its promoters it seemed to me that the machine required a great deal of maintenance and several men constantly on duty to run it, and that it would be very expensive to replace the moving parts worn by the great amount of friction and to pay the crew. I saw, however, that if it were possible to reduce the cost of maintenance and simplify the mechanism this invention would be useful in a country where manpower is expensive and where the terrain makes it impossible for horses and men to haul boats upstream, as they can in France. This thought consoled Dr. Thornton, who was the object of much derision about this steamboat. He was tired of these gibes, which did indeed seem, even to me, to be out of place.

How numerous are the obstacles that talent must overcome in every field, and how meager is the encouragement! It seemed to me so obvious that America is in need of machines to supplement its manpower that I could not suppress my indignation upon see-ing Americans frustrate and discourage with sarcastic jeers the noble efforts of one of their fellow citizens. When will men ever come to each other's help and encourage one another with real assistance, rather than discourage one another with ridicule? Only when reason and universal benevolence reign supreme will this happen. Is it not, then, the duty of republicans to hasten the arrival of this happy time?

Benevolence is, in fact, already taking root and visibly spread-ing in America. One does not find in Americans the Englishmen's condescension, which discharges an obligation without any feel-ing of gratitude, that egotistical rudeness which makes the English an alien people and the enemies of all others. One does, however, sometimes find among Americans vestiges of the English indiffer-ence to other peoples and their contempt for visiting foreigners.

---

invention. I note with pleasure in the American papers of 1790 that Mr. Fitch has not abandoned his invention, and that on May 11, 1790, he made the trip from Philadelphia to Burlington in three hours and fifteen minutes, against the wind but with the tide, at a rate of seven miles an hour.

For instance, should a foreigner find himself in a group of Americans and should he have the misfortune not to speak English, he is ignored by everyone present.[3] I earnestly believe that such behavior is both uncharitable and shortsighted, uncharitable because one owes sympathy and kindness to a man who is far from home, especially since he is without means of making friends and amusing himself, and shortsighted because foreigners, hurt by such rudeness and indifference, are glad to leave the country and to give unfavorable reports to others who may wish to visit it.

I do not think I am wrong in saying that this rude indifference to foreigners is most characteristic of the English. I have lived a good deal among them, I have learned to know them, and I have been accused of, if anything, too much partiality toward them. So my impressions can be trusted.

I have noticed that many of the English of the West Indies also have this same fault, and I am afraid that all these English vices, which seem to become accentuated in the islanders, may corrupt Americans, who appear to be very eager to have closer relations with them. I once overheard a West Indian ask some Americans the following question during a parade of volunteers in Philadelphia: "Can you tell me whether these brave officers are barbers or cobblers?" This vulgar joke revealed a prejudiced man, an insolent and base European, the servile valet of European despots or aristocrats.

Such jokes ridicule and destroy the idea of equality, which is the basis of republics. Why then do sensible men who hear such jokes fail to react to them vigorously? Why this weakness which cowardice adorns with the name of politeness? Is it not evident that it encourages the corrupt man, and that a complacent silence may allow to grow in weaker souls prejudices which a vigorous rebuttal would have destroyed?

[3] I do not imply that this is always true, but I have seen it happen quite often.

THE AGRICULTURAL SOCIETY
AND THE LIBRARY

September 2, 1788

I have attended a meeting of the Agricultural Society, which, although newly established, has considerable funds and a large membership, though there were not many present. If ever there was a country in which such a society would be likely to prosper, it is here. Agriculture is the mainstay of Pennsylvania, and, although there are many good farmers in the state, the great majority of them need instruction and information, which can be supplied only by a group of men well versed in theory and practice.

A very interesting topic was discussed at this session, namely, the moth or worm called the "Hessian fly,"[1] which for a long time has ruined the wheat in various parts of the United States. The king of England, fearing that this insect might be brought over to his country, has just forbidden the importation of American wheat. The Pennsylvania Executive Council, in order to counteract the effects of this prohibition, applied to the Agricultural Society for information, specifically to determine whether or not this insect attacked the wheat grains and if it were possible to prevent its ravages.

Several farmers who were present at this meeting declared, on the strength of their own experience as well as that of their neighbors and correspondents, that the insect deposited its eggs not in the ear but in the stalk. They were also convinced that during the threshing of the wheat there was no chance that the eggs might be mixed with the grain, and consequently no risk of the insect being carried abroad with the wheat. Most of them testified, moreover, that flour derived from wheat which had been attacked by this worm lost nothing either in quality or quantity. As this question was most urgent not only for Pennsylvania but also for the entire country, for the fly has spread to almost all the states, the society resolved to study the history and nature of this insect, the means

[1] So called because it is believed that it was brought over during the last war either in wheat of German origin or in wheat intended for the Hessians, who had been hired to hunt down Americans.

of destroying it, and the possibility of replacing the type of grain it attacked by another which would be immune. Several promising experiments along the latter lines have already been made; bearded wheat and yellow wheat, which have been grown in several places, have not been attacked by these insects.

Mr. Powel,[2] president of the society, and Mr. Griffitts,[3] its secretary, seemed to me to do equal honor to their offices, the former by the clarity of his summaries and the elegance of his style, the latter by his indefatigable zeal.[4]

Among the other useful institutions which do honor to Philadelphia I must speak of the public library, which, as I mentioned earlier, owes its origin to the celebrated Franklin. It is supported by subscriptions. Subscribers pay ten pounds on joining and have the privilege of borrowing books. Half the books are always in circulation. I noticed with pleasure that the remaining volumes on the shelves showed signs of frequent use.

Beside the library there is a small museum of natural history,[5] in which I saw nothing noteworthy except a huge femur and some equally monstrous molar teeth discovered near the Ohio in an enormous mass of "big bones." These bones nature had heaped together in an age hidden from the eye of history by an impenetrable veil, and they have occasioned long but fruitless investigations by our naturalists.

I shall only mention here another establishment, which is much more valuable from my point of view and which gave me great joy. I refer to the Friends' school for young Negroes, of which I shall speak at greater length in a later letter to be devoted entirely to this subject.

---

[2] See M. Chastellux's eulogy of him [*Voyages* (Paris, 1786), I, 168–169. Samuel Powel was also mayor of Philadelphia.]

[3] [Samuel Powel Griffitts, M.D.]

[4] This society continually offers large prizes for the encouragement and investigation of all branches of agriculture. I note in the *American Museum* of May 1790 a list of interesting proposed subjects; I also see that a similar society founded in Burlington offers a prize for the improvement of American cheeses.

[5] [Peale's Museum, of which the proprietor was Charles Willson Peale.]

THE MARKET IN PHILADELPHIA AND THE PRICE OF FOODSTUFFS

September 3, 1788

Franklin used to say that any atheist in the world would be converted if he could see Philadelphia, a city in which everything is so much for the best; and that if an idle man were born here, where he would constantly have before his eyes the three amiable daughters of Diligence, namely, Wealth, Learning, and Virtue, he would soon fall in love with them and try to obtain them from their father.

Such ideas spring naturally to mind on a market day in Philadelphia, for this market is without a doubt one of the finest in the world. It combines everything one might wish—variety in agricultural and manufactured products, orderly displays, honest dealing, and quiet trading. One of the outstanding beauties of the market is the cleanliness of the merchandise as well as of those who sell it. Here, cleanliness is evident in everything. Even meat, which looks so disgusting in all other markets, has an attractive appearance, and the spectator is not revolted by the sight of streams of blood that infect the atmosphere and befoul the streets. The women who bring in produce from the country are all dressed modestly, and their fruit and vegetables are displayed with the greatest care in handsomely woven baskets. Everything can be found here, all kinds of agricultural and manufactured products: meat, fish, fruit, vegetables, grain, etc., as well as pottery, shoes,[1] ironware, wooden tubs, very well made buckets, charming little baskets, etc.

A foreign observer never tires of watching this multitude of men and women all moving about and going in every direction, but without bumping into each other and without any tumult or abuse of one another. One would think that it is a market of brothers, the meeting place of a nation of philosophers, of disciples of the silent Pythagoras. It is a crowd which moves in uninterrupted silence. Your ears are not assailed by harsh shouts as in other markets. Everyone buys and sells in silence. These people are com-

[1] Shoes made of local leather cost approximately 7 livres 10 sous. A good pair of boots of English leather costs about 36 livres.

199

posed and orderly in everything they do, even in the way the produce wagons and horses are lined up in the neighboring streets in order of their arrival. There is no quarreling and no congestion, and when the wagons leave they do so in silence. You hear no drivers and porters swearing at one another; you see no madmen galloping at full speed down the streets. Here is one of the most striking effects of habit, a habit inspired by the Quakers, who have implanted morality in this country, the habit of performing everything quietly, reasonably, and above all without injury to anyone and without need for the intervention of a magistrate.[2] To maintain order in a market of this size in France you would need three or four police officers and a dozen soldiers. Here, law needs no muskets; education, morality, and habit do everything. Two police clerks walk in the market to keep an eye on the produce offered for sale. Should they suspect that a pound of butter is short in weight they weigh it, and if it is short it is seized and given to the hospitals, etc.

The market is roofed for a considerable distance, and between each pillar of the arcade is a stall in which merchandise is displayed or hung. A kind of portico is thus formed which is used as a promenade in rainy weather.

Here you can still see heads of families going to market as our fathers used to do. In France, women first replaced the men, and now they too, thinking this task beneath them, are sending their servants instead, a change which is neither economically profitable nor morally beneficial. Here mothers take their daughters to market to teach them how to shop, which proves, incidentally, that domestic skills and virtues are respected in this country.

Some people criticize the citizens of Philadelphia for having established the market in the middle of a street and would prefer to see it in a large square, which would indeed have been better. Such as it is, however, this market is almost without disadvantages. The lack of cleanliness which one would expect does not exist because great care is taken in cleaning up the refuse.

[2] At Newport I saw how powerful reason is. A Quaker had concluded an arrangement with the captain of a packet, from Albany I believe, to have some furniture shipped there. It was natural for the furniture to be placed in the cabin or in the hold, but the captain wanted to stow it on deck and talked very rudely to the Quaker, who, however, merely kept telling him, "Friend, this furniture would be ruined by the air and rain and the sailors going about their work, but the wood thou hast put in the hold would not be spoiled were it stowed on deck. Think of what I have told thee; I shall return tomorrow morning." By the next morning the furniture was in a safe place.

This reminds me of something which surprises all foreigners. They are shocked to see pigs wandering in the streets and rooting in the garbage. There is a law prohibiting them but it is not observed. I have read in an American review that it is both sanitary and economical to let pigs roam in the streets.

This is the place to list current prices of foodstuffs in Philadelphia, reminding you that a shilling is worth fourteen sous, and the pound a little over fourteen livres. Bread costs 2 to 3 sous; beef, from 4 to 6 sous a pound, the meat at 4 sous being very good; about the same price for lamb; veal, 2 to 3 sous; hay, from 30 to 40 shillings a ton (2,000 pounds); butter, 6 to 10 sous a pound; coal, from 16 to 18 shillings; wood, from 10 to 12 shillings a cord. Vegetables are plentiful and inexpensive; potatoes are especially delicious; venison is sometimes cheap. European, and particularly French wines, cost less than anywhere else. I have had some Provençal wine, said to be made by M. Bergasse, at 15 sous a bottle. Prices in inns are, however, very high, especially at the Moyston Tavern, where the meals are, indeed, excellent. Luxury items are also expensive. A hairdresser costs a shilling each day, or 20 shillings a month. I hired a one-horse chaise for three days at a cost of 3 louis. Laundry, which is very nicely done, costs 3 shillings 6 pence for a dozen pieces.

THE GENERAL ASSEMBLY OF PENNSYLVANIA AND A DESCRIPTION OF A FARM OWNED BY A FRENCHMAN

Saturday, September 6, 1788

In New York I met General Mifflin, who is Speaker of the Pennsylvania Assembly, and I have seen him again in Philadelphia. The Marquis de Chastellux described him well: he is an amiable, obliging, active, and popular man who performs his duties with dignity and firmness. Outspoken and an enemy of artifice and deception, he is also courageous, wholly disinterested, and devoted to democratic principles. He is no longer a Quaker, for having joined the army he was forced to leave the Society, yet he is none the less attached to it and still professes the greatest admiration for the sect, to which his wife has remained faithful.

The general [1] had the kindness to accompany me one morning to the General Assembly, where I saw nothing noteworthy. The building is far from being as magnificent as M. Raynal claims.[2] It is undoubtedly a handsome edifice if you compare it with the others in Philadelphia, but it is not the equal of any of the public buildings which we consider beautiful in Europe. There were about fifty members at this session, seated on wooden chairs in an area enclosed by a balustrade, behind which was the spectators' gallery. If a Parisian fop should suddenly stumble upon this Assembly, he would undoubtedly find it quite ludicrous and he would be scandalized by the simplicity and even the negligence of the members' dress. Any thinking man, however, would wish that such simplicity might long continue and become universal. For instance, a man was pointed out to me, a farmer by the name of Findley, who had a nondescript face and wore common clothes yet displayed great talent and eloquence.[3] The session was de-

[1] General Mifflin is at present president of Pennsylvania.
[2] [In his *Histoire philosophique et politique des établissements européens dans les deux Indes.*]
[3] [William Findley (1741–1821), who held various offices on the Council of Censors, the Assembly, and the Executive Council of Pennsylvania and in 1791 was elected to Congress.]

voted to the reading of various memoranda and documents transmitted by the Executive Council.

We later went to dine at General Mifflin's property, which is five miles from Philadelphia opposite the Schuylkill Falls. These falls are formed by a rather large stratum of rock and are not visible when the river is high. The general's house is situated halfway up a hillside and has a lovely and very "romantic" view of the river and the surrounding area. Along the road the general pointed out to me the ruins of several houses burned by the English. The countryside is bare and without trees; the English destroyed them all.

While at General Mifflin's place I met an old Quaker who said that he took particular pleasure in shaking my hand because I resembled Anthony Benezet. This resemblance was later confirmed by other Quakers. I mention this without vanity, for you will recall Chastellux's description of Benezet. But Benezet's eyes were kind and full of humanity.

Spring Mill, where we were to spend the night, is a hamlet eight miles farther up the Schuylkill. The handsomest house is one belonging to a Frenchman, M. Le Gaux.[4] It commands one of the most magnificent views you can imagine and is situated on a hill to the southeast, with the Schuylkill flowing below in a magnificent channel between two wooded mountains. On the hillside one sees a few scattered houses and some cultivated fields.

The soil of this region contains large quantities of talc, quartz, granite, and yellow gravel, and in many places there is a very black earth. In the neighborhood are quarries of a rather fine marble which adorns many of the village fireplaces.

I shall enter into some detail, my friend, in my description of the farm of this Frenchman. Besides giving you an idea of the price of land and of a farmer's life, I feel that these details may be useful to those of our friends who may wish to settle here. Surely for a philosopher observations on means of improving the well-being of men are at least as valuable as observations on methods of assassinating them methodically.

M. Le Gaux's well-designed house is solidly built of stone with two stories and with five or six rooms with fireplaces on each floor.

---

[4] [Brissot probably visited Le Gaux's farm with the idea of purchasing it, and in fact his brother-in-law, François Dupont, bought the property in 1789 in partnership with another Frenchman, M. Duplaine. Throughout this letter Brissot identifies the owner as "M. L——."]

From its two gardens, laid out in the form of an amphitheater, one can enjoy the superb view I have already described. These gardens are well cared for and contain a quantity of beehives. A German who after many travels has settled down with M. Le Gaux takes care of these hives and is a very skillful and industrious man, always to be seen either working in the garden or at the lathe or with a plane in his hand, making or improving something.

The road separates the house from the farm, where I saw nineteen cattle, ten to twelve horses, and other animals. All the gates and doors are left open or unlocked, which proves to me how rare is theft in the country.

The farm comprises approximately two hundred and fifty acres of land, a very large part of it in woods. The remainder consists of meadows and fields of wheat, corn, and buckwheat. M. Le Gaux showed us an acre of well-manured meadowland from which he had already mowed eight tons of hay.[5] He calculated that this meadow after three cuttings had earned about £12 (158 *livres tournois*). The other meadows, which have been less well fertilized, are less productive.

The weather was miserable on Sunday, so we had to remain indoors and talk about his adventures and former friendships. M. Le Gaux told me about his misfortunes, of which I was already aware. He had been victimized by a slick intendant in Guadaloupe who, in order to conceal evidence of his own involvement in some sort of underhand business, had tried successively to have M. Le Gaux imprisoned, assassinated, and poisoned. At Spring Mill he was safe from this man's persecution and able to enjoy security, but he was not happy, for he lived all alone, and what is the life of a farmer without a wife and a family?

The workers on the farm are a Negro, a German couple, a German woman, two little boys aged ten to twelve, and a little girl aged eight. The Negro is not a slave. M. Le Gaux has built him a small log house and allows him as much land as he can cultivate in return for a share of the crops he raises. This is a profitable arrangement. The Negro is a hard worker and has the hope of buying some land and bettering his lot. What miracles can be wrought in even the laziest of men by such a hope! A busy man rarely falls into evil ways. The German is a good worker but is indolent. M. Le Gaux purchased his and his wife's services for a period of four years under a kind of contract which is very common

---

[5] A ton equals two thousand pounds.

called a bond or indenture. A European who has come to America without money sells himself for a period of four or five years to pay for his passage, and the master who buys his services undertakes to give him at the end of his time a suit of clothes and some money. If the indentured person is a woman, she sometimes receives a cow. M. Le Gaux, as an added incentive, gives his indentured woman a share in the proceeds from the sale of the calves. If the master moves away or finds he has no more need of his servants' services, he sells the remainder of their time.

These indentured servants must not be confused with Negro slaves, and one must not imagine that they are unhappy. One may judge their lot by the kind of life led by M. Le Gaux's servants. They do not get up to go to work until sunrise, and they stop work at sundown. For breakfast they have tea or coffee with plenty of sugar, butter, cream, and bread or cakes made of corn meal or buckwheat, of which they are rather fond; for dinner, vegetable soup, a good piece of meat, potatoes, cabbage, butter or cheese, and cider [6] or beer; for supper, butter, tea or coffee, and meat. When the work is particularly heavy, as at harvest time, they get rum as well. I realize that it is difficult to believe these facts and that they will appear surprising when compared with the food of our farm hands or even of French farmers who own their own land, but they are the exact truth. Many a rich farmer in Europe does not live as well as an American servant or hired hand.

Nevertheless, and incredibly, despite their masters' kindness toward them and despite the excellent treatment they receive, these servants are lazy. I do not think, however, that this is characteristic of Germans generally,[7] but M. Le Gaux's servants are slow, indolent, and dirty. The horses, wagons, stable, barn, kitchen, and rooms are all in poor condition from neglect and want of order. Nor is this for lack of a good example of hard work set by the master. M. Le Gaux told me that when George has his pipe in his mouth and a glass of rum by his side no mortal can pull him out of his complacent apathy. He has given up trying.

[6] Cider is inexpensive, as one can see by the following incident: General Mifflin showed me a large quantity of fallen apples which he had offered free to one of his neighbors to make cider. The neighbor told him that cider was so cheap in Philadelphia that it was not worth his while to make his own.

[7] I was shown a beautiful house near Spring Mill belonging to a German who had come to America twenty years ago as an indentured servant and who through his thrift and hard work had made enough money to buy a large amount of land and build the house.

These indentured servants, he told me, know perfectly well that their master is forced to keep them whether they work hard or not, and they also know very well that servants are scarce. Man of his own nature will never be honest and true, and he can become so only when he himself cultivates his reason and becomes a thinking being. Unfortunately the German immigrants are far different in this respect from Americans and Quakers. M. Le Gaux told me that there were also two other disadvantages in having this sort of servant. They often sham illness, and they often run away, and it is very expensive to find them and bring them back. In fact the newspapers are full of advertisements for runaway indentured servants.

The only good work he gets is from the little boys and the little girl, whom he is training. It was one of the conditions of the contract that these children were to stay with him until they were eighteen or twenty to repay him for the time lost by their mother when she was pregnant and could not work. In order to prevent their parents from spoiling them he has the children sleep in his own room. There is nothing the little twelve-year-old boy is afraid to do. He gallops on horseback, drives a wagon, steers the ferry all by himself, goes to town on errands, speaks three languages, etc.

I asked M. Le Gaux about the wages of the other workers he employs. He told me he pays them from one and a half to two and a half shillings a day, or five to six dollars a month, the latter rate amounting to 378 livres a year, not counting their food, which is what I have described above. It should be noted that two or three years ago daily wages were from three to four shillings, that is, forty-two to fifty-six sous. The current wages for Negro servants in Philadelphia are from four to five dollars a month, not including food. One can see that servants' wages here are much higher than those paid to our country workers or even to our city servants, who at the most do not make more than 200 livres. The reason for these high wages is the scarcity of workers in this country, while in Europe the labor competition is depressing wages, which would be even lower if money were not plentiful.

M. Le Gaux pays from eight to nine pounds in taxes on all his property, and from this figure you can judge how exaggerated are the stories about American taxes which are being spread by disparaging critics of the United States. His property consists of 120 acres of woodland, 80 acres of arable land, 25 acres of meadowland, 3 acres of garden, the large house, and the small houses for his workers. For all this, only 134 livres in taxes! Compare this with what one would pay in France on a similar piece of property.

M. Le Gaux has tried to grow grapes and has planted vine sets from Medoc on a slope with a south-southeastern exposure near his house.[8] Although the vineyard is only four months old, it seems to be doing very well. Something you notice everywhere you go in America is the rapid and sturdy growth of the vegetation. Peach trees, for instance, grow quickly and yield large quantities of fruit. A month after wheat is cut you cannot recognize the field, so covered is it with high, thick grass. I told M. Le Gaux, however, that it would be a long time before he made much profit from his vineyard because, on the one hand, grapes require a lot of attention and labor is going to be expensive in America for a long time,[9] and, on the other, European wines will be cheaper for years to come. He himself gave me proof of this when he served me a very good Roussillon which cost less than twelve sous a bottle bought through an agent and only eight or nine sous, all expenses included, when bought directly. Birds are one of the principal obstacles to the cultivation of grapes. You often see in America clouds of blackbirds, which when they descend upon a vineyard can devastate it in a few minutes. It would be necessary, therefore, to find a way of keeping these birds away from the vines.

All pastures and fields in America are, as I have already mentioned, enclosed by wooden fences. These are made of four pieces of wood eleven feet long and about seven or eight inches in circumference which are placed one above the other with a space between and rest on posts. In Spring Mill, oak fence rails cost ten livres ten sous and chestnut rails, twenty-one livres. If the farmer supplies the wood, eleven feet of fence costs him close to two shillings, or twenty-eight to thirty sous. In other words, wooden fences are very expensive. M. Le Gaux, who is aware of this and realizes that the wood could be put to better use and that it ought to be employed sparingly because of its growing scarcity, has had the idea of digging six-foot ditches and bordering his fields with piles

[8] Some were planted in Pennsylvania and in Virginia a long time ago, and I have learned that they produce good grapes and a passable wine.

[9] In the region around Orleans, tilling an acre of vineyard costs thirty livres, and you do not have to feed the workers. This operation is necessary, at most, five times a year, which makes 150 livres per acre. Compare this cost with wages in America and the price of imported French wine, and you will see whether it is possible to grow grapes on a large scale in the United States. They will be raised here only in small vineyards or in hothouses.

of dirt, on which he will plant hedges and so form a barrier livestock cannot get through. This is a very advisable idea. Undoubtedly Americans will some day give up wooden fences, but in the meantime they consider ditches too expensive because of the constant need of repairs caused by rainstorms and frost. It may be that fences are less expensive in areas far from cities and more in the woods. It is estimated that a Negro can split 130 to 150 rails a day.

There are many springs in this part of the country, and we saw some fine ones. M. Le Gaux told us that one could not dig two feet into the ground without finding water. He showed us a spring from which flows a stream big enough to turn a fairly large mill day and night and also to water the surrounding meadows whenever necessary.

Having a mill in the neighborhood of a farm is a great advantage. M. Le Gaux explained that he sent his grain to a nearby mill and that the miller paid him in cash. Since everyone in the area brings him wheat this miller is kept very busy. Being also a flour merchant, he has a good-sized storage room and ships his barrels of flour by water on the Schuylkill. M. Le Gaux mentioned that he has always wondered why the miller sells his flour so cheaply when wheat is so high. The explanation is that he obtains his wheat locally mainly by barter, but sells his flour to other areas for cash. The value of money is so high that, although nominally the miller has paid more for the wheat in barter, he still makes a profit even when he sells it cheaper, if he sells for cash. It is possible also that the savings on labor in the milling contributes to the low price of the flour.

I asked M. Le Gaux where he bought his meat. He told me that when a farmer slaughters an ox, a sheep, or a calf he tells his neighbors, who take what they need and salt down as much as they wish to store. Payment is made in cash, or else through a current account, return being made when there is an opportunity. M. Le Gaux also buys meat from Philadelphia.

As he is without a family he does not have any poultry or pigeons and makes no cheese; nor does he have any spinning done or collect goose feathers. It is a great disadvantage for him not to be able to profit from these domestic farm industries, which can be carried on well only by women. Instead of raising oats he feeds his livestock either Indian corn or ground buckwheat. I saw growing in large fields of Indian corn an immense quantity of cucumbers. They chop them up and feed them to the cattle. M. Le Gaux has a small carpenter's shop and a lathe, which is a necessary tool in the country. As there is a great deal of limestone on his land, he has been making lime and selling it in Philadelphia, where it gets a good price because of the great amount of building being done there. He finds that this is the best way to get rid of his wood, and he claims that with the profits he will be able to pay for his land. He has still another activity. He has received from the General Assembly permission to run a ferry across the Schuylkill to carry passengers and freight. He thinks the ferry will some day bring in over fifty pounds a year, for there is going to be a lot of traffic at this crossing. The toll is two sous for a man, nine for a horse, and one shilling (fourteen sous) for a wagon. He was also busy building a sawmill. All these undertakings conducted at the same time are costing him a lot of money and are taking his attention away from what ought to be his main interest, namely, the good organization of his farm.

His newly cleared fields produce considerably more than French farmland. But he has had a poor wheat crop this year; the ears are shriveled and thin, although the stalks grew very high and at first it promised to be a good harvest. M. Le Gaux said the trouble was mildew and that he had lost more than 300 bushels. Mildew is caused by the heavy summer fogs and dews. When the sun suddenly breaks through it evaporates too quickly the drops of water on the ears, and this too sudden passage from cold and humidity to dry heat weakens and dries out the plant. Mildew is very common in Pennsylvania, and there is no way of fighting it, M. Le Gaux tells me, except to sow early so that the plants will be more vigorous by the time the mildew season arrives.

M. Le Gaux assured me that, except for the special expenses incidental to his taking over the farm and those caused by his ignorance and necessitated by the improvements he has made, the land produces an income well over his investment. The farm cost him £3,300, or 46,000 livres, only a part of which was paid in cash —an important point, for there is often a difference in price of a third or even more when payment is made entirely in cash. M. Le Gaux assured me that the house alone had cost as much as this to build, and I think this is very likely.

In general, those who wish to make a good bargain should purchase lands with buildings, for although the buildings cost something to build they count for little in the purchase price. For his money M. Le Gaux has acquired a beautiful stone house, three gardens, 250 acres of meadowland, good arable land, fine wood-land, fishing rights on a part of the Schuylkill, etc. I am told, how-ever, that he paid too much, and that the man who sold it to him paid only £2,800. This was because the former owner had bought it during the war, while M. Le Gaux bought it in 1784 or 1785, when the price of land had gone up. At present, prices have de-clined greatly.[10]

M. Le Gaux had to overcome great disadvantages when he settled in this country. He was alone and without family, and he spoke little English. Since he could not understand the language and could not make himself understood, he had misunderstand-ings with his neighbors. If it is a misfortune to quarrel with your neighbors in the city, it is an even greater one in the country, where you more often need to give and receive help. This assistance you deprive yourself of by having enemies. When neighbors do not understand each other and yet have similar concerns, and in-terests that may conflict, it is so easy to become enemies and to try to do each other harm. Even if nothing as serious as this hap-pens, the difference of language will still lead to indifference, and indifference is poison in a rural community. I therefore never would advise foreigners to settle on a farm in this country unless they know the language.

Luckily, M. Le Gaux's neighbors are all Quakers, and although he has had litigations with them he has only praise for the sect, saying that he would rather have legal trouble with Quakers than any other kind of people, because if you go to see their elders you can reach a just settlement much more quickly and easily.

M. Le Gaux assured me that, although isolated and struggling against all these difficulties, he is happy, and he added that in order to be completely happy he needed only to have with him his family, which has remained in France.

He is very interested in meteorology, and it is he who composes the monthly meteorological tables published in the *Columbian Magazine*. These are undoubtedly the most careful and most cor-rect tabulations to appear on this continent. He told me that he did not think there is much difference between the climate in Pennsylvania and that in Paris. The cold here, he said, is drier and

---

[10] Since this letter was written I have learned that M. Le Gaux is trying to sell his land. He could not have chosen a more favorable moment. Philadelphia having been selected as the seat of Congress for the next ten years, the price of land in the surrounding area has gone up tremendously.

less humid, and the snow and ice do not last very long. There is not a week without some fair days and sunshine. He says that it rains more here than in France, but rarely for two consecutive days. The heat is sometimes more intense and oppressive and causes more sweating and a greater feeling of lassitude. Finally, he told me, the changes in temperature are more frequent and more abrupt. Indeed, while I was at Spring Mill the temperature dropped from twenty-six to eleven degrees [11] in twenty-four hours. This shows why one should always wear wool clothes in this country.

He told me also of a strange metereological phenomenon. In America the changes in barometric readings are the reverse of those observed in Europe. There the atmospheric pressure rises for a period of twenty-four hours before the arrival of good weather, and falls in like manner before bad weather. But here the opposite occurs; when the weather is to be bad the barometer rises very rapidly and abruptly and then gradually falls.

The following are the results of M. Le Gaux's observations over a period of four years: In this part of Pennsylvania the lowest temperatures are 10 to 12 degrees below freezing on M. Réaumur's scale; the highest are 26 to 28 degrees above. The average temperature during the four years of observation was $9\frac{6}{10}$ degrees. The average height of the barometer was 29 inches, $10\frac{1}{10}$ lines (based on the English foot); the maximum variation was 22 lines. The prevailing wind was west-northwest. During the average year there were approximately 15 days of thunderstorms, 76 days of rain, 12 days of snow, and 5 days of strong winds and rain. The total average precipitation for the 81 days of rain and the snowstorms was 35 inches (based on the French foot). The sky was never totally obscured for three consecutive days. This is a very healthy and fertile country. Wheat is harvested around July 8–12. No epidemic disease was observed during the four years.

[11] [Reaumur.]

A JOURNEY BY TWO FRENCHMEN
TO THE OHIO

September 10, 1788

I have had the good fortune to meet an enlightened Frenchman who is traveling in these parts, not in order to make money but to gain knowledge. His name is Saugrain and he is from Paris.[1] You have met his charming sister at the home of M. Hardouin.[2]

M. Saugrain is an active and enthusiastic naturalist. Various circumstances first led him to enter the service of the king of Spain, who sent him to Spanish America to make investigations in the fields of mineralogy and natural history. After the death of his protector, Don Galvez,[3] he returned to France, and in 1787 he and a M. Picquet, a botanist, decided to travel in Kentucky and along the Ohio River. One of their purposes was to find out whether it would be possible to establish in that part of America a settlement for some French families who wished to emigrate.

In April 1787, on the very day of their departure from Paris, I had lunch with the two men at the home of Dr. Guillotin.[4] As soon as they arrived in Philadelphia, they hastened on to Pittsburgh, but they were prevented from going any farther by the unusually cold winter. The Ohio froze over, which happens rarely.

[1] [Dr. Antoine François Saugrain (1763–1820). After the adventures recounted here Saugrain returned to France in 1789 but came back to America the following year to settle with the Scioto group of French Emigrés at Gallipolis on the Ohio and spent the rest of his life in the United States. See H. Fouré Selter, *L'Odysée américaine d'une famille française, le docteur Antoine Saugrain*, Baltimore, 1936, and G. Chinard, "Gallipolis and Dr. Saugrain," *Franco-American Review*, 1 (1937), 201–207.]

[2] A famous lawyer who died in the prime of life and who will long be missed by his friends. [Louis Eugène Hardouin de La Rayrerie (1748–1789).]

[3] [Don José de Galvez, in charge of the Department of the Indies during the ministry of Florida Blanca.]

[4] This doctor, who, at the time, did not imagine that the French Revolution was so imminent or the role that he would play in it, was trying, like myself, to organize a settlement in the United States in order to escape from the intolerable tyranny of the French viziers. [Dr. Joseph Guillotin (1738–1814), physician and professor of anatomy in the University of Paris, who was largely responsible for the adoption of the guillotine, was a principal backer of Saugrain's first trip to America. See J. F. McDermott, "Guillotin Thinks of America," *Ohio State Archeological and Historical Quarterly*, 47 (1938), 129–158.]

Picquet and Saugrain established quarters a few miles from Fort Pitt in a house that gave them little or no protection from the weather and in which they suffered greatly from the cold. Even though they had a blazing fire and kept themselves wrapped in several blankets, they had great difficulty in keeping warm. The thermometer dropped to thirty-two degrees below zero Reaumur and then burst. During February, when this happened, the average temperature in Philadelphia was sixteen degrees [below zero]. The young men were forced to split their own wood and cook their own meals, which consisted usually of venison and potatoes. Bread was scarce and expensive.

During their rather long stay in the area they conducted a number of different experiments. M. Saugrain weighed, by means of a hydrostatic balance which he had brought with him, the different kinds of wood. He also tried to find out which kinds of wood yielded the largest quantity and best quality of potash. A number of experiments convinced him that the potash yield of corn stalks was proportionately the largest. He examined the various mines in the area and found that there were iron, lead, copper, and silver mines both on this side of Pittsburgh and down the Ohio. He was told of a rich iron mine belonging to a Mr. Murray, but he was not allowed to visit it.

With the coming of spring, navigation down the Ohio again became possible, and the travelers could continue their journey. They were joined by another Frenchman, a M. Raguet, and a Virginian, and they set out in April in a boat, provided with food, weapons, and money. When they reached the mouth of the Muskingum River they landed and visited the settlement that was being begun there by General Harmar,[5] who had with him soldiers from New England.

Proceeding down the river, they saw a kind of raft on which were a large number of Indians, who hailed them. Since they did not suspect the Indians of hostile intentions, they swung their boat around to wait for them, attaching a white handkerchief to the mast as a sign of peace. Suddenly M. Saugrain saw that one of the Indians with a knife between his teeth was about to jump into their boat, so he shot him with his pistol, knocking him backward. The Indians immediately answered with a volley which killed a horse in the Frenchmen's boat, broke one of M. Saugrain's

[5] [General Josiah Harmar (1753–1813), who fought the Indians in the Western territories.]

fingers, and wounded M. Picquet. The French defended themselves, firing thirteen shots and killing or wounding a number
of Indians. But since the savages were about to board the small
boat, the Frenchmen thought it wiser to jump overboard and
start swimming. Several Indians followed them and reached the
riverbank at the same time. They attacked M. Picquet and stabbed
him to death. M. Saugrain tried to defend himself but he was taken
prisoner. Probably the Indians killed M. Picquet because he was
older but spared M. Saugrain because of his youth, with the idea
of taking him back to their village and sacrificing him, though
this thought did not immediately occur to M. Saugrain. He let
the Indians tie him up, but he still had strength enough to take
various belongings from the pockets of his unfortunate companion. He then was forced to run with the Indians for a mile to
catch up with the raft, which was being carried downstream by
the current. When they reached it, the Indians made him jump
into the water and swim out, and they tied him alongside the raft.
Then an Indian hit him hard on the head, and this blow made
him realize the fate in store for him. Terrified but still courageous,
he resolved to escape. He broke the flimsy ropes that bound him
to the raft and began swimming with unbelievable strength
against the current. No Indian dared follow him, but they shot at
him several times, and a bullet grazed his neck without wounding
him seriously. Finally he reached the bank, where he found the
Virginian. The two men were almost naked, without food and
without means of getting any. After four days in the woods they
began to fear that it would be a long time before a boat would
come by, so they began to build one. While they were working
on it they were discovered by the same Indians, who shot at them
several times from the river but did not hit them. At last they
sighted an American boat, which rescued them from their cruel
predicament and took them back to Fort Pitt.

M. Saugrain never could find out what Indians had attacked
them. He suspects that there were among them white men who
either through informants in Pittsburgh or even by being in the
town had managed to learn of their trip and, suspecting they had
money, had made plans to steal it. In any case, he lost all he had,
his money, his clothes, and his papers, and was forced to return to
Philadelphia, where I met him, and from where he planned to return to Europe.

He shared with me various observations he had made. The valley of the Ohio had appeared to him the richest and the most fertile he had ever seen. The luxuriance and rapid growth of the vegetation were incredible. He saw the most magnificent trees, of an infinite variety of species. Settlers were sowing hemp and tobacco in order to dry out and impoverish the overly rich land and make it suitable for raising wheat, which grows to stalk and leaf. Indian corn grew to a prodigious height. The cattle were extremely fat; even in winter they can feed on a kind of cane or succulent reed which pierces through the snow and grows in abundance. The winters are never cold enough to prevent the cattle from grazing.

It is so easy to grow all the grain you need and fatten cattle and make whiskey, beer, and cider, and there are so many other advantages, that new settlers are constantly coming in. They work very hard to build their first cabins, but afterwards they lazily enjoy the fruits of their labor. A man living in these areas still surrounded by wilderness works scarcely two hours a day to support himself and his family, and he spends almost all his time loafing, hunting, or drinking. The women spin and make clothes for their husbands and children. M. Saugrain saw some very good woolens and linen made in these cabins. There is very little money in circulation and all trade is done by barter. You buy whiskey with wheat or exchange mutton for pork.

M. Saugrain met a Norman lawyer named Pintreau who lives with his wife and three children five or six miles from Pittsburgh in a house built on a sort of great rock. His wife was pretty, well bred, and well educated, and yet a true housewife. The whole family seemed happy. The husband worked in the fields, went to sell his produce in town, and for relaxation read some book from his small library, which was a source of much pleasure to him. He had arrived in Pittsburgh with fifty louis, and with twenty-five of these he had bought two or three hundred acres with a small cabin and a garden, both of which he had improved by his own labor. He lived on potatoes, bread, pork, eggs, and beef and drank whiskey.

Indians are still to be seen around Fort Pitt and they infest the Ohio. M. Le Gaux told me that they would very quickly cease their attacks if Congress would only show firmness and punish them. He added that the settlements which are multiplying beyond the Ohio will force them to withdraw.

The active nature of Americans is always pushing them forward. After they have spent some time on one piece of land, they move on to another where they hope to do better. In this way they will spread to the west and to the south. M. Saugrain has not the slightest doubt that sooner or later the Spaniards will be forced to abandon the Mississippi and that the Americans will cross it and establish themselves in Louisiana. He has been in Louisiana and he considers it one of the richest and most beautiful countries in the world.

M. Saugrain returned from Pittsburgh to Philadelphia in seven days on horseback, but in a chaise the trip from Philadelphia to Pittsburgh had taken him two weeks. A mail route has now been established and there are good inns along the road.

A LATER ADDITION TO THIS LETTER

Despite the disaster of his first journey, M. Saugrain was so delighted with the independent sort of life to be led in Kentucky that in 1790 he returned alone to settle there.

THE SCHOOL FOR NEGROES IN PHILADELPHIA— AMERICAN AUTHORS WHO HAVE WRITTEN IN DEFENSE OF NEGROES[1]

There exists, then, a land where these poor Negroes are believed to have souls and intelligence, where there is felt an obligation to shape their character to virtue and to give them instruction, where men do not consider them beasts of burden in order to have the right to treat them like animals. In this country Negroes, by their virtue and diligence, disprove the slanderous lies which their oppressors utter about them elsewhere.

There appears to be no difference between the powers of memory of a curly black head and those of a white one with straight hair, and today I had the proof of this. I have seen, questioned, and listened to Negro children; some read well, others recited from memory, others did sums quite rapidly. I was really surprised at the quality of a painting done by a young Negro who had never received instruction. I also saw in this school an octoroon, whom it was impossible to tell from a white boy. I seemed to detect in his eyes an extraordinary vivacity, which is a fairly common characteristic of these little Negro children.

I was no less edified by the school for Negro girls. In addition to reading, writing, and religion, they are taught manual skills, spinning, needlework, etc., and their teacher assured me that on the whole they show great skill. The girls seemed modest, well behaved, attentive, and obedient; this is a school that produces an

---

[1] A Free American, Mr. [Samuel Stanhope] Smith, who has written a rather profound study on the varieties of the human species, maintains that skin color is the result of local physical and climatic conditions. The Negro has the darkest skin, next comes the Kafir, and then the Indian, a gradation which can be explained as follows: Below the equator the winds follow the course of the sun, and when they reach the eastern coast of Africa they have been cooled by the wide oceans they have crossed, giving to Ajan, Zanguebar, and Monomotapa [regions on the east coast of Africa] a comparatively temperate climate. But after crossing three thousand miles of continent and absorbing all the burning heat of the desert, these winds bring this heat to the inhabitants of Senegal and Guinea. See *An Essay on the Causes of the Variety of Complexion and Figure in the Human Species*, by Samuel Smith, Professor of Ethics at the New Jersey College [Philadelphia, 1787].

abundance of good servants and virtuous housewives. How criminal are the planters in the West Indies who train to debauchery and shame creatures who can so easily be fashioned to virtue!

America owes this useful establishment to Benezet, that same Benezet whom M. Chastellux was not ashamed to ridicule, to the impious applause of those vile sycophants that are spawned by despotism and aristocracy. The life of this extraordinary man should be known to thinking men, that is, to those who respect more the benefactors of humanity than they do the flattered and basely idolized oppressors of mankind.

Anthony Benezet was born at Saint-Quentin in Picardy in 1712. France was then a prey to fanaticism under a bigoted king counseled by a villainous confessor and an ambitious woman.[2] Benezet's parents, who were fervent Calvinists, fled with their son to England, where Benezet was converted to Quakerism. In 1731 he went to America and settled in Philadelphia. Having been brought up in a family of merchants, he continued in trade, but his integrity and his inclinations being at odds with the spirit of commerce, he abandoned business and in 1736 accepted a position in the academy run by the Friends in Philadelphia. From then on all his time was devoted to public education, to the relief of the poor, and to the defense of Negro slaves. Benezet's philanthropy was of a universal sort still not very common at that time; he regarded all men of every country and of every color as his brothers. Whatever time he did not devote to teaching he spent gathering all the passages he could find that could be used against slavery and the slave trade. He wrote several treatises which were instrumental in converting his brethren to his views and winning them over to the abolition of slavery.

It was not enough to free the unfortunate Negroes from slavery; it was also necessary to educate them and to provide teachers for them. But where was he to find people willing to undertake a task which prejudice had made appear so difficult and unpleasant? No obstacle could defeat Benezet's zeal. He set the first example himself and devoted his small fortune to the establishment of the school. His brethren supported him, and thanks to their generosity and to that of the Society of Friends of London, the Negro school of Philadelphia now has an income of 5,000 *livres tournois*.

Not content with giving freely his entire fortune, Benezet devoted his knowledge and time as well to the education of these

[2] [Father François de La Chaise (who in fact died in 1709) and Mme de Maintenon.]

poor Negroes. He became their teacher, and death surprised him
in 1784 still engaged in this saintly occupation. No, it did not
surprise him. Benezet had lived too well ever to be surprised.
Death was for him only the passage to the reward he deserved. The
tears of the Negroes falling upon his tomb and the grief of his
friends must have been for his departing soul a much sweeter
reward than all the laurels ever bestowed on conquering heroes.

Two other traits will give you a picture of the charity of this
virtuous man and of his firm adherence to his principles. He wore
only coats of plush, for two reasons, first, because the sturdiness of
this cloth saved him money which he could give to the poor, and
secondly, because even when worn out, the coat could still serve
to clothe a poor person. He always carried in his pocket one of his
works and an abolitionist tract, which he gave and recommended
to everyone he met who was not already familiar with them. This
is a practice that the societies of Friends generally follow; they
distribute profusely good works. It is the true way to make proselytes.

I must also speak of the predecessors of this philanthropic
Quaker who also befriended the Negroes. First, let me mention the
famous George Fox, the founder of Quakerism. He went from
England to Barbados in 1671, not to preach against the slave trade
or against slavery, but to bring Negroes to the knowledge of God
and to urge their masters to treat them more kindly. In those days,
however, men's minds were not yet ripe for such reform, nor were
they ready even in 1718, when William Burling of Long Island
published the first treatise I know of against slavery.[3] Burling was
a highly respected Quaker. He preached, but in vain, for the hour
had not yet come.

Should not these facts console and encourage the friends of
Negroes in France? It took sixty years of struggle to overcome
the forces of greed in America. Barely a year has passed since the
foundation of our society in Paris,[4] and already I see apostates
because success has not crowned our first endeavors.

Burling was followed by Judge Sewall, a Presbyterian from New
England, who submitted to the General Court in Boston a memoir

[3] [William Burling (b. 1678) of Flushing, Long Island, wrote in 1718 "An Address
to the Elders of the Church upon the Occasion of Some Friends Compelling Certain Persons, and Their Posterity, to Serve Them Continually and Arbitrarily . . . ,"
published in Benjamin Lay's All Slave Keepers, That Keep the Innocent in Bondage,
Apostates . . . , Philadelphia, 1737.]
[4] [The Société des Amis des Noirs.]

in defense of Negroes entitled "The Selling of Joseph, a Memorial." [5] In it, he professed the highest principles and refuted most forcefully the trite arguments of the slavers about the alleged wars among the African princes.

Writers who have devoted their pens to the defense of Negroes have been often accused of not having themselves witnessed the suffering they describe. This criticism could not be made of Benjamin Lay, an Englishman who as a young man was in the slave trade and who then became a planter in Barbados, but who soon left because of the horror he felt at the sight of the atrocious treatment endured by Negroes. He went to Philadelphia, became a Quaker, and spent all the rest of his life preaching and writing in favor of the eradication of slavery. His most important treatise on this subject appeared in 1737.[6] He has been reproached for excessive zeal, for giving exaggerated descriptions produced by a too vivid imagination, and for being too vehement in his declamations against ministers of other sects. These shortcomings, however, were fully expiated by his blameless life, by his indefatigable zeal in the service of humanity, and by his profound meditations. Lay dressed very simply, wearing only cloth which he had made with his own hands. His delivery was animated and became fiery when he spoke of slavery. He died in 1760, a few miles from Philadelphia, in his eightieth year. His temperance and his love of solitude undoubtedly helped him reach such a ripe old age. Meditation was his only pleasure, his almost habitual occupation. There exists a portrait of him (which is quite extraordinary, for Quakers reject paintings as useless), in which he is shown reading at the mouth of a cave, as an emblem indicating his love of solitude.

One of the most distinguished men in this career opened by humanity was another Quaker, John Woolman, born in 1720. Trained in meditation at an early age, he was considered by the Friends worthy to be a minister at the age of twenty-two. He traveled a great deal, spreading the doctrine of his brethren, but always on foot and without provisions, for he wished to emulate the apostles. Moreover he wished to serve those who most needed his teaching, particularly laborers and the unhappy slaves. He so

[5] [Samuel Sewall (1652–1730) published this memorial in Boston in 1700.]

[6] [Benjamin Lay (1677–1759), an eccentric opponent of slavery, was in fact born of Quaker parents. Brissot is referring to his *All Slave Keepers, That Keep the Innocent in Bondage, Apostates. . . .*]

abhorred the slave trade and Negro slavery that he always refused
to taste any food produced by slaves. Their cause, he used to tell
his friends, was always present in his thoughts, he could not put
it out of his mind, and both in public and in private he tried to
gain supporters for it. The last sermon he ever gave was on this
subject. In 1772 he made a voyage to England to see his Quaker
brethren. He died there of smallpox, leaving several good works
on slavery, such as *Considerations on the Keeping of Negroes,* of
which there are several editions.

I have thought I should give you, my dear friend, a few details
on these saintly men who are so little known in France before
discussing the condition of the Negroes in this immense country.

EFFORTS TO ABOLISH THE SLAVE TRADE IN THE UNITED STATES

The letters of recommendation with which I was honored by the French and English societies concerned with the fate of the Negroes have procured me a most flattering welcome and the communication of information which can enlighten us on the work of these societies. Unfortunately, too many things claim the attention of the hurried traveler, and I cannot go as deeply into these important matters as I should like.

Having written in my preceding letter of the noble men who have defended Negroes in America, I should now like to tell you what has been done here in order to have the slave trade abolished and to liberate and regenerate Negroes.[1] I shall explain what have been the results of these benevolent efforts and what plans have been made to ensure to Negroes for evermore the blessings of liberty.

Under the English government, Woolman and Benezet had labored in vain to have the slave trade abolished. A mistaken sense of national self-interest caused England to reject all their petitions. But the minds of men in the various states of America had been prepared, and as soon as independence was proclaimed a general outcry arose against this traffic. To men who were taking up arms to defend their own liberty it seemed inconsistent to rob other men of this same blessing. Opportunely, and to prove this point more completely, a pamphlet was printed in which the principles on which slavery was based were contrasted with those which formed the foundation of the new constitution.[2] This comparison

[1] Part of the following is reprinted from a paper I read before the Société des Amis des Noirs on February 9, 1789. I have made important additions and changes. Moreover, very few copies of the original printing of the speech were issued. [*Mémoire sur les Noirs de l'Amérique Septentrionale, lu à l'Assemblée de la Société des Amis des Noirs, le 9 février 1789,* Paris, 1789.]

[2] [Brissot is probably referring to *A Serious Address to the Rulers of America, on the Inconsistency of Their Conduct Respecting Slavery; Forming a Contrast Between the Encroachments of England on American Liberty, and American Injustice in Tolerating Slavery,* Trenton, 1783. This work is attributed to David Cooper.]

enjoyed a complete success, and the new Congress soon declared that Negro slavery was incompatible with the basic tenets of republican government,[3] a principle to which the various legislators hastened to give their adherence.

Three quite distinct stages can be noted in the revolution which is taking place in the American treatment of Negroes: first, the prohibition of the importation of slaves; second, their emancipation; and third, their education. Not all the states are equally advanced toward the attainment of these three objectives.

The importation of Negroes has been permanently prohibited in the Northern and Middle states, while in the others it has been limited to a certain period of time. In South Carolina, where the prohibition was to last only three years, it has just been renewed for three years more. Georgia is the only state which has not followed the example set by the others and which continues to import slaves. Yet when General Oglethorpe laid the foundations of that colony at the beginning of this century, he required and decreed that the importation of rum and slaves be forever forbidden. These prohibitions were soon violated; the poison of spirituous liquors was thought necessary to repair the spirits of the indolent colonists, and it was believed that whites could not work in the hot climate and that to till the soil it was necessary to import workers and that this justified slavery.[4]

When we examine the motives which have led the legislatures of the various states to prohibit the importation of Negroes, either permanently or for a limited number of years, let us be neither overly enthusiastic nor too critical. Undoubtedly, the selfish interests of the individual states have had a great influence in bringing about this revolution. The Northern and Southern [Middle?] states can certainly be suspected of having adopted this measure more quickly and enthusiastically because they have less need of slaves for the kinds of crops they raise, because their needs are more limited, and because their ever-rising population makes it unnecessary for them to recruit workers from abroad in order to

[3] See the resolution of Congress of October 8, 1774.

[4] This idea is beginning to disappear, even in Georgia. A Georgia plantation owner wrote in September 1790 the following remarkable words: "Now that peace has been re-established between us and the Creeks (a very large Indian tribe), the greatest prosperity is impending, and the vast stretches of land on both sides of the Altamaha will increase in value. Nothing is lacking here except workers. *If we can get the sort of white men who are not too proud to till the soil instead of slaves, who are both very scarce and very expensive,* the country will grow rich."

grow a quantity of agricultural products proportionate to their needs. Perhaps South Carolina's recently extended prohibition of the importation of slaves is due less to humanitarian than to political considerations, that is, to the legislators' conclusion that the citizens of the state already owed a great deal of money to England for cargoes of Negroes, and that further importations would ruin them.

On the other hand, let us be just and acknowledge that Americans are, more than any other nation, convinced that all men are born free and equal. Let us acknowledge that, on the whole, their actions are directed by this principle of equality. Let us acknowledge that the Quakers, who originated, propagated, and are still spreading this revolution, have been guided by religious principles and that they have sacrificed their own personal interests.

Unfortunately, their ideas have not yet become universal and are still being successfully resisted in the Southern states by the forces of self-interest. There is still a large party which maintains that it is impossible to cultivate the soil in the South without slave labor and that it is impossible to increase the number of slaves and to clear more lands without recruiting Negroes in Africa. The strenuous efforts of this party at the recent Convention were responsible for the only article which tarnishes that glorious monument to human reason, the new federal Constitution of the United States. It was this party that proposed to bind the hands of the new Congress and make it impossible for it to prohibit generally the importation of slaves for a period of twenty years. They told that august assembly, "Sign this article, or we withdraw from the Union." In view of the evils which such a political schism would have caused, without improving the lot of the slaves, the Convention was forced to depart from the great principle of universal liberty and from the earlier declarations of Congress. It decided it should imitate Solon and make not the best possible law, but the one most suitable to the circumstances.

This puzzling article has, in truth, caused great astonishment in Europe, where people were not informed of the hidden reasons behind it, and has greatly grieved the Society in England,[5] which, being uninformed of the local circumstances which dictated the decision, was ready to accuse the new legislators of cowardly defection. Nevertheless, the general and irrevocable proscription of

[5] [The Committee formed in 1787 by Clarkson, Wilberforce, and Sharp for the suppression of the slave trade.]

the slave trade in all the United States must be considered as very near at hand. It will come about both from the nature of things and from the above-mentioned article in the new Constitution. Indeed, nine out of the thirteen states have forbidden the importation of Negroes, and any Negroes who enter these states are free. Thus there are nine asylums open to the slaves brought into Georgia and to those who may be brought into the three other states, should they revoke their temporary proscriptions. In addition, there are the Floridas, owned by Spain, where slaves from Georgia constantly flee in hopes of being better treated by the Spaniards; and there are also the vast forests and the inaccessible mountains of the Southern states, where the persecuted Negro can easily escape from slavery. It is so easy everywhere for a man to make his way from any of the states into the back country that it is impossible to prevent slaves from escaping. The expense of pursuing them would be out of proportion with their value, and although the free states do not openly oppose such pursuit, in reality the people hold the slave trade and even slavery in such horror that the master in pursuit of his human property is never welcome, finds little assistance, and is almost always thwarted. So the possibility of escape, which raises the price of Negroes and the cost of their labor, is another deterrent operating against the importation of slaves. It is probable that Georgian and Carolinian planters will be persuaded by real losses of this sort that it is simpler, more reasonable, and less expensive to cultivate their lands with the help of Free Americans rather than with Africans. *The nature of the land here is opposed to slavery.* I was thus correct in saying that the nature of things in America is against the importation of Negroes.

Moreover, in twenty years Congress will be authorized to pronounce definitely on this matter. Then no doubt the sentiments of humanity and the calculations of reason will prevail. Then Congress will be free; it will no longer be forced to sacrifice equity to expediency and will no longer fear either strong opposition or secession. Nine states have already taken a stand in support of this law, and the admission of the state of Vermont will add a new and decisive vote. The Southern states will not be able either to form a formidable opposition (they cannot outweigh the North) or ask for an amendment, since for an amendment to be passed nine states or two thirds of both houses of Congress must vote in favor of it. One must therefore consider it certain that the prohibition of the importation of Negroes will become the law throughout the United States, at least in twenty years.

I must mention here a crime peculiar to the United States, conceived by the cupidity of the dealers in human flesh. Being unable to import any more Negro slaves, they attempt to kidnap those who are free and sell them in countries where they bring an established price. The English set the example for this horrible speculation during the last war. They used to steal Negroes from Americans and sell them in the West Indies. This was an injury both to the master and the slave, but especially to the latter, who was taken from a mild and tolerable servitude and placed under infernal tyranny, for at that time public opinion was still silent and had not forced the planters to treat their slaves better. At the end of the war, there were in America men barbarous enough to abduct, mainly from the rural areas, Negro women and children and sell them to captains of ships sailing for the islands. Under one pretext or another, Negroes were enticed aboard these ships, put in chains, and transported to the West Indies. The repetition of these crimes aroused the indignation of the societies organized for the protection of Negroes in America, and even the clergy added their voices in protest. The societies denounced the practice to all the state legislatures, and almost all have recently passed very severe laws against this theft of human beings. One of the most remarkable was enacted last October by the Connecticut General Assembly.

This same law is also aimed against another crime with which the legislators of Massachusetts and Pennsylvania have already dealt severely, a clandestine and indirect continuation of the slave trade. A merchant ships a cargo of rum from Boston to Guinea, where he buys or steals Negroes. He then sells these Negroes in the West Indies in exchange for sugar and molasses, which he then sells in the United States. I must pay homage to the American societies for the protection of Negroes, which, though they have been unable to prevent this trade, are making every possible effort to discourage it. I had a proof of this during my stay in Philadelphia. The owner of a cargo acquired through the sale of slaves had great trouble in finding a buyer, for his story was known, the word had been spread, and he was everywhere treated with the greatest contempt.

THE LAWS FOR THE EMANCIPATION OF SLAVES ENACTED BY THE VARIOUS STATES

Slavery, my friend, has not defiled all of the United States, as is generally believed. In New Hampshire and Massachusetts there have never been laws authorizing slavery and there are no slaves. Therefore when these states prohibited slavery they were merely declaring what already existed. In Connecticut there are few slaves. The austere Puritanism which reigns in that state could not be conciliated with slavery; and farming with free workers was more successful and cheaper than with slaves. So everything combined to induce the farmers to free their Negroes, and almost all have done so. The children of those that have not been liberated are to have their freedom when they are twenty-five years old, that is, when they have reached the age when they can take care of their own needs.

The condition of Negroes in the state of New York is about the same, although the number of slaves is larger. This is because the base of the population is made up of the Dutch, that is, of a people less willing than others to part with property. Nevertheless, freedom is assured to the children of slaves when they reach a certain age.

The slave trade in the state of Rhode Island was formerly very large. It is now forbidden and no longer exists, and a new law reaffirming the prohibition has recently been passed. Would to God that the wisdom which has guided the legislature of that state on this point had led it to abolish that horrible banditry, paper money, which has transformed Rhode Island from the most flourishing, the most active, and the most densely populated state into a wilderness where rules indolence side by side with poverty and dishonesty. Fortunately, and this is what makes hope possible, there are many Quakers on the island, that is to say, there are few slaves and a prevailing spirit of order and economy.

In the Jerseys the base of the population is Dutch, and consequently you often find traces of the Dutch character, which I have already described. The people in the western part of the state are, however, inclined toward emancipation; those in the eastern part are opposed. There is still hope of persuading the latter to change their minds; at least this was the feeling expressed by Mr. Livingston in a letter he wrote to the Philadelphia Society.[1] Mr. Livingston is a man respected and celebrated for the part he played in the Revolution, and he himself has freed all of his many slaves and is one of the most ardent apostles of emancipation. Being, however, familiar with the character of his fellow citizens and convinced that nothing can be gained by a frontal attack upon public opinion, he is willing to temporize, reason, and compromise in the hope of winning in the end.[2]

The Quakers have been more successful in Pennsylvania. As early as 1758 their General Meeting unanimously voted to expel any member of the society who persisted in keeping slaves. In 1780 at their request, seconded by a large number of supporters from other sects, the Pennsylvania General Assembly permanently abolished slavery, required owners to register their slaves, declared the children of slaves free at the age of twenty-eight, and until they reached that age raised them, with their consent, to the status of hired servants for a specified number of years, assured them the benefit of trial by jury, etc.

This law could not, however, foresee all the abuses and subterfuges to which the forces of greed would resort, and several of its provisions have been evaded. Greedy speculators continued the slave trade outside the state and barbarous masters sold their slaves in distant places. Others sent the children of slaves to neighboring states under various pretenses, but in reality to sell them and prevent them from benefiting by the law when they reached twenty-eight years of age. Others achieved the same purpose by a different means, namely, by sending pregnant Negro mothers to give birth in other states. Finally, as I have already mentioned, others abducted free Negroes and sold them in the West Indies.

The Pennsylvania Society, which keeps a close eye on the en-

[1] [The Pennsylvania Society for Promoting the Abolition of Slavery, for the Relief of Free Negroes Held in Bondage, and for Improving the Condition of the African Race.]

[2] Mr. [William] Livingston is better known in Europe for his criticism of the learned work by Mr. [John] Adams on constitutions [*A Defence of the Constitutions of Government of the United States of America*, London, 1787]. It has been translated into French and published with judicious notes by good political writers. This respected American died in 1790 and was mourned by the United States. [Brissot is referring to John Stevens' *Observations on Government*, which was erroneously attributed to Livingston. See note p. 154.]

forcement of the laws and which was aroused by these abuses, again petitioned the Assembly, which on the 29th of last March passed a new act to prevent effectively these evasions. It stated that a slave could not be sent to a neighboring state without his consent, imposed heavy fines on anyone who sent the child of a slave to another state in order to sell him, ordered the confiscation of ships engaged in the slave trade, condemned to hard labor those who abducted Negroes, etc.

It is, to be sure, impossible to bestow too much praise on the constant and indefatigable zeal of the Pennsylvania Society, which solicited this law, and on the spirit of equity and liberty which inspired the Pennsylvania Assembly with the humanitarian principles expressed during the debates preceding its enactment. Nevertheless we may be permitted to add to this well-deserved praise certain reservations. Why did this respectable assembly not go further? Why, for example, did it not grant freedom, or at least the hope of freedom, to Negroes who were slaves at the time of the enactment of the first law? They are property, it is said, and all property is sacred. But what can be the nature of a property obviously acquired by theft? What is the nature of a property contrary to divine and human laws? I am willing to grant that this property deserves some consideration, but why could not the right to it have been limited to a certain number of years? Why not grant the slave the right to buy his own freedom? What! The child of a Negro slave in Pennsylvania can hope to enjoy liberty some day and his master cannot withhold it from him when he has worked for him till the age of twenty-eight, yet the unhappy father of this child is forever deprived of his freedom! The son, who has not, like his father, suffered the pain and the despair of being torn from his native land, from his family, and from everything he holds dear, the son, who has not been racked by all the torments so common before the present reforms—this son is favored by the law! And this biased law condemns his father to lifelong misery! No! Such injustices cannot long sully the laws of a country where the voices of reason and humanity make themselves heard. We must hope that the day will come when the self-interest of the masters will be brought to terms and these enslaved fathers will be torn from their clutches.

Again, why is it stated in the law of March 1, 1780, that a slave may not bear witness against a free man? Either you believe that this slave is less truthful than a free man, or else you believe that he has a different nature and belongs to a species different from your own. The latter opinion is absurd; the former, if it be true, testifies against you. For why would he be less truthful, more corrupt, or more depraved? It is, without contradiction, because he is a slave. His crimes and his vices are on the head of his master. And the master punishes and degrades the slave for his own crime! What a horrible injustice!

Finally, how can this law make the concession of ordering that the master be reimbursed from the public treasury for the value of a slave condemned to death? If, as can be easily demonstrated, almost all a slave's crimes are the result of his more or less harsh enslavement, does it not seem absurd to recompense a master for his own tyranny? And when one recalls that masters have until now considered their Negroes as a kind of cattle and that according to long-established law the master is responsible for damage caused by his cattle, does it not seem inconsistent to pay the master the value of his black cattle which have caused damage to society and which society believes it has to exterminate? Are we then to pay the man responsible for the damage, instead of making him pay for it?

Let us have no doubts, these blots on Pennsylvania's Negro legislation will disappear. The State Assembly is too reasonable a body and the Pennsylvania Society too zealous a one for us not to have this hope.

The small state of Delaware has followed the example set by Pennsylvania. It is peopled in large part by Quakers, and manumissions have therefore increased. It is in this state, well known for the wisdom of its laws, the honesty of its people, and its loyalty to the Union, that dwells that angel of peace Warner Mifflin, of whom I have already written. Like Benezet, he devotes all his efforts to propagating the ideas of the Quakers on the necessity of freeing the Negroes and of providing for their support and their education. It is, in part, to his zeal that we owe the formation of a society [in Delaware] for the abolition of the slave trade and of slavery, organized on the model of the Pennsylvania Society.[3]

Legal protection of Negroes ends in Delaware. There are, however, a few freed Negroes in Maryland, for there are some Quakers in that state. If you compare the tobacco and corn fields of these

[3] [The Delaware Society for Promoting the Abolition of Slavery and for the Relief and Protection of Free Blacks and People of Colour Unlawfully Held in Bondage, organized in 1788.]

Quakers with the fields of other farmers you can easily see how superior free workers are to slaves for the development of agriculture.

When you travel through Maryland and Virginia you think you are in a different world, and you think so again when you speak with the people of these states. Here there is no talk of freeing the Negroes, no praise of the antislavery societies in London and America. Nobody reads Clarkson's works. Instead, everywhere indolent masters view with nothing but concern the efforts being made for universal emancipation. Virginians are convinced that it is impossible to grow tobacco without slaves, and they are afraid that if Negroes regain their freedom they will cause trouble. If the Negroes are freed they have no idea what place to assign them in society, whether to settle them in a separate county or to send them away. These are the objections that you hear repeated everywhere against the abolition of slavery.

The strongest obstacle to abolition is in the character, inclinations, and habits of Virginians. They like to live off the sweat of their slaves, to hunt, and to display their wealth without having to do any work. This way of life would change were there no longer any slaves, for the plantation owner would have to work himself. It is not that slave labor is more productive than other labor, but that by increasing the number of slaves, by feeding them badly, by not providing them with clothing, and by wasteful use of the best land, Virginians succeed in compensating for the lack of good workers.

THE GENERAL CONDITION OF
NEGROES IN THE UNITED STATES

In the four Northern [New England] states and in the Southern [Middle?] states, free Negroes are either domestic servants, small shopkeepers, or farmers. Some work on coasting vessels, but few dare to ship on long voyages because they are afraid of being carried off and sold in the West Indies.

Physically, these Negroes are in general vigorous. They have good constitutions, are able to perform the hardest labor, and are generally active.[1] As servants, they are sober and faithful. All these traits are equally characteristic of Negro women. I have not seen any distinction made in respect to these qualities between Negro and white servants, though the latter always treat Negroes with contempt as if they belonged to an inferior race.

Those who are shopkeepers earn a moderate living but never expand their businesses beyond a certain point. The simple reason is that, although Negroes are everywhere treated humanely, the whites, who have the money, are not willing to lend a Negro the capital necessary for a big commercial establishment. Moreover, to succeed in a larger enterprise, a certain amount of preliminary experience is necessary and one must have had training in a countinghouse; but the forces of reason have not yet opened to Negroes the doors of countinghouses, in which they are not allowed to sit down alongside a white man. If, then, Negroes here are limited to the small retail trade, let us not attribute it to their lack of ability but rather to the prejudices of the whites, who put obstacles in their way.

For the same reasons Negroes in the country cannot own large farms. Their fields are small but usually well cultivated. European travelers are impressed by their good clothes, their well-kept log houses, and their many children, while the eye of the philosopher lingers with pleasure on these homes where tyranny causes no tears to flow.

---

[1] Married Negroes certainly have as many children as whites, but it has been observed that in cities the death rate of Negro children is higher. This difference is due not so much to their constitutions as to poverty, neglect, and particularly to lack of medical care.

In this part of America Negroes are certainly happy, but let us have the courage to admit that their happiness and their abilities have not reached the levels they are capable of attaining. There still is too great a distance between them and the whites, especially in the eye of public opinion, and this humiliating barrier frustrates all the efforts they make to elevate themselves. This discrimination is apparent everywhere. For instance, Negro children are admitted to public schools but they cannot cross the threshold of a college. They themselves, even though they are free and independent, are still in the habit of considering themselves inferior to the whites, who have rights they do not have.[2] Thus, it would not be fair to estimate the nature and extent of Negroes' abilities on the basis of the achievements of the free Negroes in the North.

Yet when we compare them with the slaves in the Southern states, what a tremendous difference we find! The brutalized and degraded condition of the latter is difficult to describe. Many are naked, underfed, and forced to sleep on straw in miserable huts.[3] They receive no education and no religious instruction whatsoever. They are not married, but coupled. The result is that they are brutish and lazy, lack energy, and have no ideas. They will not go to any trouble to get themselves clothes or better food, pre-

[2] The aversion the whites have toward their daughters' marrying Negroes would in itself be enough to give a sense of humiliation. There are, however, a few examples of such marriages. In Pittsburgh there is a white woman of French origin who had been taken to London as a child and who at the age of twelve had been abducted by pirates who made a practice of kidnapping children and selling them in America for a fixed period of service. Through some strange circumstances this young woman married a Negro, who purchased her freedom and rescued her from a barbaric and libidinous white master who had made every effort to seduce her. Their child, a mulatto girl, married a surgeon from Nantes who had settled in Pittsburgh. This family is one of the most respected ones in the city. The Negro husband has a prosperous business, and his wife makes a point of welcoming and being kind to foreigners, especially Frenchmen that chance brings to that part of the world. In the North, however, such a marriage would be considered revolting. In the settlements along the Ohio there are many Negresses living with unmarried white men, but I was told that such unions are frowned upon even by the Negroes themselves. When a Negress quarrels with a mulatto woman, the insult she hurls at the latter is her mixed blood.

[3] Dr. [Benjamin] Rush, who has had the opportunity to treat these Southern Negroes, shared with me a very important observation which proves how much the moral and intellectual energy of a man influences his health and physical condition. He told me that it is much more difficult to treat and to cure Negro slaves than white people and that the Negroes have much less resistance to serious and prolonged illnesses. This is so because they do not have the will to live; they are virtually without vitality and life force.

ferring to wear rags rather than mend them. Sunday, their day of rest, they spend doing absolutely nothing. Total inactivity is their supreme happiness, and as a consequence they do little work and perform their tasks listlessly.

In all fairness, I must admit that Southerners do not treat their slaves harshly; this is one of the effects of the general diffusion of the idea of liberty. Everywhere the slave works less, but that is all. Neither his food, nor his clothing, nor his morality, nor his thinking has improved; thus the master is the loser but the slave gains nothing. If Southerners followed the example set by Northerners, both slaves and masters would benefit by the change.

In describing Negroes of the South, a careful distinction must be made between those who work in the fields and those who work as house servants. The preceding description applies only to the former; the others, few in number, are generally better clad, more energetic, and less ignorant.

It has been popularly believed until recently that Negroes are intellectually inferior to whites. Even respectable writers have supported this theory.[4] This prejudice is now beginning to disappear, and the Northern states can furnish examples to prove its falsity. I shall cite only two striking cases, the first proving that through education Negroes can be made fit for any profession, and the second showing that a Negro's brain can accomplish the most astonishing mathematical calculations and can, therefore, deal with all the sciences.

During my stay in Philadelphia I saw a Negro named James Derham, a doctor who practices in New Orleans.[5] His life story, confirmed by several doctors, is as follows: He was born in a family in Philadelphia, in which he was taught to read and write, and instructed in the principles of Christianity. When a boy he was transferred by his master to the late Dr. John Kearsley, Jr. of Philadelphia,[6] who employed him to compound medicines and to

---

[4] I have already refuted this idea several times, especially in my *Examen critique des Voyages de M. Chatellux*. The argument has, moreover, been invalidated in a large number of excellent works.

[5] [James Derham (b. 1762) appears to be the first Negro physician of which there is any record. The following sketch of his life was translated by Brissot, with a number of changes, from a paper read by Dr. Benjamin Rush to the Pennsylvania Society for Promoting the Abolition of Slavery, on January 5, 1789, and published in the *American Museum*, 5 (1789), 61–62. The reported conversation between Brissot and Dr. Wistar is fictitious; Wistar's purported words are taken, like everything else in these paragraphs, from Rush's paper.]

[6] [Dr. John Kearsley was the founder of Christ Church Hospital in Philadelphia and helped draw the plans for Independence Hall.]

administer them to his patients. Upon the death of Dr. Kearsley, he became (after passing through several hands) the property of Dr. George West, surgeon to the Sixteenth British Regiment, under whom, during the late war in America, he performed many of the menial duties of medicine. At the close of the war, he was sold by Dr. West to Dr. Robert Dove of New Orleans, who employed him as an assistant in his business, in which capacity he gained so much of his master's confidence and friendship that Dr. Dove consented to liberate him, after two or three years, upon easy terms. By his numerous opportunities of improving in medicine Derham became so well acquainted with the healing art as to commence practicing in New Orleans with success. He is now about twenty-six years of age, has a wife but no children and does business to the amount of $3,000, or about 16,000 livres, a year.

"I conversed with him," Dr. Wistar [7] told me, "upon the acute and epidemic diseases of the country where he lives and found him perfectly acquainted with the modern simple mode of practice in these diseases. I expected to have suggested some new medicines to him; but he suggested many more to me." He is very modest and engaging in his manners. He speaks French fluently and has some knowledge of the Spanish language. By some accident, although born in a religious family, he was not baptized in his infancy, in consequence of which he applied to Dr. Withe [White] [8] to receive baptism. He found him qualified, both by knowledge and moral conduct, to be admitted to baptism.

The other case was reported to me by Dr. Rush, a famous doctor and writer of Philadelphia, who has published an account of it.[9] Several of the details have since been confirmed by the wife of the immortal Washington, in whose neighborhood this Negro has long been living.

Thomas Fuller was born in Africa and can neither read nor write.[10] He is now seventy years old and has lived all his life on Mrs. Cox's plantation, four miles from Alexandria. Two gentlemen, natives of Pennsylvania, Messrs. [William H.] Hartshorne and Samuel Coates, having heard in traveling in Virginia of his

[7] [Dr. Caspar Wistar (1761–1818), a Philadelphia physician and anatomist.]

[8] [Dr. William White of the Protestant Episcopal Church in Philadelphia.]

[9] This doctor is also famous in America for his excellent political writings. He is an indefatigable apostle of liberty.

[10] [Thomas Fuller, or "Negro Tom," was brought from Africa at the age of fourteen and died in 1790. The following paragraphs on Fuller are, in the original, a slightly abbreviated translation into French of an account published in the *American Museum*, 5 (1789), 62–63. We have given the original English text, with such deletions and additions as Brissot chose to make.]

extraordinary powers in arithmetic, sent for him, and had their curiosity sufficiently gratified by the answers which he gave to the following questions:

First. Upon being asked how many seconds there are in a year and a half, he answered, in about two minutes, 47,304,000, counting 365 days in the year.

Second. On being asked how many seconds a man has lived who is seventy years, seventeen days and twelve hours old, he answered, in a minute and a half, 2,210,500,800. One of the gentlemen, who employed himself with his pen in making these calculations, told him he was wrong, and that the sum was not so great as he said. This was true, because Fuller had overlooked the leap years, but with the greatest speed he corrected his figures.[11]

Third. Suppose a farmer has six sows and each sow has six female pigs the first year, and they all increase in the same proportion to the end of eight years, how many sows will the farmer then have? In ten minutes, he answered 34,588,806. The difference of time between his answering this and the two former questions was occasioned by a trifling mistake he had made from a misapprehension of the question.

After he had correctly answered all the questions, he told how he had discovered and developed his arithmetical talent. He began his application to figures by counting ten, and then when he was able to count a hundred, he thought himself (to use his own words) "a very clever fellow." He next amused himself counting, grain by grain, a bushel of wheat. From this he was led to calculate how many rails were necessary to enclose and how many grains of corn were necessary to sow a certain quantity of ground. From this application of his talents his mistress has often derived considerable benefit, and he spoke of her with great respect and mentioned in a particular manner his obligations to her for refusing to sell him, which she had been tempted to do by offers of large sums of money. He said his memory was beginning to fail him. When one of the gentlemen remarked in his presence that it was a pity he had not had an education equal to his genius, he said: "No, massa, it is best I got no learning; for many learned men be great fools."

[11] [We have translated the last sentence as Brissot wrote it, but he had misunderstood the English original, which read: ". . . not so great as he said—upon which the old man hastily replied, ' 'Top, massa, you forget de leap year.' On adding the seconds of the leap years to the others, the amount of the whole in both their sums agreed exactly." *American Museum*, 5, 62.]

These examples prove beyond a doubt that the mental capacity of Negroes is equal to any task, and that all they need is education and freedom. The difference between those who are free and educated and those who are not can also be seen in their work. The lands of both whites and Negroes in the free states, as for example in Connecticut or Pennsylvania, are infinitely better cultivated, produce larger crops, and present in general an impression of well-being and contentment. But cross over into Maryland and Virginia, and, as I have said before, you think you are in a different world. No longer will you see well-cultivated fields, neat and even elegant farmhouses, large, well-designed barns, and big herds of fat, healthy cattle. Everything in Maryland and in Virginia bears the stamp of slavery: the parched soil, the badly managed farming, the ramshackled houses, and the few scrawny cattle that look like walking skeletons. In short, you find real poverty existing alongside a false appearance of wealth.

Even in the Southern states men are beginning to see that it is poor economy to feed a slave badly, and that capital invested in slaves does not pay its interest. The introduction of free labor into a part of Virginia, in the area along the lovely Shenandoah River, may be due more to these considerations and particularly to the economic impossibility of importing more slaves than to humanitarian motives. When you see the Shenandoah you think you are still in Pennsylvania.

Let us hope that all of Virginia will look like this in the perhaps not distant future, when it is no longer sullied by slavery. There are slaves in Virginia only because it is believed that they are necessary for raising tobacco. But this crop is decreasing every day in this state and will continue to decrease. The tobacco grown near the Ohio and Mississippi is infinitely more plentiful, of better quality, and requires less labor. When it finds an outlet to the European market, Virginians will be forced to abandon this crop and raise instead wheat, potatoes, and cattle. Intelligent Virginians are anticipating this change and are beginning to grow wheat.

Chief among them must be listed that astonishing man who, though a beloved general, had the courage to be a sincere republican and who is the only one not to remember his own glory, a hero whose unique destiny it will be to save his country twice and to open for it the road to prosperity after having set it on the road to liberty. Now *wholly* occupied with improving his land, developing new crops, and building roads, he is giving to his fellow citizens a useful example which will no doubt be followed.[12] Nevertheless he does own, I am forced to say, large numbers of Negro slaves. They are, however, most humanely treated. Well fed, well clothed, and required to do only a moderate amount of work, they continually bless the master God gave them. It would undoubtedly be fitting that such a lofty, pure, and disinterested soul be the one to make the first step in the abolition of slavery in Virginia. This great man, when I had the honor to talk with him, told me that he admired everything that was being done in the other states and that he desired the extension of the movement in his own. But he did not conceal the fact that there are still many obstacles and that it would be dangerous to make a frontal attack on a prejudice which is beginning to decrease. "Time, patience, and education," he said, "and it will be overcome. Nearly all Virginians," he added, "are convinced that the general emancipation of Negroes cannot occur in the near future, and for this reason they do not wish to organize a society which might give their slaves dangerous ideas." Another obstacle which he pointed out is that most of this part of the country is made up of large plantations and people live far apart, so that it is difficult to hold meetings.

"Virginians are wrong," I told him. "It is evident that sooner or later Negroes will win their freedom everywhere, and that this revolution will extend to Virginia. It is therefore to the interest of your fellow citizens to prepare for it and to try to reconcile the restitution of the Negroes' rights with their own right to property. The necessary steps can only be worked out by a society, and it would be fitting that the savior of America be its head and restore liberty to 300,000 unhappy inhabitants of his country." This great man told me that he was in favor of the formation of such a society and that he would support it, but that he did not believe the moment was favorable. No doubt there were greater problems which demanded his attention and preoccupied him at the time; America's destiny was about to be placed a second time in his hands.

It is certainly a misfortune that no such society exists in Maryland or Virginia, for it is to the constant zeal of those in Philadel-

---

[12] Washington was not at that time President of the United States. I am anticipating here several conversations which I had with this great man and which I shall describe subsequently.

phia and New York that we owe the progress of this revolution in America and the birth of the society in London.[13]

Would that I were able here to describe to you the impressions that crowded upon me as I attended the meetings of these three societies! How earnest were the faces of the members! How simple were their speeches! How frank were their discussions! What benevolence! What strength in their resolution! Everyone was eager to take part, not in order to shine, but in order to be of use. How great was their joy when they learned that a society similar to theirs was being formed in Paris, in that immense capital, so famous in America for its opulence, for its pomp, and for its influence over a vast kingdom and over almost all the states of Europe! How quickly did they publish this news in all their gazettes and circulate everywhere the translation of the first speech read before the Paris society! [14] How great was their joy when they saw on the list of members of that society a name dear to their hearts, one which they pronounce only with affection,[15] as well as the names of other persons known for their energy and patriotism! They were certain that if this society grew, if it faced the obstacles bravely, and if it united with the London society, then the information spread by these two groups on the slave trade and its unprofitable infamy would enlighten governments and persuade them to suppress the traffic.

It was no doubt this enthusiasm, and also the flattering recommendations I had brought with me from Europe, rather than my own feeble achievements, which won me the honor of being elected a member of these societies. They did not however limit themselves merely to words and gestures of support; they appointed committees to assist me in my work and opened their archives to me.

[13] [The Society for the Relief of Free Negroes Unlawfully Held in Bondage was founded in Philadelphia in 1775. It was revived in 1784 and reorganized in 1787 as The Pennsylvania Society for Promoting the Abolition of Slavery, the Relief of Free Negroes Unlawfully Held in Bondage, and for Improving the Condition of the African Race. The New York Abolition Society was established in 1785, and in London the Society for the Abolition of the Slave Trade was organized in 1787 under the presidency of Granville Sharp.]

[14] ["An Oration Upon the Necessity of Establishing at Paris a Society to Promote the Abolition of the Trade and Slavery of the Negroes," in Thomas Clarkson, An Essay on the Impolity of the African Slave Trade (Philadelphia, 1789), pp. 135-155.]

[15] [Lafayette.]

These beneficent societies are at present engaged in new projects to achieve their humanitarian ends and are endeavoring to create new societies in the states where there are none, as in Delaware, where one has just been organized.[16] They are also working on new ways to discourage slavery and the slave trade. For example, in order to put a stop to the shameful public auctions of slaves still held in the state of New York, all members have undertaken never to employ the services of any public auctioneer who presides over such sales.[17] The Philadelphia society is particularly ingenious in rescuing slaves from the hands of rapacious owners who have no right to hold them. If a slave is mistreated by his master, the society provides him with sure and free protection. If a slave has completed his time of servitude and is still detained by his master, the society demands that his rights be respected. Should strangers bring Negroes into the state and not comply with the provisions of the law, the society sees to it that these poor Negroes receive the legal benefits to which they are entitled. One of the best-known lawyers in Philadelphia, whose talents I admire and of whose friendship I am very proud, Mr. Miers Fisher, donates his services to the society and is almost always successful in the cases he undertakes.[18] The society, having observed that many associations become ineffective because they become too large, has formed several committees which function permanently. It encourages the organization of similar committees in all the states to press for the enforcement of the laws forbidding the slave trade and regulating the freeing of slaves, and to keep submitting to the legislatures petitions for new laws to meet unforeseen cases. I have no doubt that the activities of this society will eventually lead to the formation of similar societies in the South.

[16] [See p. 230.]

[17] At the meeting of the New York Society on November 9, 1787, a resolution was passed to award a gold medal for the best oration delivered at the commencement of the College of New York on the subject of the injustice and cruelty of the slave trade and on the harmful effects of slavery.

[18] [Miers Fisher, a distinguished Quaker lawyer, became a devoted friend of Brissot, with whom he continued to correspond after Brissot's return to France, and later of François and Nancy Dupont, Brissot's brother- and sister-in-law. In one of the last letters Brissot wrote before his execution he asked François and Nancy, then in the United States, to convey "un souvenir de moi à Miers et à sa femme." In 1819 Miers Fisher, still loyal to this memory, wrote Nancy of the death in Albany, N.Y., of Sylvain, Brissot's son. See Brissot's own character sketch of Fisher, pp. 304–305.]

THE CONDITION OF NEGROES

My hopes have not been disappointed; the progress made by the various societies in the United States has been rapid. One has even been established finally in Virginia,[20] where men have dared to declare openly the truth which has so often put greed to shame, the truth which formerly would have been stifled in a Bastille, though it is taught by the Bible: *That God created men of all nations, of all languages, and of all colors equally free, and that slavery, in any form and in any degree, is a violation of divine law and a degradation of human nature.*

Let us have faith, my friend, that this truth, published in every journal, will succeed in extirpating this odious slavery, which is in fact already being rapidly destroyed by the very nature of things. For you may well imagine that in this mania of migration, which has seized all the United States, Negroes find it easy to flee from slavery and are welcomed wherever they go.

The solemn examples set by great men will greatly contribute toward bringing about this revolution in public opinion. What slaveowner can escape feeling the shadow of shame fall upon him from the actions of the famous General Gates, who called together his numerous slaves and amidst their tears and expressions of love set them all free, but in a way which would prevent the fatal consequences that the enjoyment of this inestimable blessing might bring upon them? [21]

The Philadelphia Society, which may be considered as the mother of these holy institutions, has just adopted some very effective means of providing for the education of Negroes and their preparation for various occupations. In "An Address to the Public" it states: "The unhappy man, who has long been treated as a brute animal, too frequently sinks beneath the common standard of the human species. The galling chains, that bind his body, do also fetter his intellectual faculties, and impair the social

[19] It seemed to me necessary to introduce this addition here in order to complete the history of these important societies.

[20] [The Virginia Society for Promoting the Abolition of Slavery, organized under the Quaker leadership of Robert Pleasants about 1790.]

[21] [General Horatio Gates (1728–1806), who in 1790 freed the slaves on his Virginia plantation.]

affections of his heart." [22] The great objectives of the Philadelphia Society are to educate and advise Negroes who have been freed and to make them capable of exercising and enjoying civic freedom; to awaken in them industriousness; to provide them with occupations suitable to their age, sex, abilities, and other circumstances; and finally, to procure for their children an education suitable to the kind of life they will lead. To achieve these objectives, the society has appointed four committees:

I. A Committee of Inspection, who shall superintend the morals, general conduct, and ordinary situation of the free Negroes, and afford them advice and instruction, protection from wrongs, and other friendly offices.

II. A Committee of Guardians, who shall place out children and young people with suitable persons, that they may learn some trade or other business of subsistence.

III. A Committee of Education, who shall superintend the school instruction of the children and youth of free blacks.

IV. A Committee of Employ, who shall endeavor to procure constant employment for those free Negroes who are able to work.[23]

What friend of humanity will not rejoice at such a pious and sublime project? Who can fail to see that it is dictated by that perseverance which inspires earnest men induced to do good not by vanity but by a sense of duty? Such are the men who compose these American societies.[24] They will not abandon this good cause until they have carried it to the highest degree of perfection, that is, until they have by the most moderate and equitable means succeeded in making Negroes the equals of whites in every respect. Yet these are the holy societies which the infamous forces of greed are not ashamed to slander!

The protectors of the Negroes in Pennsylvania let nothing escape their solicitous attention. Some slaveowners were taking advantage of a provision in the law of 1780 to force the children

[22] [From "An Address to the Public; From the Pennsylvania Society for Promoting the Abolition of Slavery, and the Relief of Free Negroes Unlawfully Held in Bondage," November 9, 1789, signed by the Society's president, Benjamin Franklin. See The Writings of Benjamin Franklin, ed. A. H. Smyth (New York, 1907), X, 67.]

[23] [The descriptions of these committees were taken from Franklin's "Plan for Improving the Condition of Free Blacks." See Writings, X, 128.]

[24] Such also are the respectable Moravians, who have successfully educated and trained so many Negroes and Indians in the West Indies.

of their slaves, who had been freed by this act, to serve them until the age of twenty-eight instead of twenty-one. The society successfully fought for the correction of this abuse; now such children will serve their masters as servants only until the age of twenty-one.

It is to be hoped that this society will also find a way to improve the situation of those unhappy slaves who do not fall under the categories specified by the law of 1780. These wretches have no other choice but to die of grief or seek freedom by running away, which is what frequently happens.

These societies have succeeded so well in propagating and publishing their principles that this year (1790) a kind of peaceful revolution took place in Congress, where a demand was made for the repeal of that article in the Constitution which suspends for twenty years any legislation by Congress generally prohibiting the slave trade.

I should have mentioned earlier that the Philadelphia Society submitted to the Constitutional Convention a very eloquent address, which met with no success whatsoever, and from which I quote the conclusion:

By all the attributes of the Deity, which are offended by this inhuman traffic;

By the union of our whole species in a common Ancestor, and by all the obligations which result from it;

By the apprehensions and terror of the righteous vengeance of God in national judgments;

By the certainty of the great and awful day of retribution;

By the efficacy of the prayers of good men, which would only insult the Majesty of Heaven if offered up in behalf of our country while the iniquity we deplore continues among us;

By the sanctity of the Christian name;

By the pleasures of domestic connections, and the pangs which attend their dissolution;

By the captivity and sufferings of our American brethren in Algiers, which seem to be intended by Divine Providence to awaken us to a sense of the injustice and cruelty of dooming our African brethren to perpetual slavery and misery;

By a regard to the consistency of principle and conduct which should mark the citizens of republics;

By the magnitude and intensity of our desires to promote the happiness of those millions of intelligent beings who will probably cover this immense continent with rational life;

And by every other consideration that religion, reason, policy, and humanity can suggest, the Society implore the present Convention to make the suppression of the African slave trade in the United States a part of their important deliberations.[25]

Congress has been flooded by letters from all parts of the United States, signed by the most worthy men. Never was a question more hotly debated. What was unprecedented in America was that the most atrocious invectives were uttered by the adversaries of humanity. You can well imagine that these adversaries were the representatives from the South, with the exception, however, of the virtuous Madison and especially of Mr. Vining, brother of that respectable American lady so unjustly insulted by M. Chastellux.[26] Mr. Vining has defended the cause of liberty with vehement eloquence. Nor must I fail to mention among the defenders of the Negroes Messrs. Scott, Gerry, and Boudinot.[27]

You will no doubt be astonished to find among their adversaries the man who first denounced the Cincinnati, Mr. Burke, who so forcefully demonstrated the fatal consequences of the inequality which that order would introduce among the citizens of the United States.[28] This same man defended the much more revolting inequality established between whites and Negroes. You will be even more surprised to learn that he has nearly always employed invective. This is the weapon which the partisans of the slave trade and of slavery have always used in America, in England, and in France. Thus greed takes the same appearance everywhere, it respects nothing in its rage, and it thinks that insults are argu-

[25] ["To the Honourable the Convention of the United States Now Assembled in the City of Philadelphia. The Memorial of the Pennsylvania Society for Promoting the Abolition of Slavery, etc." Philadelphia, June 2, 1787. MS in the library of the Historical Society of Pennsylvania.]

[26] [John Vining (1758–1802), member of the Continental Congress, senator, and brother of Mary Vining, of whom Chastellux wrote: "I met a rather ridiculous woman who nevertheless is a well-known figure in Philadelphia. This was Miss V——, famous for her coquetry, her wit, and her spitefulness. She is thirty years old and seems to have no idea of getting married. Meanwhile she puts red, white, and blue and every other possible color on her face, wears the most extraordinary dresses and hairdos, and like a good Whig puts no limits upon her own liberty." *Voyages* (Paris, 1786), I, 264–265. Chastellux was right, for Miss Vining maintained her independence to the end and died an old maid.]

[27] [Gustavus Scott (1753–1801) of Maryland, Elbridge Gerry (1744–1814) of Massachusetts, and Elias Boudinot (1740–1821) of New Jersey.]

[28] [Aedanus Burke of South Carolina, *Considerations on the Society, or Order of Cincinnati* . . . , Philadelphia, 1783. The translation, or rather imitation, of this work by Mirabeau and Chamfort, *Considérations sur l'Ordre de Cincinnatus*, London, 1784, which included material supplied by Franklin and was written at his suggestion, was one of the important attacks in France on the principle of aristocracy during the period just prior to the French Revolution.]

ments. Serious men and thoughtful statesmen have felt only pity for these mad tantrums, so there is little doubt that during its December session Congress will finally reach a decision in favor of humanity.

One of the most ardent advocates of the cause before Congress is the worthy Warner Mifflin, whose zeal has been repaid with the most atrocious calumny. Yet what is his answer? Patience, kindness, forgiveness, and logic. I cannot resist the pleasant temptation of quoting here a few fragments from a letter written by this man of peace to one of his most vicious enemies, whom Mifflin wished to see and attempt to convert and who refused absolutely to receive him.

Friend,

I can call thee by this name for thou hast not offended me in spite of what thou hast said of our society; I love thee, I wish thee happiness, I wish thee no more ill than I wish for myself . . .

Thou wouldst not let me visit thee; thou fearest perchance lest I corrupt thy slaves . . . far from me this thought, I would not render them dissatisfied with their lot. It is not that I am unaware that most of them know full well that their slavery is against all principle; but whenever I have the opportunity, I tell them to be patient, to be resigned, to expect all things from God and their liberty from the law. I have often met slaves a hundred miles from the houses of their masters, fleeing from their servitude. I preached to them, I exhorted them to return; I gave them money and letters requesting that they not be punished; their masters have thanked me. This is the man that thou fearest. Our brothers do as I do whenever the occasion presents itself.

For a long time I believed that one could own slaves; I was raised in this prejudice, my cradle was surrounded by slaves; but God has enlightened me, and I have obeyed Him. "Thou shalt love," He tells us, "thy neighbor as thyself." This commandment includes all the children of Adam, whatever be their color, whatever be the language they speak.

My conduct for the last sixteen years since I set my Negroes free has not belied my profession of faith on these matters. I have since set free as many more as it has been in my power to do. I do not say this in order to boast, but to show thee that I have been constant in my practices and my principles regarding the slave trade and slavery, and that I have sought every way to expiate the part I formerly had in the latter of these crimes. Ah, what crime is blacker! . . . I can hardly bear to think of it, as I wrote the other day to my dear wife. What if she and I had been thus seized, cast into a ship, and condemned to be separated from each other in the West Indies! A horrible idea! So I always put myself in the place of these poor Negroes. Canst thou find it surprising that I plead their cause warmly and that I do so constantly?

MAPLE SUGAR AS A SUBSTITUTE FOR CANE SUGAR

On this continent, defiled and most cruelly tortured by slavery, Providence seems to have placed two powerful means for the inevitable destruction of this evil, namely, the societies of which I have written and the sugar maple.

Of all the various plants containing sugar, the maple, next to sugar cane, produces the largest amount. This tree is native to the United States and seeds itself very easily, especially in the North. The whole of America seems to be covered with maples, from Canada to Virginia, where they begin to become rare but are still plentiful in the back country. This valuable tree for a long time compensated the happy settlers in this part of the world for their lack of the choice sugar of the French West Indies. They inherited this resource from the Indians, who have so often been repaid with death for their gifts to the white men.

The Canadian Indians mixed maple sugar with wheat or corn flour and made a very nutritious kind of dough which they carried for food on long trips. Kalm, who reports this fact, says that sugar is also made from a kind of birch, which does not, however, yield as much as the maple.[1] Settlers living in the American forests have up to the present time limited themselves to a very simple procedure for gathering the sap and producing a coarse brown sugar; but now that the Quakers think they have discovered in this tree a substitute for cane sugar and a weapon against the slave trade and have pointed out the necessity of bettering the quality, more attention has been given to the methods of preparation, and success has crowned these efforts.

You know, my friend, all the conditions necessary for raising cane sugar, the constant and varied care that it requires, the diseases and accidents to which the plant is subject, and the heavy labor of the unhappy Negroes in gathering the cane and manu-

---

[1] [Peter Kalm's *En Resa til Norra America* (Stockholm, 1753–1761), translated into English, *Travels in North America* (Warrington and London, 1770–1771), and abridged and adapted by Rousselot de Surgy in his *Histoire naturelle et politique de la Pensylvanie* (1768), was a frequently cited authority on the British colonies.]

facturing the sugar. Compare these disadvantages with the advantages offered by maple sugar, and you will be convinced once again that men often go to a great deal of trouble in order to commit unnecessary crimes. Maples grow wild and the extraction of the sap requires no preparatory work. It flows in March, at a time when bad weather normally prevents farmers from working. Each tree yields quite easily without being harmed fifty to sixty pints of sap, which produces at least five pounds of sugar. A man with the help of three or four children, either girls or boys, can easily make fifteen hundred pounds of sugar during the three or four weeks that the sap is flowing.[2] His helpers need only be able to carry the buckets and keep a small fire burning under the kettles in which the sap is boiled down. If a tree is tapped with care it can produce for several years.

All these advantages have inevitably impressed the enemies of slavery here. Consequently, independently of the antislavery societies, an association has been formed whose special purpose it is to perfect the production of maple sugar. From the very start it has been very successful.

Mr. Drinker of Philadelphia [3] last spring produced sixty barrels [4] of maple sugar from trees on his lands on the Delaware, and he has published a pamphlet on the methods which he has found to be the best.

Edward Pennington, now of Philadelphia but formerly a sugar refiner in the West Indies, thinks that maple sugar is equal to cane sugar from the islands in texture, color, and taste. The chemist Benjamin Rush, whom I have already mentioned, sees nothing

---

[2] M. Lanthenas, one of the worthiest men among those who have devoted themselves to the defense of Negroes, who has most strongly recommended the cultivation of the maple tree in France, has made the following calculations which cannot be too often repeated: "If, as has been estimated, a family can produce 1,500 pounds of maple sugar in a season, about 80,000 families could produce without any trouble, so to speak, a quantity of sugar equal to that exported from Santo Domingo in the most productive years, which seems to be 122 million pounds. This would suppose 25 million trees, at 5 pounds per tree, which is the estimated yield. Taking the American acre to equal only 38,476 French square feet and assuming that the trees are planted seven feet apart, an area of about 32,000 acres would be sufficient to produce this quantity of sugar." [François Lanthenas (1754–1799) was a friend of Brissot and the Rolands and an ardent member of the Société des Amis des Noirs.]

[3] Some of the facts given below date from 1789 and 1790 and were written to me by friends in Philadelphia. I did not wish to separate them from this letter, to which they pertain. [Henry Drinker was a prominent Quaker merchant.]

[4] Each barrel weighs about 300 pounds.

extraordinary in this. He believes cane sugar and maple sugar to be of the same nature.

I myself tasted some maple sugar at the home of the good Quaker whose farm I have described earlier [5] and who because of religious scruples refuses to eat West Indian sugar. It seemed to me little different from our coarse brown product, and I have no doubt that when the methods of preparation are perfected it will be as good as ordinary sugar. I have been told by reliable persons that even some planters in Jamaica, where some maple sugar was taken, came to the same conclusion.

The state of Pennsylvania is not the only one in which strong efforts are being made to perfect the production of maple sugar; New York farmers are aware of all the advantages of this industry. They have produced this year a quantity of sugar in Cooperstown on Lake Oswego [Otsego].

If only a holy coalition, a holy competition were organized from north to south to increase the production from this divine tree! If, above all, it were considered impious to cut down such a useful plant, either for firewood or in order to clear the land,[6] America would be able not only to supply her own needs but would flood the markets of Europe with a product priced so low that it would drive out the sugar produced by the tears and blood of slaves, for it would cost only about six sous a pound.

How much will this revolution be hastened if the maple is naturalized throughout all Europe! [7] In America it grows in vast forests, but in France the trees could be planted in orchards, under which it would also be possible to grow all kinds of fruits. Spaced regularly twenty feet apart, at least one hundred and forty maples could be grown on one acre. A tree of average age yields three pounds of sugar, which would come to 420 pounds to the acre. At a selling price of six sous a pound, the net profit, after deducting half for labor, transportation, and other expenses, would be sixty-three *livres tournois* per acre, not including the return from other crops, which the maples would not in any way prevent from being grown on the same land. I could reasonably increase these figures, but I prefer to give the lowest estimate.

Thus we should obtain a large quantity of sugar, which would

[5] [Mr. Richardson. See Letter 10.]
[6] Figures have been published indicating that three million maple trees are destroyed annually in the state of New York alone.
[7] Maples have been planted in the garden of M. Noailles [Louis, Vicomte de Noailles?] at Saint Germain and have done well.

reduce by that much the lashings the Negroes have to endure to grow sugar cane to satisfy our gluttony. Why is it that in our great cities, where delicacy of sentiment is often as great as refinement of senses, no society has been formed to speed the arrival of the day when it will be possible to put sugar in our coffee without being saddened by the thought of all the toil, sweat, tears, suffering, and crimes that have hitherto been necessary to procure this product for us? Such thoughts cannot fail to present themselves a thousand times to the imagination of every man with any education or humanity.

Had Americans acquired all the means which are available to Europeans, they would have undoubtedly brought about in a very few years this glorious revolution. They would have saved our bigots and our ignorant and inhuman priests, always great lovers of sugar and coffee, from the horrible part they play in the most enormous crime the sun has ever shone upon. In consuming these products, do they not, in effect, join hands with the blind or perverse men who take a more active part in the iniquities without which these products would not be produced? Yet with what coldness, with what culpable indifference did these pious men look upon the establishment of our Société des Amis des Noirs!

A PLAN TO TRANSPORT AMERICAN NEGROES BACK TO AFRICA

I have already briefly mentioned to you, my friend, Dr. [William] Thornton's ideas on this subject.[1] This energetic friend of the Negroes is convinced that we cannot hope to see a sincere union between them and the whites in the United States as long as the difference in color exists and as long as both do not enjoy the same rights. He does not attribute to any other causes the sort of apathy to which many Negroes are reduced, even in Massachusetts, where they enjoy great freedom. Deprived of the hope of suffrage and of being elected to the legislature, or of rising to any position of responsibility or honor, they are condemned either to drag out their days as domestic servants or to languish as small shopkeepers. The citizens of that state reproach them for being dirty and indolent and for neglecting their children. Yet how can they be expected to be active and industrious when an insurmountable barrier separates them from other citizens and when prejudice has marked a point beyond which they are forbidden to rise? I am not certain that a lasting and sincere union could be achieved even if Negroes were admitted to all the privileges enjoyed by other citizens. We have so strong a tendency to love those who resemble us and to prefer them to those who are different from us! There would always be between whites and Negroes jealousy, suspicions of partiality, and perpetually recurrent disagreements. We must therefore come back to Mr. Thornton's plan to resettle Negroes in their native land, to encourage them to grow sugar, coffee, cotton, etc., to set up factories, and to establish trade with Europeans. This plan was first conceived by the great philanthropist Fothergill[2] and was carried out by the society organized in London for the abolition of the slave trade, or rather by that benefactor of humanity, Granville Sharp.[3]

Dr. Thornton is devoting much time to this benevolent idea and

[1] [See pp. 146, 149.]

[2] [Samuel Fothergill (1715–1772), a leader of the English Quakers, who became an ardent abolitionist as a result of a visit to America in 1754–1756.]

[3] [Granville Sharp (1735–1831), a leader of the English abolitionists, who helped establish in 1787 a colony of freed slaves in Sierra Leone.]

is himself planning to act as the leader of the Negroes returning from America to Africa. He proposes to unite this settlement with the new colony of Sierra Leone. To avoid mistakes he has sent to Africa at his own expense an enlightened man who has spent several years making observations on the products of the country, inquiring into the manufactures most suitable to it, looking for the most convenient location for this re-emigration, and deciding on the necessary means to be taken to protect the settlement from any unfriendly activities, etc. Everything is now ready, and Dr. Thornton has communicated his plan to several members of the legislature of Massachusetts, who, at first, did not like it. They preferred to grant land to Negroes and encourage them to establish farms. "But," the doctor said to them, "what will they do with these lands, unaccustomed as they are to defending themselves with arms and surrounded by Indians who will harass them and by frontiersmen who will be even more cruel? Suppose they do succeed. Will you allow their representatives to sit in your assemblies and preside over you? No. Then return them to their native land."

The doctor is convinced that when his project becomes known thousands of Negroes will follow him. He bases his conviction on the requests submitted to him by the majority of the Negroes who have heard of his ideas.

He has, like myself, noted the injustice of the accusation that Negroes are lazy. "If they are so lazy," he says, "why do men abduct them from their homeland and condemn them to the hardest and most painful kind of work?" Arguments such as these are beginning to convince right-thinking men. His plan offers the solution to the problem posed by Mr. Jefferson (see his *Notes on the State of Virginia*).

The state of Massachusetts has recently received a request from Negroes that this project be carried out, and has promised to support it as soon as a site in Africa suitable for a good settlement is assured. It has even promised to supply ships, tools, loans, etc.

What advantages Africa, Europe, and even America would reap if this emigration took place! The African Negroes would gradually become civilized with the help of the American Negroes, for the whites, whom they must hate, will never succeed in civilizing them. By this settlement Europe would open up a vast market for its manufactures and would obtain, cheaply and without bloodshed, the products which it now buys from the West Indies at the cost of so much money and so many iniquities. God grant that this idea may soon become a reality! [4]

[4] On the advantages of this project read the work entitled *M. Lamiral réfuté par lui-même* [by François Lanthenas, Paris, 1790], and see the efforts made in England to establish colonies in Africa and to civilize the Negroes. A society has been formed in England to manage the settlement established at Sierra Leone and to trade in the local products. This establishment is on English territory and is under the English government. Mr. Hunter is the president. Another society has also been formed whose purpose is the same but which wishes to make its establishment independent of any European government. It has just published its proposal under the title *Plan for a Free Community Upon the Coast of Africa, Under the Protection of Great Britain; But Entirely Independent of All European Laws and Governments, With an Invitation, Under Certain Conditions, to All Persons Desirous of Partaking the Benefits Thereof* [London, 1789]. It is declared in this *Plan*, which must surely win the good wishes of all friends of humanity, that this society is founded on the principle of universal philanthropy and is not organized merely in order to gain commercial advantages, the latter being, the society says, greatly overrated, as if the happiness of all mankind consisted in the mere acquisition of wealth! All this confirms the contention put forward by the Société des Amis des Noirs in a letter to M. Necker dated June [14] 1789 [*Lettres de la Société des Amis des Noirs à M. Necker, avec la réponse de ce ministre d'état*, 1789] and in an address to the National Assembly [*Adresse à l'Assemblée Nationale pour l'abolition de la traite des Noirs, par la Société des Amis des Noirs de Paris*, Paris, 1790], and also expressed by the author of the refutation of M. Lamiral, namely, that the English ministry is secretly working on a plan whereby, the moment that the abolition of the slave trade is passed, a substitute will be ready which will provide all the English who have been engaged in the African trade with a new commerce to take the place of the one they have lost. [Brissot's reference to "Mr. Hunter" is perhaps an error for Henry Thornton (1760–1815), banker, member of the Evangelical party, and philanthropist, who in 1791 founded the Sierra Leone Company, for the purposes Brissot describes. See p. 65. The group which published the utopian *Plan for a Free Community* was headed by August Nordenskjold, Charles Bernhard Wadstrom, Colborn Barrell, and Johan Gottfried Simpson.]

PHILADELPHIA

When Voltaire considered the vices which corroded the Old World and the tender brotherly love which united the Quakers, he sometimes would cross the seas in his imagination and long to spend the rest of his life in the "city of brotherly love." [1] What would he have said had he been able for a few days to realize his dream and witness the peace which reigns in Philadelphia?—No, I am wrong; Voltaire would have hastened to return to Europe, for he was consumed with pride and lived on adulation, and he would have got very little of that here. The seriousness of the Quakers would have seemed to him a kind of gloomy pedantry; he would have yawned at their meetings; he would have been mortified to find that his epigrams went unapplauded; he would soon have been homesick for the glittering witticisms of his polite Parisian roués.

Philadelphia may be considered the metropolis of the United States. It is certainly the most beautiful and best-built city in the nation, and also the wealthiest, though not the most ostentatious. Here you find more well-educated men, more knowledge of politics and literature, more political and learned societies than anywhere else in the United States. Many other American cities are older but Philadelphia quickly surpassed them all.

The Swedes were the first settlers on the land where the city is today. Their church, the first to be built here more than a hundred years ago, still stands on the banks of the Delaware. Penn, as I have already mentioned, was reluctant to choose this angle of land formed by the Schuylkill and Delaware Rivers. As the proprietor of an immense grant of territory, he found it hard to have to build his city on land which did not belong to him. But the arguments in favor of this site persuaded him to buy it from the Swedes, and he gave them in exchange some land in the interior of Pennsylvania. Several Swedish families settled there, but their posterity have not prospered and no longer are the owners of these grants. Today there are few descendants left of the original Swedes, who numbered over one thousand and made a number of other settle-

[1] [See the article "Quakers," in *Questions sur l'Encyclopédie*, 1772.]

ments. The Swedish church still exists, however, and has been for many years in the care of a Swedish minister, Dr. Collins, a learned man of rare merit. He writes very well in English and has produced several books and pamphlets in that language, such as *The Foreign Spectator,* in which he outlines the soundest republican principles. He is a fervent apostle of liberty.[2]

Penn introduced in his new colony a truly fraternal regime, a familylike sort of government. Brothers who live together need for their defense neither soldiers, nor forts, nor police, nor any of those formidable constructions which give to most towns the appearance of fortresses. Until recently Philadelphia had not felt the need of a public governing body or of a city hall; now, however, the necessity is beginning to be apparent because of the many foreigners and members of other sects who have established themselves here. For some time there have been complaints of disorders and of robberies committed at night on the outskirts of Philadelphia by thieves escaped from prison.

At ten o'clock in the evening all is quiet in the streets, and the profound silence is interrupted only by the cries of the few watchmen who form the only patrol. The streets are lighted at night by lamps placed at intervals, like those of London. On each street there are brick sidewalks and narrow gutters of brick or wood on both sides. Between the gutters and the street there are strong posts to prevent carriages from running up on the sidewalks, which are level with the street. These stout posts are made of a kind of cedar imported from the Carolinas. On all the streets one sees a surprisingly large number of public pumps.

At the door of each house there is a pair of benches where the family sits in the evening to enjoy the fresh air and watch the passers-by. This is certainly a bad habit, for the evening air is not always very healthy and its ill effects are not counteracted by exercise. People never take walks here; instead they have parties in the country.

There are few private coaches in Philadelphia,[3] but one sees many attractive wagons which are used to convey families to the country; they are long, lightly built, and open, and can hold twelve persons. Also very common in the country are small chaises, open

---

[2] [Dr. Nicholas Collins, minister of the Swedish Church in Southwark. Brissot gives the title of his pamphlet as *Le spectateur étranger.*]

[3] There is only one public cab, and it does not make much money.

on all sides. One kind, known as the sulky, has a seat for only one person.

The horses which pull the carriages are in general neither handsome nor strong, but they travel well enough. I have not seen any of the fine horses mentioned by M. Crèvecoeur, which I thought would rival the enormous Belgian horses. I suspect Americans do not take good enough care of their horses and feed them badly; they are not bedded down with straw in the stable, and after a long and tiring trip they are allowed to graze.

Philadelphia is built on a regular plan of long, broad streets which cross each other at right angles and run from north to south and from east to west. This truly ornamental regularity is at first confusing to the stranger, for it is difficult to find one's way, especially since there are no street signs and no numbers on the doors. It is inconceivable that the Quakers, who are so fond of order, have not borrowed these two practices from the English, from whom they have adopted so many other things. This lack of signs and numbers is the bane of foreigners.

The shops which adorn the principal streets are remarkable for their cleanliness. You find here the same taste and the same quality as in London. The State House, in which the General Assembly meets, is, as I have already said, a fairly handsome building. Next to it a magnificent court of justice is now being constructed. M. Raynal's descriptions of the State House, the library, and other public buildings are exaggerated. He was deceived by the information he had been given. He speaks of streets 100 feet wide, of which there are none, except for Market Street; they generally have a breadth of 50 to 60 feet. He also speaks of 200-foot wharfs, of which there are none either; in fact they are in general rather small and unimpressive. He states that Penn's plan has been followed everywhere in the city. On the contrary, it was violated in the building of Water Street instead of the beautiful wharfs which Penn had planned. Raynal also speaks of slate-roofed houses and of marble monuments in churches and meeting halls. I have seen nothing of the sort.

Behind the State House there is a public garden, the only one in Philadelphia. It contains large squares of greenery intersected by pathways, and although it is not large, it is pleasant and one can breathe there.

All the space from Front Street on the Delaware to Front Street on the Schuylkill is already divided into streets and blocks for houses. Building is going on, but not as fast as in New York. The inhabitants of Philadelphia apparently wish to see the city grow. In this they are wrong, for it is already too big. When the population of a city becomes large, it is necessary to have almshouses, prisons, soldiers, police, and spies. Soon luxury begins to appear, that very luxury which Penn wished to avoid. Indeed, it has already begun to be apparent for some time, and you see carpets, and fine ones, in the houses. They are treasured by Americans; this is a taste they have inherited from their luxury-loving former masters, the English. A carpet in summer is an absurdity, yet it is kept on the floor out of vanity. The excuse is that it makes the house look better, which is to say that good sense and utility are less important than "show." Sensible people, however, are beginning to take up their carpets during the summer and leave the floors bare or covered with mats.

Quakers too have carpets, but the rigorously orthodox disapprove. I was told of a Quaker from Carolina who when he went to dine at the house of one of the wealthiest Quakers in Philadelphia was so offended at seeing the front hallway to the stairs covered with a carpet that he refused to enter the house. He said that he would not eat in a house of luxury, and that it was far better to clothe the poor than to clothe the floor.

If this Quaker justifiably criticized this ridiculous prodigality in carpets, how much more severely must he have censured the extravagance of the women of Philadelphia! I am not referring to the wives of the Quakers, of whom I shall speak later in a special chapter on the Society of Friends, but to the women of other sects, who wear hats and bonnets almost as varied as those seen in Paris. These women pay a great deal of attention to their dresses and hairdos and are too obviously affected to be pleasing. It is a great misfortune in a republic when women waste so much time on such foolishness and when men attach any importance to these things.

A very clever woman in this city is accused of having contributed more than any other to this taste for extravagant show. I am truly sorry to see her husband, who seems an agreeable, well-educated man, display in his house and furniture an ostentation which ought to have remained forever unknown in Philadelphia. And why does he do this? To attract a few European fops and empty-headed parasites. What does he gain by it? The jealousy and the censure of his fellow citizens and the criticism of foreigners. When a man of great wealth is intelligent, educated, wise, and benevolent, how easy it is for him to make himself loved and esteemed by devoting his fortune to useful public enterprises.

Despite the fatal consequences that might be expected from this luxury, we may say with assurance that there is no city in which morals are more respected than in Philadelphia. Adultery is unknown here, and there is no single instance of a wife of any sect failing in her duties.

This is perhaps due, as I was told by an American, to the civic status of women. They marry without doweries and bring only household goods to their new homes; only after the death of their parents can they expect to own any property. They are therefore entirely dependent on their husbands.

I was told, however, of a Mrs. Livingston, a daughter of Dr. Shippen, who lives separated from her husband. But this separation was arranged by an amicable agreement. The young woman married Mr. Livingston only in obedience to her father, a kind of obedience which is very rare in this country. The father promised to take his daughter back if she were not happy with her husband. She was not, she returned to her father's home, and she lives today the life of a virtuous and respected woman.[4]

I was also told of a lady from Rhode Island once famous for her extravagance. There is, however, no proof of the accusation, and if one examines closely the circumstances one will find that this anecdote belongs to the history of English rather than of American manners.

You would not have as good an opinion of the morals of this country if you read a recently published satire entitled *The Times*, by Mr. Markoe.[5] It reveals an unmistakable poetic talent, similar to that of our satirist Gilbert, who died recently in a charity hospital.[6] But, like Gilbert, Markoe paints with exaggerated strokes, and, like all poets, often substitutes fables for truth. Mr. Markoe's satire is all the more unworthy of confidence because he dishonors his writings by a dissolute life. A satirist if he is to be believed and useful must be a man of the strictest morals.

---

[4] [Nancy Shippen (1763–1841), the daughter of Dr. William Shippen (1736–1808), fell in love with Guillaume Otto, secretary to the French minister, but her family opposed the match and forced her to marry Lieutenant Colonel Henry Beekman Livingston, with the unhappy results Brissot recounts. See Ethel Armes, *Nancy Shippen. Her Journal Book*, Philadelphia, 1935.]

[5] [Peter Markoe, *The Times. A Poem*, Philadelphia, 1788.]

[6] [Nicholas Joseph Laurent Gilbert (1751–1780).]

Paine, the celebrated author of *Common Sense,* who is so revered in France, is cruelly mistreated in Markoe's satire. This was not the first attack on Paine to be published; I have seen another very severe one written by a citizen of North Carolina.[7] It is generally agreed that Mr. Paine is a talented and powerful writer, but he is accused of having taken the major portion of his famous letters from a pamphlet published at the beginning of the troubles in Holland and quoted by Sir William Temple.[8] He is also accused of having copied the plan of his iron bridge, which is attracting some attention in Europe, from a collection of architectural designs published in London some fifty years ago by Swan.[9] Mr. Paine has achieved great success here, so it is not surprising that so many satires have been written against him. Whether or not these satires are justified, it cannot be denied that his writings played an important part in the Revolution, and this fact places him among the benefactors of America.

In Philadelphia I saw another writer of imagination and wit, Mr. Crawford.[10] He has published several poems and some sensible and humane observations on Negro slavery, and he has republished an address to the Jews by the famous George Fox.[11] His inclination toward mystical ideas, combined with his devotion to study and his inflammable imagination, have brought on attacks of insanity. Formerly a deist, he was converted by the famous Dr. Jebb.[12]

There is no other city on this continent where as much printing is done as in Philadelphia. There are a great many printing presses, gazettes, and bookstores in the city, and likewise a large number of paper mills in the state. Pennsylvania is truly the general emporium of the United States.

Among the printers and booksellers of Philadelphia I took particular note of Mr. Carey, an Irish printer who was persecuted

---

[7] [It is not known to what work Brissot was referring.]

[8] [William Temple (1628–1699), English Ambassador to The Hague, *Letters* (London, 1699). "Famous letters" presumably refers to Paine's *The American Crisis,* 1776–1778.]

[9] [Abraham Swan, *A Collection of Designs in Architecture: To Which Are Added . . . Designs of Stone and Timber Bridges,* London, 1757. Thomas Paine conceived the idea of a single-arch iron bridge, and after failing to obtain financial backing in America and France finally did succeed in erecting one in England in 1790.]

[10] [Charles Crawford (b. 1752).]

[11] [George Fox, *A Looking-Glass for the Jews* (Philadelphia: Joseph Crukshank, 1784).]

[12] [John Jebb (1736–1786), the English divine.]

and forced to flee to America for having published in his *Volunteer's Journal* an article which hurt some important people, among them a Mr. Forster.[13] Having no money, he was in great difficulty until M. Lafayette came to his assistance and enabled him to establish a press, on the condition that this act of generosity would remain a secret. Mr. Carey kept his word until two years later when, in a public quarrel with another newspaper publisher, Mr. Oswald,[14] who quarrels with everybody and who raised doubts about the sources of Carey's money, he was forced to reveal the secret.

Mr. Carey, who combines great industry with much knowledge, publishes the *American Museum,* a monthly magazine which is equal to the best periodicals of Europe. It contains information on America's most important achievements in the arts and sciences and in politics; the part which deals with agricultural developments is given the greatest attention.

There are today far fewer French merchants in Philadelphia than there were during the war. The bankruptcies of the first to establish themselves here discouraged others from following their example and put Americans on their guard. But who should be blamed for the failures of these French merchants? I have gone to a great deal of trouble to collect information on this subject, and the conclusions from my investigations are these: Most of the French who set up businesses in Philadelphia either had brought insufficient capital, or bought stock unwisely, or indulged in extravagant expenses. The majority did not know the language and were unfamiliar with the customs and the laws of the country. They were enticed by the *apparently* high prices they were being paid in paper money for their European merchandise. Thinking that this paper would soon be redeemed by the state or Congress, they accumulated as much as they could and, computing enormous profits, kept encouraging with high expectations their correspondents in Europe. These hopes came to nothing. Had these Frenchmen known anything of business, of human nature, of politics, of revolutions, or of this country, they would have perceived that many years were to pass before the public debt would be paid. It soon became necessary for them to abandon their illusions and sell the paper at a loss in order to meet notes due. They had, however, made a parade of wealth and had incurred considerable ex-

[13] [Mathew Carey (1760–1839) came to the United States in 1784.]
[14] [Eleazer Oswald, printer, bookseller, and publisher of the *Independent Gazetteer.*]

penses, and now they thought they had to keep up this front in order to maintain their credit. For, judging Philadelphia by Parisian standards, they foolishly imagined that well-informed and reasonable men could, like the subjects of an enslaved nation, be duped by vain show. There were no more profits, expenses were multiplying, and the moment of bankruptcy arrived. They had to justify themselves to their correspondents, to other merchants, and to their own country. So what did they do? They accused Americans of dishonesty, perfidy, and fraud. These slanderers should have blamed only their own ignorance, ineptitude, and extravagance.

Frenchmen have been seen appearing in public with harlots who flaunted their wanton, frivolous, and impudent airs just like the *filles* of Paris.[15] You can imagine the scandal this indecent spectacle caused in a country where women are so modest and where morals are so pure. The first reaction was one of contempt, the second one of distrust. And without the trust of the public, how long can a merchant maintain his business?

Some French merchants arrived in Philadelphia during a period of prosperity, in 1783. Continental paper money had disappeared, and hard cash was plentiful in Philadelphia and was not rare in other parts of the United States, because of the expenditures being made by the European armies. At that time obligations were being met faithfully. But the foreign merchants spent their money as fast as they made it, thinking that the source was inexhaustible. Then peace came, the flow of money dried up, and new bankruptcies ensued. I must point out, by the way, that not a single bankruptcy sullied the Quakers, for they combine prudence with thrift, two virtues which are the foundation of a solid business.

Since the peace, the Quakers have been very active in business. Capital, which for so long was hoarded because of fear, is now being released and is stimulating industry and encouraging commercial speculations. The flags of all nations can be seen floating over the Delaware, and ships are sailing to all parts of the world. Factories are rising in the city and in the country; everywhere there is activity, industry, and competition. Although Baltimore, on the Susquehanna, which was only a village a few years ago, has drawn

---

[15] One of these Frenchmen dared to introduce his mistress in the best houses, pretending not that she was his wife but his business associate. Later this same woman was publicly kept by the ambassador, who did not have enough respect for the morals of the country to conceal his turpitude.

some trade away from Philadelphia, the presence of established sources of capital, the universally good reputation of the Quaker merchants, the extension of new settlements, and the progress of industry are all bringing in so much business that any loss to Baltimore is scarcely noticeable.

You can now easily see the reasons for the prosperity of Philadelphia. Its geographical position on a river navigable by large ships makes it a center for foreign trade, and at the same time it is the market place for the products of the fertile lands of Pennsylvania and the neighboring states. The vast rivers with their numerous branches that flow through Pennsylvania connect almost all points in the state, making easy the transportation of goods, which in turn raises the value of land and attracts settlers. One of these rivers can carry to the capital the produce of the remotest farms and even products of the forest trapped or hunted by the Indians. The climate, warmer than it is in the Northern states but cooler and more comfortable than in the Southern, also is a considerable attraction.

Yet I firmly believe that Pennsylvania does not owe its prosperity merely to these geographical advantages, but rather to the private morals of the inhabitants; to the universal toleration which has been practiced here since the very foundation of the colony; to the Quakers' simplicity and thrift; to their firm virtues; and to their industry, which, concentrated on two activities, farming and trade, has necessarily produced better and faster results than other sects have achieved. Many more children are born in the simple cabin of a hard-working farmer than in a gilded palace, and fewer of them die. Since population has always appeared to you to be the most exact index to the prosperity of a country, compare the following figures on the number of inhabitants paying the poll tax in Pennsylvania in four different years fairly close together:

1760	1770	1779	1786
31,667	39,765	54,683	66,925

You can see that the population has more than doubled in twenty-five years, in spite of the fearful depopulation caused by a seven-year war. Note also that these figures do not include the Negro population, which is about one third as large as the white. According to the calculations of the recent federal convention, the white population of the state was 360,000, which means that there were about three children per family.

Let us take another point of comparison: Albany was founded in 1614, Philadelphia in 1681. The latter now has 7,000 houses and over 50,000 inhabitants.[16] Albany, on the other hand, has only seven hundred houses although it enjoys almost the same geographical advantages as Philadelphia. To what is this difference due? More to moral than to physical causes. The spirit of the Quaker religion keeps the people constantly and directly aware of the public good; while in Albany such a spirit is almost unknown, and everyone seeks his own enjoyment and cares little about others.[17] This, I repeat, is the Dutch character, and the Dutch as founders of Albany form the base of the city's population.

The public spirit which the Quakers, more than any other sect, exhibit in all their activities has given birth to several useful institutions in Philadelphia. It is to this spirit that Philadelphia owes its Dispensary, which distributes free medicines to the sick who cannot afford to buy them. How easy, and often how inexpensive it is to do good! Let those blush who dissipate their fortunes on ostentation and idleness! Between December 12, 1786, and December 12, 1787, 1,647 patients were treated in this Dispensary, and the average treatment per person cost 5 shillings 9 pence. Thus with a little over 5,000 livres, 1,647 people were made happy.

To this same public spirit, so ingenious in varying its good deeds, is owed the Benevolent Institution, whose purpose is to bring help to needy women in labor and to deliver them in their own homes. It is to this spirit also that is due the formation of another society, whose object it is to aid prisoners. The rules and regulations of this society were drawn up at a meeting held on May 8, 1787.[18]

Philadelphians do not limit their charity to their brethren but extend it to strangers as well. They have formed a Hibernian Club for the assistance of immigrants from Ireland, like the similar group for Germans in New York.[19] Members of these societies inquire about the nationality and plans of arriving immigrants and make efforts to find employment for them.

[16] According to the 1790 census, the present number of inhabitants is 53,000.

[17] This inertia of the people of Albany is, however, disappearing. There is great activity there now; roads are being built, mountains leveled, and new ferries established, there is a plan for building a bridge over the Mohawk River, and the channel has just been made navigable for ships. This change is due to the immigration into this area by people from Massachusetts. The rapid progress achieved by the new town of Hudson, built by Quakers, supports these observations.

[18] [The Society for Alleviating the Miseries of Public Persons.]

[19] [The German Society for Encouraging Immigration from Germany.]

PHILADELPHIA

Philadelphia has formed a fire insurance company. The houses are built of brick and wood and therefore are especially inflammable.[20] It is a society in which the insurers are the insured, an arrangement which makes impossible such abuses as those which occurred in your insurance company in Paris.

Among all these things which warm my heart and arouse my admiration, I nevertheless have found one injustice which grieves me, since it seems to tarnish all of Pennsylvania and particularly the city of Philadelphia, which exercises a great influence on the legislative body. Penn left to his family an immense property in America. During the last war his descendants sided with the English and withdrew to England. The government of Pennsylvania ordered the confiscation of their lands and revenues, with payment in compensation of £150,000 for all their property. This sum was to be paid in paper money, which was then greatly depreciated. Only the first payment was made. It cannot be denied that a very great injustice was done in the estimate of the property, in the form of payment, and in the delay. The state of Pennsylvania has too much respect for property and too much devotion to justice not to make eventual reparations for the wrongs done to the Penn family, which is now wholly dependent upon payments from the English government.[21]

---

[20] [Brissot is referring to the Philadelphia Contributionship for the Insurance of Houses Against Fire, founded in 1752, or to the Mutual Assurance Company for the Ensurance of Houses from Loss of Fire, founded in 1783.]

[21] The English Parliament, by an act passed in May 1790, has allotted this family a pension of £4,000 sterling. It is estimated that the Penns lost £500,020,000. This is an additional expense to be added to the enormous losses suffered by England in the American War and to the compensations she has granted to Loyalists. An accounting of these latter compensations has just been made:

Claims	£10,358,413
Parliament has granted only	£ 3,033,091
In 1790, Parliament had paid only	£ 2,096,326
Still due	£ 936,091

We cannot refrain from praising here the magnanimity of the English people and their sense of justice. There are few free governments, and no despotic ones, that after an unsuccessful and very costly war would have thus compensated their ruined partisans, whose complaints could easily have been silenced or disregarded. This sense of justice is an inevitable result of the spirit of liberty.

FARMING LIFE AND THE SETTLEMENT OF THE FRONTIER IN PENNSYLVANIA

Until now, my friend, I have described to you only well-established farms and land in a state of full cultivation close to the cities. We now must go farther, plunge into the forests, and observe man in isolation, axe in hand, felling the revered and ancient oak of the Indians and replacing it with humble ears of wheat. We must follow this man, his progress, and his improvements; we must note how his cabin changes as it becomes the center for twenty other cabins which rise around it. An American farmer has communicated to me the principal elements of the following picture of rural life: [1]

The first settler in the woods is generally a man who has outlived his credit or fortune in the cultivated parts of the state. His time for migrating is in the month of April. His first object is to build a small cabin of rough logs for himself and family. The floor of this cabin is of earth, the roof is of split logs; the light is re-

[1] A part of the following observations has since been printed and translated into French with deliberate inaccuracy. [These "observations," which seem partially to anticipate Frederick Jackson Turner's thesis respecting frontier democracy, are actually Benjamin Rush's "An Account of the Progress of Population, Agriculture, Manners, and Government in Pennsylvania," first written in 1785 as a letter to the Maine physician Benjamin Vaughan (1751–1835), then in London, and in 1786 expanded into an epistolary essay addressed to Thomas Percival, M.D. (1740–1804), of Manchester, England, president of the Manchester Literary and Philosophical Society. This second version was published in the *Columbian Magazine* in November 1786, I, 117–122; in Jedidiah Morse's *American Geography* (Elizabethtown, 1789), pp. 313–318; and in the *Memoirs* of the Manchester Literary and Philosophical Society, 3 (1790), 183–197. A third revised version appeared in Rush's *Essays, Literary, Moral and Philosophical* (Philadelphia, 1798), pp. 213–225, and is reprinted in the *Letters of Benjamin Rush*, ed. L. H. Butterfield (Princeton, 1951), pp. 400–407 (q.v.). Brissot indicates that there was at least one other French translation besides his own, and Joel Barlow's note (*New Travels*, London, 1792, p. 330) that "the translator recollects to have seen this fanciful description many times published in America" suggests that there were several additional printings. Brissot's translation was made from the second version, but it contains, in addition to some rather free renderings, a number of changes, omissions, and interpolations, and it omits the introductory and final paragraphs. The following retranslation gives the wording of the second version as printed in the *Columbian Magazine*, except where Brissot obviously departed from this text. Most of Brissot's alterations are insignificant except in respect to factual accuracy; interpolations and omissions which do throw light on his ideas and opinions are indicated in footnotes.]

ceived through the door and, in some instances, through a small window made of greased paper. A coarser building adjoining this cabin affords a shelter to a cow and pair of poor horses. The labor of erecting these buildings is succeeded by killing the trees on a few acres of ground near his cabin; since removing them entirely would require too great an effort, this is done by cutting a circle around the trees two or three feet from the ground. The ground around these trees is then plowed and Indian corn planted in it. The season for planting this grain is in May. It grows generally on new ground with but little cultivation, and yields in the month of October following from forty to fifty bushels per acre.[2] After the first of September it affords a good deal of nourishment to his family, in its green or unripe state, in the form of what is called roasting ears. His family is fed during the winter by a small quantity of grain which he carries with him, and by fish and game. His cows and horses feed upon wild grass or the succulent twigs of the woods. For the first year he endures a great deal of distress from hunger, cold, and a variety of accidental causes, but he seldom complains or sinks under them. As he lives in the neighborhood of Indians, he soon acquires a strong tincture of their manners. His exertions, while they continue, are violent, but they are succeeded by long intervals of rest. His pleasures consist chiefly in fishing and hunting. He loves spirituous liquors, and he eats, drinks, and sleeps in dirt and rags in his little cabin.

In this situation he passes two or three years in idleness, independence, and an alternation of pleasure and labor. In proportion as population increases around him, he becomes uneasy and dissatisfied. Formerly his cattle ranged at large, but now his neighbors call upon him to confine them within fences to prevent their trespassing upon their fields of grain. Formerly he fed his family with wild animals, but these, which fly from the face of man, now cease to afford him an easy subsistence, and he is compelled to raise domestic animals for the support of his family. A growing society requires the establishment of government, taxes, and laws, and our settler revolts most against all these shackles.[3] He cannot bear to surrender up a single natural right for all the benefits of government, and therefore he abandons his little settlement and seeks a retreat in the woods, where he again submits to

[2] The bushel is equal to sixty English pounds.
[3] [This sentence replaces Rush's "Above all, he revolts against the operation of laws."]

all the toils which have been mentioned. Such is the attraction of independence that there are instances of many men who have broken ground on bare creation not less than four different times in this way, in different and more advanced parts of the state.

It has been remarked that the flight of this class of people is always increased by the preaching of the gospel. This will not surprise us when we consider how opposite its precepts are to their licentious manner of living. If our first settler was the owner of the spot of land which he began to cultivate, he sells it at a considerable profit to his successor; but if (as is oftener the case) he was a tenant to some rich landholder, he abandons it in debt; however, the small improvements he leaves behind him generally make it an object of immediate demand to a second species of settler.

This species of settler is generally a man of some property. He pays one third or one fourth part in cash for his plantation, which consists of three or four hundred acres, and the rest in gales or installments, as it is called here; that is, a certain sum yearly, without interest, till the whole is paid. The first object of this settler is to build an addition to his cabin; this is done with hewed logs; and as sawmills generally follow settlements, his floors are made of boards; his roof is made of what are called clapboards, which are a kind of coarse shingles split out of short oak logs. This house is divided by two floors. His next object is to clear a little meadow ground and plant an orchard of two or three hundred apple trees. His stable is likewise enlarged, and, in the course of a year, he builds a large log barn, the roof of which is commonly thatched with rye straw. He moreover increases the quantity of his arable land, and instead of cultivating Indian corn alone, he raises a quantity of wheat and rye. The latter is cultivated chiefly for the purpose of being distilled into whiskey. This species of settler by no means extracts all from the earth which it is able and willing to give. His fields yield but a scanty increase, owing to the ground not being sufficiently plowed and never being manured. The hopes of the year are often blasted by his cattle breaking through his half-made fences and destroying his grain. His horses perform but half the labor that might be expected from them if they were better fed, and his cattle often die in the spring from the want of provision and the delay of grass. His house as well as his farm bears many marks of a weak tone of mind. His windows are unglazed, or, if they have had glass in them, the ruins of it are supplied with old hats or pillows. This species of settler is seldom a good member of civil or religious society; with a large portion of an hereditary, mechanical kind of religion, he neglects to contribute sufficiently toward building a church or maintaining a regular administration of the ordinances of the gospel. He is equally indisposed to support civil government; with high ideas of liberty, he refuses to bear his proportion of the debt contracted by its establishment in this country. He delights chiefly in company—sometimes drinks spirituous liquors to excess—will spend a day or two in every week in attending political meetings; and thus he contracts debts which compel him to sell his plantation, generally in the course of a few years, to the third and last species of settler.

This species of settler is commonly a man of property and good character—sometimes he is the son of a wealthy farmer in one of the interior and ancient counties of the state. His first object is to convert every spot of ground over which he is able to draw water, into meadow. Where this cannot be done, he selects the most fertile spot on the farm and devotes it by manure to that purpose. His next object is to build a barn, which he prefers of stone. This building is in some instances 100 feet in front and 40 in depth. It is made very compact, so as to shut out the cold in winter; for these farmers find that their horses and cattle when kept warm do not require near as much food as when they are exposed to the cold. He uses economy, likewise, in the consumption of his wood. Hence he keeps himself warm in winter by means of stoves, which save an immense deal of labor to himself and his horses in cutting and hauling wood in cold and wet weather. His fences are everywhere repaired so as to secure his grain from his own and his neighbor's cattle. But further, he increases the number of the articles of his cultivation, and, instead of raising corn, wheat, and rye alone, he raises oats and buckwheat. Near his house he allots an acre or two of ground for a garden, in which he raises a large quantity of cabbage, potatoes, and turnips. Over the spring which supplies him with water he builds a milkhouse; he likewise adds to the number and improves the quality of his fruit trees. His sons work by his side all the year, and his wife and daughters forsake the spinning wheel to share with him in the toils of harvest. The last object of his industry is to build a dwelling house. This business is sometimes effected in the course of his life, but is oftener bequeathed to his son or the inheritor of his plantation; and hence there is a common saying among these farmers, "that a son should always begin where his father left off"; that is, he should begin his improvements by building a commodious dwelling house, suited to the improvements and value of the plantation. This dwelling house is generally built of stone—it is large, convenient, and filled with useful and substantial furniture. It sometimes adjoins the house of the second settler, but is frequently placed at a little distance from it. The horses and cattle of this species of settler bear marks in their strength, fat and fruitfulness of their being plentifully fed and carefully kept. His table abounds with a variety of the best provisions. His very kitchen flows with milk and honey—beer, cider, and wine are the usual drinks of his family. The greatest part of the clothing of his family is manufactured by his wife and daughters. In proportion as he increases in wealth, he values the protection of laws. Hence he punctually pays his taxes toward the support of government. Schools and churches likewise, as the means of promoting order and happiness in society, derive a due support from him.[4]

Of this class of settlers are two thirds of the farmers of Pennsylvania. These are the men to whom Pennsylvania owes her ancient fame and consequence. If they possess less refinement than their southern neighbors who cultivate their lands with slaves, they possess more republican virtue. It was from the farms cultivated by these men that the American and French armies were chiefly fed with bread during the late revolution; and it was from the produce of these farms that those millions of dollars were obtained from Havana after the year 1780 which laid the foundation of the Bank of North America and which fed and clothed the American army till the peace of Paris.[5]

This is a short account of the happiness of a Pennsylvania farmer. To this happiness this state invites men of every religion and country. It does not pretend to offer emigrants the pleasures of Arcadia or of the great cities of Europe. It is enough if affluence, independence, and happiness are ensured to patience, industry, and labor. The moderate price of land, the credit which arises from prudence, and the safety from the courts of law of every species of property render the blessings which I have described objects within the reach of every man.

From a review of the three different species of settlers, it ap-

[4] [Rush: ". . . from him; for benevolence and public spirit as to these objects are the natural offspring of affluence and independence."]
[5] [Rush: "glorious peace of Paris."]

pears that there are certain regular stages which mark the progress
from the savage to civilized life. The first settler is nearly related
to an Indian in his manners. In the second, the Indian manners
are more diluted. It is in the third species of settlers only that we
behold civilization completed. It is to the third species of settlers
only that it is proper to apply the term of *farmers*.

While we record the vices of the first and second settlers, it is
but just to mention their virtues likewise. Their mutual wants
produce mutual dependence; hence they are kind and friendly to
each other. Their solitary situation makes visitors agreeable to
them; hence they are hospitable to strangers. Their want of
money (for they raise but little more than is necessary to support
their families) has made it necessary for them to associate for the
purposes of building houses, cutting their grain, and the like;
this they do in turns for each other, without any other pay than
the pleasures which usually attend a country frolic. Perhaps what
I have called virtues are rather *qualities,* arising from necessity
and the peculiar state of society in which these people live. Virtue
should in all cases be the offspring of principle.

I do not pretend to say that this mode of settling farms in Pennsylvania is universal. I have known some instances where the first
settler has performed the improvements of the second and yielded
to the third. I have known a few instances likewise of men of enterprising spirits who have settled in the wilderness and who, in the
course of a single life, have advanced through all the intermediate
stages of improvement that I have mentioned and produced all
those conveniences which have been ascribed to the third species
of settlers.[6] There are instances likewise where the first settlement
has been improved by the same family in hereditary succession
till it has reached the third stage of cultivation. There are many
spacious brick houses and highly cultivated farms in the neighboring counties of the city of Philadelphia which are possessed
by the grandsons and great-grandsons of men who accompanied
William Penn across the ocean.

I dare say this passion for migration which I have described will
appear strange to you. To see men turn their backs upon the houses
in which they drew their first breath—upon the church in which
they were dedicated to God—upon the graves of their ancestors—
upon the friends and companions of their youth—and upon all

[6] [Rush: ". . . of settlers, thereby resembling in their exploits not only the
pioneers and light infantry but the main body of an army."]

the pleasures of cultivated society, and exposing themselves to all the hardships and accidents of subduing the earth and thereby establishing settlements in a wilderness, must strike a European philosopher as a picture of human nature that runs counter to the usual habits and principles of action in man. But this passion, strange and new as it appears, is wisely calculated for the extension of population in America; and this it does, not only by promoting the increase of the human species in new settlements but in the old settlements likewise. There is a languor in population as soon as farmers multiply beyond the number of farms into which a township is divided. To remove this languor, which is kept up alike by the increase of the price and the division of farms, a migration of part of the community becomes absolutely necessary. And as this part of the community often consists of the idle and extravagant, who eat without working, their removal, by increasing the facility of subsistence to the frugal and industrious who remain behind, naturally increases the number of people, just as the cutting off the suckers of an apple tree increases the size of the tree and the quantity of fruit.

I have only to add upon this subject that the migrants from Pennsylvania always travel to the southward. The soil and climate of the western parts of Virginia, North and South Carolina, and Georgia afford a more easy support to lazy farmers than the stubborn but durable soil of Pennsylvania. Here, the ground requires deep and repeated plowing to render it fruitful; there, scratching the ground once or twice affords tolerable crops. In Pennsylvania the length and coldness of the winter make it necessary for the farmers to bestow a large share of their labor in providing for and feeding their cattle, but in the Southern states cattle find pasture during the greatest part of the winter in the fields or woods. For these reasons, the greatest part of the western counties of the states that have been mentioned are settled by original inhabitants of Pennsylvania. During the late war the militia of Orange county in North Carolina were enrolled, and their number amounted to 3,500, *every* man of whom had migrated from Pennsylvania. From this you will see that our state is the great outport of the United States for Europeans, and that, after performing the office of a sieve by detaining all those people who possess the stamina of industry and virtue, it allows a passage to the rest to those states which are accommodated to their habits of indolence and vice.

The unoccupied lands are sold by the state for about six guineas in certificates per hundred acres.[7] But as most of the lands that are settled are procured from persons who had purchased them from the state, they are sold to the first settler for a much higher price. The quality of the soil—its vicinity to mills, courthouses, places of worship, and navigable water—the distance of land carriage to the seaports of Philadelphia or Baltimore—and the nature of the roads all influence the price of land to the first settler. The quantity of cleared land and the nature of the improvements, added to all the above circumstances, influence the price of farms to the second and third settlers. Hence the price of land to the first settler is from a quarter of a guinea to two guineas per acre; and the price of farms is from one guinea to ten guineas per acre to the second and third settlers, according as the land is varied by the before-mentioned circumstances. When the first settler is unable to purchase, he often takes a tract of land for seven years on a lease, and contracts, instead of paying a rent in cash, to clear fifty acres of land, to build a log cabin and a barn, and to plant an orchard on it. The tract, after the expiration of this lease, sells or rents for a considerable profit.[8]

The third species of farmers I mentioned are generally Germans, who compose a large part of the population of Pennsylvania. The oldest German colony in the state is over one hundred years old. They are considered the most honest, the most industrious, and the most thrifty of farmers. They avoid contracting debts and of all Americans are the least given to the use of rum or spirits. As a result, they have large families, quite commonly of as many as twelve to fourteen children.[9] Their only shortcoming is that they do not have the education of other Americans, an education which is necessary for participation in a democratic government. Never-

[7] [This paragraph appeared in Rush's text as a footnote earlier in the essay.]

[8] [Rush's final paragraph, omitted by Brissot, read: "I shall conclude this letter by remarking that in the mode of extending population and agriculture which I have described we behold a new species of war. The third settler may be viewed as a conqueror. The weapons with which he achieves his conquests are the implements of husbandry, and the virtues which direct them are industry and economy. Idleness, extravagance, and ignorance fly before him. Happy would it be for mankind if the kings of Europe would adopt this mode of extending their territories. It would soon put an end to the dreadful connection which has existed in every age between war and poverty and between conquest and desolation."]

[9] According to M. Moheau [*Recherches et considérations sur la population de la France*, Paris, 1778], out of every 27,000 French families only one has thirteen children and two have twelve.

theless several men respected for their acquirements have arisen from among them—Rittenhouse, Kuhn, and Muhlenberg.[10] There are proposals to bring the Germans into closer relationship with Americans and improve their education.

One of the reasons for emigrating to the back country of Pennsylvania is the hope of escaping land taxes, even though they are not very high, being less than a penny, or two *liards,* per pound of the appraised value, which is very low. Although this tax is modest, it still weighs heavily on large landowners and on the land jobbers. Rather than pay the accumulated taxes in arrears some allow their lands to be sold by the public treasury, and then repurchase them through a dummy at public auction for less than they would have had to pay in taxes.

You can well imagine that in a country where the government is so new and where men are so spread out and so intoxicated with liberty it is easy to evade taxes. Furthermore, there are many irregularities in the apportionment, so that you find landowners around Philadelphia who each year pay two per cent on the value of their land while others pay much less. The same is true of the poll tax, which is even more irregular because the regulations for its assessment are very vague. These faults can disappear only in time, but I did note with pleasure that bachelors pay higher taxes than married men.

Land in Pennsylvania varies in price, just as it varies in quality and in products. Around Lancaster there is some land which sells for four to twelve pounds an acre, but there is also a great deal which is stony and barren. Good virgin limestone land yields fifteen to twenty bushels of wheat an acre, and prime land, known as bottomlands, which has a thick layer of topsoil rich in vegetable matter, yields nine to ten quintals of hemp or forty to fifty bushels of corn per acre.

There is still much vacant land in the northern and western parts of the state, but I am told that there are very few good pieces that are not already taken. In remote woodlands you can see people searching for such land, which, if they find it, they take possession of by virtue of a warrant issued by the land office. This warrant orders the surveyor of the county where the land is located to sur-

[10] [David Rittenhouse (1732–1796), professor of astronomy at the College of Philadelphia and first director of the Mint; Adam Kuhn (1741–1817), physician, botanist, and professor at the College of Philadelphia; Frederick Muhlenberg (1750–1801), first speaker of the federal House of Representatives.]

vey it if it is vacant and to forward a copy of the survey so that
the property may be registered. The buyer pays the state ten
pounds in state debt certificates for 116 acres, which at the present
rate of this paper amounts to two and a half pounds.[11] Including
the fee for the survey, the expense of the patent, etc., these lands
cost approximately fifteen pence or sous an acre, and are then
resold at a profit.

From this description of the different kinds of farming in this
state, it is apparent that European families wishing to settle in
America would not be well advised to attempt to clear land in the
interior, or even to buy a farm that is only at the second stage of
development.

1. A man who needs to think, to keep himself informed, and to
exchange ideas with others would be unhappy isolated in a region
where there are no means of communication and where all his
neighbors are either far away or are lazy or ignorant.

2. It is almost impossible if you live so far inland to get articles
from Europe, and if you do they are extremely expensive.

3. Above all it is impossible to accustom European women to
such a way of life.

4. You are forced to build your own house and in the meantime
you are uncomfortable waiting; you run risks, and your workers
cheat you.

5. It is wrong to consider only the cost of the land without any
buildings. Your calculations should be based rather on what it will
cost after all building is finished. When you make the comparison
you will see that you have much to gain in buying land with
buildings.

Prudent Frenchmen who would like to become farmers in America ought to rent a farm in a settled region and spend a year there
before they buy, getting to know their neighbors and learning how
much income the land produces. Above all they must bring from
Europe *families* of peasants used to farm work, for, I repeat, help
is scarce here and very expensive. The usual price for indentured
servants, whose time is bought for three years, is as follows: twelve
to fifteen pounds for men over eighteen, and six to eight pounds
for children between nine and twelve. I am not sure that the difference between the lower cost of an indentured servant and the
higher wages paid to a free servant is not compensated by the better
work done by the latter.

[11] The value of these certificates has since increased greatly, as I shall show later.

LETTER 29

CLIMATE AND DISEASE
IN PENNSYLVANIA

I have already written, my friend, of the climate of this happy
city,[1] but the estimable Dr. Rush has just communicated to me
some new and curious details which I wish to give you.[2]

This enlightened observer has succinctly summarized for me the
variations of climate in Pennsylvania. "We have," he told me,
"Great Britain's humidity in the spring, Italy's temperature in
June, Africa's heat in the summer, the sky of Egypt in the autumn,
Norwegian cold and snow and Dutch ice in the winter, the storms
of the West Indies occasionally in any season, and the variable
winds of Great Britain in every month of the year." Despite all
these variations, the doctor claims that the climate of Philadelphia
is one of the healthiest in the world.

The air when dry has a peculiar elasticity, which renders both
heat and cold less insupportable than the same degrees of both
are in moister countries. It is in those cases only when summer
showers are not succeeded by northwest winds that the heat of the
air becomes oppressive and distressing, from being combined with
moisture.

I had been warned that I would experience a certain apathy and
weakness commonly felt in Philadelphia during hot spells, and the
descriptions I had heard reminded me of the ravages of the oppressive sirocco. Yet during the three weeks I spent in Philadelphia,
in August and September, I did not suffer any lethargy or mental
depression, and although it was very hot I found the heat bearable
and somewhat similar to that of Paris, the only difference being
that I perspired more.

Perhaps I was not subject to the general rule because I was so

[1] See Letter 19, pp. 210–211.
[2] I learn from American newspapers that Dr. Rush has published a work on the
climate of Pennsylvania, and it was from this that came the observations with
which he favored me. It deserves to be translated into French and will be useful for
comparative studies in meteorology and hygiene. [Brissot refers to Rush's "Account
of the Climate of Pennsylvania and Its Influence Upon the Human Body," *American Museum*, 6 (1789), 250–254; 7 (1790), 333–340. Brissot drew most of the material for this letter from this account.]

274

busy and active going around talking to enlightened men and making notes of their remarks that I did not have a moment's rest. Dr. Rush, like many European doctors, has observed that one's state of mind has a great influence upon one's health and that it often is stronger than the effects of external circumstances. As proof of this he gave two striking examples. He had learned from a surgeon that the English soldiers wounded in the famous naval battle of April 12, 1782,[3] were cured with the greatest ease, for the intoxication of victory seemed to restore vigor and health to their bodies. Rush himself had noted the same speedy recovery among American soldiers wounded in the battle of Trenton.

Variability is, as I have said, the essence of the climate of Pennsylvania. It has changed, especially as a result of the clearing of the land and the draining of the waters which used to flood this part of America. Numerous creeks and even rivers have gradually disappeared, as was to be expected in a country where forests are giving place to cultivated fields and meadows.

These climatic changes have had a favorable effect on the health of individuals. An old man of this state told me that Pennsylvanians are growing healthier as more lands are being cleared, that in the last thirty to forty years people's faces have become less pale, that for some time the number of centenarians has been increasing, and that septuagenarians are very common. These established facts may seem difficult to reconcile with the variability of the weather, which is so great that not only is it true that no two successive years are alike, but even that the same seasons and months have no resemblance to one another in successive years. The climate has only one constant characteristic, namely, its inconstancy, for which Ovid's line seems to have been written:

Et tantum constans in levitate sua.[4]

In 1782 there was an extraordinary drought. The Indian corn did not ripen and the fields turned brown. The earth became so inflammable in some places that it burned below the surface. In contrast, this summer (1788) has been excessively rainy. On the eighteenth and nineteenth of August seven inches fell in Philadelphia, causing great damage to the wheat.

Fortunately the various parts of the state are not subject to the

---

[3] [Rodney's defeat of De Grasse off Dominica.]
[4] [Consistent only in its fickleness. *Tristia* V, viii, 18.]

same variations of weather, with the result that there are never any general shortages, for if the harvest fails in one place it will be abundant fifty miles away.

If you wish to compare the temperature of Philadelphia with that of other countries on about the same latitude, here are some good comparative meteorological observations: The heat is about the same in Philadelphia as in Paris, but it is never as great as in Rome, where the temperature rises to thirty degrees or more. Winters are not considerably colder than in Paris, for in both cities the thermometer frequently drops to ten or twelve degrees below freezing.[5] Much more rain falls here than in Paris, where the average rainfall is twenty inches a year and has been known to reach twenty-five inches only once in sixty years, while the average in Philadelphia is thirty-five inches. If one compares the climate of Philadelphia with that of Peking, which is on about the same latitude, one learns from the tables of the famous Kirwan [6] that the winters in that part of China are much colder and the summers much warmer than in Pennsylvania. Dr. Rush attributes these differences to local circumstances. There are vast forests to the northwest of Pennsylvania, while the country around Peking is entirely and extensively cultivated.

Still another fact adds to the general confusion which makes it impossible to devise reliable systems for explaining variations in temperature. I have mentioned temperatures on the Ohio and in Pittsburgh,[7] and have said that in the winter of 1788 the cold there was greater than in Philadelphia and almost equal to that of Siberia. Usually, however, the cold and heat are less intense on the other side of the mountains than on this side. During that same winter there were such variations that on February 5 it was much colder in Philadelphia than in Pittsburgh, according to the comparative observations of Dr. Bedford for Pittsburgh and by M. Le Gaux in Spring Mill.

The variation of temperature is felt not only from day to day but also during the hours of the morning and of the afternoon. One day in early November 1788 I noted that the thermometer stood at eleven degrees below freezing; two days later, the heat of the sun was unbearable. The twenty-third of that same month was very hot, the twenty-fourth was very cold and below freezing; the

[5] See Letter 19, p. 211. [These are readings on the Reaumur scale.]
[6] [Richard Kirwan, *An Estimate of the Temperature of Different Latitudes*, London, 1787.]
[7] See Letter 20 [p. 213].

difference in temperature was certainly fifteen or twenty degrees.

These variations are due to the geographical situation of Philadelphia, to its soil, the surrounding bodies of water, and the prevailing winds. The city seems to be situated on the border line between two zones, at a point where two opposing winds, one from the east and the other from the northwest, constantly meet in violent opposition. It is also located at the confluence of two rivers; the terrain is marshy; and the soil is clay. The current of the Delaware is swift at this point.

My friend [Miers] Fisher, who is interested in explaining the character of men by their permanent physical environment, has told me that the activity of a region's inhabitants can be measured by the swiftness of its rivers and by the variations of its climate. He saw the Virginians' slowness and indecision in the sluggishness of the Potomac, while the swift flow of the Northern rivers mirrored for him the activity of New Englanders.

He also told me that one's health is related to atmospheric variations and can be improved by the observance of wise precautions. This is, he assured me, part of the Quaker discipline. In fact, according to him, one could measure the longevity of the citizens of Pennsylvania by the sects to which they belong, and if a table of longevity were established, the Quakers would come first, followed by the Moravians, then by the Presbyterians, etc.

Dr. Rush, who has made many observations on the effects of weather on health, has told me that sudden changes in temperature cause many more illnesses and deaths than does constant excessive heat or cold. He pointed out as proof the cold winter of 1780, the burning summer of 1782, and the rainy summer of 1788, when there were few or no illnesses, the occasional cases being most often due to imprudent acts such as drinking cold water in summer or spirits in winter.

According to elderly residents, cases of pleurisy and inflammatory diseases have greatly decreased in the last forty or fifty years. It is interesting that these diseases were on the increase while lands were being cleared and trees were being cut down, but that they have diminished as these lands have become cultivated.

Dr. Rush considers night air most unhealthy, especially after the twentieth of August, when man's *anima vitalis* is in a passive state. He therefore believes that it is very dangerous to sleep with open windows because the air, besides having imponderable qualities, changes temperature too frequently and too suddenly during the night.

Dr. Griffitts,[8] who has the same views on the effects of night air, disapproves of sleeping without a nightcap, as many of his fellow citizens do. He told me that since he started wearing one he no longer suffers from the frequent toothaches he used to have.

Dr. Rush considers May and June the healthiest months, and he has noticed that valetudinarians feel better in summer and winter than during the rest of the year. He agrees, however, with Dr. Huxham [9] that the other seasons, which are the ones with the greatest variations of temperature, could be rendered less dangerous by taking proper precautions in dress and in the design of houses and construction of doors and windows. The residents of Pennsylvania who acquire the habit of making their dress, diet, and daily activities conform to the changes of weather reach, he told me, an age as old as that attained in any other part of America.

If you wish a general idea of the climate of this part of the New World, read the following description by Pownall, a learned man who served for a long time as a colonial governor and to whom the public is indebted for his excellent observations:

Its seasons are summer, autumn, or what the Americans more expressively call the fall, and winter. The transition from the locking up of all vegetation in winter to the sudden burst of it again to life at the beginning of the summer excludes that progressive season which in the more moderate climate of Europe we call spring.

The season begins to break soon after the fall of the leaf, and temporary cold rains and sleets of snow fall in November, the northwest winds begin, and towards Christmas winter in all its rigor sets in; the ground is covered with snow, the frost is settled, the sky becomes clear and one continued expanse of azure, with constant sunshine; temporary blasts and storms are at intervals exceptions to this. Towards April the currents of the air begin to change to north, and round to northeast, and the season of hazy, foggy, and rainy squalls from northeast begins towards the latter end of April in some parts, towards the beginning of May in others. The frost breaks up, the snow melts, and within a week or ten days after the woods and the orchards are in the full glow of bloom. About the middle of September the mornings and evenings begin to grow cool, and from that time to the beginning of the winter season it is the climate of Paradise.[10]

[8] [Samuel Powel Griffitts, M.D., Professor of Materia Medica at the College of Philadelphia.]

[9] [John Huxham (1692–1768), *Observations on the Air and Epidemic Diseases from 1728 to 1737*, London, 1759–1767.]

[10] [Thomas Pownall, *A Topographical Description of . . . Parts of North America . . .*(London, 1776), p. 45.]

COMMON DISEASES IN THE
UNITED STATES

Of all the diseases in the United States consumption undoubt-edly wreaks the greatest ravages. As it was unknown to the Indians, it is not caused by the climate but must be the result of certain ways of life practiced in Europe and brought over by Europeans to this continent. Since it is common in towns and less frequent in the country, it must be connected with certain urban habits, and since it kills more women than men it must be more specially related to the pattern of women's lives. Consumption is a lan-guishing disease which gradually undermines the health and drags its victims step by step to the grave. Its ravages become more ap-parent each day as the knife sinks deeper and deeper into the breast of the victim, who can only stare death in the face, unable to evade it, imprisoned for the rest of his life in an inescapable shroud. The world and its pleasures fade away; only the ties of love are strengthened, but as they become stronger and dearer the bit-terness of their imminent dissolution is redoubled. Consumption is, in a word, a slow agony, a protracted and living death.

The doctors in this country attribute it to a number of different causes: to an excessive use of hot drinks, such as tea and coffee; [1] to the habit of staying too long in bed and of sleeping in feather beds (for mattresses are unknown); to eating too much meat; and to drinking too many spirits. Women are more subject to the disease than men because, in addition to the above causes, they take little exercise, which is a powerful remedy against the stagna-tion of the humors, the principal cause of marasmus. They do not enjoy walking, an activity which by varying the sights of nature refreshes and pleases the senses and seems to quicken the flow of blood and lend new vigor to the soul.

A cause of consumption peculiar to the wives of the Quakers is the solemn immobility they maintain for many hours on end in their silent meetings, a habit they learn early in life.

The fashionable women of Philadelphia also have consumption, but in their case the disease has other causes: they dance too much

[1] The coffee they drink here is very weak, merely colored water.

279

and then drink cold or iced water, or eat cold unripe fruit when they are hot; they drink boiling tea; they dress too lightly in winter and pay no attention to the changes of temperature so frequent in Philadelphia.

The wives of the Friends avoid these excesses and are usually suitably dressed for the weather, but they rarely go for walks, know no pleasures, and take none of the exercises which are so necessary in order to shake up and recharge from time to time this frail physical structure of ours, which for lack of movement sinks into mortal apathy.

To be healthy, a woman of Philadelphia ought to adopt a bit of the gaiety of the fashionable woman as well as the devotion of the Quaker woman to her home and family life.

There is another reason of a moral or political nature which could further explain why women are more subject to consumption than men. This is their infirmity of will, their lack of any civic life. The submission to which they are accustomed, or rather condemned, acts on them like chains which compress their limbs, gnaw at their flesh, cause obstructions, deaden their vitality, and impede circulation. The gradual depression of the soul results in a weakening of the body. And since submission to their fathers and husbands is more characteristic of Quaker girls and wives, they are as much subject to consumption as are fashionable women, although they do not taste the pleasures which cause the disease in the latter. No doubt, the time will come when men will be convinced that the great source of physical health is equality among all beings and freedom of individual thought and will.

Consumption is common throughout America. I have found it even in the states with the coldest climate, such as New Hampshire, a fact which must prove that the disease is due to the general way of life of Americans. For it would seem that the healthful frosts by giving a good tone to the nerves ought to prevent the torpor of the body and the stagnation of humors which are characteristic of this disease.

Consumption is not, however, as common in America as is generally imagined. Through ignorance this name is improperly given to many other diseases that cause the same loss of weight that follows pulmonary phthisis. This symptom is likely to, and in fact does, deceive the nurses that give information to those who make up mortality tables.

Another very common ailment is sore throat, which if the

throat is putrid can be fatal. It is almost always caused by excessive heat, cold drinks, and lack of proper clothing. A few years ago an epidemic of sore throats broke out in Boston and spread throughout the state of Massachusetts, killing many people, particularly members of old families.

It has been noticed that from time to time, and almost always at regular intervals, certain miasmas rise in the air causing widespread sickness. At other times, however, these diseases strike only certain places or certain classes of people. An epidemic which occurred a few years ago on the island of Nantucket attacked only the Indians who were still living there and killed almost all of them but spared the whites.

When one recalls that Europe in the past was subject to these regularly recurring epidemics, and that they have become less frequent as cultivation of the land and civilization have progressed, is one not tempted to believe that these epidemics are characteristic of countries where land is being newly cleared?

The epidemic disease known in Europe as influenza or grippe is even more common in America. The epidemic of 1789 caused everywhere tremendous havoc. Beginning in Canada in the fall, it spread into New York and soon infected Pennsylvania and the Southern states. The symptoms were fatigue, weakness, chills, fever, and headache. It attacked people of both sexes and of all ages and was especially fatal to those already suffering from consumption.

The fever and ague, which I mentioned previously, may be classified among these cruel epidemics, but this disease is much worse because it recurs every year. It occurs mainly from June to November and is most common in marshlands and along the seacoast but has broken out even in Albany, where the climate is so healthful. The customary treatment is quinine, but the most effective remedy is a trip to the mountains or to the north. More humane than human beings, the ague respects Negro slaves, an exemption attributed to their stubbornly preserved custom of keeping a fire in their cabins even in the hottest weather. Negroes consider excessive heat a guarantee of health, and this is why you will see a Negro woman working in the fields expose her child to the burning sun rather than place him under the refreshing shade of a tree. Although she is ignorant of the interesting experiments conducted by Ingenhousz [2] on the harmful effects of shade and darkness, she nevertheless knows what these effects are.

[2] [John Ingenhousz (1730–1799), Dutch chemist and physician.]

We must also mention here pleurisy and peripneumonia as common diseases in the United States, though less frequent now than they used to be.

Smallpox, which used to cause such terrible destruction in the United States, is no longer so dangerous since the introduction of general inoculation, first tried in Chester, England, and particularly now that this beneficial practice is surrounded by precautions preventing the spread of the infection.

There are many doctors in Philadelphia, a fact which you might consider responsible for so much sickness. You would be wrong, however, for they are said to be skillful and almost none of them are charlatans. I myself know several who are highly respected both for their character and their skill, such as Drs. Rush, Griffitts, and Wistar. The latter two are Quakers.

Most of these physicians are apothecaries as well, and they continue to combine these two professions out of consideration for the prejudice of the people who require that their prescriptions be filled by the same man who orders them. There are, however, special apothecaries, from whom the physicians purchase their drugs. Bloodletting is performed by barbers. All these facts must remind you of the beginnings of the healing art in our country.

The English school of medicine is practiced here; that is, the physicians use many violent remedies. Laxatives are seldom prescribed. Almost all the doctors in this country were trained at Edinburgh, which explains their predilection for English medical practices. I know a Dr. Bailey, a very intelligent man, though perhaps too excitable and caustic, who is greatly irritated by the unjust preference shown by his countrymen for English methods. He is resolved to establish communications between his country and the French schools, an intention which does him all the greater honor since he is known to be an Anglophile and staunch Loyalist.

LIFE EXPECTANCY IN THE
UNITED STATES

After the account I have given of the diseases prevalent in America, you may think, perhaps, that the human life span is shorter here than in Europe. This misconception, which has been spread by many writers, even by some who have traveled in America, must be destroyed.

One of these travelers, the Abbé Robin, wrote that American women appear old after twenty-five, that infant mortality is greater in America than in Europe, that there are few old people, etc.[1] I believe M. De Pauw had told these same tales earlier.[2] They are completely false. I have carefully observed American women between the ages of thirty and fifty; most of them are plump, healthy, and even attractive. I have seen fifty-year-old women who looked so fresh and young you would not have thought they were even forty, and some of sixty and seventy who sparkled with health. This is true particularly of the women of New Hampshire, Massachusetts, and Connecticut. It is correct, however, that Quaker girls and women in Pennsylvania, though attractive, do not have as good color. In general they are pale. I have noticed some women with fine teeth, but you can not make this a general observation, and American women, like English women, are not without defects in this respect. The cause is drinking hot liquids rather than the climate.

Not only are there more old people here than in Europe, as I shall prove, but they generally retain their intellectual faculties and even their physical health. I was told of a minister in Ipswich, Massachusetts, who at ninety years of age still preached very well, and of another, equally old, who walked twenty miles to meeting every Sunday. I heard also of a Mr. Temple who died a centenarian in 1765, leaving behind him four daughters and four sons aged 86, 85, 83, 81, 79, 77, 75, and 73.

[1] [Charles César Robin, *Nouveau voyage dans l'Amérique Septentrionale*, Paris, 1782.]

[2] [Cornelius de Pauw, *Recherches philosophiques sur les Américains*, Berlin, 1768; *Défense des Recherches philosophiques sur les Américains*, Berlin, 1770; "Amérique," *Supplément à l'Encyclopédie*, 1776.]

I shall not, however, confine myself to these superficial observations, but shall give, in order to provide definite data, tables of mortality and life expectancy in this country. Longevity tables ought to be the touchstone by which all governments are judged, the scale against which their strengths and weaknesses are measured, and the criteria for determining the progress or decadence of the human race.

The general causes of longevity are:

1. A healthy climate.
2. Abundant and nutritious food and drink.
3. A regular, active, and happy life.

Moreover, one must take into account such external circumstances as a man's work, his morals, his religion, and the government under which he lives. Wherever property is concentrated in the hands of a few and where employment is precarious, dependent, and uncertain, human life is briefer. It is shortened by worries and cares, which, even more effectively than actual want, cut off the very source of life. Wherever government is arbitrary, where tyranny, descending and subdividing itself at each rank of society, stops only at the members of the very lowest classes, to crush them all, there the life of the common people must be shorter. For such people are slaves, and a miserable slave, forever trodden under the feet of his masters, enjoys neither the material well-being, nor the regularity of existence, nor the inner contentment that are necessary to the sustenance of the principle of life. Nor is life long even for the power-hungry ruling class, for their days are shortened by excesses and worries.

If you apply these moral and political considerations to the United States you must conclude that there cannot be any country in which life expectancy is longer, for, in addition to all their natural advantages, the people enjoy the benefits of a liberty unequaled in the Old World, and it cannot be sufficiently stressed that it is liberty which is the source of health.

If any government should wish to revive the speculation of life annuities issued to selected risks, I should advise it to issue its policies to citizens of the northern United States, were this not impossible because of the great distance from Europe.[3]

It is difficult to draw up very exact tables of births and deaths

---

[3] [The sale of annuities, or *rentes viagères* as they were called, for lump-sum payments was a common and often abused form of government financing in France under the Ancien Régime.]

in the United States. As for births, in some sects children are not baptized and inaccurate records are kept; in other sects, only adults are baptized. As for deaths, many sick persons do not have a physician or surgeon but are cared for by nurses, who are not reliable as sources of information. In addition, the perpetual migrations cause constant fluctuations of population within all the states that make it impossible to draw totally accurate conclusions from the comparative tables of births, marriages, and deaths for a given region. It is possible, however, to obtain approximately correct figures by selecting as bases of comparison towns with relatively small emigration, such as seaports, particularly ones whose seamen sail in the coastwise trade rather than on long sea voyages. For these reasons, I am giving you figures on the towns of Salem and Ipswich in Massachusetts, taken from the *Memoirs* of the Academy in Boston,[4] a publication little known in France.

Dr. Halley chose Breslau, Germany, as the standard for his mortality tables because of that city's peaceful inland position and because of the regular employment of its inhabitants.[5]

According to the calculations of this political mathematician, five out of twelve children die in Breslau before reaching the age of five. In Ipswich, a village north of Boston, not far from the sea, only six out of thirty-three children die. Hence we conclude that Ipswich has a more favorable death rate than Breslau.

In Breslau, one person in thirty reaches the age of eighty, and in Ipswich one in eight, which is an enormous difference. This sort of longevity can also be found in many other parts of New Hampshire and Massachusetts.

In Woodstock, Connecticut, according to authentic records, 113 persons died in a period of eleven years, twenty-one of whom were over seventy years of age or older, and thirteen of whom were eighty years of age or older. This gives approximately one octogenarian in nine deaths.

I learned from a well-informed minister in Andover, New Hampshire [Massachusetts] that many men and especially women in that town live beyond the age of seventy. Basing his estimate on long experience in his own and neighboring parishes, he judged the proportion to be certainly better than one out of eight.

[4] See Dr. [Edward] Wigglesworth's memoir in vol. I [of the *Memoirs* of the American Academy of Arts and Sciences.]

[5] [Edmund Halley, *Degrees of Mortality of Mankind*, London, 1693. Brissot probably used the French edition *Tables . . . sur la mortalité dans les différens âges de la vie*, n.p., 1778.]

NEW TRAVELS IN THE UNITED STATES

Compare these figures with those of M. Moheau,[6] who stated that out of 14,000 inhabitants on the island of Oléron [7] only five or six were octogenarians, and that on the island of Ré,[8] which has a very healthful climate, there was only one octogenarian out of forty-two deaths.

The minister in Andover mentioned another of his observations (which confirms a theory of an author whose name escapes me), namely, that men of letters enjoy the greatest longevity, and that for the most part the oldest men are ministers. Another fact confirms this observation, as you will see from the tables below: men who have been graduated from the university in Cambridge live the longest. From these facts one can logically induce the causes of longevity: regularity of morals, an enlightened mind, independence of spirit, and freedom from want.

You will have a clearer picture of longevity in the United States from the attached life expectancy table given me by the respected Dr. Wigglesworth of the university in Cambridge, which shows comparative figures for New England, England, Sweden, Germany, Holland, and France.

The first column gives the ages; the following ones give in years and decimal parts of a year the life expectancy for the inhabitants of the different places indicated. You will see that life expectancy in this part of the United States is higher than in England or in Sweden, and is even higher than that of the annuitants on whose lives Kersseboom's tables are based,[9] and is almost equal to that of the annuitants on whose lives M. De Parcieux [10] has established his calculations for life annuities.[11]

The second column shows the life expectancy of graduates of Harvard College in Cambridge, which is a sort of hotbed for producing New England's ministers. Although they are dispersed

[6] See his *Recherches et considérations sur la population de la France* [Paris, 1778], p. 192.

[7] [Off La Rochelle, Department of Charente-Maritime, France.]

[8] [Also off La Rochelle.]

[9] [Willem Kersseboom, *Proeven van politique rekenkunde, vervat in drie verhandelingen over de meenigte des volks in de provintie van Hollandt en Westvrieslandt; de probable leeftyt der weduwen, de duurzaamheid der huwelyken, de relatie van de meenigte des volks tegen het getal der geboorene, en dat der gehuwde paaren, etc. . . . ,* The Hague, 1748.]

[10] [Antoine de Parcieux, *Essai sur les probabilités de la durée de la vie humaine,* Paris, 1746.]

[11] Of course the life expectancies of the general populations in France and Holland are much lower than those of the annuitants. The figures for France are slightly lower than those for Breslau.

throughout almost all the states in this area, although they hold the highest positions in the church and in the state, and although they conform to the customs and way of life of the towns in which they settle, you will see that, with the exception of Dover, New Hampshire, they have a higher life expectancy than any of the regions studied. In this column the life expectancy figure has been calculated from the list of all graduates since 1711 and has been computed by comparing the number of deaths with the number of graduates alive over a period of ten years.

The data in the third column is for Hingham, a town situated southeast of Boston. The occupations and way of life of the inhabitants are about the same as those of Massachusetts as a whole. These calculations have been made from a mortality table carefully compiled by Dr. Gay over a period of fifty years.[12]

The figures in the next column are for Dover, located on the Piscataqua River in New Hampshire, ten or twelve miles from the sea, and have been taken from mortality tables carefully composed by Dr. Belknap, the pastor at Dover,[13] for a ten-year period.

The other columns for European countries have been taken from Dr. Price's work.[14]

This comparative table should give you a definite picture of longevity in the United States. It would be desirable to have similar tables for the rest of the nation, and I have good reason to believe that, thanks to Dr. Wigglesworth of the Academy in Boston and to the other American academies, we shall have within a few years regular and complete tables for all the thirteen states.

I have given you a general picture of life expectancy. Now to satisfy your curiosity more completely I shall give a detailed table of births, marriages, and deaths in a single town in order to show you the relationships between births, deaths, the ages at which death occurs, and the various diseases. I shall take Salem. Since it is considered a very unhealthful place, there is no risk of our erring on the side of optimism if we induce from these figures conclusions about other towns.

Salem is a seaport, situated forty-two degrees latitude north, five leagues northeast of Boston, and between two tidal rivers. The land is flat, lying about twenty feet above high tide—two

[12] [Ebenezer Gay (1696–1787), for sixty-nine years pastor of the First Parish in Hingham.]

[13] [Jeremy Belknap (1744–1798), author of *The History of New Hampshire*.]

[14] [Richard Price, *Observations on Revisionary Payments, on Schemes for Promoting Annuities for Widows . . . and on the National Debt . . .* , London, 1771.]

A COMPARATIVE TABLE OF LIFE EXPECTANCY IN NEW ENGLAND AND IN EUROPE

Age	New England			England					
	Graduates of Harvard College	Hingham, Massachusetts	Dover, New Hampshire	London, Simpson's Tables	Norwich	Northampton	Chester Males	Chester Females	Holy Cross, near Shrewsbury
25	36.07	35.46	37.89	26.1	31.56	30.85	32.00	34.78	35.58
30	33.40	33.81	34.97	23.6	28.93	28.27	29.25	32.27	32.66
35	30.70	30.83	31.89	21.5	26.05	25.68	25.97	29.26	29.43
40	26.45	28.28	28.74	19.6	23.18	23.08	22.92	26.37	26.40
45	22.90	25.11	25.80	17.8	20.78	20.52	20.20	23.50	23.35
50	19.86	22.08	22.79	16.0	17.55	17.99	17.64	20.62	20.49
55	17.75	18.47	19.22	14.2	14.87	15.58	15.14	17.52	17.47
60	14.63	15.20	15.49	12.4	12.36	13.21	12.36	14.20	14.86
65	11.31	12.29	12.98	10.5	10.05	10.88	10.79	11.94	12.30
70	10.01	9.68	10.46	8.8	8.12	8.60	8.05	8.81	10.00
75	10.39	7.63	8.40	7.2	6.44	6.54	7.00	7.14	7.87
80	6.96	6.03	6.87	5.0	5.14	4.75	5.43	5.20	5.75
85	3.06	5.02	4.96		3.50	3.37	4.25	4.85	

| Age | Sweden | | | | Germany | | Holland | France |
| | Stockholm | | In the Kingdom | | | | Kersseboom's Tables of Annuitants | M. De Parcieux's Table of Annuitants |
	Males	Females	Males	Females	Breslau	Brandenburg		
25	21.40	26.80	33.63	35.58	30.88	31.76	33.27	37.01
30	19.42	23.98	30.34	32.17	27.80	28.70	30.92	33.96
35	17.58	21.62	27.09	29.03	24.92	25.56	28.36	30.73
40	15.61	19.21	23.75	25.21	22.13	22.65	25.49	27.30
45	13.78	17.17	20.71	22.57	19.56	19.65	22.34	23.77
50	11.95	15.12	17.72	19.26	17.07	16.55	19.41	20.24
55	10.36	12.89	14.98	16.15	14.77	13.68	16.72	16.88
60	8.69	10.45	12.24	13.08	12.30	11.28	14.10	13.86
65	7.39	8.39	9.78	10.49	9.86	9.15	11.56	11.07
70	5.81	6.16	7.60	7.91	7.45	7.48	9.15	8.34
75	4.09	4.39	5.89	6.03	5.51	6.17	6.81	5.79
80			4.27	4.47	4.08	5.06	5.05	4.73
85			3.16	3.40	2.36	4.18	3.38	3.45

EXPLANATION:

The first column gives the ages; the following ones give, in years and decimal parts of a year, the life expectancy for the inhabitants of the different places mentioned. The second column regards the graduates of Harvard College, in Cambridge; Hingham, which forms the third, is located to the south-east of Boston; and Dover, which forms the fourth, is in New Hampshire on the Piscataqua River, ten or twelve miles from the sea. The other columns regarding the European countries are taken from the work of Dr. Price.

very small hills near the town—the soil light, dry, sandy—no swamps—the residents are not subject to endemic diseases. They are at present complaining of nervous troubles and hysteria, which were formerly unknown there.

Mr. Holyoke [15] sent the Academy of Boston the two following excellent mortality tables for the town for the years 1781 and 1782.

TABLE FOR 1781		TABLE FOR 1782	
Deaths	175	Deaths	189
Births	317	Births (approximate)	385
Baptisms	152	Baptisms { Girls 78 / Boys 80 }	158
Marriages	70	Marriages (approximate)	84
Taxed persons, that is, male residents over 16 years of age	897	Taxable persons	1,000
Transients	200	Number of inhabitants (approximate)	9,000
Ages at Death		*Ages at Death*	
At birth	6	At birth	14
In the first month	6	In the first month	11
1 month to 1 year	30	1 month to 1 year	27
1 to 2 years	20	1 to 2	29
2 to 5 years	2	2 to 5	28
5 to 10	7	5 to 10	12
10 to 15	3	10 to 15	5
15 to 20	6	15 to 20	2
20 to 25	5	20 to 25	8
25 to 30	7	25 to 30	8
30 to 40	24	30 to 40	9
40 to 50	10	40 to 50	8
50 to 60	7	50 to 60	7
60 to 70	2	60 to 70	6
70 to 80	7	70 to 80	6
80 to 90	6	80 to 90	2
Ages unknown, mostly children	27	Ages unknown	9

In 1781, the greatest mortality occurred in the months of September, October, and January. Deaths in September, 35; in October, 22; in January, 21. The most favorable months were May, 8 deaths, and March, 9 deaths.

In 1782, May and June were the months with the highest mortality, because of an epidemic, with 33 and 24 deaths respectively. January had the lowest with 5 deaths.

[15] [Dr. Edward Augustus Holyoke (1728–1829), one of the foremost physicians of New England and one of the founders of the American Academy of Arts and Sciences.]

In 1781, the disease called cholera or dysentery killed 20 people; consumption, 4; pulmonary phthisis, 13. In 1782, the same number died of phthisis and consumption, while the measles, a kind of chest disease, killed 16, and dysentery only 8. It has been noted that 1782 was a worse year for sickness than any other. I have mentioned in an earlier letter that that year was very dry in Pennsylvania.

I have already given the mortality tables for Salem for two different years. Below is a table for the single month of September 1788, when 20 persons died:

1 woman aged	67
1 woman aged	80
1 man aged	88
1 man aged	79
1 man aged	66
1 man aged	85
1 man aged	75

Three others were 23, 16, and 30 years old, and the ages of the other ten are unknown.[16]

Keep in mind, my friend, the fact that Salem is one of the most unhealthful towns in America. Are you not surprised to find four octogenarians out of twenty deaths?

In another respect, the two mortality tables for the two years suggest some other striking thoughts. In 1781 there were 175 deaths. If we estimated the population of Salem by the general rule of one death for every thirty persons, Salem should have only 5,250 residents. Now, in fact it has over 9,000. This means that we must estimate that in Salem there is about one death for every fifty persons. In London, the rate is one out of twenty-three, and in the English rural areas about one in forty. The average death

[16] American periodicals give lists of deaths for all the states. Here is one taken at random from the *American Museum* for May 1790:

	Deaths
New Hampshire	one at 70 yrs.
Massachusetts	several at 71
Southborough, [Mass.]	106
Stockbridge, [Mass.]	92
Dorchester, [Mass.]	87
Lisbon, Conn.	91
Canterbury, [Conn.]	98
New York	104
New Jersey	80
Pennsylvania	84 yrs., 3 mos.
Elsewhere	76

rate in Paris is one in thirty, and in the French rural areas one in twenty-four.

Comparing the number of births in Salem in 1781 to the number of inhabitants, we find there is one birth for every twenty-seven persons, while the average in France is one in twenty-six.

As to marriages, M. Moheau estimates that there is one marriage for every 121 inhabitants in the French rural areas, and one in 160 in Paris. In Salem in 1781 there was one marriage for every 128 inhabitants, while in 1783 [1782?] the rate was the same as in rural France. This is, however, far from being normal for American rural areas. We do not yet have accurate tables; we must wait.

As you have told me, we cannot hope to have a mass of complete information until there are life insurance companies in every country which compile statistics according to a uniform procedure and whose tables can serve, at the end of certain periods, as exact bases for calculations on life expectancy.

I do not wish to end this lengthy letter on longevity without giving you the birth and death tables for the Lutheran congregation in Philadelphia over a period of fourteen years, from 1774 to 1788. You will notice an interesting progression:

		Births	Deaths
From 1774 to	1775	379	156
1775	1776	338	175
1776	1777	389	124
1777	1778	298	169
1778	1779	303	178
1779	1780	348	186
1780	1781	320	158
1781	1782	323	162
1782	1783	398	219
1783	1784	389	215
1784	1785	426	153
1785	1786	420	157
1786	1787	419	150
1787	1788	425	178
		5,175	2,369 [2,380]

I do not know the number of Lutheran families in Philadelphia. If we apply the common rule of one birth per twenty-five people, the number of Lutherans in Philadelphia in 1788 should have been 10,525 [10,625]. But if we apply the common rule for deaths of one in thirty, we arrive at a figure of only 5,340 inhabitants, that is, one half less. In order to reconcile this discrepancy of one half we must either diminish our estimate of the number of inhabitants based on the number of births, or else increase our estimate based on the number of deaths. If we do the first, the conclusion must be that the Lutherans are very fertile; if we do the second, we must conclude that they have a longer average life span than the French.

You will notice from this table that in the years 1782–1783 and 1783–1784 the mortality was highest. If we apply this observation to the Salem tables, made for these same two years [sic], we must conclude that two particularly unhealthful years were chosen for the calculations. You will also note that during the war years there were fewer births, which was natural. This is a consideration to be borne in mind by all those calculating mortality rates in America.

Finally, my friend, I should like to give you an idea of the rapid general increase in population in the United States with the following tables for Rhode Island and the Jerseys, which you may compare with those I have already given you for the states of New York and Pennsylvania.

POPULATION OF RHODE ISLAND AND PROVIDENCE

Years	Whites	Negroes
1730	15,302	2,603
1742	29,755	4,373
1761	35,939	4,697
1774	54,435	5,243
1783	48,538	3,361

NEW JERSEY

1738	43,388	3,981
1745	56,797	4,606
1784	139,934	10,501

You will see from these tables that the population of Rhode Island, which doubled in the twelve years from 1730 to 1742, decreased from 1774 to 1783. This decline was due to the seven years of war and to the emigrations caused by bad government and the scourge of paper money. But with what pleasure will you note that the population of New Jersey has tripled in forty years, despite the horrors of a bloody war! And how delighted you will be, my friend, you who are a champion of the Negroes, to see that the Negro population in New Jersey has much more than doubled during the same period, although the slave trade has been forbidden since 1775, although the war cost the lives of many Negroes, and although many of them were stolen by the English to be sold in the West Indies.

Even supposing that the figures may not be rigorously exact, what conclusions can we draw from all the facts and all the tables I have given you?

That the life of man is much longer in the United States of America than it is in the healthiest countries of Europe.

THE PHILADELPHIA PRISON

Philadelphia too has its prison! I like to think that thirty or forty years after the foundation of this city, when the Quakers were the magistrates, or rather when there was no need for magistrates, no prison existed here. But since the decision of the English to rid themselves of all the bandits infesting their island by setting them loose in the United States, since the inundation of America by a greater number of foreign adventurers, and since the last war, which increased the number of these adventurers, reduced many persons to poverty and habituated others to crime, it has become necessary to restrain them with prisons. It is to the honor of the state, however, that less than a tenth of the prisoners in Philadelphia are native Americans. During my stay in this city only one theft has been committed, and this by a French sailor. Almost all the other prisoners are either Irish or French.

This prison is a kind of house of correction where the prisoners are forced to work and receive the proceeds of their labor. This is the most effective method of improving men and is the one employed by the Quakers. Those who manage the house of correction in New York, when they consented to take charge of the malefactors condemned by the law, asked to be allowed to substitute their humane method of correction for lashings and mutilations. They were permitted to do so, and they have succeeded in persuading these misguided men to work and in bringing them back to the paths of reason.

"What do you do," one of these Quakers was asked by an American, "to reform these men who degrade human nature and refuse to work?"

"Don't we have hunger, thirst, and the torch of hope?" the Quaker replied.

The small number of native Pennsylvanians in the prison of Philadelphia makes it evident that if there were no foreigners there would be no need of a jail. There could be, as in Nantucket, a prison where the door would stand unlocked and where honor and repentance would be the only guardians.

But why must there always be prisons? Why these tombs in

which men are buried alive? The Indians have none and do not suffer from the lack. If there is any country where one could and where one ought to change this system, it is indeed the United States. So it is to Americans in particular that I now speak:

Prisons are destructive of the health, liberty, and goodness of man. To be healthy, a man needs fresh air, frequent exercise, and good food. In prisons the air is foul, there is no room for exercise, and the food is often detestable. A man is healthy only when he is with those who love him and whom he loves; in prison he is with strangers and evil men. There can be no social relationship between prisoners; and if there is, one of two things must happen: either he must ceaselessly struggle against the fearful influence of these evil men and thus engage in a constant and agonizing battle; or else he becomes like them, which subjects him to equal torments. A man who lives with madmen becomes mad. Everything in life is contagious and interrelated.

When you imprison a man, you tear him away from his wife, his children, and his friends; you deprive him of their help and their consolation; you plunge him into bitterness and boredom; you cut off all his ties. It is like severing a plant from its roots and its nourishing soil. How can you expect it to exist?

A man who has vegetated long in prison and who has passed through frequent fits of rage and despair is no longer the same person when he leaves as he was when he entered. He returns to the family from whom he has been separated so long and finds that he no longer has the same feelings. He may no longer find the same understanding, the same affection; he may not be able to respond to their love; in his absence, others may have formed new ties with his family, and new needs may have dominated and shaped their lives.

When you put a man in prison you subject him to the power of the keeper, of the jailer, the turnkey, and the commissary of the prison, before all of whom he must abase and restrain himself in order not to worsen his lot. This constraint and humiliation are horrible, and the jailers become habituated to injustice and cruelty and turn into evil men.

To force a free man to plead for his own well-being is a crime. The tree once it has been bent never regains its natural form.

From all I have said, it follows that the *habeas corpus* law is wise and in accordance with nature, but unfortunately it does not apply to all cases. A man who is imprisoned for debt and who is unable to furnish bail is forced to remain in prison. A man accused of a capital offense, even though he will probably be acquitted, cannot take advantage of this law. These are injustices.

Would it not be simpler to let each man's house be his prison, as the Indians do, even if it should mean placing a sentinel at his door? But what about those who have no home? Let there be a public refuge for them, and they will have no cause to complain. And how many expenses would be saved!

If such a system as this is necessary at all, it is surely necessary for a society which has good morals and wishes to preserve them. If it is at all practicable, it is practicable in a nation where serious crime is rare, as is the case in North America. Remember, my friend, that for nineteen years before the war no capital punishment was inflicted in Connecticut.

I am indeed surprised that capital punishment has not been totally abolished in this country. Morals here are so pure, material well-being is so general, and poverty is so rare! Is there any need of such terrible punishments to prevent crime?

Dr. Rush recently stressed all these arguments in asking for the abolition of the death penalty when sentences were imposed on two unfortunate brothers who were guilty of criminal assault on several occasions during and after the last war. He was not successful, however. The Executive Council referred the matter to the legislature, and it is to be hoped that Pennsylvania, and all the other Northern states as well, will free themselves of their superstitious respect for English law and will have the courage to give to Europe a great example of justice, humanity, and political wisdom. Any objection which could be made in Europe against this reform does not apply, for here everything supports it.

QUAKERS AND THEIR CUSTOMS

I have promised you, my dear friend, a letter specially devoted to this worthy society, and today I shall keep my word.

You recall the insulting frivolity with which M. Chastellux discussed the Quakers in his most superficial *Travels*. You will also recall my stern criticism of his errors, lies, and calumnies,[1] the underhanded persecution I suffered for this criticism, and the attempts to block its success made by that clever marquis and some Academicians seeking to tyrannize public opinion and inflate their own reputations. Nor will you have forgotten those petty letters published in the *Journal de Paris,* a sheet which served the cause of every sort of despot, in which the Quakers were pitilessly lacerated while the biased censors and journalists cravenly suppressed every reply to these virulent diatribes.[2]

---

[1] See my *Examen critique des Voyages dans l'Amérique septentrionale de M. le marquis de Chatellux; ou Lettre à M. le marquis de Chatellux, dans laquelle on réfute principalement ses opinions sur les Quakers, sur les Nègres, sur le Peuple et sur l'Homme* . . . , [London,] 1786.

[2] Perhaps this would be the place to give an account of all these maneuvers and to publish the correspondence which this affair occasioned between M. Chastellux, several other persons, and myself. However, as I am forced to abbreviate what I have to say on the Quakers, I shall postpone this publication to another time. [Brissot is referring to the letter by Filippo Mazzei published under the name Ferri in the *Journal de Paris* November 16, 1786, which defended Chastellux's opinion of the Quakers. Brissot, according to his own account, sent "letter after letter" in reply to the editors of the *Journal de Paris* but none was printed (*Mémoires*, II, 183). He never published a complete account of this controversy, but see his amusing description of his encounter with Mazzei (p. 309n) and the relevant passages in his *Mémoires* (II, 46–47, 183). Although the quarrel was ostensibly over the Quakers, the real issue was between what might be called democratic and aristocratic Americanism, two positions best exemplified by Brissot and Chastellux respectively. Crèvecoeur, who had connections with Chastellux, was embarrassed by a controversy in which he had no wish to be involved; Lafayette felt obliged to apologize for Brissot's brochure in his letter of introduction to Washington (Brissot, *Correspondance,* p. 192); the Abbé Morellet published a defense of Chastellux but was persuaded to destroy all but two copies lest he add unwanted fuel to the conflagration (A. Morellet, *Mémoires* [Paris, 1823], I, 322); and the Marquis de Moustier, French minister to the United States in 1788, felt that the fact that Brissot had authored this "brochure . . . full of invectives" was ample reason why "it was not fitting that such a man should be received by the king's minister" (Brissot, *Correspondance,* p. 177). On the other hand, Mirabeau, citing his own "antiaristocratic sentiments" called it "a vigorous reply" and Mme Roland thought it an "excellent letter" (*Ibid.,* pp. 102, 222). Despite Brissot's implication, the truth is that the

QUAKERS AND THEIR CUSTOMS

I now have had the opportunity, my friend, to compare the portrait I formerly made of the Quakers with the Quakers I have seen in America, and I am convinced that, with the exception of a few details, I did not flatter them. You will be convinced of this as you read the following observations and impressions. I have tried as much as possible not to be influenced by the flattering manner in which they received me because of their gratitude for the apology of their sect which I had published. It has been translated into English here in America by some worthy members of the Society and has been widely distributed among the Friends.[3] I was happy to see that my work had helped to dispel the unfortunate prejudices against our nation which had been occasioned by the indiscretion, boasting, and indecent sarcasm of that frivolous Academician.

I first must quote from the general description I wrote when in England of the private conduct and public morals of the Quakers.[4] You yourself have had opportunity to become more intimately acquainted with Quakers during your frequent trips to England and your extended stay in Ireland. I wrote as follows:

Simplicity, candor, and honesty characterize their actions and speech. They are not affectionate, but they are sincere; they are not polite, but they are humane; they lack the scintillating wit without which a man cannot exist in France and with which he can do anything, but they have common sense, balanced judgment, integrity, and honest hearts. In short, for friends and associates, give me Quakers; for diverting companions, give me the French. As for their women, they are what all women ought to be: faithful to their husbands, tender with their children, simple in their dress, and thrifty and conscientious housewives. Their main characteristic is that they are not in the least interested in courting the attention of other individuals or of the world at large. Their whole life is directed inward, not outward.

There are still a few countries where such simplicity of manners exists; it is preserved, for instance, by the Arabs, who lead the nomadic life of the early patriarchs. I cannot repeat too often that it is only among people fol-

only anti-Quaker article the *Journal de Paris* published during the years 1786–1788 was Mazzei's letter. On November 26, 1786, it printed a warm defense of the Quakers by the Abbé Robin, and the following year it published a sympathetic review of the second edition of Crèvecoeur's *Lettres* as well as several long extracts from this work.]

[3] [The *Examen*, translated as *A Critical Examination of the Marquis de Chatellux's Travels in North America, in a Letter Addressed to the Marquis; Principally Intended as a Refutation of His Opinions Concerning the Quakers, the Negroes, the People, and Mankind . . . with Additions and Corrections by the Author*, Philadelphia, 1788.]

[4] See vol. II, no. 4, p. 196 of the *Journal du Licée de Londres, ou Tableau de l'état présent des sciences et des arts en Angleterre* (Paris: Périsse, 1784).

lowing this way of life that one finds happy families and public virtue. We, unhappy and diseased in the midst of our civilization and polite manners, have renounced these virtues. And indeed, who among us is happy except the man who has the strength to return to nature and live as did the good people of ancient times? "Ad naturam si vives," Seneca says, "numquam eris pauper; si ad opinionem, numquam dives." [5]

I shall not repeat here everything that M. Crèvecoeur wrote about the Quakers; I wish to tell you only what he did not say.

Simplicity is the Quakers' main virtue, and the men still adhere quite closely to Penn's advice: "Choose thy clothes by thine own eyes, not another's. The more plain and simple they are, the better. Neither unshapely, nor fantastical; and for use and decency, not for pride . . . If thou art clean and warm, it is sufficient; for more doth but rob the poor and please the wanton." [6]

I have seen James Pemberton, one of the wealthiest Quakers and a man whose virtues place him among the most respected of their leaders. His coat was threadbare but spotless; he prefers to clothe the poor and spend his money in defense of the Negroes rather than have a large wardrobe.

You are familiar with Quaker dress: a round hat, almost always white; a coat of fairly good cloth; cotton or woolen stockings; and their hair cut round and without powder. A Quaker usually carries in his pocket a small comb in a case, and if his hair is in disorder when he enters a house he simply combs it in front of the first mirror he finds.

The white hat which the Quakers prefer has recently become more common since Franklin has proved its advantages over black ones. They still insist on not wearing buttons on their hats. They have nothing against this custom in itself, but since they despise vanity and superfluity and wish to have only well-tried members who are above the fear of appearing ridiculous, they require of all Quakers that they do not dress as other men. A test at first, this practice ends by becoming a distinctive sign of the truly devout.

The country Quakers usually wear homespun cloth. It was called to my attention that at their General Meeting in September

[5] [If you live in accordance with your nature, you will never be poor; if in accordance with opinion, you will never be rich. *Moral Epistles* II, 4.]

[6] William Penn, *Some Fruits of Solitude; or Reflections and Maxims Relating to the Conduct of Human Life* [London, 1693, nos. 74, 75]. This excellent manual, which ought to be in the hands of all those who seek to practice virtue, especially the virtue of republicans, has been lately translated by M. Bridel and is on sale in Paris, at Gras's, Quai de Conti.

of this year nine tenths of the nearly 1,500 persons present wore this domestic cloth, thus setting a good example for other sects to follow.

There are Quakers who dress with greater care and elegance, who wear powder, silver buckles, and ruffled cuffs. They are called "Wet Quakers" and are regarded by the others as schismatic or weak. Though allowed to attend the Sunday Meetings, they are never permitted at the Monthly or Quarterly Meetings.

Not more than fifteen years ago it was still considered a sort of crime by all the sects in America to wear powder. A mother would send her daughter to the theater and forbid her to wear any. Since the last war, however, manners have changed in almost all sects because of the influence of the European armies. Let it be said to the honor of the Quakers that theirs have changed less, because of the strictness with which they adhere to their discipline and repudiate those who stray from it.

On the fifteenth of September Quakers put on woolen stockings. This is part of their system of discipline, which applies even to their clothing, and they attribute their longevity to the regular observance of this custom. There is also another fact which I forgot to mention, and which proves that they are right. Of the Quakers who were Penn's contemporaries in 1693, there are six who are still alive at the moment I write. One named Drinker, born in 1680, lived to be a hundred. It is this deep-seated conviction of the advantages of their ways that causes the Quakers to keep their dress unchanged. Their so-called eccentricities are in reality customs inspired by the counsel of reason and by long experience. Yet writers who are presumed to be serious have had the effrontery to ridicule their simple dress.[7]

Quaker women usually dress more warmly than other American women and consequently are less subject to diseases, as I have

---

[7] [Jean Antoine] Rigoley de Juvigny, in a very weighty book, *Sur les décadences des lettres et des moeurs* [Paris, 1787], complains about the frequent trips we French make to London, about the simplicity of English dress which we have brought back to France, and about the dire results of this simplicity. "Might one not mistake for a Quaker," he writes, "this courtier or that great lord who conceals his identity under rough clothes, wears a round pointed cap pulled down over his nose, and walks about the streets without any mark of his dignity, running the risk at every moment of some unpleasant accident or of being elbowed and shoved aside by some mere passer-by?" An even better idea of this writer can be had from his opinion that the writings of the *Philosophes* are unconcerned with the public welfare, that the people are a mass of brutish beasts, and that it is to the general interest to leave them in their ignorance.

already noted. Age and wealth do, however, introduce differences in their dress which are far more noticeable than in men's clothing. The matrons wear very dark, even dismal, colors and small black bonnets, with their hair simply brushed up. On the other hand, the young women often curl their hair with so much care that they spend as much time, I am told, as they might on the most elegant toilettes. I noticed with sorrow that they wear small hats covered with silk or satin. These young Quakeresses, who are so well endowed with natural beauty and whose charms have so little need of artifices or added adornments, make themselves conspicuous by their choice of the finest linens, muslins, and silks. Their fingers play with elegant fans, and the luxury of the Orient would not disdain their fine linen. Is all this in accordance with Penn's precepts? "Meekness and modesty," he said, "are the rich and charming attire of the soul; and the plainer the dress, the more distinctly, and with greater lustre, their beauty shines." [8]

Since I will not flatter even my friends, I must say frankly to the Quakers (for I am sure they will read me and I know they always profit by good counsel) that if anything can discredit their principles abroad it is this gradual and imperceptible relaxation of their morals and customs. Their liking for fine cloth appears as an ill-disguised and hypocritical love of luxury, which is, to say the least, inconsistent with their loud professions of simplicity and austerity.

Luxury begins where utility ends. Now, of what use is fine linen to the body? And to what use could not be put the money which is spent on this luxury! There are so many good deeds to be done! So many people in need!

Luxury in simple things betrays even more vanity than the usual sort of luxury, for it appears to be a measure of that very wealth which the Quakers would have us believe they scorn to parade. Such luxury proclaims that the mind is no longer imbued with great moral principles; it proves that one believes that happiness depends on appearances and show rather than on virtue.

What a poor example the Quakers, who have been the models of simplicity, set for other Americans! The United States does not now nor will it for a long time manufacture fine linens, delicate fabrics, and almost transparent muslins; these must be imported from the foreign countries on which Americans already rely for so

[8] [*Some Fruits of Solitude,* no. 77.]

many other more essential needs. Thus these luxury goods drain away money which is badly needed for extending the settlements and establishing new industries. Let the Quakers who read this letter meditate on my words; may they realize that the use of rum, which they so strongly oppose, cannot harm America any more than will the introduction of luxury into their society. I have noticed the same sort of thing in the furniture of wealthy Quakers; it seems plain, but there are many fine and expensive pieces.

Fortunately this luxury has not yet found its way to the tables of the Quakers. I must describe a dinner given by one of the richest men of the sect at the time of the General Meeting in September; it presents a curious contrast with our splendid French banquets. At the time of this meeting Philadelphia is filled with Quakers from the country and the neighboring towns, and their brethren lodge and feed them and welcome them with the most affectionate hospitality. About twenty guests were gathered around the table, the master of the house sitting at one end and the mistress at the other. Before the meal was served there was a moment of silence during which the Quakers silently gave thanks to the Supreme Being. The first course consisted of a large piece of beef placed at one end of the table, a ham placed in the middle, a leg of lamb at the other end, two soups, and four dishes of potatoes, cabbage, vegetables, etc., as well as cider, Philadelphia porter, and beer. The master of the house spoke to each Friend, saying: "Help thyself, ask for what thou likest, make thyself at home." The second course consisted merely of various kinds of pies and cakes, two bowls of cream, two dishes of cheese, and two of butter. The servant then poured a glass of wine for each guest, but there were none of those tiresome toasts which are more incitements to drunkenness than expressions of patriotism. We chatted quietly. It is true that at this simple meal there was none of the sparkle and gaiety of our noisy French dinners and suppers. But everybody seemed happy and comfortable and felt at home. Good Thomas —— seemed very happy indeed to be able to welcome in this way his brothers from the country.

Those who have reproached Quaker men and women for being sad and morose can have known them only superficially and not intimately. I, who have been received by them as their own son and have shared their family life, have found that they have moments of open, frank emotion and of gaiety, as well as periods of pleasant and affectionate conversation. They do not lead lives of mad joy, but they are serene and happy, and, if gaiety is the expression of the happiness of the soul, they are gay.

We Frenchmen have the reputation of being gay because we laugh at everything and find consolation for misfortune in a vaudeville.[9] This is not gaiety but folly. Laughter is the sign of gaiety, and gaiety is the outward expression of pleasurable sensations, or of a sense of well-being, or of thoughts which awaken such pleasurable sensations. One should therefore not be gay except when one is happy. A man who is gay in the midst of misfortune is mad; but if he is serene and imperturbable he is wise. One should not be crushed by misfortune, nor should one laugh at it; the former is weakness, the latter madness or stupidity.

Seneca seems to have well depicted the Quakers' gaiety in the following philosophical passage: "Above all, my dear Lucilius, make this your business: learn how to feel joy . . . I do not wish you ever to be deprived of gladness. I would have it born in your house (*domi nasci*, or home-born, as the English say with inimitable concision); and it is born there, if only it be inside of you. Other objects of cheer do not fill a man's bosom; they merely smooth his brow and are inconstant, unless perhaps you believe that he who laughs has joy. The soul must be *happy* and confident, lifted above every circumstance. *Real joy, believe me, is a stern matter.*" [10]

The composure of the Quakers in their gaiety is also theirs in the midst of misfortune, during their discussions, and in all their undertakings. This they owe to their special training, which teaches them at an early age to curb their passions, and especially to check hasty temper or anger. Their aim is to make themselves, as they say, "immovable," that is, impervious to sudden emotions, impassive, imperturbable. As a result, they are at all times complete masters of themselves, and so in discussions they have a great advantage over those who lose their tempers. "Nothing does reason more right," Penn said in his manual, "than the coolness of those that offer it; for truth often suffers more by the heat of its defenders than from the arguments of its opposers." [11]

I have seen in my friend Miers Fisher, whom I have mentioned before, a sample of the excellent effects of this coolness in discus-

[9] [A gay popular song, usually topical and satirical.]
[10] *Moral Epistles* XXIII.
[11] [*Some Fruits of Solitude*, no. 142.]

sion. I must first tell you something about his life. He was born a Quaker and belongs to one of the largest and most respected families in Philadelphia, among whom there are several distinguished merchants. He first went into trade and then studied and practiced law. During the last war he consistently adhered to the pacifist neutrality of the Quakers and refused to side either with the Americans or the English. As a result he became most unpopular. He was one of the Quakers who were exiled to Virginia, and he lost at that time a large part of his fortune. After the peace he returned to Philadelphia, where he continues to practice law. Even his enemies think highly of his ability, and not only in legal matters. This estimable man has a great fund of information, which is rare among Quakers, who rather study the Bible and moral questions, and is indeed rare among Americans generally. His political sentiments, however, still make him an object of considerable suspicion, and we can only hope that this hostility will vanish and that he will someday play the part in Congress for which his talents and virtues have created him. I heard him in the Pennsylvania General Assembly defend the cause of the pilots, who were opposing a bill to reduce their fees. Clarity, close reasoning, and erudition were the distinctive marks of his plea, which was successful. He constantly maintained his calm even though interrupted by sudden and sometimes rather sharp attacks from members of the Assembly.

This composure accompanies Quakers to the very edge of their graves. Even the women do not lose it at this sad moment. It is the fruit both of their religious principles and of right conduct constantly maintained. After a death the survivors seem either to abandon themselves to grief less than do most people or else to contain it within themselves. They hold Heaven their home and do not believe that death, which leads to it, can be a misfortune.

You must understand, however, that this habitual composure in no way diminishes their sensibility. The worthy James Pemberton described to me the death of his beloved daughter on the very next day after this misfortune had struck him. I saw steal down from his eye a tear, which reflection immediately wiped away. He loved to talk to me of her virtues and of her resignation during her long suffering. "She was an angel," he said, "and she is now in her home."

This good father did not exaggerate. In this society you will find a far greater number of those happy, angelic faces on which you can read serenity, the sign of peace of soul, and therefore of virtue.

I cannot explain why, but it is true that with a pure soul, a great soul, I am at once at ease. I feel that we have known one another for centuries; we understand each other without speaking. But a corrupt man, a rake, a man of the world, immediately produces upon me the opposite impression. My soul shrinks and recoils like a sensitive plant. In the company of Quakers I have almost always experienced the first of these two impressions.[12]

The portrait I have given of the Quakers is a summary not only of my own observations, but also of information I have gathered from the best-informed men, including ones of other sects.

Once, in company, I asked: "Is there greater purity of morals, more simplicity, and more honesty and integrity among the Quakers than in any other sect?" A man distinguished for his knowledge and his devotion to the new constitution answered me, "Although I was born a Presbyterian, I must admit that the Quakers excel all other sects in these respects."

Of course, they are not all pure and irreproachable, and there have been rascals among them, for the use to which their reputation can be put has inevitably drawn to them hypocritical proselytes and knaves. A man would rather counterfeit a guinea than a halfpenny. But Quakers are very strict in expelling from their

[12] I find in the *Bhagavad-Gita*, a work translated from the Sanskrit, a portrait of a true servant of God, which is applicable to many Quakers: "He my servant is dear unto me, who is free from enmity, the friend of all nature, merciful, exempt from pride and selfishness, the same in pain and pleasure, patient of wrongs, contented, constantly devout, of subdued passions, and firm resolves, and whose mind and understanding are fixed on me alone. He also is my beloved of whom mankind are not afraid, and who of mankind is not afraid; and who is free from the influence of joy, impatience, and the dread of harm. He my servant is dear unto me who is unexpecting, just and pure, impartial, free from distraction of mind, and who hath forsaken every enterprise. He also is worthy of my love, who neither rejoiceth nor findeth fault; who neither lamenteth nor coveteth, and, being my servant, hath forsaken both good and evil fortune. He also is my beloved servant, who is the same in friendship and in hatred, in honor and in dishonor, in cold and in heat, in pain and pleasure; who is unsolicitous about the event of things; to whom praise and blame are as one; who is of little speech, and pleased with whatever cometh to pass; who owneth no particular home, and who is of a steady mind. They who seek this *Amrĕĕtă* of religion even as I have said, and serve me faithfully before all others, are, moreover, my dearest friends." [Brissot's source was a long quotation, identical with this passage, which appeared in the *Journal de Paris*, May 2, 1787, in an article reviewing *La Bhaguat-Geeta, ou Dialogues de Kreeshna et d'Arjoon* . . . , London, 1787, a translation by Parraud of Charles Wilkins' translation from the Sanskrit, *The Bhăgvăt-Gēētā, or Dialogues of Krĕĕshnă and Arjŏŏn* . . . , London, 1785. The above English version is from this latter text, pp. 99–100.]

community those who have been found guilty not only of crimes but even of breaches of delicacy and probity that are not punishable by law. The public is often unaware of these expulsions because the rejected Quaker continues to attend Sunday Meetings. The Quakers cannot prevent him from doing so, but they no longer consider him a member of their society, and he is no longer admitted to their Monthly and Quarterly Meetings.

I should like to be able to summarize here all the characteristics of the Quakers, but I must choose from the most striking. Among these is orderliness, which they are taught from childhood to observe in their work, their thoughts, and in every moment of their existence. They apply this principle of order to every aspect of their life; it teaches good behavior and it saves time, effort, and money.

Quaker homes are remarkable for their orderliness and cleanliness. They instill these virtues into their young people at an early age. This is the very opposite of our French education and habits. Look at the room of a French bachelor—everything is thrown about, books, papers, stockings, clothes, shoes, etc., and everything is covered with dust. The consequence of this disorder is that he gives no care to his linen or clothes; they are dirty, worn out, and flung in a heap. So he has to buy new ones. And so he has to spend more, he needs more money, and as a result he is less able to aid the unfortunate and contribute to good works. Then too, in buying new clothes more often he acquires a taste for new and frivolous fashions and loses the habit of simplicity. Nor is this all; the final consequences are even worse. Since his needs are greater he requires more money, and if he cannot make enough in trade or farming or industry he tries his luck, he gambles or he borrows, and soon he is overwhelmed by inevitable ruin. Nor is even this the end. For a man with simple tastes, the modest inheritance of his ancestors or the wages of his own work are sufficient. Such a man is independent, he is free to vote as he pleases and to criticize any public official. But once he falls into luxury he must combine the salaries of several positions to meet his expenses; but these positions can be obtained only by flattering either men in power or the people, or else by compromising with all parties—in a word, by sacrificing his independence. You who aspire to independence, then renounce luxury! Inspire in your children at an early age an aversion to it; teach them to love simplicity and orderliness in all their doings and all their occupations. Only then will they achieve a sufficiency of goods and be humane, hospitable men and women. My friend Miers Fisher is a living example of this precept: His house is ever open to strangers, particularly to Frenchmen, to whom he is like a father, ever ready to help with either his wisdom or his purse. Truly, orderliness is the mother of all virtues.

ATTACKS UPON QUAKERS BY VARIOUS WRITERS

The spectacle of virtue is painful to the wicked, and they seek to avenge themselves by decrying it. You should not then be surprised that some writers have tried to vilify the Quakers. One of their most pitiless critics is the author of *Recherches sur les Etats-Unis,* published early this year.[1] In a long chapter he has spun out all the insults he had already directed against them in a letter published under the name of one of his fellow citizens in the *Journal de Paris* of November 16, 1786.[2] The writer is an Italian, a M. Mazzei, who is now living in France and who has spent a few years

---

[1] [Filippo Mazzei,] *Recherches historiques et politiques sur les Etats-Unis de l'Amérique septentrionale . . . par un citoyen de Virginie* [Colle, 1788], 4 vols., 8º.

[2] I must report here a conversation which will give the reader an idea of the mentality of the Academicians who were persecuting me at that time. It is a faithful transcript from notes I made immediately afterward.

Early in September 1786, M. Mazzei, who had dictated the letter, met me at the Palais Royal and said, "I have read at the house of the Duke de L[a Rochefoucauld?] my letter on your criticism and on M. Chastellux's *Travels.* Several Academicians were present. They advised me to delete all my criticisms of the Marquis and retain only those that applied to you. *I thought I ought to comply.* My letter would not have been translated and defended except on that condition. You have," he added, "terrible enemies in the Academy. They complain that you are always attacking them and that you have tried to associate them with the Marquis in your criticism of him. You are young, you are in danger, take care."

"And what will they do to me?" I asked. "Put me in the Bastille?"

"Maybe something worse."

"Then you advise me to be a coward, to sacrifice truth to these paltry considerations? What would you do in my place?"

"Placate them."

"No, I shall never lend myself to this. Have I been unjust? Look at the advice they give you. Isn't it proof of their baseness? I am not afraid of them, I have no hopes of a pension or a seat in the Academy. Ministers have never seen my name on the shameful list of beggars pestering them for favors. Heaven knows, I have never had thoughts of the Academy, and all I have sought has been the truth. Whatever happens, I shall do my duty, and I am sure, M. Mazzei, that you will do yours."

"You are right," he said. "I am fifty years old and I am still not cured of the need to tell the truth."

Yet this vigorous teller of truths lent himself to quashing the criticism of a marquis and to censuring the commoner who had made it! And this is the man who jokes about the Quakers, calling them Jesuits and hypocrites! Here indeed is the place for the apologue of the beam and the mote.

in Virginia, where he must have absorbed the prejudices against Quakers common among plantation owners. These planters, spend-thrifts, advocates of slavery, and lovers of luxury, pleasure, and show, regard with nothing but dislike a society which preaches and practices thrift and simplicity.

Moreover, M. Mazzei has met few Quakers and has never known any intimately, so his words can carry little weight. He quotes as authorities Virginians and Frenchmen, and especially French offi-ers. It seems to me that the French, who love to indulge in ridi-cule, and particularly French officers, whose lives are far removed from Quaker principles, make superficial observers and unreli-able judges. I must, however, say in praise of the French army that it always respected the Quakers. A French general, for in-stance, was preparing to use their meetinghouse in Newport as an armory but returned it to them when they protested. An English general on a similar occasion behaved differently. In another in-stance, a French officer who was quartered with his soldiers in the home of a Quaker did not allow any arms to be taken into the house out of respect for the Quaker's principles.

M. Chastellux did not sympathize with these principles. The reason for his bias against the Quakers was that at the time when he was traveling in America the Friends were very unpopular. He became infected with the current prejudices against them, without meeting or talking to any of them. He allowed himself to be carried along by the current of public opinion, and to amuse pretty women he made jokes about the Inner Light. What faith can we place in such a traveler?

In order to be well informed about Quakers, I have associated with both English and American Friends. I have also questioned reliable and respected men of other denominations and of various professions, and although they agreed that not all Quakers were above reproach, they told me that the sect was the most respected of all and the one least infected by the general corruption of our day.

English journalists, to whom nothing is sacred, make fun only of Quaker dress. Now, were there anything scandalous to report, these malicious scribblers would not fail to reveal it. If Quakers were really hypocrites and swindlers, would it not have been a miracle indeed if during the period of two years that I was in England the scandal sheets of London that I used to glance through had failed to mention them?

ATTACKS UPON QUAKERS

Among the defenders of the Quakers I have cited Voltaire himself, Raynal, Mrs. Macaulay,[3] and above all M. Crèvecoeur. What names can one oppose to these?

Here is how the Quakers are described by a French traveler, whom I suspect of being a noble because of his contempt for *le peuple canaille*, and whose testimony, I am sure, M. Mazzei will not reject when he learns that he is rather harsh on the Quakers' religious enthusiasm:

In speaking of them in these general terms, I do not mean to confuse them with the rest of humankind, from whom they differ in their social way of being in such a way as to make them most valuable citizens. Indeed they owe to the exercise of certain ideas, in part moral and religious, which are implanted in them at birth, a routine kind of virtue which, even if it gives them no merit, is at least an advantage for society, in which, *being peaceful subjects always submissive to the sovereign whoever he may be, they serve as models of good morals to the nation and as ministers of fraternal beneficence to individuals.*[4]

Do you not recognize here, my friend, the peevish tone aristocrats adopt when they feel obliged to pay homage to virtue? It is "a routine kind of virtue"! What does it matter, pray, whether virtue be the product of habit, of circumstances, or of the blood that flows in a man's veins, so long as it makes the individual and society happy? Is it not, in fact, better that virtue should be produced by habits implanted by education, since this is a means that can be used to shape men of all climates, of all societies, and of all times?

M. Mazzei even while abusing the Quakers is forced to admit that their strange ideas "have in certain matters raised them well above other men." [5]

He also states that they have some faults. Have I ever denied it? *Ubi homines, ibi erunt vitia,* says Tacitus,[6] and Quakers are men.

[3] [Catherine Macaulay (1733–1791), an English historian for whom Brissot had great admiration.]

[4] [De La Coste,] *Voyage philosophique d'Angleterre fait en 1783 et en 1784* ([London,] 1786), II, 117. The pretentiousness of this bizarre style apart, can anything truer and more sensible be said of the Quakers? Since I have mentioned this book, I must note that I am far from agreeing with all the opinions expressed by its author, who seems to me imbued with all the pernicious principles of aristocracy, which must render suspect his point of view, his observations, and his conclusions.

[5] [*Recherches historiques et politiques*, III, 63. What Mazzei actually wrote was, "(Their) eccentricities have made them superior to other men in some respects and inferior in other ways."]

[6] [Apparently a misquoting of "Erunt vitia, donec homines." Wherever men exist there will be vices. Tacitus, *Histories* IV, 17: 11.]

But I do say that their precepts render them more impervious to vice than others are.

M. Mazzei admits that, as far as thrift and attention to business are concerned, "their conduct is truly exemplary and praiseworthy." [7] Now it is from these two sources that all private and civic virtues flow; for a man who is by principle thrifty and businesslike is not afraid, for this very reason, of having a large family. If he has many children, he loves them and he sees ways of planning for their future. Such a man is neither a gambler nor a profligate. He is a good husband, for, putting his whole happiness in his family life, he is forced to be good in order to be loved, and he can be happy only by making those around him happy.

How could this critic fail to see all the implications of such an admission? How could he fail to see that it canceled out all the evil he later said of the Quakers? Did he not see that he was establishing their superiority over all other sects? For men of other beliefs are made thrifty and diligent in their work by example, habit, or other variable circumstances, while with the Quakers these virtues are practiced from religious principles from which they cannot depart without ceasing to be Quakers. Thrift and attention to business form part of their religious principles. How much stronger are such motives than all others which elsewhere may produce thrifty and diligent men!

M. Mazzei also acknowledges that the Quakers "are not inferior to others in hospitality and good works." [8] He ought to have said that they are superior, for charity and hospitality are the consequences of thrift and wealth. A man who has greater financial means, fewer needs, and no extravagant desires and who moreover truly loves his fellow men is necessarily charitable and hospitable, as indeed the Quakers are.

But, M. Mazzei says, and this is his great accusation against them, they are supreme hypocrites. To judge this grievance, let us examine the nature of hypocrisy.

When a man makes a show of feelings which he does not really have and of virtues which he practices only in the public eye; when he appears humane but is really selfish, austere where he is really a libertine, a good Christian when he is really a materialist, then he is a hypocrite. In short, hypocrisy is *to appear what one is not*.

[7] *Recherches historiques et politiques,* [III,] 63.

[8] [*Recherches historiques et politiques,* III, 63. Actually Mazzei wrote, "As far as hospitality and good works are concerned, they are like other people."]

Now, the question to be answered is whether the Quakers are or are not what they appear to be. To convict them of religious hypocrisy one would have to prove that they do not believe in the Holy Ghost and in the Gospel although they show outward signs of respect for them. One would have to prove that they are unbelievers and atheists under the mask of Christianity.

If moral hypocrisy is meant, one would have to prove that they hide libertinism, dissipation, and cruelty toward their families under the veil of austerity, thrift, and apparent tenderness.

Or is it, finally, political hypocrisy? It would then have to be proved that they secretly covet the positions and honors they have renounced; that they long to massacre their fellow men while professing horror of bloodshed; that they are really egotists disguised as friends and benefactors of humanity; that they are proud and haughty behind their appearance of simplicity.

It seems that it was this latter kind of hypocrisy which M. Mazzei wished to ascribe to Quakers when he quoted one of them as confessing that there was a great deal of pride in their avoidance of show.[9] If this Quaker was not one of those who try to unburden themselves of their own faults by attributing them to others, if he told the truth, and if this pride is general among Quakers, it is a saintly pride which every virtuous man ought to feel. This kind of pride is simply an awareness of the good one does and of the evil one has avoided, and without it good actions would be mechanical and without merit. It is not vicious so long as it does not become vanity. Notice also that this reasonable pride puts to shame the petty vanity of other men, who are forced to yield and to render homage to it.

In short, hypocrisy is only a vague word which signifies nothing so long as it is not applied to facts. To justify an accusation of hypocrisy, it is not enough to say that the Quakers are "Protestant Jesuits." This is merely an insult, another prejudice, and I ask for facts. If Quakers resemble Jesuits in their mildness, indulgence, tolerance, and art of persuasion, that simply means that they share these good qualities. M. Mazzei at least does them the justice of admitting that they do not resemble the Jesuits in everything, thus canceling what M. Chastellux frivolously said on this point.

I am not surprised that Quakers possess the art of persuasion. They have had it for one hundred and fifty years, and this fact is proof that they are worthy of public confidence. For they would

[9] *Recherches historiques et politiques*, [III,] 64.

have lost this confidence had they been merely charlatans and hypocrites. The Tartufe is not a man to slit his own throat with his own hands, and a sect of Tartufes could not exist for nearly two centuries, especially in these enlightened times.

In our own day there is a great outcry against hypocrisy. This is the common reproach made against earnest and devout sects by men who have yielded to the corruption of our times and who try thus to justify their own guilty weakness. It seems that having renounced all virtue they do not wish even to take the trouble of feigning it. Perhaps finding the burden of respect for virtue too heavy, they think it simpler to deny the existence of virtue. Or perhaps is not this charge of hypocrisy merely a new and subtler form of hypocrisy which hopes to escape unnoticed under the cloak of the accusation?

M. Mazzei accuses the Quakers of lacking "scrupulousness" and even "equity" in their commercial dealings; and he adds that this is their "national character." [10] Notice, my friend, that M. Mazzei, like M. Chastellux, adduces no facts and quotes no authorities. This is, then, pure calumny. Were this indeed the Quakers' character would facts be lacking to prove it?

I have so often heard repeated this accusation that the Quakers are dishonest that I have very carefully questioned on this point Englishmen and Americans of other denominations, as well as French merchants who had had dealings with Friends, and I have not heard of a single instance of dishonesty. They limited themselves to saying that Quakers are in general sharp, strict, and inflexible, and that they do favors only for members of their own sect. I was also told what M. Mazzei wrote, that they are shrewd dealers and that they sell dear. In my *Examen de Chatellux* I have shown how absurd it is to blame them for this. To be sharp is not to be dishonest; it is the essence of business. I will go even further and say that it is the essence of the American spirit. Americans are a shrewd people. I shall explain the reasons for this elsewhere.

Mr. Bingham, one of the wealthiest citizens of Philadelphia, who by his tastes and his love of luxury ought to be the last man to be partial to Quakers, had only the highest praise for them.[11] He told me that they are most scrupulous in fulfilling their obliga-

[10] *Recherches historiques et politiques,* [III,] 63.
[11] [William Bingham (1752–1804), a wealthy Philadelphia banker who served in the Continental Congress, the Pennsylvania Assembly, and the U.S. Senate.]

tions, that they never dip into capital, etc. This may explain the saying you hear so often in Philadelphia that Quakers are so shrewd that even the Jews cannot compete with them. Just as a pork merchant would go bankrupt if he lived among Jews, so a Jewish moneylender will always fail if he lives among thrifty men who have no need to borrow.

During a conversation I once had with M. Mazzei he mentioned a certain Quaker custom in support of his accusations. He must have been ashamed to make much of this point in print, for in his book I find it mentioned only obliquely. He told me that Quakers never close a bargain definitely, but merely say, "It can be done." He claimed that if later the bargain turns out not to be profitable, they refuse to go through with it, saying "It can no longer be done." "However," added M. Mazzei, "this Quaker phrase 'It can be done' means in ordinary speech 'I agree to the bargain.' So in this case they are being dishonest, and it happens often." This is probably the custom M. Mazzei is referring to when he writes, "It has happened several times that the Quakers' reserved way of making contracts, which is part of their religion, has given them excuses for not keeping their word." [12]

If it is true that the Quakers have this custom and do not make agreements otherwise, then either they respect such engagements, or else, if they often violate them, other merchants must refuse to make agreements with them. For this petty subterfuge of which they are accused could scarcely serve two or three times, and once it were known all the Quakers would be ruined, and they would be detested and avoided in the commercial world. Yet it is an unquestioned fact that Quakers are very active commercially and that business connections with them are sought by other manufacturers and merchants. Instead of criticizing this custom, which is the rejection of all oaths, bargains, and written agreements, we should admire it. How noble it is, how befitting the dignity of man! It recalls all the simplicity, all the good faith of the golden age, or rather of rural life. With such a custom as this there is no need to bind oneself by written documents that are an insult to the honor of both parties, and one is free of all the formalities which entail so many expenses, inconveniences, and litigations. If only trade throughout the world could return to the point where it would be possible to adopt and sanction without risk so saintly a practice!

[12] *Recherches historiques et politiques,* [III,] 66.

So this custom, which is practiced by Quakers only in some cases, should do them honor. Everywhere they have constantly proved that they keep their word even though nothing has been put down in writing. During my first stay in New York I saw the launching of a beautiful six-hundred-ton ship which had been built by a Quaker who had refused to give a written guarantee that the ship would be delivered at a specified date and had merely expressed the hope that it would be completed on time. Yet he was punctual. I find a similar case in an English newspaper:

Last Friday was launched at Gravesend the ship *Nottingham,* the largest to be built for the East India Company. It is of 1,152 tons, and what will appear most extraordinary is that it was built in seven months, the time agreed upon by the contractor.

This fact can be cited as an example of the Quaker spirit. The builder absolutely refused to guarantee under any conditions at all the date when it would be completed, but on March 7 he delivered it in accordance with the wishes of his employers in as fine a condition as any other shipbuilder on the Thames could have done.

A worthy old man, Mr. Rotch of Nantucket, told me of the following case.[13] During the last war various Nantucket Quakers sent to sea about a hundred ships, some of which they owned and some of which they leased from owners of other sects. The lessors assumed responsibility at a fixed amount for the risks run by the vessels but signed no written obligations. Yet when the ships were taken and confiscated by the English, the accounts were settled amicably between the parties without any discussion.

I have already said that this custom is followed only in some cases, such as when the outcome depends on too many uncertainties to warrant assuming obligations for a fixed time. In such cases, there are some Quakers who are too scrupulous to sign written contracts. In general, however, Quakers do make written contracts and sign and accept bills of exchange. Otherwise how could their banks, which are so numerous in England, exist? M. Mazzei, then, has been misinformed, or rather he has too broadly generalized a special practice.

M. Mazzei does not as openly accuse Quakers of acquisitiveness as does M. Chastellux, but he assumes it.[14] I must set down here

[13] [Probably either William or Benjamin Rotch, who together headed a group of Nantucket whalers in Dunkirk from 1787 to 1793, and whom Brissot apparently met in Paris.]

[14] [The word whose meaning Brissot discusses in the following paragraphs is *cupidité,* which has, like its English cognate, the derogatory connotation of inordinate

a few reflections which I failed to include in my criticism of M. Chastellux's *Travels* on this word *acquisitiveness*, with which businessmen are being attacked today.[15] The term is used without consideration of its true meaning. Acquisitiveness consists in accumulating a lot of money, in saving it, in keeping a constant eye on one's business, in missing no possible speculation or opportunity. This acquisitiveness is considered a crime, particularly by nobles, who, concerned only with the problem of dissipating wealth and always hungry for the gold they pretend to despise, seek to dishonor those whose occupation it is to accumulate money in order to put it to profitable use.

This then is the crime of which Quakers stand accused, that they accumulate wealth and are conscientious businessmen. But when people reproach them for their diligence and perseverance, they disregard the circumstances. Since Quakers are excluded by their religious principles from all ambitious careers, positions of honor, and official employment, they must rely wholly on their industry for their subsistence and the security of their children. They therefore have a greater need to accumulate money than other citizens, who can find positions for their children in government offices, the army, the navy, or the church.

Besides, Quakers avoid luxury and show on principle. Their only expenses are for food, fine linen, and good furniture; having less occasion to spend, they have more money than other citizens.

Finally, since Quakers do not indulge in clandestine love affairs,

---

desire for wealth. We have translated it "acquisitiveness" throughout this passage. It is obvious that Brissot, handicapped by the impoverished French vocabulary of the eighteenth century, was groping unsuccessfully for a term to designate the operation of the profit motive in either undesirable or desirable (capitalistic) social forms.]

[15] The author of the *Voyage philosophique d'Angleterre*, quoted above, says on p. 237, vol. I, that France is fortunately protected from the acquisitive spirit by the pride of the large noble class. Today, more fortunately, we no longer possess such a useful class! But I might ask this noble traveler what kind of spirit used to inspire these proud nobles to beg for pensions and lucrative political appointments? What kind of spirit prompted them to speculate, to gamble on the exchange, to become involved in deals, to ask for bribes for their protectors, favors on their taxes, and shares in every sort of enterprise? Was this not that "acquisitive spirit" which they find so vile and base in a businessman? These nobles have the businessman's mind but are twice as base, first because they are hypocrites and pretend to despise a metal which they ardently covet, and second because of the wasteful use they make of their wealth. Most of the money earned in commerce is employed again for trade or for useful speculation, but money earned by a noble is spent only on ostentation, vanity, and debauchery, and it only serves to generate a thousand poisons in the social body.

entertainment, science, or literature, they devote themselves wholly to their business and consequently appear more concerned with it, or, in the language of prejudice and the idle nobility, they are more "acquisitive."

Hence the Quakers' kind of acquisitiveness, far from deserving censure, is praiseworthy, for it springs from an absence of ambition and from a horror of extravagance and luxury. Here we have then a word truly misused; with a word you can cut the throat of a virtuous man.

M. Mazzei indeed agrees that Quakers are virtuous, but no more than other men. He believes that other sects have produced equally fine persons. I agree; Fénelon's name touches me as much as does that of Fothergill or Benezet. But, going further than he, I maintain, first, that Quakers have, in proportion to their number, produced more such great men and have done so more constantly; and second, that no sect presents so perfect, harmonious, and pure an assemblage of virtuous men or so constant a series of good and great actions. To prove this latter assertion, I need only recall the abolition of Negro slavery, which they carried out by unanimous agreement and with a single mind, and the numerous efforts they have since made to abolish the slave trade and improve the condition of Negroes. Let any one show me any other sect which has achieved such a prodigy of equity, disinterestedness, and humanity. Name a sect which like the Quakers has made it a rule never to engage in privateering or in smuggling, even in foreign countries, in order not to tempt other men to violate the laws of their country.[16] I have known Quakers here who even refuse to engage in the new India trade, because its main purpose is fraudulent.

Here is another case which will show both the disinterestedness and the honesty characteristic of this society. During the last war the Quakers passed a resolution that whoever repaid his debts in Continental paper money (then much depreciated) would be expelled. This resolution was voted at a time when it was a crime to question the value of Continental paper, when few people had scruples about repaying their debts in this currency, and when the Quakers like everyone else had to accept payments from their debtors in these depreciated notes.

[16] I must remind the reader of the letter published during the last war by a Quaker who returned his share of a prize taken by chance by a merchant ship in which he had an interest.

THE GROWTH OF THE SOCIETY OF FRIENDS—THEIR RELIGIOUS PRINCIPLES AND SYSTEM OF DISCIPLINE

A society whose members lead simple, thrifty lives and devote themselves mainly to farming and trade must necessarily grow rapidly. Consequently there are many Quakers in Pennsylvania and they have extended their settlements to all the other states.

Pennsylvania, where they constitute the majority of the population, may be considered their capital or metropolis. There are, however, also many Quakers in New York, the Jerseys, Delaware, and Maryland, but fewer in Massachusetts and New Hampshire.

Many Quakers have gone to set up their tabernacles in the beautiful valley of Shenandoah beyond the first range of mountains. Since they own no slaves and employ Negroes only as hired servants, they have given up growing tobacco. This valley is said to be the best-cultivated part of Virginia.

Quakers have also pushed their settlements as far as the two Carolinas and Georgia, and many are beginning to settle near the Ohio River. There is already a meeting at Red Stone on the Monongahela, about twenty miles from Pittsburgh. Seventy-five persons have emigrated to this place in one month, as is proved by the certificates presented at the Monthly Meeting there. For when a Quaker emigrates, he asks from the meeting which he is leaving a certificate of his good conduct and religion and takes it to the new meeting which he is joining. In this way a perpetual correspondence is maintained between all the meetings.

It would be much better, for the sake of the happiness of the Indians and the peace of America, if all the settlers close to Indian territory had the Quakers' pacifist principles, for then a lasting union would be soon formed between the Indians and the whites. Blood often stains the furrows which American industry traces in the wilderness.

The fact that new settlements established by Quakers are almost always successful is to be attributed to their thrift, to their sense of good management, which prevents them from investing everything they own in a new enterprise, and, above all, to the perseverance which is instilled in them by their religious beliefs.

The Quakers' religion consists in one phrase, the voice of conscience, the Inner Light, the divine instinct which they believe God has given to everyone. This instinct, this light, this grace, which each man receives at birth, seems to them to be the only guide man needs to consult and follow. But to be heard this guide must be known, and to be known it must be frequently interrogated. Hence the need for frequent meditation; hence the uselessness of any kind of ceremony or formal worship,[1] which they consider obstacles that turn the soul's attention away from the Inner Light; and hence also the uselessness of priests, who do not possess more than anyone else the divine spark and who can add nothing to the resources of meditation.

I pointed out in my *Examen critique des Voyages de M. Chatellux* how superior this meditative worship of divinity is to the mechanical ceremonies of other sects. I showed that a man whose entire adoration of the Divinity consists in perpetual meditation on his duties necessarily becomes good, tolerant, just, and beneficent. Here you have the key to the Quakers' moral character and to its extraordinary consistency. Their virtue is a habit, a second nature.

The Quakers have been often laughed at for their faith in this Inner Light. The scoffers, some of whom call themselve philosophers, do not know that this belief is not peculiar to Quakers and can be found in the writings of many philosophers who have earned mankind's admiration. With Pythagoras, it was the Eternal Word, the Great Light; with Anaxagoras, the Divine Soul; with Socrates, the Good Spirit, or Daemon; with Timaeus, the Uncreated Principle; with Hiero, the Author of All Light, the God within Man; with Plato, the eternal, ineffable, and perfect principle of Truth; with Zeno, the Creator and Father of All; and with Plotinus, the Root of the Soul. When these philosophers

---

[1] For instance, no bell is rung to call Quakers to worship. The Dutch Presbyterians have the wearisome custom of ringing a bell, one stroke at a time, for a whole half hour. This practice bears witness to the disinclination of the congregation to go to church. Quakers have no more need of such a stimulant than they have of a beadle to keep order. So M. Raynal was correct in saying that Quakers do not have churches, in the literal sense of the word, and M. Mazzei was wrong to refute him on this point by comparing the building in which the Quakers hold their meetings to a church. Can one apply this term to a room containing only benches and devoid of any ornament, paintings, altar, or pulpit—in short, without any of the objects seen in churches of other religions?

wished to characterize the influence of this principle upon and within us, they used corresponding expressions. Hiero called it a domestic god, an inner god; Socrates and Timaeus, the genius, or angel; Plato, the light and spirit of God. According to Plotinus, it was the Divine Principle in man, and according to Plato, the law, the living rule of the soul, the inner guide, the fountain of virtue.

I do not claim to explain here all the religious beliefs held by Quakers, for this would lead me too far afield, though the number of their dogmas is not very large and they have been credited with many more than they actually have. Their doctrine is simpler and even briefer than their moral code. But this subject deserves, as does their history, to be treated separately. For I can assure you that all the French authors who have written about it, Voltaire not excepted, were ignorant of the sources on which they should have relied.[2] They have merely seized upon the points which could be turned to ridicule and have disregarded all those that could show the Society in a good light.

Do you not admire, for example, the practice that the Quakers have adopted and from which they never depart of not arguing about points of dogma? They put a quick end to most such disputes by refusing to accept either the Old or the New Testament as superior to the Inner Light, and by not supporting men whose only function is to wrangle and dictate under pretext of instructing. How much bloodshed would have been avoided if Catholics and Protestants had had this wise rule! If only instead of quarreling over unintelligible words and dubious texts and the authority of the Pope and Church, they had believed in an Inner Light which

---

[2] Among the works to be consulted, the following are the more important: George Fox, *A Journal* [London, 1694], fol.; [William] Sewel, *The History of the [Rise, Increase, and Progress of the Christian People Called] Quakers* [London, 1722], fol.; all the works of Penn, which consist of six [five] large octavo volumes [*The Select Works of William Penn*, 3rd ed. (London, 1782), 5 vols., 8°]; [Robert] Barclay, *L'Apologie de la véritable théologie chrétienne, ainsi qu'elle est soutenüe[, et prêchée, par le peuple, appellé par mépris, les Trembleurs]* (London, 1702), 8°, p. 654; [William Penn,] *Exposition [succincte] de l'origine et des progrès des Quakers* (Phillips: London, 1784), 8°; [Anthony] Benezet, *Observations sur l'origine [. . .] des Quakers* [Philadelphia, 1780; London, 1783]; Mary Brook, *Des Raisons de la nécessité d'attendre en silence pour le culte solonnel de Dieu* (Phillips [London, 1782]), 8°. Those who seek books which will give them a better knowledge of the Society should address themselves to James Phillips, bookseller, George Yard, Lombard Street, London. They may also find some translations in Paris, chez Gras, bookseller, below the Pont Neuf. [In this bibliographical note Brissot gave all the titles in French. Where he was apparently referring to a French edition we have given that title; where he seemed to refer to an English edition we have identified it as accurately as possible.]

is each man's surest guide! Since this guide speaks little about dogma and much about man's conduct, there would have been fewer hairsplitting arguments and quiddities and more brotherly love and virtue.

[Joseph] Priestley, who likes to puff his own sect, claims that Quakers are true anti-Trinitarians. I discussed this subject one day with a learned Quaker, who denied the charge. "It is true," he told me, "that we do not believe in the Trinity, but we believe in a union between God and Christ; we believe that God resides *corporally* in Christ." This word *corporally* did not seem clear to me. I wished to discuss it further, but my Quaker stopped me. "It would be a waste of time," he said. "Return within thyself, consult thy Inner Light, and believe what it tells thee."

Among the Quakers' political principles there are two which especially set them apart from other men. The first is that they never swear oaths, and the second is that they refuse to bear arms for any cause whatsoever. In a separate letter I shall discuss the latter and the persecution they have suffered in America for their constant refusal to fight for independence. As to their refusal to swear oaths, they are justified in this by the Christian religion, by philosophy, and by political wisdom. An oath adds nothing to the declaration of an honest man, and perjury costs a dishonest one nothing.

Their forms and ceremonies are as simple as their system of discipline. In their marriages, births, and funerals they employ only the formalities necessary to certify these happenings. A month prior to a marriage, the banns are published in meeting in order to permit anyone who may have any objection to have the time to make it. A Quaker may not marry a person of another sect. I once asked the reason for this rule, which seemed to me a sign of intolerance. "The survival of our Society," a Quaker told me, "depends on the preservation of the customs which distinguish us from other men. Our singularity forces us to be more strict in our conduct, and if we admitted among us strangers who were not members of our Society, they would not follow our customs and they would be confused with others. A Quaker woman who marries a Presbyterian submits herself to the authority of a man over whom we have no influence, and our Society exists only through this voluntary and reciprocal domestic influence."

How is this influence exercised? Through the various meetings, whose object it is to maintain the system of discipline in all its purity. There are Monthly, Quarterly and Yearly Meetings. The Monthly Meetings are generally composed of several individual congregations at some distance from one another. Their principal functions are to provide for the support of the poor and for the children's education; to examine the new converts who present themselves and to test and judge their morals; to sustain the zeal and religion of the members and to inquire into and judge their shortcomings reported by overseers appointed for this purpose; and to arbitrate differences arising either between Quakers or between a Quaker and a stranger, when the latter agrees to submit to such arbitration. The arbitration of differences is one of the Meeting's most important functions; it prevents the plague of lawyers which so cruelly ravages other countries and is the source of so much corruption and of so many scandalous quarrels. This is a practice which must make the presence of Quakers in a neighborhood a great advantage to others. The Meeting expels those who refuse to submit to arbitration.

Sometimes appeals from the decisions of the Monthly Meetings are taken to the Quarterly Meetings, whose main duty is to watch over the Monthly Meetings. The general supervision of the entire Society, however, is the function of the Annual Meeting. It receives from all the lower meetings reports which taken together inform it of the state of the Society as a whole; it gives advice; it makes what regulations it thinks necessary; it sometimes appoints committees to visit the Quarterly Meetings; it gives final judgment on appeals from the lower meetings; and it writes letters to the other Annual Meetings in order to maintain with them a fraternal correspondence.

There are seven Annual Meetings: one in London, to which the Quakers of Ireland send representatives; a second in New England; a third in New York; a fourth in Pennsylvania and New Jersey; a fifth in Maryland; a sixth in Virginia; and a seventh in the two Carolinas and Georgia.

As the Quakers believe that women can be called to the ministry as well as men, and as there are, moreover, certain articles of discipline which concern only women and whose observance can be supervised and maintained only by them, the women too have their Monthly, Quarterly, and Annual Meetings, but they are not given the right to make regulations. This system is much more apt to maintain good morals among women than that used by our Catholic confessors and directors of conscience, who subject the weaker sex to the whims, trickery, and tyranny of a few men, opening the door to the most scandalous scenes and often bringing inquisitions and fatal dissension into the bosom of the family.

Quakers have no paid priests, as I have said; they follow to the letter the word of the Gospel, "Freely ye have received, freely give." [3] They do, however, have ministers. These ministers are those who are most often moved to speak and who are received in their function by the Monthly Meetings. They are not admitted lightly; they must be tested, and time must have manifested in them the necessary qualifications. It sometimes happens that persons who have not been approved still wish to speak as ministers. They are suffered long and patiently, but if the discontent caused by their speaking is considerable, then the Meeting publicly "disavows" them.

The ministers together with elders approved by the Monthly Meeting also hold monthly meetings for their own instruction. They are no less subject to the same general and reciprocal supervision than are the other members, and at meetings they cannot prevent anyone who is moved to speak, man or woman, from doing so.

It is usually these meetings of ministers and elders which are entrusted with examining and publishing works to be distributed by the Society. They do all they can to see that useful books are sold at the lowest possible prices so that all the brethren may buy them and be enlightened.

In all these meetings there is no president because the Quakers believe that only Divine Wisdom should preside and that no member has the right to claim pre-eminence over the others. But, you will ask, how is order maintained? By itself, without a president, without a bell, through the force of habit, and by the seriousness and calm which all Quakers are taught from childhood.

The Annual Meeting in Philadelphia is composed of three hundred deputies and is also attended by about twelve hundred members who have the same right to speak as the deputies. Who would believe it? In this assembly of fifteen hundred persons, which has no president, everything is conducted with perfect order. You never hear two persons speak at once, animosity or pride never pierce through the speeches, and all the discussions are brotherly. But what will surprise you even more is that in these very large meetings, and in general in all their meetings, all decisions are unanimous. Each member has a kind of suspensive veto, and it is

[3] [Matthew 10:8.]

enough for him to say, "I have not yet clearness." The meeting is then adjourned and no decision is taken until there is perfect unanimity.

This custom, it seems to me, does great honor to the Society, for it demonstrates the unity that exists among all these brothers and proves that all are moved by the same spirit and the same concern for truth and the general welfare. My friend, men would not have such long and violent arguments if, like the Quakers, they were free of all ambition and if to resolve their questions they appealed only to their consciences.

You might conclude that because it can act only by unanimous consent the Society achieves very little, but you would be wrong. No group has done as much for the public good.[4] It is through their efforts that Philadelphia has so far been preserved from the danger of theaters. This year they successfully petitioned that permission to erect one be withheld.

I have not attended a Quaker meeting, for they are closed to strangers, but I have been to a meeting of the Society for Promoting the Abolition of Slavery, which is composed almost wholly of Quakers. Every one of the almost two hundred members present spoke whenever and as often as he wished. When a member made a motion and when it had been seconded, the president repeated it and asked whether there was any objection. Then he waited a few moments. Often a member would get up, utter three or four sentences, and sit down again. I heard no long speeches, for vanity alone inspires long perorations. When a committee is to be elected, the president requests that the assembly designate the members. Names are suggested by various persons and, if there is no objection, they are appointed. In this way little time is lost in selecting a committee.

Yet this is the society that has been subjected to so much

[4] A Quaker named Mill, a simple bookseller of Bristol, is responsible for a truly humane institution in this city. He had seen that many poor women died in childbed for lack of care and money, and that the children who survived these miserable conditions were weakly and degenerate. So in 1787 he undertook to form a society to care for these women in their homes and to pay out of contributions for doctors, surgeons, etc. It has been very successful.

This is one of the advantages of the Quaker religion. One cannot be a Quaker without having a greater love for one's fellow men and without being aware of their misfortunes, and seeking means to alleviate them. Witness, for instance, all the good accomplished in England by Drs. Fothergill and Lettsom. It was not vanity that guided them. Lettsom is a simple man who dreams constantly of new ways of being useful to men, as others dream of glory and fortune. [John Coakely Lettsom (1744–1805), a Quaker physician, was the author of a number of medical and philanthropic works.]

calumny in our country! Voltaire used to say that if you repeat something often enough, even if it is false, you can make the French believe it. He knew his century, and the Quakers are the proof. They have been judged on the strength of trivial anecdotes, petty witticisms, and groundless rumors.

A thorough knowledge of the Quakers and an impartial opinion about them cannot be had by touring a few meetinghouses in the course of two hours, as M. Chastellux did, but by meeting the Quakers themselves in London, Dublin, and Philadelphia. Go in their houses, and you will always find that they are abodes of peace, calm, harmony, kindness, and frugality; you will find that their children are brought up with tender care and that their servants are treated with humanity and as equals. Go into their hospitals, and you will see the most touching manifestations of true charity: good beds, help and attention for the sick, and a scrupulous cleanliness unequaled anywhere else. Go in their alms-houses for the aged and infirm, and you will see that the clothes and linen of the poor are as seemly as those of their benefactors, that every person has his own room and receives not only necessary attentions but many pleasant superfluities as well. If you leave the city and visit Quaker farms, you will find in their houses more orderliness, cleanliness, and well-being than anywhere else, sleeker and better-groomed horses, fields better fenced, and beds for guests which are at the least clean and neat. If you investigate the internal organization of the Society, you will find in all the congregations a charitable fund whose size is proportionate to the means of the people in the neighborhood and which is always maintained. It is used to help young men in business or those who have suffered unexpected bankruptcies, fires, accidents, etc. You will find that many wealthy Quakers consider it their duty to contribute to this charitable fund a tenth of their incomes. You will find that these Quaker farmers are better educated than those of other sects.

I am sure, my friend, that after having read all these facts about this society you will exclaim: "If tomorrow I were to lose all my money and be helpless and friendless, may God grant that I spend the rest of my days in a Quaker almshouse! If tomorrow I were called to be a farmer, may God grant that my neighbors be Quakers, for by their example they would edify and instruct me, their advice would be useful to me, and, above all, they would not involve me in lawsuits!"

QUAKER POLITICAL PRINCIPLES

As I have already said in my *Examen Critique des Voyages de M. Chatellux,*[1] these wise Quakers have seen that the foundation of universal happiness is universal peace, and that the road to peace is total rejection of warfare. The Bible told them that the time would come when "nation will not lift up sword against nation." They have understood that the best way to hasten the fulfillment of this prophecy is to set the example; that talking will do no good if we do not suit actions to our words, and that sovereigns will always find a way to perpetuate war as long as they can pay men to kill. The Quakers, therefore, have resolved never to take up arms and never to contribute money to the support of any war. They have been tortured, martyred, robbed, and imprisoned; they have endured all, until at last tyranny, wearied by their constancy, has exempted them from military service and has even been reduced to subterfuges in order to extort contributions from them.

I ask you, what would become of our military heroes if all religious sects took this antimilitarist stand, if all denounced war, and if no man would consent to become an automaton trained in the infernal art of killing his fellow creatures? What would become of the ambitions of conquerors if all men became Quakers and in common accord and with unshakeable stubbornness refused to fire a shot in support of the lust for power?

If we love the good of mankind, let us pray that this peaceful society will spread over the whole world, or at least that its humane principles will be universally adopted. Then will become universal that peace which the Quakers have already achieved wherever they are the majority.

The Quakers of Pennsylvania did indeed succeed in protecting their state from the scourge of war until hostilities broke out in 1755 between England and France. Although they lived surrounded by Indians, no quarrels had ever arisen, nor had there been any bloodshed.[2]

[1] Pp. 69ff.

[2] M. Mirabeau was unaware of this fact when in February 1791 he replied for the National Assembly to a deputation of French Quakers who had requested to be

In spite of all its maneuvers, the English government never could persuade the Quakers to support that war. Not only did the Friends refuse to participate in it, but they even resigned all the positions they had hitherto held in the administration, which had been almost entirely in their hands. For they had conducted a peaceful administration and so economical a one that the revenue from customs and excise taxes had been sufficient to cover all the expenses of the civil government, and neither the Quakers nor anyone else had been subject to any other taxes.

All this was changed by the war of 1756 [the French and Indian War], which led to expenditures that the colonies were forced to pay for. The Quakers like everybody else were assessed, but not only did they refuse to pay taxes levied to support the cost of the war; they even expelled those who did pay them.

They followed the same policy again during the last war, and it was at that time that a hostility to them was kindled which is not yet fully extinguished. Faithful to their religious principles, they declared that they would take no part in the war and they disavowed or expelled all those of their society who served in either the American troops or the British army.

I must admit that, fully convinced as I am of the sacred and divine principle which sanctions armed resistance to oppression, and also fully convinced that in this case the oppression was manifest, I cannot help but disapprove of the neutrality maintained by the Quakers while their brothers fought for independence. But in spite of this principle, I none the less believe that it was wrong to persecute them so ruthlessly for their pacifist neutrality.

Had this been the first time they had refused to fight, had this refusal been dictated by devotion to the British cause,[3] and had it been only a cloak to cover their true feelings, then they would have certainly been guilty and the persecution would have perhaps been justified. But their neutrality was dictated by religious

---

excused from bearing arms and told them: "What would have become of your brethren in Pennsylvania if vast distances had not separated them from the Indians, if the savages had murdered their wives and children?" The Indians were for a long time neighbors of the Quakers and never attacked them, for they had full confidence in the Quakers' good faith and they respected their love of peace. The French Quakers submitting this petition to the National Assembly were from a colony in Languedoc. There are also a few Quakers in Dunkirk, but these came from Nantucket. [See pp. 165–166 and 316.]

[3] It would have been very natural for the Quakers to side with the English, who had always treated them well. During the war, however, the Quakers suffered much at their hands.

beliefs which they had always professed and have continuously practiced. Whatever prejudiced or misinformed writers may say, the truth, which I have well substantiated, is that the majority of Quakers did not favor more one side than the other, and that they helped anyone who needed help, no matter who he was. If a few Quakers did serve in the English army, a few such as Generals Greene, Mifflin, and Lacey [4] also served in the American army, and the Society expelled indiscriminately all who bore arms.

The following episode will show you that no human force can prevail against the inflexible will of an individual who adheres to his principles. In Virginia it was decided to form a company of drafted Quakers. When they refused to be enrolled, they were rounded up by force; when they were given guns they refused to touch them, and the weapons had to be tied to them; when they were ordered to guard some military equipment and shoot whoever attempted to steal it, they answered that they would not shoot, but that they would warn the thieves and preach to them, or denounce them if they persisted; when they were imprisoned, they made no complaint; when they were offered soldiers' rations, they refused them, saying that since they were not soldiers they had no right to the rations. In truth, they did not suffer from this last act of resistance, for their Quaker brethren sent them an abundance of food. Finally, with their hands bound and their guns tied to them they were led before General Washington, who, appalled by this persecution, sent them back home and reprimanded his own men.

Nobody spoke to me with greater impartiality about the Quakers than that famous man, who is distinguished by his sense of justice. He admitted that during the war he had had a poor opinion of the Society. He had not known much about it, for there were then few Quakers in Virginia. He had attributed to their politics actions which were really expressions of their religious beliefs. When the army was encamped in Chester County, which is inhabited mainly by Quakers, he thought he was in enemy territory, because he could not persuade any Quaker to spy for him, although, on the other hand, neither did they spy on him for the English army.[5]

[4] [Nathanael Greene (1742–1786), Thomas Mifflin (1744–1800), and John Lacey (1755–1814).]

[5] The Quakers have also been charged with selling Continental paper money at a very depreciated rate to get gold. M. Chastellux hazarded this accusation ([*Voyages*, Paris, 1786,] I, 273), and M. Mazzei picked it up in his book. It seems quite reasonable that at a time when there was general lack of faith in the de-

You will hear the contrary alleged by detractors of the Quakers but their error can be easily explained. Since Quakers visited both camps frequently and without passes and came to be regarded without suspicion, spies, in order to escape detection, disguised themselves as Quakers. Several were caught and hanged in Quaker dress; hence the accusation.

When General Washington understood the Quaker spirit better he came to have a high regard for them. He told me that because of their simple way of life, their thrift, their fine moral standards, the excellent example they set, and their support of the Constitution, he considered them to be the strongest pillars of the new government, which requires of its citizens both full loyalty and frugality.

It was not in this light that the Congress which declared American independence regarded the Quakers. Angered by their resistance, it sided with their persecutors and, it must be admitted, without any justification banished the leaders who were most suspect, among them my esteemed friend Miers Fisher, to Staunton, Virginia, two hundred miles from their families. These Quakers tried to justify themselves, but when they failed they obeyed the order. M. Mazzei in his *Recherches sur les Etats-Unis* quotes the violent attack on them that Paine published,[6] but carefully refrains from giving Fisher's reply. Such, however, is the logic of this calumniator of the Friends. Elsewhere in order to disparage Penn [7] M. Mazzei quotes a stricture written against him by Franklin, the spokesman for the adversaries of the Penn family.[8] It is as if we were asked to believe today that the famous Duke de Rohan, the

---

preciated paper Quakers should try to exchange it for gold, which is always current everywhere. Such action was not criminal but merely prudent. It is also important to bear in mind the Quakers' religious principles. Convinced that Continental paper money was merely a kind of tax levied to finance the war, they had refused to take it in payment, and when some of them were forced by circumstances to do so, they took the first opportunity to get rid of it at a loss. This was perfectly logical.

[6] See his *Recherches* [. . .] *sur les Etats-Unis*, III, 67. [The "attack" was in Paine's *Common Sense*.]

[7] M. Mazzei and his various mouthpieces made outrageously unjust accusations against Penn in the *Journal de Paris*, but it would take me too far afield to enter into a defense of Penn. I am forced to omit it here, but perhaps I shall some day have a chance to take up this question again. [See note pp. 298–299.]

[8] [*Recherches . . . sur les Etats-Unis*, I, 71–72, contains a reference to *An Historical Review of the Constitution and Government of Pennsylvania, From Its Origins* published in London in 1759, "under the eyes of Franklin," as Mazzei quite accurately said, for it is possible Franklin was not the author. See P. L. Ford, *Franklin Bibliography* (Brooklyn, 1889), pp. 109–111.]

pillar and ornament of the French Calvinists, was seeking his own advantage at the expense of his party and that he was dictatorial, merely because the minister Babat, the mouthpiece of his enemies, made such assertions at the 1622 Assembly.[9]

When people grew tired of persecuting the Quakers, the exiles of Staunton were allowed to return to Pennsylvania, but the permission did not specifically mention Philadelphia, where their families lived but which at that time was still occupied by the English. This was of course a trap, for had they gone to Philadelphia they would have been accused of treason and of conspiracy with the English. General Washington, who here deserves the highest praise for his integrity, saw the snare and issued them passports specifically to Philadelphia.

When the English evacuated this city and the Presbyterian party became its masters, the persecution of Quakers was renewed in an even more violent form, and two of them were condemned to be hanged for high treason. The English translator of M. Chastellux's *Travels* [10] has in his notes strangely and venomously altered the circumstances of this incident, using it to try to prove that the Quakers betrayed the American cause. It is, therefore, important to clarify matters with the help of the following facts, for which I can vouch.

One of the executed men, John Roberts, was a respected miller from near Philadelphia, known for his straightforwardness and integrity. He had strongly supported the party organized by Dr. Franklin in opposition to the Presbyterians, and this was undoubtedly the reason for their inveterate hatred of him, which brought about his death. At the outbreak of the War of Independence Roberts could not hide his true feelings, but he remained neutral. When, however, the English became masters of Philadelphia he did go there but limited his activities to helping those in need of assistance. Later Roberts was accused of having guided the English to a place where some American soldiers were in hiding. He admitted having done so but maintained that he had

[9] See *Mémoires [du Duc] de Rohan*, I, 160. [Brissot may have been referring to any of a number of different editions. Henri, Duke de Rohan (1579–1638), was a leader of the Huguenots during the reign of Louis XIII. Protestant General and Provincial Assemblies were authorized by the Edict of Nantes, 1598.]

[10] This translator [George Grieve (1748–1809)] is a young Englishman more witty than precise and more sarcastic than truthful. He spent four years in America during the war, but I have been unable to find out what his mission was. The reader should beware of everything he says, pro or con. Had I his translation at hand, I would often have occasion to refute his statements.

been taken from his house at night, threatened, and forced at gun's point to do so. He proved another point which attested his innocence, that at that time the secret papers and archives of Congress were hidden in his mill, where the English headquarters were located, and he never betrayed this secret.

The second man was Abraham Carlisle, a carpenter of Philadelphia, much less well known than Roberts, who, disregarding the advice of his brother Quakers, accepted employment as a watchman at the northern entrance to Philadelphia, thinking that the position was a civil and not a military one. This was the crime of which he was accused.

But the accusation was nothing but a tissue of injustices. The jury was in part composed of enemies of these two Quakers. There was at the time in Philadelphia a committee of inquiry whose task it was to uncover enemies of the new government and which was directed mainly against the Quakers. It transmitted denunciations to both the attorney general and the jury. Only two of the jurors thought Carlisle and Roberts guilty, and the ten others wished to acquit them. The two succeeded in persuading the other ten to change their votes only by promising that a pardon would be granted and by persuading the others of the necessity of a conspicuous example. Accordingly a request for a pardon was submitted to the Executive Council, which agreed to grant it. But at this juncture the Quakers' worst enemy, Reed,[11] was elected President [of the Council]. He was in a hurry to accept the position in order to forestall the granting of the pardon, which he succeeded in doing. The two wretches were executed, though the public generally disapproved of the sentence. Reed was an ambitious man with the soul of a Cromwell. He made a show of being an ardent republican because he hoped some day to seize power. He died of remorse, I have been told, for having ordered the execution.

Slowly and with a great deal of patience the Quakers succeeded in overcoming their enemies' resentment and won the right to live as brothers with both parties. They held a meeting every three years at Flushing on Long Island, which almost all of them attended in spite of the war and the fact that Long Island was behind the English lines. M. Crèvecoeur once met a Quaker on his way to this meeting, and having learned the reason for his trip warned him of the danger he was running. "But I am not a spy,"

---

[11] [Joseph Reed (1741–1785), president of the Pennsylvania Executive Council, 1778–1781.]

said the Quaker, "I am no man's enemy. I carry neither papers nor weapons."

"It makes no difference, they will arrest you and put you in prison."

"So be it," said the Quaker. "They will do as they please, but I shall have done my duty."

The English general having learned of the meeting sent spies, who reported that the Quakers talked only about the congregation's affairs, so he did not disturb them and none were arrested.

M. Crèvecoeur has told me that most of the Quakers worked hard to alleviate the suffering caused by the war and that in New York they provided prisoners of war with money, food, and even bail when necessary. He also told me about having met in Dutchess County in New York on a very cold day some Quakers who were driving a wagon carrying food for free distribution to prisoners.

After the war the Quakers were subjected to another kind of persecution. Every citizen between the ages of sixteen and forty-five was required by law to serve in the militia under penalty of a fine. The Quakers refused either to serve or pay the fine. The officials charged with collecting these fines would enter their houses, seize a piece of furniture, and sell it. The Quakers made no effort to prevent them.

It is obvious that such a procedure encouraged dishonesty, and indeed collectors were known to seize goods worth three to six times the amount of the fine, sell for a shilling what was worth a pound, and never return the difference. Occasionally the collectors would even pocket the fines and then declare themselves bankrupt. This led to another iniquity, for the collectors' creditors would demand of the Quakers the fines already paid. The Quakers decided to complain to the legislature, and a law has just been passed (November 1788) suspending the collection of these fines until September 1789. A study of the irregularities in the collecting of these fines is to be made. The needs of the state, the duty of each individual to contribute to them, and the Quakers' religious principles could be easily reconciled if the Quakers were required to pay only taxes for nonmilitary purposes but were made to pay a larger proportion of these. This is what has already been done in Virginia, where Quakers are exempt from militia taxes.

Honest men of other sects disapprove so strongly of the manner in which the Quakers have been robbed that many of them refuse to buy furniture thus extorted. It must be admitted, however, that there do exist honest collectors who take only what is needed to cover the Quaker's tax.

Considering all the characteristics of the Society of Friends, you will agree, my friend, that the government ought to make every effort to bring about its establishment in France. Everything there is likely to appeal to the Quakers, and their example could serve to regenerate our morals, without which liberty cannot be preserved for long, even if it can be won without them. The fact that Catholicism is the predominant religion in France can be no obstacle, for Quakers do not hate any sect. On the contrary, they love all men. The Quakers have always been on good terms with the Catholics of Pennsylvania and of Maryland, who for their part have always treated the Quakers well. James Pemberton told me that during the War of 1740 he saw a crowd of Presbyterian fanatics, axes in hand, bent on destroying a Catholic chapel. Ten or twelve Quakers stopped them, preached to them, and they dispersed without carrying out their purpose.

As they live in peace with the other sects, they do not harbor resentment against apostates from Quakerism, in spite of the vexations they often suffer at the hands of such men. Their only weapon is reason.

During the last war a sect called Free Quakers was formed by persons who even before the war had been "disavowed" by the Quakers for misconduct. This sect found new recruits among Quakers who fought in the war. When they thought their group was large enough, they submitted a petition to the legislature asking to share the old Quakers' meetinghouses, cemeteries, and other properties. The Quakers opposed this move and won. The Free Quakers were forced to build a meetinghouse at their own expense. They are not numerous.

This schism gave rise to various writings, among which I have noted a very sensible letter published in the *Pennsylvania Journal* of September 28, 1782, written by a Quaker who, although disavowed, was just to his former friends. Had M. Mazzei read it, he would not have repeated so many of the calumnies so well refuted in this letter.

POSTSCRIPTUM, 1790

If it was in the interest of the former French government to attract Quakers to France, it is doubly important for the present regime now to do so, for there are many things that free France has in common with the Society of Friends:

The Society has established important settlements without bloodshed; the National Assembly has renounced the policy of conquest, which has caused almost all wars.

The Society practices universal tolerance; the Assembly orders it.

The Society requires simplicity of worship; the Assembly is restoring it.

Finally, the Society practices virtue, the strongest pillar of free governments; the political regeneration of France, which the Assembly will achieve, will necessarily lead to moral regeneration.

If Frenchmen from north to south have taken up arms, it is for the sake of their liberty, to strike fear in the heart of despotism, to fulfill the design of Heaven itself, for God has willed that man be free, since He has made him rational. He therefore wishes man to use every means to defend himself from that tyranny which destroys what is greatest in God's eyes, what brings man closest to God, namely, his virtues and his talents.

Yet with all their ardor to take up arms in such a holy cause, the French people will none the less respect the Quakers' religious ideas, which forbid them to shed the blood even of their enemies. Their error, which results from their humanity, is almost as beautiful as truth. We are all moving toward the same goal, universal brotherhood; the Quakers follow the road of meekness and we follow that of resistance. They travel as a society, we as a great nation.

JOURNEY TO MOUNT VERNON

On November 15, 1788, I left Philadelphia by private stage for Wilmington, where I planned to spend two days visiting several people. Wilmington is twenty-eight miles from Philadelphia, and the road though hilly is in general fairly good.

Before reaching Gray's Ferry on the Schuylkill, one crosses the vast section between the Schuylkill and the Delaware which Penn included within his plans for the city. Although the land has already been divided into lots, there seems to be no likelihood that this immense area will be built up in the near future. This, as I have said before, is a blessing for Pennsylvania and even for the nation, for a large city is always a source of many evils. This truth was not well enough known at the time when Penn was founding this haven for the Quakers. Besides, when you consider that the vast empire of the United States is divided into many sovereign states and that its trade will inevitably be shared by many cities, it is difficult to see what could make Philadelphia grow to be as big as Paris or London, as some persons hope and as Penn seems to have hoped, if we may judge by his plans.

The ferry over the Schuylkill has been replaced by a wooden bridge, from which one can see Mr. Hamilton's beautiful house, which enjoys a very fine view.[1]

Travelers like to stop at Chester, a town fifteen miles from Philadelphia where the inns are good. It is on a creek which flows into the Delaware and does a certain amount of trade. A much more important commercial center is found in Wilmington, also on a creek and near the Delaware. Its most important trade is the exportation of flour to the West Indies.

On the road to Wilmington one passes through Brandywine, a name which calls to mind a victory of the English over the Americans. The site of the battlefield is eight miles away. Today Brandywine is known for its mills, which exist because of the falls there.

[1] [Gray's Ferry, a short distance below the mouth of Mill Creek, was west and south of what was then the city of Philadelphia. Alexander Hamilton did not own a house in this vicinity in 1788; perhaps Brissot was referring to Robert Morris' place, "The Hills," about a mile from Gray's Ferry, where Hamilton was frequently a guest.]

The establishment likely to become the most important someday is the paper mill owned by Mr. Gilpin and Mr. Miers Fisher, the Quaker lawyer I have previously mentioned. This talented orator is also a craftsman and a scientist. He has introduced into the manufacture of paper, and especially into the process of pounding the rags, much simpler techniques than ours, and he produces beautiful writing and printing paper equal to the finest made in France. His mill is supplying the paper for the edition of classical English authors now being published in Philadelphia by Dr. Franklin's grandson.[2]

Wilmington, only a mile farther on, is a beautiful town with fine houses, most of whose inhabitants are Quakers. Several most worthy Quakers, among them a Dr. Way, came to see me as soon as they had learned of my arrival. The famous Mr. Dickinson, also a resident of Wilmington, was unfortunately away in Dover.[3]

I spent two evenings in the company of Miss [Mary] Vining, the charming American lady to whom M. Chastellux has slanderously attributed too great a taste for gallantry.[4] It was an inexcusable libel, particularly since Miss Vining, although she may have been slightly flirtatious, has always led a blameless life. Even the Quakers, who do not like her, recognize that her conduct is irreproachable. Such slander is particularly undeserved coming from a Frenchman, for she has always shown great partiality for the French nation, her house is always open to French visitors, and during the winter when Lauzun's Legion was quartered in Wilmington she constantly extended her hospitality to all the French officers. It is all the more unforgivable in view of the fact that Miss Vining was always most civil to M. Chastellux. Even if she did wear rouge and powder, what business was it of his? Miss Vining is pretty, amiable, affable, and witty. He should have been satisfied with that, and should not have tried to hurt her. I must pay this American woman still another tribute. In recounting several conversations in which her wit and sensibility shone in turn, M. Chastellux claimed that she was malicious. As for myself, I never heard her speak ill of anyone, not even of the women who snub her

[2] [Benjamin Franklin Bache (1769–1798).]

[3] Mr. [John] Dickinson, formerly president [of the Supreme Executive Council] of Philadelphia [i.e., Pennsylvania], is the author of *Letters from an American Farmer*, published before the last war, which contributed greatly to open the eyes of Americans to the injustices committed by the English. [Dickinson's *Letters* were translated into French by Barbeu Dubourg and published in 1769.]

[4] See Chastellux's *Voyages dans l'Amérique septentrionale*, I, 264. [Also see p. 244.]

today. It seemed to me that M. Chastellux's shafts had wounded her deeply.

In Wilmington I also met a French surgeon practicing there by the name of Cappell. He had served as a surgeon in Lauzun's Legion, from which he resigned to settle in America, where he is married and is, according to his own statement and to all appearances, happy.

Wilmington suffered a terrible gale while I was there. The damage extended as far as the Susquehanna River and prevented the stage from getting through. I was forced to take a chaise to continue my journey.

Nine miles from Wilmington I came to Christine [Christiana] Bridge, where there is some commercial activity. From there to Elkhead there are fewer farms than around Wilmington. You travel through eight miles of woods, with here and there a few log houses, before you reach Henderson's Tavern, a very good inn, standing alone in the midst of this vast forest. There I found a stage for the Susquehanna, which I took. It is twenty-two miles from there to the ferry on the Susquehanna. Before reaching it you pass through a good-sized town called Charlestown, and a smaller one located at the head of the Elk River [Elkton].

A beautiful view met my eyes some four miles from the Susquehanna. We had reached a rocky eminence and had to get down and cross on foot some falls which were dry. Through the trees, I saw balls of fire rising in the air. They were produced by the furnaces of some ironworks nearby. The sight of these globes, whose light seemed to paint the azure moonlit sky, in the midst of that vast, dense forest, together with the sound of the water flowing between the rocks and the loud blows of the hammers of the ironworks, kindled my imagination to great and imposing thoughts. I was happily abandoning myself to these meditations when I was forced to quit them and return to the stage.

We reached the ferry at night. A big fire and good cheer, which cost us thirty-four sous apiece, compensated us for the uncomfortable night we spent there.

We had to leave at six o'clock in the morning, and from the banks of the Susquehanna we glimpsed the magnificent spectacle of the moon shining on the vast expanse of water, dotted here and there by a few islands.

A town, Havre de Grace, is already rising on the opposite bank. I was told that it had been named by a Frenchman who bought land there and built houses but was later forced to give them up. It consists of only about a hundred and fifty houses scattered about within the limits of the town, but there is no doubt that when the Susquehanna has been made navigable the town will be advantageously located and will be well populated. A Frenchman who was traveling with me told me that three years ago, when he had passed through, there were not three houses here. I saw a very fine garden belonging to the owner of the ferry, and from it I enjoyed casting my eyes over the delightful view of this magnificent river. The Susquehanna is over a mile and a half wide at this point. The stage does not cross with the passengers, and one has to take another stage on the other side.

From the Susquehanna ferry to Baltimore is about sixty miles. It took us a day to cover the distance; the roads were almost all terrible, clayey and full of deep ruts. We traveled all the way through woods and were often forced to clear a way for the stage around trees blown down across the road by the gale. It is surprising that the coaches do not frequently overturn. The fact that they do not is probably due to their special construction with few springs and therefore little sway, as well as to the drivers' skillful handling of the horses, which are used to this sort of road. But why are not the roads kept in repair? There are inspectors of roads, and sometimes even fines are imposed. But collusion and the difficulty in collecting the fines make the law inoperative, and so everything is allowed to run down. This is one of the effects of slavery. The slave does as little work as he possibly can, and the master, who cares only for his own pleasure, finds better things to do than send his Negro to repair the roads. We saw some of these masters, ill-clad but riding good horses, hunting like madmen through the woods.

The general picture we saw in Maryland was one of uncultivated or poorly cultivated land, occasional large fields of Indian corn, people with pale, drawn and feverish faces, naked Negroes, and wretched huts. I met a man who had had a fever for three months and could not cure it although he took a great deal of quinine. He told me that he had heavy sweats, which weakened him greatly. The best remedy, as he knew from his own experience, was to spend some time in the Eastern or Northern states.

There are places in the Southern states where the inhabitants are not subject to fever. This same traveler pointed out to me two houses built on two hills facing one another across a river, both of which belonged to the same man, and he told me that the people in one house always had fever but that those in the other never did.

In view of the unhealthfulness of the air of Maryland and of the indolence of the citizens, who will not take the trouble to improve this condition, it is not surprising that many of the inhabitants are emigrating to Georgia, where land is cheap and where they probably imagine they will be better off and live in idleness. We met several such emigrant families. There were pretty, well-dressed young women riding good horses and slaves driving the wagons loaded with the family's belongings. These caravans had an appearance of gaiety that surprised me. Apparently for Americans a migration to a place several hundred miles away is no more serious than moving from one house to another and is taken in the spirit of a pleasure party.

We reached Baltimore at night, and I saw this city much better on the way back. There are almost two thousand houses and fourteen thousand inhabitants. The town is very irregularly laid out and stands on a slight elevation above the Patapsco River, forming a crescent along the north shore of a large bay which is not deep enough to accommodate large ships. The anchorage is at Fell's Point, two miles from the center of the town. There still are stagnant waters within the city, and most of the streets are unpaved and are dreadfully muddy after a rain. Everything indicates that the air must be most unhealthful, but if you ask the inhabitants they claim it is not. One might say, like the Swiss in the midst of the battlefield, "If you believed them, nobody would be dead." Ask the inhabitant of a town where there is fever, and he will tell you they never have had a case.

A large part of the trade of Philadelphia has shifted to Baltimore, which before the war was no more than a village. This is the head of navigation for the largest ships, and much freight comes down to it by the Susquehanna. When this river is made navigable Baltimore will be a major port. At the time of my visit, the city was split over the question of Federalism and the new Constitution, and the two parties had almost come to blows during the elections.

Geants' [Grant's] Tavern, where I stayed, is good but expensive. Nearby there is a large house for the stage offices, where I lodged on my way back and fared no worse than at Brant's [Grant's].[5]

[5] [In 1782 Daniel Grant kept the Indian Queen Hotel and in December of the same year took charge of the Fountain Inn.]

Sometimes travelers have to wait for the stage here, but there are a lot of newspapers, which help to while away the time.

At four o'clock in the morning we left Baltimore for Alexandria, some sixty miles away. The roads were about as bad as those we had traveled over the day before—a primitive wagon, excellent horses, skilled drivers—and the same sights too: poorly cultivated fields, wretched huts, wretched Negroes. A plantation belonging to a Quaker was pointed out to me; there were no slaves on it.

We passed through Brushtown [Bushtown], a new town where the state of Maryland plans to establish a college. The building was almost completed and is situated at the top of a hill, where it enjoys good air.[6]

Having lunched at Brushtown we dined at Bladensburg, sixteen miles from Alexandria. Bladensburg is on a small river which flows into the Potomac and which is deep enough for twenty- to thirty-ton vessels. We found nothing to drink except *eau de vie* [whiskey?] or rum and water. In slave country there are no manufacturing or domestic industries, and people have no idea of making beer or cider at home.

Before reaching Bladensburg, one has to cross a river on a small ferry at a place called, I believe, Elksbridge [Elkridge Landing]. It is a very small river in summer but large in winter. The fact that no bridge has been built as yet seems strange, until one recalls the political effects of slavery. For the use of the ferry the stage pays, the driver told me, a yearly toll of thirty pounds, which is enormous.

Georgetown is the last town in Maryland. It has a pleasant situation overlooking the Potomac and does considerable trade. Regulations and taxes foolishly imposed on commerce by the state of Virginia have brought to Georgetown a large part of the trade which would have normally gone to Alexandria, eight miles farther down the Potomac. From Georgetown, and even from vessels lying in the middle of the river, goods are smuggled into Virginia. This increase in trade has attracted to Georgetown many merchants, among them some Frenchmen. One of the latter by the name of Casanauve is building a beautiful house. The river is

[6] [There is good evidence here that Brissot wrote this letter considerably after the event, at a time when his memory could no longer supplement his rough notes. He passed through Bushtown, the present Abingdon, on the Bush River, the day *before* he arrived in Baltimore, not the day after. The college he describes was Cokesbury College, founded in 1785 by the Methodists.]

superb here and the views to be had from both sides are infinitely delightful. The channel is deep and can accommodate large vessels.

From the ferry landing across the river to Alexandria there are eight miles of very good roads. Alexandria, which thirty or forty years ago had only one or two houses, is not as large as Baltimore but ought to be even bigger. It is laid out in almost as irregular a fashion and the streets are just as muddy. There is a greater display of luxury, but it is a tawdry sort of ostentation: servants in silk stockings, men wearing silk stockings inside their boots, and women most elegantly arrayed and with feathers in their hats.

The people of Alexandria believed that their city was destined to become a big center of commerce at the end of the war because of all its natural advantages—good air, a well-protected port with water deep enough to take the largest ships and permit them to anchor near the docks, and an abundance of agricultural products in the surrounding area. Consequently they did a great deal of building and constructed superb wharfs and vast warehouses. But trade is still stagnant. This is attributed to the unwise taxes I have mentioned, from which Maryland, across the river, is exempt. As a result, many residents are leaving or trying to do so. Some trade, however, is carried on by ships sailing to the West Indies and New Orleans.

As soon as I arrived in Alexandria I set out for Mount Vernon, the beautiful house of General Washington ten miles down the river. After passing through many woods and crossing two hills, I caught sight of an elegantly simple and beautiful mansion with well-kept lawns in the front. On one side there were stables and cattle barns, on the other a greenhouse and buildings in which Negroes worked. In a sort of farmyard there were turkeys, ducks, geese, and other fowl. On the side of the mansion overlooking the Potomac was a vast and very high portico, from which there was a most beautiful view of the river. Inside, the arrangement of the rooms was well planned and convenient. The exterior was painted with a kind of varnish covered with cement [paint and sand finish to give the effect of stone], which makes an almost completely waterproof covering.

The general did not arrive home until evening and came in very tired from riding around a part of his estate where he was having a road laid out. You have often heard him likened to Cincinnatus; the comparison is accurate. This famous general is now merely a good countryman entirely devoted to the care of his farm, as he calls it, to improving his agricultural methods, and to constructing barns. He showed me a huge one he was building, about one hundred feet long and of an even greater width, which was to store all his grain, potatoes, turnips, etc. Around it he had also built stables for all his cattle, horses, and donkeys. The latter are a breed unknown in this country which he is trying to increase. The barn is so well planned that a man can fill the racks with hay or potatoes easily and without any danger. The general told me that he had used a design sent him by the famous English agriculturalist Arthur Young, but that he had added many improvements. The building was made of bricks baked on the estate. With the exception of the rafters and the roofing shingles, which he had had to buy because he was in a hurry, all the materials came from his own place. The total cost of construction, he told me, amounted to no more than £300. In France, it would have cost over 80,000 livres. This year he had planted 700 bushels of potatoes. All these things were innovations in Virginia, where they have no barns and do not store fodder for cattle.

His horses, mules, and donkeys were grazing in nearby meadows. He told us that he also intended to show his fellow Virginians how to raise hay as a crop, which is so rarely done and yet is very necessary, for the cattle often lack feed in winter. His mules were doing very well, and he owns a magnificent stallion which will sire a line of beautiful horses for this area. He also took us to see his two handsome donkeys, one from Malta and the other from Spain.

His three hundred Negroes live in a number of log houses in different parts of the estate, which contains over 10,000 acres.

Colonel Humphreys, the poet I mentioned earlier, who is General Washington's secretary, told me that the general owns altogether over 200,000 acres in various states.

General Washington had brought over from England a good English farmer with his family and put him in charge of the farming.

Everything was simple in the general's home. He provides a good table but not a sumptuous one, and his household is run with regularity and order. Mrs. Washington keeps an eye on everything. She combines with the qualities of an excellent countrywoman the simple dignity which befits a wife whose husband has played the greatest role in his country's history. She is gracious as well, and she shows strangers that courtesy which is the flower of hospitality. The same virtues are mirrored in her niece, who is charming but unfortunately seems to be in very delicate health.[7]

You have heard me criticize M. Chastellux for having put so much art in his character sketch of the general. To paint a pretentious portrait of an unpretentious man is nonsense. The general's kindness of heart shines in his eyes, which, although they no longer have the piercing gleam his officers knew when he was at the head of the army, still grow animated in conversation. His face has no distinctive features, which is why it has always been difficult to paint a good likeness of him, and why few of his portraits resemble him. His answers to queries are full of common sense. He is very cautious and hesitant about committing himself, but once he has made a decision he is firm and unshakable. His modesty is astonishing, particularly to a Frenchman.[8] He speaks of the American War as if he had not been its leader, and of his victories with a greater indifference than even a foreigner would. I saw him lose his characteristic composure and become heated only when he talked about the present state of affairs in America. The schisms within his country torture his soul, and he feels the necessity of rallying all lovers of liberty around one central issue, the need to strengthen the government. He is still ready to sacrifice his peaceful life, which gives him such happiness. "Happiness like this," he told me, "is not to be found in great honors or in the tumult of life." This philosopher believed in this truth so strongly that from the moment of his retirement he severed every political connection and renounced all offices. And yet, despite his spirit of abnegation, his disinterestedness, and his modesty, this astonishing man has enemies! He has been viciously attacked in the newspapers and has been accused of being ambitious and conniving, when all his life, when indeed all America, can testify to his selflessness and integrity. Virginia is perhaps the only state where he does have enemies, for everywhere else I have heard his name pronounced with nothing but respect mingled with affection and gratitude. Americans speak of him as they would of a father. Perhaps Washington is not to be compared to the most famous military

---

[7] Fanny (Bassett) Washington.

[8] In Tacitus' portrait of Germanicus there are many of Washington's traits: "Tanta illi comitas in socios, mansuetudo in hostes, visu que et auditu juxta venerabilis, cum magnitudinem, et gravitatem summae fortunae retineret, invidiam et adrogantiam effugerat." [So great, then, was his friendliness towards allies and his clemency toward enemies; inspiring in both appearance and speech, he maintained the dignity and seriousness of his high position and yet avoided jealousy and arrogance. *Annals* II, 72.]

leaders, but he has all the qualities and all the virtues of the perfect republican.

He spoke to me of M. Lafayette with affection. He regards him as his son and foresaw with both joy and anxiety the role he was to play in the forthcoming revolution in France. He could not clearly predict the outcome of this revolution, for on one hand he knew well the ardor of the French and their tendency to resort to extreme measures, but on the other he was also aware of their deep veneration for traditional government and for monarchs, though he regarded the belief in the sacredness of the throne as a bizarre idea.

After spending about three days in the home of this famous man, who showered me with kindnesses and gave me a great deal of information both on the recent war and on present conditions in America, I reluctantly returned to Alexandria.

OBSERVATIONS ON MARYLAND
AND VIRGINIA

Chesapeake Bay divides Maryland into two almost equal parts, of which the western is the more populated. Lakes and many navigable rivers provide good avenues for trade. Maryland would be a very prosperous region if slavery were abolished, if tobacco were replaced by a more moral and profitable crop, and, lastly, if the influence of Catholicism had not corrupted the instinct for order, method, and frugality which is characteristic of the other sects and is so essential to the orderly management of political and civic affairs. The Catholics are a well-behaved people and they conducted themselves well during the Revolution.

Since I passed rapidly through Maryland, I did not have the opportunity to verify the truth of the story which claims that some Jesuits before the destruction of their order owned superb establishments in Charles and May [Saint Mary's?] Counties and were accused of keeping harems of Negro women, from whom was born a mixed race. I was told that several of these Jesuits had married and now owned large estates.[1]

Cotton is grown both in Maryland and in Virginia, but in general there is no effort either to improve the methods of cultivation or the product or to clean it. Thrifty families merely make a plain but warm cotton cloth, which General Washington's Negroes, for instance, wear. I also saw on his estate some very fine cotton which could be made into beautiful muslin. A Frenchwomen in Alexandria has started making fine cotton cloth, but her example has had no imitators. When there are so many slaves, why not use them to clean and spin cotton? Because, as I have already said, the slave does as little as he possibly can, the master cares about nothing, and the overseer is busy making his own little fortune.

These disadvantages, as well as the recently invented machines which will cost less than slaves, will probably end by turning people against slavery. In South Carolina, for instance, there has just

---

[1] The good nuns from Flanders who, prompted by a holy despair, have just boarded ship for Maryland, are not going to find there the religious fanaticism whose disappearance in their own country they so deplore.

been invented a machine to thresh and plant rice which will make the importation of Negroes unnecessary.

There is certainly some excellent land in Maryland and Virginia, including even that where tobacco has been grown and which has been abandoned. All that is needed to make it productive is to fertilize it and rotate the crops, growing, for instance, Indian corn the first year,[2] wheat the second, alfalfa the third, etc. But that would require some extra work, and slave owners do not wish to make the effort.

You see in these two states few good meadows, although the land is of the right kind, sloping and well watered. The inhabitants will not take the trouble to grow hay except in small quantities; most of it is mediocre or poor, and there is not enough to feed their cattle. Nor do they raise potatoes, carrots, or turnips for fodder, preferring to buy them from the North, where they are grown. In winter they feed the cattle with the "tops" of Indian corn, that is, with the leaves and a kind of fine grass which grows in the ears. Horses are very fond of this fodder. Cattle are neither kept in barns nor fed during the winter. Consequently, I am told, a number starve or freeze to death, and those that survive into the spring are terribly thin. Another result is that meat in winter and spring is very poor.

Virginians live in a kind of tawdry luxury. Persons who have known them intimately assure me that the richest do not have more than five or six shirts and generally have only two or three, wearing one while the other is being washed. (The washerwomen are very fast.) These shirts are of fine quality, and so are their silk stockings. The trousseau of a girl who is getting married consists of only a few chemises. Virginians do not use napkins, but they wear silk cravats, and instead of carrying white handkerchiefs they blow their noses either with their fingers [3] or with a silk handkerchief which also serves as a cravat, a napkin, etc.

These customs surprised me. I searched for an explanation and I think I found it in the state of commercial bondage in which England used to hold this country. The English supplied all the imports to America, and they preferred to ship merchandise which they manufactured themselves or which they could buy directly

---

[2] The tilling of the land for planting Indian corn makes an excellent preparation for a crop of wheat the following year, for the soil has been well stirred up and freed of weeds. That is why farmers usually alternate Indian corn and wheat.

[3] I have seen the best-bred Americans do this.

and cheaply. Since the English had little linen, especially before the establishment of the linen mills in Ireland, they preferred to get Americans used to doing without linen rather than buy it for them in France or Holland, which would have required large capital investments they did not wish to make. This is also why American women wear so many shawls, but no mantelets; the English have shawls but little silk.

The English have introduced in this country their method of inoculation, but Americans have improved the precautions that are required. For instance, in Virginia they have an excellent way of preventing contagion by requiring that after an inoculation the neighbors for two miles around be warned. Inoculation is not dangerous there; General Washington told me that he had several times had a general inoculation of his Negroes and had never lost any.

The general also told me that the population is increasing everywhere in Virginia in spite of the large emigrations to the Ohio.

This state undoubtedly has the finest horses in the country, but they are twice as expensive as those in the North. Horse racing, which Virginians borrowed from the English, has greatly declined. There used to be several famous race courses, but almost all have been abandoned, which is all for the best, for they were an occasion for gambling, drunkenness, and brawling.

General Washington told me that in this respect he had noticed a great improvement in his countrymen, that there was less drunkenness, that people no longer forced drinks on their guests or made it a point of honor to send them home drunk, that there were no longer the rowdy parties at the taverns there used to be, that people were dressing more simply, that the sessions of the courts no longer occasioned scenes of gambling, drunkenness, and bloodshed, and that at last class distinctions were beginning to disappear.

It is estimated that the consumption of salt in Virginia is about half a bushel, that is, forty pounds, per person. The salt is imported mainly from Liverpool. If the same amount is consumed in all the other states of America, you can see that we underestimated in *De la France et des Etats-Unis* the per capita consumption of salt in the United States when we said it was only twenty pounds. A great deal of salt meat is eaten in Virginia, and I was informed that it constitutes seven eighths of all the meat consumed. General Washington told me that his household, composed of twenty persons in his family and of three hundred slaves, consumes about four hundred bushels of salt. He uses a lot more in addition for salting the shad he catches in the Potomac.

There are no markets and no butcher shops either in the towns or in the country. This is because of slavery and because the plantations are so large and so far apart.

I was told that the towns in Virginia are small, even Norfolk and Richmond with its "capitol," which has turned the heads of Virginians. They imagine that, like the Romans, they will some day dictate the laws of the whole world.

There is little manufacturing in Virginia. General Washington told me, however, of a glasswork forty miles from Alexandria which exported last year over ten thousand pounds of glass.

In spite of the general indolence which prevails in this state, progress has, however, been made in digging the famous Potomac canal. The small falls have already been passed, and the company is now working near the big ones.

One hears of more crimes in Virginia than in the Northern states, which is another consequence of the large plantations, luxury, and slavery. During my stay there I was told of a man who although well off had murdered his brother to get his property.

The number of criminals may perhaps also be due to the fact that the English prefer this state as a place to get rid of their convicts. I read the following in an American paper: "Thirty-eight convicts have been embarked in London on the *Secret,* Captain Burke, headed for Virginia." Does that not amount to poisoning a country? Does a nation have the right to infect even an enemy country, much less a friendly one? Would it not be better to work with the American Quakers to reform these convicts gradually? Everyone would profit.

Wherever you find luxury, particularly luxury in the midst of poverty, all goods, even prime necessities, are expensive. I found this to be true in Virginia, where I paid at an inn 5 livres 5 sous, or one dollar, for a supper which in Pennsylvania would have cost 3 livres and in Connecticut 40 sous. Porter, wine, and everything else is very dear; but these high prices are due to causes which I shall discuss later.

VIRGINIA TOBACCO AND TOBACCO NOTES

I was glad to find, my friend, that the excellent article "On Tobacco" which you included in our work *De la France et des Etats-Unis* is, except for a few minor errors, correct in all its details.

It is quite true that tobacco requires a heavy and fertile soil and also continual attention in transplanting, weeding, and protecting it from the insects that attack it, in picking it at the right time, and in curing, rolling, and packing it.

Because of the various expenses before the tobacco reaches the warehouse, only a very large yield and the utter destitution and near starvation to which the poor Negroes are condemned can make this crop profitable. So, as the good land becomes exhausted and as the Negroes, with the progress of humanitarian principles, are less exploited, tobacco growing is declining. You can already see in Virginia fences rising around the fields and wheat and hay replacing tobacco. Farmers are all the more inclined to switch to wheat because of the high yield; one bushel of seed produces twenty to thirty bushels of grain. Wise plantation owners are making this change, among them General Washington, who has completely given up growing tobacco.

If only Virginians were well informed about European needs and about the products in which we are more interested and for which we are willing to pay higher prices, they would surely try, for example, to improve the quality of the cotton they grow, for which the market in Europe is increasing at such a prodigious rate.[1]

I shall not discuss here in detail tobacco growing, the method of picking and preparing it, or the different varieties, for these details have already been described by several writers, and it would be useless to repeat what they have written. I should like, however,

---

[1] Georgia cotton is, however, in greater demand. It is not surprising that this state draws so many immigrants, for it is singularly favored by nature. It produces everything: indigo, rice, hemp, flax, tar, excellent lumber, dye wood, wood for inlaid work, orange trees, olive trees, mulberry trees, etc. As a result land there is at a premium.

to dwell on a subject which no one has treated, namely, "tobacco notes," a kind of artificial currency, the use of which proves that there is no need to be so concerned, as some people are, over the lack of coinage. Under a free regime and in a fertile country the constant produce of the land can give the value of money to any kind of token.

The state has public warehouses where tobacco is deposited. They are run by inspectors responsible for examining the quality of the tobacco. When tobacco is judged "merchantable" it is received for storage and the owner is given a note for the number of hogsheads deposited. These notes circulate like real money and are accepted at the current market price of the tobacco. If they are exchanged for goods the holder of the notes receives a discount.

The price of tobacco depends not on the locality where it was grown [2] but on the place where it is stored, for the relative strictness of the different inspectors alone determines differences in prices. These are the warehouses, ranked in descending order: Hanover Court, Pittsburg, Richmond, and Cabin Point. When Richmond tobacco is worth sixteen to seventeen shillings, Hanover tobacco is worth twenty-one to twenty-two. When tobacco is not of first quality it is transported from place to place until it is accepted, or if it is not acceptable anywhere it is sold locally or smuggled to the West Indies. There are two tobacco crops a year, and only the first one is submitted for inspection. The second is used locally or is smuggled to the West Indies.

Since Virginia produces about 80,000 hogsheads of tobacco, the equivalent of their value circulates in the state in the form of notes. At 10 Virginia pounds per hogshead, these notes amount to about £800,000, or between 13 and 14 million livres, the pound being worth 17 livres 10 sous. For this reason Virginia does not need much silver or copper coinage, for the fast circulation of the notes takes its place. Before the tobacco is delivered the note has often gone through as many as thirty hands.

There is another reason why small coins are scarce and are not necessary. Large plantations are common in Virginia, and the owners get almost all the products they require either from their own land or by opening accounts with others who can supply their

---

[2] There are various kinds of tobacco, each distinguished by different qualities. Here are the names of a few: Thick Joint, Shoestring, Thickset, Sweet Scented, and Oronoko. Virginia tobacco is black and not oily, with thick leaves, and is good for grinding into snuff. Maryland tobacco is yellow and dry and is preferred by the Dutch, who chew it.

needs. In the second place, small coins are necessary where there are many small families and where there are artisans and independent journeymen; but these classes do not exist in Virginia, for almost all the work is done by slaves who are fed by their masters or who live off what they grow themselves and who never go to market. In the towns merchants buy in wholesale lots what they need or else resort to makeshift arrangements to get around the lack of copper coins. For instance, in Alexandria when an ox is slaughtered every citizen buys a large piece which he salts down. To pay for small objects, pistereens [3] and sixpences are cut into two or three pieces, each of which circulates at its proportionate value. This custom leads to a great deal of dishonesty. A man will often cut a dollar into three pieces, keep the middle part for himself, and give the two others as half dollars. People who do not have scales, or do not have the time or patience to weigh the money, are forced to accept them, and later when they spend the money the coin is weighed and they lose the difference.

Before the war England sent over a cargo of well-minted pennies, but the legislative assembly refused to accept them.

Although the pitiful resource of cutting silver coins does some good, still the shortage of coins causes losses to Virginians; it is estimated that because of this situation it is doubly expensive for a family to live in town. Thus the lack of copper coinage is a true sign of both poor government and economic distress.

To return to tobacco and the tobacco notes: There are two kinds of tobacco, rolled and wagoned. The former is that which is placed in a hogshead and rolled from the place where it is grown to the place where it is to be stored or sold.[4] To protect the hogshead, they put a couple of heavy hoops around it to roll it on. This method is used by the poorer farmers, and the price paid for this tobacco is lower than that paid for tobacco packed in hogsheads and transported in wagons.

Although tobacco exhausts the soil, Americans make no effort to restore what is lost. They take and make no return, and simply abandon the land when it becomes unproductive.

In rich soil four or five plants yield a pound of tobacco; in poor

[3] [A popular form of the word *peseta*, a small Spanish silver coin.]

[4] Also sometimes the hogsheads are dragged on two pieces of wood. Both these methods are indications of the great poverty of the country. A traveler once met a tenant farmer who was rolling his tobacco in a hogshead and asked him if he was satisfied with the price of tobacco. "I wish to God," he answered, "I could take all this tobacco and burn it and have done with it. I would be better off."

land it takes ten plants. In the region of the Mississippi, two or three plants give a pound.

You see many abandoned fields in Virginia and Maryland, for the owners prefer to clear new land rather than to try to bring back the old, although the abandoned fields would still be productive if they were manured.

Since tobacco notes constitute real money in circulation, during the last war the Virginia government, relying on the people's confidence in them, put in circulation many tobacco notes that were not backed by tobacco in storage. At the end of the war it established a fund to cover these notes and part of them have already been paid off.

The state of Virginia accepts tobacco in payment of taxes, at a price of twenty-eight shillings, which is very advantageous to the grower, though it is not clear why the price should be forced up in this way. The state then sells the tobacco, two thirds for military warrants, a kind of bond, and one third for money, which is then used to pay interest on other warrants and to cover government expenses.

The cost of storing a hogshead (the legal hogshead contains 1,000 pounds) is 13 shillings, payable by the buyer when he removes the tobacco. These payments cover the salaries of the inspectors and are used to create a fund for self-insurance against fire. A large warehouse burned down in Richmond some time ago, and the state paid for the loss and built a new brick building. The state has also undertaken to pay the counterfeit notes that formerly circulated. All these facts prove how valuable such a system is for the circulation of money and for the promotion of business in general.

When foreigners buy tobacco for shipment to France, they must note that two deductions will be made: the first of about twelve livres per quintal, and the second, a fairly large and very arbitrary sum, for tare.

Virginians do not use snuff or chew tobacco, but some of them smoke it, although this is not as widespread a habit in Virginia as it is in the Carolinas, where people smoke to excess.

I shall not speak here of the tobacco trade with Europe, but I must point out that Virginians would very much like to see free trade established in France. They complain of being subjected to the monopoly of the farmers-general. If they could sell tobacco freely in France and if they had to pay only small import duties, they would surely use France as the distribution center for all the enormous quantities of tobacco with which they flood Europe and which amount to over 100,000 quintals. At present this tobacco is being warehoused in England, where no more than 10,000 to 12,000 quintals are consumed, the rest being re-exported. England pays for this tobacco with its own products, and you can imagine what profits it makes on the exchange. To this should be added the commissions, the money spent by the many Americans whom this trade brings to London, and all the additional incidental business that is created.

These are all advantages that France could take away from England if she abolished the farmers-general and made the customs duties light. The duty on tobacco that Americans pay in England, which is now 1 s. 4 d., or about 33 French sous, per pound of tobacco, is so high they would not prefer the English market. The example of England proves that there is no need to fear that a free tobacco trade will mean a total loss of revenue from this product, for although England herself uses little tobacco, the import duties amount to from twelve to fifteen millions.

The great financial needs of England will not allow her to reduce this duty in the near future, even in order to compete with France. So continue, my friend, to preach your doctrine.[5]

The tremendous consumption of tobacco throughout the world and the prohibitive systems of regulations enforced by almost all governments will encourage Americans to continue to raise this crop, for since their tobacco is priced as low as possible, since their ships operate cheaply, and since no people equal them in daring, enterprise, and energy, they can undertake to supply the whole world with tobacco.

Spain, for instance, will undoubtedly become a market for America. A great deal of smoking tobacco and snuff is used there, the proceeds of the sales going to the king's treasury. The author of the *Nouveau Voyage en Espagne* [6] estimates the profit at twenty

---

[5] It has been partially adopted by the National Assembly. The monopoly has been abolished and the selling and manufacture of tobacco have been made free. There is a duty of only twenty-five livres per quintal on American tobacco. Patents or licenses for its manufacture and sale have been issued, but unfortunately the effects of these excellent reforms have been counterbalanced by the creation of a *Régie Nationale* for the manufacture of tobacco on behalf of the nation. This is one of those unfortunate dreams that the last ministry succeeded in enacting in order to cover up its wasteful practices and acquire supporters, but it was unworthy of the National Assembly. A nation should be neither a manufacturer nor a merchant, for any national business enterprise is destructive of individual industry and prosperity.

[6] On sale at Regnault's, bookseller [Paris, 1789], 3 vols., 8°.

million *livres tournois*.[7] All this tobacco is supplied by the Portuguese, who get it from Brazil; Spaniards prefer it to any other kind. Under their latest contract the Portuguese sell it at less than ten sous per pound, and the king resells it at ten livres. When this contract expires, the author says, if the Americans should offer a better bargain they might well get the business.

All snuff legally consumed in Spain comes from Cuba. The king pays a somewhat higher price for it than for tobacco from Brazil, although he still sells it at ten francs a pound. About forty sous per pound should be deducted for manufacturing costs and the salaries of employees.

The high price of tobacco inevitably leads to smuggling, which is quite considerable even though it is punishable by death. This penalty, however, is actually never inflicted.

Shredded tobacco is strictly prohibited, but the above-mentioned author says that in 1785 the government considered permitting its use because it was believed that the treasury would profit.

Tobacco has been very successful in the Spanish colonies in which it has been tried, in Mexico, on the Caracas coast, and particularly in Louisiana and Trinidad, two colonies whose tobacco may someday be preferred to all others. Its cultivation in Mexico goes back no further than 1765. In this colony alone the sale (to profit of the king) brought in four million Spanish dollars in 1778, and six million in 1784, from which one should subtract expenses and taxes. The Spanish minister plans to reserve Louisiana tobacco, which is cheaper and better, for consumption in Mexico.

The tobacco which is beginning to be grown on the eastern banks of the Mississippi and along the Ohio will undoubtedly someday supply the largest part of the Spanish domestic and colonial markets. These same regions will probably also supply our needs, which will become enormous if a free system is adopted, for it has been proved by those who know the secrets of the farmers-general that the real consumption of tobacco in the kingdom of France amounts to more than thirty million pounds, and not to fifteen million as they are trying to make us believe.

[7] This author [Jean François, baron de Bourgoing (1748–1811)], who was for a long time employed in the French Embassy in Spain and is at present entrusted with an important mission in the north and who, therefore, ought to be well informed about the French government, is mistaken when, in the same article, he estimates at 120 million the profits made by the French treasury on the revenue from tobacco. It is known that this profit amounts to no more than 28 or 30 million.

THE SHENANDOAH VALLEY

I had intended, my friend, upon leaving Alexandria to visit the beautiful valley watered by the Shenandoah River in the back country of Virginia, of which Mr. Jefferson [1] and M. Crèvecoeur have given us such attractive descriptions. I then intended to come back through the Lancaster Valley and pay my respects to the virtuous Moravians. The approaching revolution in France, however, has hastened my return and I am forced, if I am to give you some idea of the land where we have been urged to set up our tabernacles, merely to borrow from the descriptions left by several travelers who have this very year visited and carefully observed this region, situated between the ranges of mountains which separate Virginia from the Western Territory.

The United States is divided into an eastern and western section by a clear natural line of demarkation. The eastern part contains the thirteen states and extends about 850 English miles (300 French leagues) along the Atlantic Ocean. The inland part is intersected by several mountain ranges running from northeast to southwest parallel to the seacoast. The area between the sea and the first chain of mountains, called the South Mountains or Blue Mountains, is about 200 to 225 miles (60 to 70 French leagues) wide. This latter region may in turn be divided into two equal parts: the first, stretching inland from the coast, is a sandy, infertile, and unhealthful plain extending from New Jersey to the south but becoming more fertile and more healthful as you progress north from New Jersey.

The second part of the coastal area rises somewhat and rests on a base of granite and quartz covered by a layer of clay, above which is a shallow layer of topsoil. Since the clay is impervious to water, the land is in general not fertile and is unhealthful, particularly toward the south. Yet one can occasionally find in this area rather large stretches of excellent land which are not too remote from the coast. There is also good land in the colder regions, but it is expensive because the settlements there are long established.

[1] See Mr. Jefferson's description of this valley in his *Notes on Virginia* [Paris, 1785], p. 29.

THE SHENANDOAH VALLEY

Between the South Mountains and the North Mountains, also called by the Indians the Endless Mountains, there is a valley thirty-five to forty miles wide, sometimes less, which runs parallel to the two ranges. The soil is of very good quality and is underlaid with limestone. The land slopes enough to allow water to drain easily, but not so much as to be washed away by the heavy rains to which America is subject and which often shatter the farmer's hopes, especially if they come just after he has plowed and seeded. The air is wholesome. This is the region where the finest settlements have been made by people from Pennsylvania and New York. The part of this valley in which land is least expensive and which promises most for the future is that between the Potomac and James rivers.

Before going into details, I must speak briefly of the lands farther west.

Between the North Mountains and the Alleghenies, which form the backbone of the continent, there is a continuous series of mountains of very hard sandstone between which there is almost no land suitable for farming and which also form serious obstacles to the transportation of products.

From the crest of the Alleghenies flow many rivers toward the west in a direction directly opposite to those which on the eastern slopes flow into the Atlantic. The quality of the western lands improves as you come closer to the Ohio and the Mississippi, and they are also cheaper than on the eastern side of the mountains, but there is not yet any outlet from this region, either to the United States ports or through the Spanish settlements. The Spaniards are now developing and encouraging the growth of a colony in Louisiana and the Floridas to counterbalance the power and the population of the United States.

It is, however, most likely that it will not be long before an important line of communication is established between the western settlements and New Orleans, and it is this hope which, together with the astounding fertility of the land, draws so many settlers to Kentucky, which Americans call "the promised land."

The region which presents more advantages than disadvantages is undoubtedly the Shenandoah Valley, situated, as I have said, between the North and South Mountains. It has almost all the advantages of the Western Territory and none of its disadvantages. This valley is located almost in the center of the United States and has nothing to fear from foreign enemies. Moreover it is close to two large rivers, both of which flow into Chesapeake Bay. It is true that these rivers are not yet navigable from their sources to their mouths, but the work begun on the canal along the Potomac is so far advanced that it is almost certain that it will be completed within five or six years.

Because it is farther to the south and has a peculiarly favorable situation, this valley enjoys a more equable climate than the Northern states. Its grain crops are superior even to those of Pennsylvania, and fruit and other European products do better here than anywhere else.

Current grain prices in the Shenandoah Valley are as follows: a bushel of wheat, 60 English pounds in weight,[2] sells for 5 s. 6 d., Virginia currency (4 livres 12 sous, French currency),[3] while the same quantity is currently worth in Philadelphia 7 s. 6 d., Pennsylvania currency (5 livres 5 sous or 5 livres 10 sous, French currency).[4] The difference between the prices of corn is about the same, although corn may be a little more expensive in the Shenandoah than in Pennsylvania because it is the staple food of the inhabitants and particularly of the Negroes.

As to land, the prices vary according to the quality, and an acre costs from 24 to 90 livres, while in Pennsylvania land of similar quality costs from 85 to 500 livres.

There are three or four kinds of land: bottom land, near the Potomac, the Shenandoah, and the Conococheague rivers; virgin limestone land of top quality; land already under cultivation; and what is called slate land, which contains no limestone and is much inferior. In the very center of the valley there are leagues of land covered with rock and not fit for farming called the Barrens.

There is a surprisingly big difference between the productivity of these lands and those in Pennsylvania. It is attributable to the large population of the latter state, to the industry, order and harmony prevailing among its inhabitants, and to its plentiful and easily accessible outlets for trade. This valley will, however, undoubtedly soon have plenty of such outlets, for already its wheat

[2] Four and four-fifths U.S. bushels equal one *setier de Paris.*

[3] A Virginia shilling equals about 16 French sous.

[4] The Pennsylvania shilling equals about 14 French sous. The high price of wheat in Pennsylvania is due to the prodigious demand in Europe and the colonies this year. The average price of wheat in Philadelphia is 5 or 6 s., that is, a *setier* of Philadelphia wheat costs in an average year 18 to 20 livres. In Virginia the average price of wheat is 14 to 15 livres, and Indian corn is 36 to 42 sous a bushel, or about 10 livres a *setier.*

and flour are transported by land and sold as far away as one hundred miles. The Shenandoah is not more than fifty miles from Georgetown, which I have described, where navigation begins, and products are transported even to Alexandria, sixty or seventy miles away, and to Richmond and to Baltimore, eighty or a hundred miles away. The future holds even greater promise. Of all the rivers which flow into the Atlantic Ocean, the Potomac is the one which most resembles the rivers of the West in navigability. This circumstance will someday transform this region into the transportation center for all the United States. It will enjoy the greatest security in wartime and will have the best means of transportation in all seasons.

Before this ideal is realized, however, the morals of the people will have to be reformed. Luxury, which is even worse here than in Pennsylvania, will have to be banished. Indolence and the love of hunting and pleasure will have to be rooted out of the hearts of Virginians. The present population should be replaced with frugal and energetic Germans. But what is needed above all is to abolish slavery, which produces three great scourges: the idleness of the few, and poor work and lack of industry on the part of the many. Slavery, this hideous, festering wound of humanity, will always deter sensitive Europeans from settling there. No such disgusting spectacle confronts them in Pennsylvania, where, although they will have to pay higher prices for land, they can make large profits raising cattle.

A wide choice of land is available in Pennsylvania, but the European who plans to buy, if he is to avoid making a mistake, should be very cautious. He should live and travel for a while in the state and should talk to many people. For instance, the lands watered by the Susquehanna are highly regarded. Read what M. Crèvecoeur says of this region in the third volume of his work, and also Mr. Pownall's description, and you will be tempted to think it is a sort of paradise. The latter writes of the area nearest to Philadelphia:

There are [. . .] between the Susquehanna and Schuylkill rivers [. . .] several valleys. A succession of such [are] divided from each other by little hilly branchings of the main hills [. . .] The lands are of a limestone good farming soil. [The farmers . . .] raise a great deal of wheat. The sides of the hills are covered with woods: the timber in general oak, chestnut, and hickory [. . .] These successions of valleys appeared to me as I rode along them the most charming of landscapes. The bottoms of the vales were full of cultured farms, with houses such as yeomanry, not tenants, live in. These were busked up with gardens, and with peach and apple orchards all around them, and with every convenience and enjoyment that property and plenty could give to peace and liberty.[5]

This description is true of the land below the Falls of the Susquehanna, but if you visit the area above the falls, you will not find many sections of which you can paint so handsome a picture. The best lands there are close to the rivers and the soil is very thin. The winters are cold and long, and since the land is very high, harvests are more likely to fail and fruit trees do less well. Navigation on the Susquehanna is interrupted by many waterfalls. It is true that in spite of these obstacles boats travel more than two hundred miles above the falls, and that since most of the waterfalls are close together canals around them can be easily built. This has already been attempted on the branch of the river in Maryland, but unfortunately the work, which was well advanced, was stopped because of the company's lack of funds and because the Pennsylvanians were slow in doing what they had promised for their part of the river. When they become convinced of the advantages they will derive from the completion of this work, they will very probably resume the execution of this project with new energy.

The farther northwest you go the fewer good lands you find, but the traveler who is a philosopher and a naturalist is rewarded by superb landscapes, such as those around the Juniata, a large river which empties into the Susquehanna. The Juniata flows through a broad and variegated countryside with many woods, mountains, and valleys quite beautiful though narrow, of which the soil is mainly of limestone. The mountains are often awesome and contain deposits of copper, lead, and coal.

Occasionally you see isolated houses, and it is there that real contentment can be experienced by those who are wise enough to make their happiness depend only on peace of mind and on the enjoyment of themselves and of nature. Compared to this delicious tranquility, what is the wearisome bustle of our great cities worth? What is the spectacle of men compared to the spectacle of nature? My friend, trees do not slander, and they do not destroy their benefactors; but deserving men have endured such treatment hundreds of times at the hands of their fellows.

[5] [Thomas Pownall, *A Topographical Description of . . . North America . . .* (London, 1776), p. 28. Brissot in his translation of this passage both condensed and embellished the original. For instance he translated "yeomanry" as "de bons *gentlemen* (messieurs)."]

But to return to my subject, what conclusion is to be drawn from everything I have said?—That a European who wishes to emigrate and settle here ought to beware of all the descriptions that he is given of these various regions? If he is interested mainly in the fertility of the soil, the beauty of the trees, the opportunities for hunting and fishing, he will surely choose Kentucky. If he is looking for large crops, inexpensive land, a more temperate climate, and the promise of good transportation by water, he will settle in the Shenandoah Valley. But if he clings to his European ways and wishes to satisfy his European tastes and needs society, his best choice will be Pennsylvania, where the disadvantages of a variable climate can be met by due precautions, where the inferiority of the crops is compensated by higher prices, and where he can enjoy both the pleasures of solitude and the advantages to be procured from the proximity of large cities.

JOURNEY FROM BOSTON
TO PORTSMOUTH

I left Boston on October 2 after dinner, in a chaise, in the company of the worthy Mr. Barrett,[1] whose good qualities and kindness I cannot praise highly enough. He made every effort to supply me with information on the objects of my investigations. We slept in Salem, a town fifteen miles from Boston, after traveling along an excellent gravel road bordered by woods and meadows. We crossed the fine Malden bridge, which I mentioned earlier, and went through Lynn, known for the manufacture of women's shoes. Almost all the inhabitants of the town are cobblers, and it is estimated that over 100,000 pairs of shoes are made there every year and exported to the South, the West Indies, and other places. They retail at fifty sous a pair and are covered with cloth. Not far from Lynn, at Reading, there is a similar factory of men's shoes.

Salem is a pretty place. There are seven churches, although the town has no more than 9,000 inhabitants. To understand the reason for the number of churches you must recall that Salem was one of the first towns established on this continent, that the most extreme form of Puritanism prevailed, and that witches were burned there about a century ago. Of these churches one belongs to the Quakers, who once were persecuted in this place.

Like all American towns, Salem has a printing press and a newspaper which copies the papers of other states. While waiting for supper I read the speech M. D'Eprémesnil was making when he was arrested in a full meeting of the Parlement.[2] What a wonderful invention the press is! It brings all nations in touch with one another, and the reports of good deeds performed in one country serve to inspire others and permit these acts to be shared by all in common. D'Eprémesnil's speech delighted the daughters of my hostess and they thought him another Brutus.[3]

[1] He is a member of a respected Boston family and has been recently appointed American consul in France.

[2] [Jean Jacques Duval d'Eprémesnil (1746–1794), Conseiller of the Parlement of Paris and deputy of the nobility to the Constituant Assembly. During the Revolution he defended the royal authority and was executed.]

[3] Heu! quantum mutatus ab illo! 1791. [Ah! How much he has changed from the man he was! *Aeneid* II, 274.]

It was cold, and we had a fire in a Franklin stove. These are very common here. When other kinds of stoves are used, the device described by M. Crèvecoeur is utilized, so that they rarely smoke.

The mistress of the tavern, Mrs. Robinson, was having tea with her daughters, and at their invitation we joined them. I repeat, nothing like that ever happens in France. Everywhere in the United States innkeepers' daughters are very neatly dressed and have a modest, proper appearance. The innkeeper himself is a respected man in a country where money is scarce, for more of it passes through his hands than anyone else's, and since money controls goods it also controls men. In American inns you find good beds, good food, and good service, but neither the servants nor the stage drivers get tips—an excellent custom, for tipping is an inexcusable practice, not only because of the vexations it occasions, but also because it teaches men to be base and instills in them a kind of servile greed.

Butter here costs eight sous a pound.

Salem has a large trade with the West Indies and there is much cod fishing.

We left at seven o'clock in the morning and crossed over the bridge from Salem to Beverly, a fine and very ingenious wooden construction which cost only £3,000 to build and was financed by a subscription of 200 shares. The toll for a horse and carriage is eight pence, Massachusetts currency (twelve French sous).

The ingenuity of this bridge, which opens for the passage of ships by a mechanism simpler than that of the Charlestown bridge, and the speed with which its construction was completed, are indications of the technical progress and the industry of Massachusetts. The bridge spans a creek almost one mile wide, which is mentioned by M. Chastellux, who in 1782 crossed it on a ferry.[4]

On the road to Beverly we saw a cotton mill which has a carding machine. The company had applied to the government for a monopoly, which was refused, or else for certain special concessions, which will be granted. I noticed along the way that everywhere more hemp and flax were being grown. The fields of New Hampshire are covered with these crops, and there is a flourishing linen mill at Londonderry, a town in New Hampshire settled partly by the Irish.

We arrived at Newbury at noon and had dinner at the home of Mr. Tracy, who owns a small country house two miles out of

[4] *Voyages* [Paris, 1786], II, 192.

town.[5] This American once had a fortune of over two millions, but he was ruined in a number of various enterprises, especially a contract to supply masts to France during the last war. He relied on untrustworthy people who cheated him. According to the most reliable information I have obtained on this episode, the cargo of masts was eventually sold in Le Havre for not more than 6,000 livres. Colonel Wentworth [6] and Mr. Dalton,[7] of whom I shall have more to say later, told me that because of either the ignorance or the dishonesty of Mr. Tracy's agents the cargo contained nothing but scrap wood fit only for burning. The clerks of the Ministry of the Navy in Versailles, prompted by personal motives, dishonestly exaggerated this incident in order to prove that American timber was worthless and prevent the government from buying any.

Mr. Tracy, ruined by this venture and by several equally unfortunate ones, now lives retired in the country, where he stoically bears his misfortune, comforted and sustained by his good wife, who maintains great dignity in the midst of their adversity.

M. Chastellux, who also visited Mr. Tracy, but at a happier time, in describing his stay launched a bitter complaint against the states which were burdening merchants with enormous taxes.[8] He said that in 1781, although Mr. Tracy had lent the state £5,000, or close to 100,000 francs, his taxes were £6,000, that is, nearly 120,000 francs.

It is difficult to see how a private citizen who has a capital of only two million can be expected to pay taxes amounting to more than his income from this capital, or even how there can be in any country citizens rich enough to pay so heavy a tax. The enigma can, however, be easily explained when you know that these £6,000 were payable in [state] certificates [of indebtedness], which at that time were tremendously depreciated. Studying the depreciation rate for New Hampshire in 1781, I find that in January £100 in money could buy £7,500 in certificates, and in June, £12,000. So if Mr. Tracy paid in June £6,000 in certificates, in reality he paid

⁵[Nathaniel Tracy (1751–1796), one of the financiers of the Revolution, who, as Brissot indicates, lost his fortune by a number of various reverses during the war and died virtually bankrupt.]

⁶[Colonel Joshua Wentworth (1742–1809), who fought in the Revolution and was a political leader in Portsmouth, N.H. Brissot appears (p. 367) to have confused him with John Wentworth, also of Portsmouth, Surveyor General of the King's Woods in North America and last royal governor of New Hampshire.]

⁷[Tristram Dalton (1738–1817) of Newbury.]

⁸[*Voyages*, Paris, 1786], II, 188.

only £50, that is, about 875 livres, a sum which is not very large for a capitalist worth two million and who operated a large number of ships. This mistake of confusing taxes payable in depreciated paper with those payable in silver has been made more than once by M. Chastellux.

Newbury is much more active than Salem. It has the same type of trade and exports to the West Indies a large amount of food-stuffs—butter, cheese, meat, and fish—as well as horses and wood. Ship construction, however, has greatly declined; in 1772, ninety ships were built on the Merrimack River; in 1788, only three. The town is turning to fishing and trade with the West Indies. The Merrimack is a magnificent stream abounding in fish. They catch cod at the mouth of the river, and in April salmon are plentiful and sell for five pence a pound. Newbury would be the best port in the United States were it not for a dangerous bar at the entrance.

During the last war they built here privateers, which captured many prizes and brought in almost the whole Quebec fleet, flooding the United States with English merchandise.

Mr. Marquant, one of the leading merchants in town, told me that business was falling off, that wood could be bought for next to nothing, that carpenters, who at the end of the war were asking one or two dollars a day, were now happy to get a few shillings, that a ship could be built and completely outfitted at a price of eighteen dollars a ton, and that money was scarce and in great demand.

While talking to this merchant and several others, I made note of a number of American traits: a great desire to make money and a willingness to risk the hazards of the sea; a tendency to complain about the disadvantages of their own state and region and talk up the advantages of other parts of the country, and a readiness to move elsewhere; and complaints about taxes and other hardships, though upon examination their grumblings appear quite unjustified. Even if business is depressed in Newbury, the towns farther south and the rural areas are expanding. It is important to keep in mind, when one compares the trade of Boston with that of other states, that Massachusetts shipping is distributed among many busy ports: Boston, Marblehead, Salem, Newbury, and Portsmouth.

Court was in session at Newbury and drew a crowd of people from all around. It was a circuit court, which is an excellent system, for it cuts down the number of cases and disposes of them faster. I met several judges at Mr. Jackson's,[9] and I asked them whether many crimes had been committed that year. "No," one of them said. "No murders and very few thefts." Everything was down in Newbury.

The town has, however, many handsome houses and presents an appearance of wealth, which is due to some thirty French families that settled here for religious reasons about one hundred years ago under the leadership of Mr. Dummer.[10]

Newbury played an important part in the Revolution. It is a noteworthy and perhaps unique fact that there was not a single Tory in the town and that no property was confiscated.[11]

There are twenty-four miles of fine road from Newbury to Portsmouth. We took ferries at Halmsbury [Amesbury] and at Salisbury. All the children I met along this road and in general in New Hampshire seemed to be in good health; they were plump and had healthy complexions, good color, and blond hair, and looked in general healthier than children in Pennsylvania. All the farmers in these parts are either sailors or shipbuilders, and I saw some fine boats being built on a farm.

Portsmouth, the capital of New Hampshire, is less active than the other towns I have described and everything shows signs of being in a state of decline. The population is small, many of the houses are dilapidated, and I saw a good number of women and children in rags, a sight I had never before encountered in America. Yet there are some handsome houses; I was told that labor is so cheap that a charming three-story house cost to build no more than 12,000 to 15,000 livres. People are complaining about the scarcity of money. They are beginning to export horses and wood to the West Indies. I heard that there are a lot of land jobbers and that they have caused many people to lose money.

Situated on the swift and deep Piscataqua River, Portsmouth has a fine port which is always ice-free as far as four or five miles

[9] [Jonathan Jackson (1743–1810), member of the Continental Congress and the Massachusetts legislature]

[10] [Jeremiah Dummer (1645–1718)?]

[11] The list of compensations paid by the king of England to the Loyalists was received in America during my stay there. The royal generosity caused a great deal of laughter, for while he paid 75 per cent of their losses to people who had indeed lost property, he paid an equal amount to many who had had none. No account was taken of the fact that some of this land had mortgages, which had to be paid off when the property was sold by the state.

above the town.[12] This was once one of the largest ports for the export of building timber. Colonel Wentworth, one of the most intelligent, honest, and esteemed men in these parts, was formerly the agent of the English government and the East India Company for the export of lumber to England. The East India Company is again beginning to show interest in this trade.

Everybody here is involved either in trading or in building, and President Langdon himself keeps a store.[13] The inhabitants are also beginning to engage in fishing, but they have not as yet been very successful. They complain about their crews and the difficulty of getting enough men, and they are not as expert as the fishermen of Marblehead at cleaning and drying the fish.

I was invited to dinner by President Langdon, who is very well informed on matters pertaining to the state. You may recall that it was he who, at the time of Burgoyne's invasion, was the first to mount a horse and persuade his fellow citizens to go meet the enemy. You probably also remember the words attributed by M. Chastellux to a Negro who followed him and who was freed.[14] Mr. Langdon told me M. Chastellux's story was untrue.

Mr. Langdon seemed strongly convinced that his state will become extremely prosperous if the new Constitution is adopted. This feeling was shared by Colonel Wentworth, who is well informed on the real situation in America.

We left on Sunday and stopped for dinner at Colonel Dalton's,

[12] See the maps of the coast from Portsmouth to Cape Ann and of the inland waters of the Merrimack River drawn by Mr. Wheeler, Engineer to the King of England. They are very detailed and exact. Almost all these states have good maps, even of their inland waters, such as the Delaware. They are on sale in London, at Faden's, near Charing Cross. [Vol. III of *The Atlantic Neptune* (1774–1781) contains "Charts of the Coast and Harbors of New England from Surveys Taken by . . . Thos. Wheeler." No. 15 shows the coast from Newbury Harbor to Cape Elizabeth. Brissot may also be referring to *A Topographical Map of the State of New Hampshire . . . by . . . Thomas Wright, George Sproule, James Grant, Thomas Wheeler, and Charles Blaskowitz.* (London: William Faden . . . Charing Cross, 1784).]

[13] [John Langdon (1741–1819) of Portsmouth, in 1788 president of the State of New Hampshire.]

[14] [*Voyages* (Paris, 1786), II, 177: "[Langdon] was marching with his troops day and night, resting only at night in the woods. One of his favorite Negro slaves, whom he had taken with him on the expedition, said to him, 'Master, you are enduring many hardships, but you are marching to fight for liberty. I too would endure all this patiently if I had any liberty to fight for.'

" 'Let that be no obstacle,' answered Langdon. 'From this moment on you are free.'

"The Negro continued with the troops, fought bravely, and has never left Langdon since."]

five miles from Newbury on the Merrimack. It is one of the most beautiful spots imaginable and the view, one of the grandest I have ever seen, embraces a panorama stretching over more than seven leagues. His farm is well kept; I saw thirty cows, a good number of very fat pigs, some sheep, a well-stocked larder, and a big vegetable garden. Artichokes do very well but they are grown only as a curiosity, for no one eats them.

Mr. Dalton told me that barley grows fairly well. I tried his beer and found it pleasant. Good cheeses are also made on his farm. He told me that his Indian corn was not doing as well as before and he attributed this failure to the fact that this crop quickly exhausts the soil. So he is giving it up and is replacing it with pastures for cattle. This country is good for raising livestock, for the farmers can grow enough hay to last all winter, as well as carrots, potatoes, and other vegetables for fodder. Beet roots grow here to an enormous size, and Mr. Dalton intends to raise more, for people like them and they also eat the leaves as salad. Peppers are also grown; Americans make from them a kind of pickle of which they are very fond. The pork is good, the best coming from a mixed breed of pig imported from the East Indies.

Mr. Dalton also has grapes and several kinds of pears and apples, and does a great deal of gardening, which is not usual in America. His grapes are sweet and his Cressane and St. Michel [Archange] pears are good, but he complained that children steal his fruit. This is a fairly common sin, easily forgiven in a free country, and a property owner here who used the infernal traps invented by the English would justly be execrated by his fellow citizens.

Mr. Dalton received me in the friendly manner which bespeaks a worthy and talented man and with the typical hospitality of the people of Massachusetts and New Hampshire, who are certainly more hospitable than the inhabitants of any of the other New England and Central states. Several people told me, however, that Salem is an exception and is known for its lack of hospitality.

Americans do not have what we call *grands repas* or *fêtes*. They simply share with visitors their daily fare, which is very good. They told me that they could not starve themselves during the week in order to feast on Sunday. These are people who live well and care nothing for show.

Mr. Dalton's family was a picture of patriarchal life and of true domestic happiness. There were four or five young ladies, pretty and modest and wearing simple silk dresses. (It was Sunday and they had just returned from meeting.) I met Mr. Dalton's brother-in-law, Mr. Hooper, a well-to-do miller, educated and intelligent. He had with him his father, a fine old gentleman of eighty years, who at this advanced age still preserved a sound memory and an excellent appetite and exercised a good deal. His face was unlined, which is quite common among old people in America; at least this was my frequent observation.

Mr. Dalton was formerly speaker of the legislature of New Hampshire. He has the reputation of being a good orator and of presiding with dignity.[15]

In New Hampshire the cold sets in early and the winters are long and rigorous, beginning in November and ending in May. When I visited the state in October I was forced to have a blazing fire. At Newport in Rhode Island, where I was on the twentieth of October, the weather was, by contrast, extremely warm. I noticed in Massachusetts the previous September that it was cold in the morning and very warm at mid-day. It is to the cold air that may be attributed the good health enjoyed by inhabitants of this state. Nevertheless, unbelievable as it may seem, there is a great deal of consumption, due to the causes I have already mentioned and to the kind of life the women lead. At Portsmouth there were twenty-five persons suffering from this terrible illness all at one time.

I heard of another disease, but a moral one, which was then sweeping Newton-Newbury, the township in which Mr. Dalton lives. This was a new sect of religious enthusiasts called the New Lights, a branch of the Methodists, who are increasing remarkably throughout America. Their principles and the terrors and convulsions they go through dispose their minds to melancholy, and the weaker souls break and go mad. There are known cases of this happening.

From Mr. Dalton's we headed for Andover but were forced to stop at a small inn on the road. In this state the inns are generally good and the food is far from being as expensive as it was when M. Chastellux was here.[16]

At Portsmouth I stayed at a very good inn run by a Mr. Greenleaf. I found a neatness and cleanliness rarely met with in France —good beds, pretty wallpaper, substantial and inexpensive food. When we were at Sandsburn [Sandown, N.H.?], we had a lunch of chicken, grilled lamb, beer, and a glass of cherry wine, and the

[15] He is at present a senator in Congress.
[16] [*Voyages*, Paris, 1786,] II, 183.

horse had his oats, and all this cost only three shillings, or forty-eight sous.

In this part of America, oats cost *retail* 2 sous a quart (there are 32 quarts in a bushel, which weighs 60 pounds); butter 8 to 9 sous; beef, 2 to 4 sous; veal, 2 sous. Pigs, geese, and turkeys are plentiful. A cord of wood costs from one to one and a half dollars.

In Andover, my traveling companion introduced me to the respected pastor of this parish, Dr. Synner,[17] in whom I found the ideal of a priest of any religion, but particularly of a Christian one, for he combines in his character purity of morals, simplicity of life, and kindness. He lives with his estimable wife, by whom he has had several children. When he is not busy studying or shepherding the souls entrusted to his care, he spends his time farming.

Andover is not a town in the European sense, nor is it even like Salem or Hartford. It is merely an area of ten miles over which are scattered farms. Some of these are excellent, with many good meadows and fine cattle. There are also some very high mountains in the area, from one of which can be seen Pidgeon Island [Pigeon Hill, in Rockport?] thirty-two miles away.

From Andover we went to Woburn, where live the "Shaking Quakers," who actually shake. Some entertaining stories have been circulated about them and about a woman who plays a leading role among them. These satirical tales, which appeal to malicious minds, should be viewed with circumspection. At any rate, this sect has not made many proselytes.

From Woburn we proceeded to Cambridge on a road that ran all the way through well-cleared and well-cultivated fields and along which we saw some lovely landscapes.

We had, in a tavern in Cambridge, the most expensive dinner I have ever eaten; about ten shillings, or eight French livres, for beef, two chickens, half a bottle of Madeira, a jug of porter, and two cups of coffee. The coffee alone was a shilling eight pence (thirty French sous). It would, however, be wrong to draw general conclusions from these prices, for Cambridge is a university town and a very popular place.

[17] [Probably William Symmes, fifth minister of the North Parish Church in Andover.]

THE AMERICAN DEBT

I have followed your advice, my friend, and have gathered valuable information on the American debt. I have enough facts to write a full discussion of this question; but time is pressing and space is short, so I shall merely sketch an outline which will at least give you a clearer idea than all that has been written by others on the subject until now.[1]

You have seen in the *Encyclopédie* [*Méthodique*] a table of the American debt up to 1784.[2] There are a few errors in this article, which was, I believe, supplied to the editor of the *Encyclopédie* by the learned Mr. Jefferson, Minister of the United States.[3] Despite these faults, you will find there reliable information on the origin and the development of the American national debt. There is, however, no work treating the changes which have occurred since 1784, and it is the purpose of this letter to fill in this gap.

You, my friend, who are so well versed in financial matters, will undoubtedly be shocked to learn what errors were committed by Congress in constituting this debt and what ineffectual steps were taken to overcome the lack of hard currency.[4] But your surprise

---

[1] The same circumstances which forced me to cut my trip short also prevented me from giving, as I had proposed, a detailed account of the present state of the American debt, although I have all the necessary material. Perhaps the time will come when it will be important to place this information before the French people, in which case I shall publish it. In order to bring up to date the figures given in this brief account, written in 1788, I have incorporated into it the new data reported by Mr. Hamilton, secretary of the treasury of the United States, in his report to Congress of September 21, 1789.

[2] ["Etats-Unis," *Encyclopédie Méthodique*, section *Economie Politique et Diplomatique*, II (1786), 345–433. The article was by J. N. Démeunier but the data was provided in large part by Jefferson.]

[3] He is now secretary of state. The judicious and patriotic address, published by Congress in 1783, was also used as a source by the editor of the *Encyclopédie* [*Méthodique*].

[4] Despite the fact that the Americans were at a great disadvantage compared with the English, it cost them much less to win their liberty than it did the English to try to deprive them of it. It would be easy to prove mathematically that the American War cost the English four times as much as it cost the Americans. This was because love of liberty has resources unknown to despotism, and because a free man has far fewer needs than does a satellite of despotism.

will disappear when you understand the critical circumstances in which Congress, to whom America owes its independence, found itself at the time.

The members of that Congress knew nothing of financial principles, having never had an opportunity to deal with such problems. The needs were pressing, and they had to choose between submitting to the British or fighting, and if they chose to fight they had to pay the men who did the fighting.

The use of paper money was the first, and perhaps the only, idea that occurred to them. Their aim was so sublime, their patriotism so fervent! The highest expectations seemed justified. Congress trusted in the power of patriotism, and if it increased the amount of paper money even while this currency was rapidly depreciating, it did so in good faith and with the expectation of being able to pay off the principal and interest. It believed that the first issue of paper money would allow the government to wait until it had the proceeds of its first requisition.

The American people fully shared this confidence at the time. It was considered almost a crime not to have faith in the paper issued by Congress, and one risked being stoned by refusing to accept it.

The states and many citizens made great efforts to help and support Congress, but as the war continued with no end in sight and expenses kept increasing, they grew weary. A revolution of opinion took place, and while in 1777 it had been a crime not to believe that the United States would redeem its paper money, in 1784, that is, after the peace was signed, it seemed a crime to maintain that it ought to be redeemed. The common enemy of the separate states having been defeated, enthusiasm collapsed, and holders of the certificates of indebtedness were no longer considered benefactors but rather leeches. Thus both times opinion was shaped by self-interest: opinion in 1777 was inspired by the desire to be freed of oppression and the fear that this freedom could be gained only with the help of moneylenders; opinion in 1784 was the result of realization of the size of the burden to be borne and of the desire to get rid of it.

Since the adoption of the new Constitution, a third revolution in opinion on the public debt has taken place. In a free nation truth and honor must sooner or later prevail. Almost all Americans are now convinced that in order to achieve the high level of prosperity to which they are destined by the nature of things and

to acquire the credit necessary for this achievement, they must fulfill most scrupulously all their obligations. Consequently the new
Congress has decided to devote most serious attention immediately
to the problem. Such is at present the state of American finances.

The public debt of the United States is divided into two categories:

1. Foreign debt: Money lent by foreign powers or by foreign
individuals.

2. Domestic debt: Money borrowed and due in America.

THE FOREIGN DEBT

The principal of this debt consists of:

24,000,000 [livres] of a loan made in France at 5% interest; [5] and 10,000,000 [livres] at 4% borrowed in Holland and guaranteed by France, both together amounting in dollars to	$ 6,296,296
From Spain, at 5%	174,011
In Holland, four loans of:	
1. 5,000,000 florins at 5%	
2. 2,000,000 florins at 4%	
3. 1,000,000 florins at 5%	
4. 1,000,000 florins at 5%	
9,000,000 florins	3,600,000
Total principal	$10,070,307
Interest due up to December 31, 1789	1,651,257
Total principal and interest	$11,721,564

[5] The secret history of the American debt to France, were it made public, would
reveal the source of many fortunes which have caused considerable surprise. It is,
for instance, a definite fact that M. Vergennes had a free hand in disposing of the
loan, that he appointed merchants who were his own secret agents to furnish
munitions and merchandise and then made reports that nobody was permitted to
question. It is also a definite fact that in his accounts with Congress one million
became missing, which he could never explain despite all the requests made to
him to do so. Finally, it is a definite fact that out of the forty-seven million [livres]
that it is claimed were provided by France to Congress, no satisfactory account has
been given for the disposition of twenty-one million. I have been given these facts
by well-informed and trustworthy persons. Many fortunes can be made with twenty-
one millions.

This brings me to the dealings of M. Beaumarchais with the United States. In
a memoir he published two years ago [*Requête à MM. les Représentants de la
Commune de Paris,* 1789] he claimed that Congress still owed him two millions.
I have in my hands a report made that year (1788) to Congress by two esteemed

THE DOMESTIC DEBT

This can also be divided into two categories: (1) the liquidated debt; (2) the nonliquidated debt.

Liquidated Debt

Principal	$27,383,917
Interest (at 6%, from 1776 to December 31, 1790, including deductions)	13,030,168
Total	$40,414,085

Nonliquidated Debt

This consists mainly of Continental certificates of indebtedness. It is estimated at approximately	$ 2,000,000
Adding to these two sums the total foreign debt	11,721,564
Total United States debt, foreign and domestic, including principal and interest to January 1, 1790	$54,124,464 [sic]

members, who are not connected in any way with M. Beaumarchais and who had no interest in blackening his reputation. They prove in this report that he owes the United States at least 742,413 livres and 16 sous, and another million in addition, if he has the lost million mentioned above. [Brissot refers to the Report on the account of Beaumarchais made by the Board of Treasury to Congress in 1788.] The authors of this report draw an amusing picture of all the maneuvers that were used to cheat the good Americans.

Will the National Assembly demand no accounting of the great sums spent in the American War, or rather of the sums which instead of being used to help those brave and proud insurgents were squandered in the boudoir of some actress or used to subsidize her insolent extravagance paraded in the Bois de Boulogne? An Adeline [a danseuse of the day] may have been a worse enemy of the Americans than a Hessian regiment. Where are the accounts of her Chevalier Veymeranges? Why did M. Necker [minister of finance, 1776–1781 and 1788–1789] fail to lift the impenetrable veil which concealed these accounts from the public's eye? Is he himself not to blame for the recourse to ruinous expedients dictated by ignorance of the country where the war was fought? Is he not to blame for the use of corrupt, incapable, and dishonest agents and for the lightheartedness with which he approved all the accounts?

Several American newspapers have attacked, in connection with all these robberies, Mr. Morris and Mr. Franklin. I am far from subscribing to the accusations made against the latter, but I wished he had given some clear answers to the writer who signed himself "Centinel." [Samuel Bryan, *To the People of Pennsylvania* (signed Centinel) and *Centinel No. II. To the People of Pennsylvania*, Philadelphia, 1787.]

French ministers of finance have for a long time considered the United States debt as a loss. Their contempt for this nation went so far that M. Calonne [minister

THE AMERICAN DEBT

The states, having their own expenses, were forced to levy state taxes or float state loans or issue paper money for circulation within their borders. Thus each state incurred a debt consisting of certificates which circulated at various depreciated prices, but everywhere at a considerable discount.

The total of all the state debts is estimated at
approximately $25,000,000

Adding to this the above sum of 54,124,464
Total $79,124,464
Annual interest, including the agreed interest on the foreign debt and allowing 4% on interest in default $ 4,587,444

This, my friend, will give you a picture of the total debt of the United States. It amounts to about 400,000,000 *livres tournois,* on which the interest is approximately 22,000,000.

To complete the picture of the total United States expenditures, we must add the public expenses of the Union. In 1790, they were as follows:

Civil list $254,892
Department of War 155,537
Military pensions 96,979
$507,408

If you are curious to know what the main items on the civil list are, in order to compare them with governmental expenses in Europe, here are a few:

Salary of the President of the United States $25,000
Vice-President $ 5,000
Chief Justice of the Supreme Court $ 4,000

The salaries of the circuit judges in the different states vary, the minimum being $800, the maximum $1,600.

The Speaker of the House of Representatives, at $12 a day for six months $ 2,190
Eighty members at $6 a day 87,600

of finance, 1783–1787] refused to sell this debt, out of pity, so to speak, for the possible buyer. He did not conceive how anyone could be foolish enough to wish to buy it, but the republican [Clavière?] who made the offer knew somewhat better than he what powerful incentives for men are justice, good faith, and honor, and he was not mistaken.

The Secretary of the Treasury and the Secretary of State each receive $3,500, and the Secretary of War only $3,000, but the expenses of their departments and the salaries of their clerks are paid separately.

You can see from these details, my friend, that the cost of government for a free people includes none of the extravagance and ostentation which are exhibited by other governments and which contribute in no way to the good of the people. I can assure you that although Washington has only about 120,000 livres to spend a year and although he is surrounded by no pomp or ceremony, he is more revered and better loved than the most ostentatious potentate of Europe. The same is true of the other officers of the Executive Branch; everything around them is kept very simple. You can see that with about 3,000,000 [livres] it is possible to govern a federation of almost four million people scattered over approximately 208,[000] square miles, a territory equal to that of Germany, Flanders, Holland, and Switzerland put together.[6] And lastly, you can see that Americans now have to pay only some 22,000,000 *livres tournois* a year in interest for the independence that they have won.

MEASURES ADOPTED TO MEET THESE EXPENSES, TO PAY THIS INTEREST, AND TO REDUCE THE PRINCIPAL OF THE DEBT

Mr. Hamilton, whom I have mentioned and praised earlier, and whose energy equals his financial acumen, has proposed to Congress in his report of September 21, 1789, five measures, all of which have been adopted:

1. An indirect and uniform tax on imports.
2. A loan.
3. Conversion of all obligations of the liquidated and non-liquidated debt into a new issue of stock with a lower rate of interest.
4. Assumption by Congress of all the individual state debts and conversion of these debts into a single debt with a lower rate of interest.
5. Application of the excess of revenue over expenditures in 1789 to the redemption of part of the debt.

[6] I am speaking here only of the territory of the thirteen states, the part of the country which has been settled.

THE AMERICAN DEBT

FIRST MEASURE. IMPORT DUTIES

I cannot discuss in detail the duties imposed on imported goods or the distribution of this tax, but in general it applies only to luxury items such as wine, brandy, spirits, tea, coffee, etc.[7]

The duties are calculated so that they offer no incentive to smuggling, which defeats the purpose of indirect taxation and which is incompatible with the principles of a free people; so that the collection of import duties is not vexatious; and that confiscation, when there is an attempt at smuggling, is governed by formalities which guarantee merchants against harassment.

Mr. Hamilton estimated that these duties, together with taxes on tonnage, would bring in about $1,700,000. He also believed that the revenue from these taxes would increase greatly in the following years because of the inevitable rise in consumption. In addition, he counted on an estimated $100,000 revenue from the Post Office Department. I can assure you, however, that he has greatly underestimated the actual revenue, for according to a statement now in my hands on imports, import duties can be expected to bring in at least $2,400,000. This figure is confirmed by the import tax revenues in Philadelphia and New York; over $400,000 were collected in the former city alone.

Although the probable revenue from these taxes might not be sufficient to pay both the civil list and the interest on the debt, Mr. Hamilton did not advocate that taxes that year be raised or levied on additional items. He thought it necessary to give Americans time to become used to the new burden, and he also wished to spare them at a time when they were still busy repairing the losses caused by the war. He therefore preferred to float a loan.

SECOND MEASURE. THE LOAN

Two kinds of expenses are unavoidable: the payment of salaries for civil and military personnel, which amount to about $600,000, and the payment of interest on the foreign debt together with the

[7] Congress cannot levy export taxes; this article [in the Constitution] was insisted upon by the states which have large exports, such as Virginia. Consequently, Congress cannot tax tobacco, although it is expected that tobacco notes can be taxed. It has been estimated from experience that a hogshead of tobacco (of 1,000 lbs.) could be taxed one dollar without hardship to the exporter. It is very likely that someday Congress will be allowed to levy taxes within the individual states.

redemption of obligations which are due. These payments on the debt are absolutely essential for a nation which wishes to establish sound credit. As the taxes are, however, too low to cover both these types of expenditures, Congress has authorized a loan of $12,000,-000. Although loans are undesirable in principle, this one is advisable, for it is justified by its purpose, and the United States can offer such vast security for this modest loan that it must be considered both safe and wise.

THIRD MEASURE. CONSOLIDATION OF THE DOMESTIC DEBT

Finally, the United States must consider their domestic creditors. Until now, the interest on this debt has been paid in indents, that is, paper coupons which have been selling at a rate of two and three silver shillings for an indent with a face value of twenty.

But several questions arose at the beginning of this operation. Should the certificates be redeemed at their full specie value? This was the first question. To the wise politician who is convinced that justice is the foundation of prosperity there could be only one answer. Self-interest, however, motivates states as well as individuals, and we must consider what the interests of the various states were in this question of full payment.

Full payment was greatly to the interest of the four New England states as well as of New York, the Jerseys, and Pennsylvania; Delaware would profit to a smaller degree, and Maryland scarcely at all, but Maryland had always distinguished itself by its adhesion to honorable and advantageous solutions and had never followed selfish motives. There were, then, nine votes on which to count.

Virginia held Continental certificates because it had assumed Congress' debt to private individuals, but it had already charged these certificates to the debit of Congress, so it had nothing to gain.

The other three states held few certificates, and so were to be expected to be opposed, but their opposition could be easily overcome.

The interest of the large capitalists who were members of Congress also weighed in the scales, but the enlightened and disinterested men who pleaded the cause of justice had the greatest influence. Hence this question never presented serious difficulties.

Should the debt be left in the chaotic and multifarious state in which it was? That was the second question. No, it had to be reconstituted and simplified in order to put an end to speculation. The drop in the value of debt certificates and indents, and the hope of a rise in price or of repayment by some operation or other was occasioning a rather large amount of speculation, and speculation is always disastrous, for it creates a profession that almost always involves shady deals which are unworthy of a free people, and it deprives agriculture and commerce of capital that could bring more stable and, above all, more moral advantages.[8] The large number and the diversity of these certificates and the variety of their prices also encouraged this odious speculation.

These were, then, the primary considerations which prompted Congress to merge all the domestic debts into one type of obligation. But Congress had yet another aim in view. The interest on this debt was six per cent, and this was considered too high in view of the strong position of the United States, the modesty of its indebtedness, and the certainty that the interest and even the principal would be paid in the future. It seemed advisable to seek a way of reducing the rate of interest. Consequently Congress passed a law on January 4, 1790, authorizing a loan for an amount equal to the total domestic debt, the new stocks to be exchangeable for the old certificates of the liquidated debt at the following rate:

The United States allocates to the subscriber who turns in a hundred dollars in certificates, stock for two thirds of this amount bearing six per cent interest payable in silver. This stock may be redeemed by the government in annual payments over a period of ten years. The remaining third of the certificates are exchanged for stock which begins to pay an interest of six per cent only after ten years. Creditors of the states who do not wish to exchange the old certificates for the new stock still receive their interest due for 1791, just as if they had subscribed, but after that period the government reserves the right to make new arrangements in the case of people refusing to accept the new stock.

Congress expressly states that it has no intention of inconveniencing any of the creditors of the United States by this law, or of modifying any of its obligations.

---

[8] Speculation in certificates has somewhat lowered moral standards in the cities. The same thing happened in 1756 when paper money was introduced, but it was noticed that this tendency disappeared with the withdrawal of paper money from circulation. The man who had paid off his debts or bought land with this paper, having become a tradesman or a farmer, wished only to preserve his property and was therefore honest. Happy country which can so easily regenerate its morals and heal its wounds!

Those who pay their subscription in indents receive a certificate for the same sum bearing three per cent interest, also redeemable by the government but not within any specified time.

It is obvious that the result of this operation is the reduction by two per cent of the interest on the whole debt for a ten-year period, or a reduction to four per cent of the agreed rate of interest.

The reasons which have prompted Congress seem to be the following:

On the one hand, there was pressure from the farmers, who were horrified that so high an interest should be paid on obligations most of which had been bought at one fourth of their nominal value. On the other hand, there was the outcry of capitalists and creditors who demanded that Congress keep its sacred promise, so often made on behalf of the people, that it would faithfully fulfill all its obligations.

In this embarrassing position, Congress tried to satisfy everybody by an act which offered an "approximate" justice to all. It considered that:

(1) in 1789 certificates whose nominal value was twenty shillings were selling at five shillings in silver, that is, at a three-fourths discount;

(2) the majority of the present owners had bought them at even lower prices;

(3) the new plan would not affect the principal, which was to be paid in full;

(4) the indents, which until now had carried no interest, were selling for this reason at half the price of the certificates, that is, at two and three shillings to the pound;

(5) under the new law they were exchanged for stock;

(6) the present financial situation and the current revenue from taxes, which would necessarily increase with the growth of industry, commerce, population, and consumption, constituted a most solid security for the public debt, in fact better security than any other nation could offer;

(7) finally, in view of all these considerations, and particularly in view of the new loan, it was most likely that the interest rate would drop to five per cent in five years, and to four per cent in twenty years.

From all these considerations, Congress concluded that it would be doing no injustice to the creditors, most of whom had bought their certificates at dirt-cheap prices, if it gave them four per cent interest on obligations which were redeemable at the full specie value, since both nations and individuals in Europe who had credit far inferior to that of the United States borrowed money at even lower rates.

Finally, Congress believed it was satisfying the protests of the farmers against an exorbitant rate of interest on the public debt by reducing the rate by two per cent.

It is impossible for a man who has sworn to adhere faithfully to principles to approve such an operation. It is niggardly, impolitic, and unnecessary. Niggardly, because it is unworthy of a free and wealthy nation to try to haggle over such sacred obligations, and for so paltry a sum. For, what is the result in the long run? It will gain for the nation a profit of $500,000 a year, or a total of $5,000,-000. Is it really worthwhile for a nation destined by the nature of things to reach the greatest heights of prosperity to dishonor itself forever for some 25,000,000 *livres tournois?*

This action is unworthy of Free Americans from another point of view. A very complicated maneuver was worked out in order to disguise the real nature of this reduction. Why could not the truth be frankly explained? These petty subterfuges may be suitable for despotic states ruined by loans and by their predatory tyrants, but they dishonor a free nation all of whose operations must be completely open because all its actions are and must be honest.

Besides, by this very measure, Congress imperils both its basic objective of re-establishing its credit in Europe and its immediate objective of borrowing money. What trust can European bankers put in its promises when they see Congress deviate from its principles and violate its obligations? [9] Should they not fear that a similar fate will befall the new loan that is being offered to them, and, if so, should they not either refuse it or else sell their money dearly, as they would to an untrustworthy debtor?

But, it may be objected, this is not a forced loan. Granted, but,

[9] It is most important for the United States to maintain its credit in Europe, for it is in Europe that the loans are sold and it is from Europe that will come the millions to buy up the American stocks. In 1788, $3,000,000 of the American debt was registered in the names of foreigners, and now that there is confidence in the American government's ability to repay this debt, such speculative investments must have doubled in England and in Holland. I have met Americans who were very upset about these speculations, but is not the effect of them to pour into America large sums of money which are used in commercial and industrial enterprises that produce profits much greater than those made by Europeans on the loan?

even so, it indicates uncertainty and groping on the part of Congress, and it is difficult to trust a government which does not have a firm attitude, which muddles along hoping that tomorrow will bring good counsel. Besides, there is an actual and imposed reduction of the rate of interest in 1791 for the creditor who refuses to subscribe to the new stock.

The uselessness of this partial bankruptcy is just as clearly demonstrated. Is there any other country whose debts are so small and which has such vast means with which to repay them? How heavy is a debt whose principal is smaller than the annual expenditure of another nation (England) whose population is only twice that of the United States? How heavily can a debt of 400,000,000 [livres] weigh when balanced against the hundreds of millions of acres that Congress has to sell? What does this sum amount to when you compare it to a population of four million people which will double every twenty years,[10] and when you consider the rapid progress of industry, of land settlement, of trade, and of imports and exports, a progress which is inevitably translated into increased revenue from taxes, which serve as security for the debt? Investors can have the highest confidence in the solvency of a nation in such circumstances, when they see how little the government spends and that it is happily incapable of misappropriating the people's money [11] or of imposing an incompetent administration or at least of keeping one long in office, and when they see the general character of this nation, its thrift and its adherence to principles. Can such a nation fail to find limitless credit?

Mr. Hamilton, let us admit it, has undervalued his country's potentialities, the probable income from taxes, and the men he is dealing with. The future is so brilliant and so secure that the na-

[10] America's ability to repay its debt should be calculated in relation to its population, for in America consumption increases in an almost direct proportion with the population, and tax revenues will increase in proportion to consumption. The American people are different from Europeans, of whom one third, and often as many as one half, consume little because of poverty, so that in Europe consumption is not proportional to population. Here in the United States everyone has approximately the same wealth and consumes the same amount. It is therefore possible to take the size of the population as a basis for our calculations. Thus in twenty years, when there will be as many Americans as there are now English, the United States in paying off the principal of its debt would spend only once what England has to spend every year on interest.

[11] Can one, from this point of view, compare the security of the American debt with that of a kingdom such as Spain, where the king, Ferdinand VI, raises the question of whether or not he is under any obligation to pay the debts contracted by his predecessor, and where a complaisant junto decides that he is not?

tion could hope to retire a much larger debt. He has underestimated the revenue from taxes, as experience has already proved to him, for instead of the expected $1,800,000, he has collected in the first year, that is, from August 1, 1789, to September 30, 1790, $2,523,868.

As for his fellow citizens, Mr. Hamilton, with all his talents, all his logic and powers of reason, could have led them to do anything he wished. He could have easily persuaded everyone that it is in the public interest to pay the debt completely. All Americans know that without credit they cannot expand their commerce, and they all wish to trade on a large scale. They all feel that in order to achieve this kind of commercial activity they must give dignity and strength to their government. But such dignity is impossible if they do not pay their debts. They all know now that it is not money they lack or will lack, that the so-called shortage of money is due only to lack of confidence and to fluctuations of the public's faith in the government. They all know that the real way to re-establish this confidence and consequently to make money flow is to pay all their debts without any reduction and without any consideration of the price at which these obligations were purchased.

Even the farmers are convinced of this truth, although at first they favored a reduction of the debt. They are convinced of this twin truth: without public confidence, there is no trade; without trade, there is no agriculture and no industry. The farmers of the United States live well. They like to have their tea, coffee, sugar, etc., and they can pay for these only with what they produce; they therefore feel the need of an export trade, the need for credit to support this trade, and the need to create public confidence to maintain this credit. Such are the thoughts and feelings I found everywhere among all the citizens I met during my travels in the United States.

How is it possible that Mr. Hamilton has not consulted and obeyed this public opinion? Why was he frightened by the outcries of a few ill-informed men? [12] Is it worthy of such an enlightened statesman to yield to the forces of ignorance and to compromise principles which should always be inflexible?

[12] Why did he not feel encouraged by the confidence with which the public anticipated his operations, a confidence based entirely on the expectation that all obligations would be met, a confidence spelled out by the rapid rise in government securities? In 1788 they were discounted seventy-five per cent, while in 1789, just

The celebrated D'Avenant indicated the road to be followed when he wrote that credit is acquired only by uninterrupted and certain payments and by strict fulfillment of the conditions of the loan:

We give over trusting the public, or private persons, then only when we perceive fraud or evil faith in their proceedings, or when we judge their affairs to be desperate; but when the interruption in common payments is occasioned only by some accidents in the state, when both the government and particular persons take the utmost care to disengage themselves, and when it can be made to appear there is a fund sufficient to satisfy all pretensions, men's minds will become quiet and appeased; mutual convenience will lead them into a desire of helping one another . . . The huge engine of credit [. . .] is not to be put in order by patching here and there; and you can never have true motion till the legislative power interpose in setting all the springs right.[13]

Mr. Hamilton is far from unfamiliar with these principles, for they all appear in his report. He recognizes throughout it the need to fulfill faithfully the nation's obligations in order to acquire credit, to make America respected, and to restore value to government stocks, public lands, etc. But unfortunately, Mr. Hamilton also believed that there are situations when states may fail to meet their obligations, provided they plan to repair in the future the harm done, and he seemed to believe that the United States was somewhat in that position. This was an error. Mr. Hamilton did not have enough trust in his own strength or in that of his country to dare attempt a large operation based on respect for good faith, which would have necessarily produced excellent credit and opened up vast resources to Americans.

In addition to the plan adopted by Congress he had proposed several others, for instance, that of giving to subscribers one third of their loan in land, an operation which would have looked less like bankruptcy since the debtor would have acquitted himself of his debt by surrendering the property pledged as security. But it would have been unworthy of the United States to impose such an arrangement on its creditors. Also, he suggested a tontine.[14] This was a much more suitable idea, but perhaps Americans are too unfamiliar with this type of speculation for it to have been a success.

---

before the report, the discount was only twenty-five per cent. The pound was formerly selling at thirteen to fifteen shillings; it is now at sixteen.

[13] See *The Political and Commercial Works of Charles D'Avenant* ([London], 1771), [I, 151–152, 163].

[14] [A loan raised on life annuities.]

THE AMERICAN DEBT

FOURTH MEASURE. UNIFICATION [15] AND CONSOLIDATION OF THE
STATE DEBTS

This was the most delicate operation of all, and it was therefore strongly opposed. There were some states whose debts were small, or which had managed their affairs better than others, and these naturally did not wish the Union to take over the obligations of those states which were deeper in debt or had greater financial problems.[16] Reason prevailed, however, over the calculations of

[15] [Brissot uses here the neologism *Adunation* (apparently from the Latin phrase *ad unum omnes,* "all to one") and explains it in the following footnote:] This word seems to me the best to express concisely the fusion into a single mass of thirteen small debts.

[16] This was the case for the states of Maryland, Connecticut, and New Hampshire. Maryland owed in 1788 a principal of only £474,944, and had £526,738 receivable. Connecticut owed between £600,000 and £700,000; its internal taxes were sufficient to cover the interest, but as these taxes were being paid at a slow rate, the state was issuing indents as payment of interest owed. At the end of the year, these indents could be exchanged for silver by those who had been able to wait. They stood at 10 s. in 1788. The tax collectors would buy them up and turn them into the treasury at their full specie value and take the difference. This was obviously a detestable operation on the part of the government. The same thing happened in Virginia with warrants and resulted in similar irregularities. Note, however, the tremendous difference in opinion in the different states on the soundness of these indents: while in Connecticut they circulated at 10 s., in Virginia they sold at 3 s. 6 d., and in South Carolina at 2 s. 6 d. These indents were thus discredited not because of the public's fear of being cheated but rather as a consequence of the ignorance of the legislators who wrote the laws.

Respect for their state debts has been most outstandingly shown by the inhabitants of Connecticut and Maryland. The citizens of Connecticut have not refused, as have those of almost all other states, to pay a direct tax to cover the interest on the debt.

New Hampshire's state debt is approximately £120,000 and certificates sell at 3 s. on the pound. There was a plan to redeem this debt and also the state's share of the Continental debt. It was estimated that to do so would cost no more than two dollars per taxable person; New Hampshire's population is placed at 100,000. Although this plan was favorably regarded, various incidents caused it to fail. It would have involved the following procedure: Each person was to have paid his share in local products, which the government was then to sell, using the income to pay off the debt.

The debt of the state of New York in 1788 was more than £800,000; but its finances were in good condition, it paid its interest regularly, and the lands it had just sold in the northern part of the state were more than sufficient to retire the principal.

Pennsylvania's debts were much larger, amounting to over £2,000,000, because the state had assumed a large part of the Continental debt; but it also had large claims outstanding.

Certificates of indebtedness of the state of Massachusetts stood at 4 s. in 1788, and it was generally believed that the debt would be devaluated. Many people seemed unwilling to submit to paying the full specie value of the debt; the greatest state interests. Creditors, trade, industry, the United States, the individual states, all stood to profit by the fusion of state debts, most of which had been incurred for the same reasons as the national debt, namely, to cover the costs of the war. It is indeed more advantageous to the creditor to have a single reliable debtor than to have five or six different ones who are of unequal soundness and who operate under a variety of financial systems. It is easier to get information on a single debtor, payments are more prompt, and the formalities fewer.

To pay off their debts the individual states would have had to borrow or to impose new taxes. Their loans would have worked at cross purposes and in competition with the federal government, and the cost of the borrowed money would have gone up. There would have been no harmony between the taxation systems of the different states, and this could have had an adverse effect on some forms of agriculture, causing them to be abandoned, and on certain industries, causing them to take refuge in neighboring states. I have given you examples. Taxes imposed by Congress cannot have such ill effects because they apply to the Union as a whole. Unification also effects great savings in debt payment and in tax collection. Congress has organized the machinery necessary for dealing with the federal debt, and this machinery can function as well for the individual debts of the thirteen states and save the work of thirteen state treasurers.

Moreover consolidation and unification of the state debts wiped out speculation in this kind of obligation. For some time past there had existed a species of men who, well versed in all these various sorts of paper, were chasing after certificates and indents from New Hampshire to the Carolinas, buying them up and peddling them. As I have said before, this is an extremely perni-

---

opposition came from landholders who were members of the legislature and who outnumbered the other members two to one. Merchants were to be expected to side with the capitalists, since they acted on the same principles, and lawyers would do the same. It was hoped, however, that discussion would persuade the merchants to change their minds, and indeed the forces of reason did triumph.

In Virginia, there was yet another reason for the opposition to the unification of the debt. People knew that the tax on tobacco, which yields £70,000, enables the state to pay the interest on its debt. They wondered whether under the new arrangement, that is, if Congress collected this tax, the money would be used as regularly to meet payments on the Virginia debt. They doubted that Congress would be able to do this and they thought that more urgent needs would force it to use the money to pay other debts. There is a general feeling of suspicion in the state. Consequently Congress' plan will cause a drop in the value of Virginia obligations and therefore will probably meet with resistance.

cious sort of activity in a free nation and one most likely to derange the financial system.

Finally, this unification of the state debts constituted a new bond between the states, strengthening federalism, and this is the main reason that all the states were in favor of it. Henceforth their interests will be common ones. Now they have the debt in common, and soon there will be for all the states only one system of taxation, including both internal revenue and duties on imports.

Nevertheless Congress, in assuming for the Union the debts of all the separate states, had no wish to infringe on the rights of any one of them. It has assumed these debts only provisionally, subject to later settlement of its accounts with each state.

It has been estimated, as I have said, that the state debts amount to $25,000,000, but Congress is floating a loan for only 21,500,000 livres [actually $21,500,000], reserving the power to settle the difference later. This loan was made on the same conditions as those for the national domestic debt.

FIFTH MEASURE. APPLICATION OF THE SURPLUS OF 1789 TO THE
REDEMPTION OF THE PUBLIC DEBT

Congress has authorized the President of the United States and various other officers to use for the redemption of whatever part of the debt they deem advisable the excess of the revenue from taxation intended for public expenses. They have even been authorized to borrow for this purpose $2,000,000 at five per cent.

It appears that the revenue for 1789 has produced a surplus of $1,764,000 over expenses.

This is one of the best ways of freeing a country from its debt without shaking public confidence. It sustains credit by the very principle which dictates these redemptions. Such an action, however, must be the natural consequence of good management; otherwise it is a useless trick. Now can it be said of a state which does not fully meet its obligations that its finances are well managed? Is it permissible to take as profits money which really belongs to the creditors of the state?

Be this as it may, the conclusion to be drawn from these various measures is that all the states are very anxious to be rid of the burden of the debt, that they are most eager to revive general credit, and that they are determined to lead the United States toward complete freedom from debt, and hence toward prosperity.

From this picture of the debt and of the finances of the United States, you can see, my friend, that the greatest hopes are justified, that order, simplification, and economy are being practiced everywhere, and that the only thing the Americans now need in order to acquire completely sound credit is more confidence in their own strength and the courage to undertake a large operation which would in one step balance their budget. If Congress has made a mistake in this respect, it is due to its timidity and not to lack of good faith. This is amply proved by the statements contained in the act and by the freedom Congress leaves to its creditors. Congress has attempted a measure which it could have avoided. The principles it has acted on should reassure us about the success of the operation, and these principles can in no way jeopardize the soundness of the credit of the United States. It is likely that the mistake will be corrected at the next session of Congress.

AMERICAN IMPORTS

If you had any doubts, my friend, about the Free Americans' capacity to pay their debts and to meet the expenses of the federal and of the state governments, they would be dissipated by the figures on their annual imports.

Some political thinkers hold it to be an incontrovertible axiom that a country must import as little as possible and export as much as possible. If by this they mean that a nation ought to produce as much as it can within its own borders, then they are right; but if they mean that a nation with a large import trade is poor, then the statement is false. For a nation imports goods for only one of two reasons, either in order to consume them, in which case the imports are an indication that the nation has the money to pay for them, or in order to re-export them, which means that it makes a profit. You see, my friend, that when we analyze this so-called axiom, it amounts to either a truism or a falsehood, as is the case with almost all the *dicta* about commerce that are mouthed by the ignorant. Who knows and has exposed their worthlessness better than you?

Imports to the United States have soared since the peace treaty, as you will be convinced by comparing the following table and the accompanying explanations with Lord Sheffield's tables of figures for the prewar period.[1] My data has been supplied by a well-informed New York merchant and the correctness of the figures has been confirmed by the records of several customhouses in the United States and by one of the most enlightened financiers in the country.

TABLE OF THE PRINCIPAL IMPORTS TO THE UNITED STATES

Rum, brandy, and spirits	4,000,000 gal.[2]
Wine	1,000,000 "
Bohea tea	1,000,000 lbs.
Hyson tea	125,000 "

[1] [John Baker Holroyd, Earl of Sheffield, *Observations on the Commerce of the American States*, New Edition, London, 1784, translated as *Observations sur le commerce des Etats-Unis d'Amérique*, London, 1789 and Rouen, 1789.]

[2] A gallon is equal to about four Paris pints.

TABLE OF PRINCIPAL IMPORTS *(Continued)*

Sugar	20,000,000 lbs.
Coffee, cocoa, chocolate	1,500,000 "
Molasses	3,000,000 [gal.]
Salt	1,000,000 bu.

Dry goods to the value of more than $20,000,000.

The above general table is an estimate from the records of imports through the port of New York during a three-year period, based on the accepted assumption that New York receives one fifth of the total imports of the United States.[3]

Spirits. In 1784 the imports of spirits, brandy, rum, etc., by New York State amounted to 1,200,000 gallons, and by Pennsylvania, 1,000,000. You can see that if the total imports are estimated from these figures, they amount to almost 5,000,000 gallons.

Mr. Swan says that France could ship 1,500,000 gallons of brandy, which would be about 30,000 casks a year.[4] What a tremendous importation! Nor is it an impossible dream, for Americans like our brandies very much and find them less expensive than Jamaica rum, whose exportation, incidentally, has been prohibited by the English, and greatly superior in quality to the rum of the French West Indies, which the Americans think is detestable but which will no doubt be improved someday under a free regime.

Wines. You will also see that I have given a low estimate of the quantity of imported foreign wines, of which Madeira constitutes about one fifth.

In 1784, the imports were as follows:

By New York	290,000 gal.
By Pennsylvania	280,000 "

Mr. Swan, who estimates that the present population of the United States is over 5,000,000, believes that this item can without exaggeration be set at more than 5,000,000 gallons, figuring one gallon per person.[5] But he advises merchants to show scrupulous

---

[3] [James] Swan in his *Causes qui se sont opposées aux progrès du commerce entre la France et les Etats-Unis* [Paris, 1790], p. 116, also subscribes to this ratio. This work cannot be too carefully studied by French merchants who wish to conduct a useful and profitable trade with the United States. It is sold by Potier de Lille, 5, rue Favard.

[4] *Causes*, p. 131.

[5] *Causes*, p. 128.

good faith in their shipments, for, he complains, the United States has been flooded with bad Bordeaux, which has prejudiced Americans against other French wines.[6]

Tea. In 1784 the following amounts of tea were imported:

Bohea tea	
By New York	400,000 lbs.
By Pennsylvania	344,000 "
Hyson tea	
By New York	15,000 "
By Pennsylvania	44,000 "

This is a heavy tribute that Americans pay to China, and their need for tea is a disease they have caught from the English and of which they will not be easily cured. The usual estimates underrate the consumption of fine teas, which amounts to an average of over 200,000 lbs. a year—proof enough that either wealth or extravagance is increasing.

Please note that Pennsylvania imports a larger amount of fine tea; this larger consumption is because wealth is more widely distributed in Pennsylvania, for the difference in price is enormous, 12 or 15 livres a pound as compared to 1 livre 10 sous for ordinary tea.

Sugar. The figure of 20,000,000 [lbs.] seems to be below the actual imports when you compare it to the quantity of tea and coffee consumed in the United States and when you consider the amount of confectionary products eaten, in which sugar is an ingredient. But even accepting this figure, if we estimate the population at four million, this would give an average per capita sugar consumption of five pounds.

Note that the lowest possible estimate has been given, and that it does not include either maple sugar, which is consumed in great quantities by American farmers, or the sugar refined in the United States. It would not be difficult to prove that consumption exceeds thirty million pounds, or eight pounds per person.

[6] Mr. Swan's preferences are the white wines of Graves, Pontac, and [Château] Saint Brice, followed by those of Sauterne, Preignac, and Barsac. Among red wines, he ranks the following: Château Margaux, [Château] Ségur, Haut-Heiss, [Château] La Fite, etc. I mention this because it discloses an American's preferences and because it is important for French merchants to find out what American tastes are. I drank some excellent champagne in Boston and in New York and good Burgundy in Philadelphia, which proves that if a few necessary precautions are taken these wines can stand the ocean crossing.

What a difference between this per capita figure and ours! Proportionately for its population, France at the same rate ought to consume 200 million pounds of sugar, while in reality consumption does not exceed 80 million.

These figures are indicative of the respective wealth of the two countries. In the United States servants eat sugar, while in France how few craftsmen even can afford this necessary commodity, which they consider a luxury!

An important conclusion, my friend, can be also drawn from the fact that the Free Americans import these twenty million pounds of sugar from our islands even though its export is strictly forbidden. What purpose, then, do these prohibitions serve, when two neighboring peoples have reciprocal needs? What purpose would they serve under a free regime, where restrictive laws are much more abhorred? Are not facts such as these an invitation to all governments to pull down barriers that can be so easily crossed?

The quantity of sugar imported into Pennsylvania in 1784 amounted to 8,207,000 pounds.

Coffee, cocoa, etc. imported in 1784:

By New York	220,000 lbs.
By Pennsylvania	704,000 "

Molasses. This item was imported free of duty in New York until August 1, 1788. After that date, records for three months show imports of 300,000 gallons. The estimated annual figures are:

New York	1,200,000 gal.
Pennsylvania	564,000 "

The importation of this item is less in Pennsylvania because its citizens are trying to discourage the consumption of rum, a reform which will be very beneficial to both the morals and the health of the state.

Salt. Importation of salt in 1786 in New York amounted to 160,-000 bushels. The estimated per capita consumption is one third of a bushel, or twenty pounds. This estimate is below the true figure. In any case, it would give a total importation of eighty million pounds, instead of the amount given in the general table above of one million bushels (sixty million pounds).

In New York in 1784, imports of merchandise on which duty is paid ad valorem amounted to over $8,000,000. Since then, however, these imports have dropped by half, either because they are entering through other ports, or because the importation of luxury goods has diminished, or because of the establishment of local manufactures of several luxury articles.

Lord Sheffield calculated that in 1774 American imports [from Great Britain] stood at £4,000,000 sterling, not counting imports from Ireland and smuggled goods. It is no exaggeration to estimate that these imports have increased by one fifth, reaching a total of £5,000,000 sterling, or 120,000,000 *livres tournois*. Records of the customhouses in England for 1787 show that that country's exports to the United States have increased prodigiously.

Can you now doubt that if America imposes even small customs duties on its imports it will be able to cover its governmental expenses and pay the interest on its debt? The experiment of 1789 should open everyone's eyes; the Act of Congress of June 1, 1789, imposed only modest duties, and yet it produced revenue beyond all expectations.

To give you an idea of these duties, here are a few examples: distilled spirits, 2 cents per pint; Madeira wine, 18 s. for 4 pints; other wines, 10 s.;[7] brown sugar, 1 s. per pound; cheese, 4 s. per pound;[8] Bohea tea, 6 s. per pound; Souchong tea, 10 s. per pound;[9] etc.

On the other hand, if you wish to have a glimpse of the prospects God has in store for America, read the figures given by Mr. Swan.[10] According to the incontrovertible figures presented by Mr. Franklin and Professor Wigglesworth, who guarantee that the population of the United States doubles every eighteen years, our [American] imports, which were 70,000,000 [livres] in 1774, will amount to 140,784,000 livres in 1792, proportionate to a population of 6,129,356; in 1810 they will reach 281,588,000 livres, for 12,258,712 consumers; and, maintaining the same proportion, which is more than probable, imports in 1846 will rise to 1,126,352,000 livres, for 49,000,000 inhabitants.

Before concluding this letter I should like to list briefly the manufactured articles which America is producing in competition with Europe: hats, boots and shoes, all kinds of carriages, harnesses, scythes, hoes and other agricultural tools, carding machines for

---

[7] You can see from this that Americans favor the French.
[8] Americans produce some cheese.
[9] The duty is higher on teas brought in on foreign vessels.
[10] *Causes,* p. 117.

wool and cotton, gloves, wallpaper, children's toys, porter, beer, butter, cheese, mustard, linseed oil, candles, sugar, etc.

The tariffs on these articles are not, however, high enough to prevent us from exporting our own products profitably to the United States, provided our merchants are careful to conform to American tastes. I shall list some of these products and this enumeration may serve to supplement, and occasionally to correct, the corresponding items listed in our work *De la France et des Etats-Unis.*

Hats. The shape of our hats and their plainness do not suit American tastes. They prefer their own product and have factories everywhere, but the hats are rather expensive. The duty on imported hats is 7½ per cent ad valorem.

Carriages. Americans make stagecoaches, coupés, phaetons, sulkies, and chaises, all of them excellent carriages with light, well-made wheels, good springs, and they are half as expensive as ours.[11] The duty on imported carriages is 15 per cent ad valorem.

Silks. Men prefer satin for their waistcoats and breeches and wear it all year round. Women wear taffetas, etc., and show a preference for French ribbons, etc. The consumption of this item may become very large, and is estimated by Mr. Swan at 3,000,000 livres. The duty is 7½ per cent ad valorem.

Hair powder. The French product is in demand.

French books. Even the best will not sell here. Very few people know French.

English books. Very expensive, much more expensive than in London. This would be a profitable item if there were many readers, but I doubt that there are. This is a business in which profits are slow and uncertain.

Paper. Wallpaper. I have said that there are many paper mills in the United States, and I have described the one owned by Mr. Fisher. He uses simpler procedures than are used in France, employs English cylinders, and does not macerate the rags. His product is less expensive than French paper, but European paper will always sell at a profit because consumption is enormous.

As to wallpaper, it is an even more profitable export because the

[11] The French who go to America often take their own carriages, for they think they are going to live among savages. M. Crèvecoeur told me that one day he saw one of our young gentry disembark with one of those heavy post chaises formerly so fashionable. It was a great surprise to the Americans, who could not conceive that such a contraption could come from a civilized country. Fortunately for the honor of our nation, the French consul hastened to hide it in a shed.

kind manufactured in the United States, where labor costs are high, is much more expensive.

Plaster of Paris. Would you believe that this is a product greatly in demand by American farmers? They have found that it is a good fertilizer. Several experiments conducted on two adjoining acres have proved that land fertilized with plaster of Paris doubles its yield. Plaster has been found on the Bay of Fundy, in Nova Scotia, but it is not as good as the kind from Paris.

Plated ware. Americans use it and will continue to use it in increasingly large quantities, first, because they like cleanliness, and second, because they cannot afford the luxury of expensive silverware. The English supply this item, but our manufacturers ought to compete in inexpensive tableware.

There is a savings of seven eighths on plated silver over silverware, as you yourself have shown. In two years you get back the price of plated silver, for this price is more than equal to the interest on the cost of the silver used in making the same amount of solid silverware.[12]

Vinegar. There is little demand for foreign vinegar. American vinegar is not strong. Imports can be expected to remain small.

Olive oil. Americans do not consume much olive oil. They do not like oil which smells of the fruit; they prefer it to be very clear. When I had a salad at General Washington's home I was surprised to find that it was made without oil; he does not use it. It is more common, however, in the North.

Dried Fruit. Americans import large raisins from Madeira and are beginning to get some from Marseilles.

Besides the above articles, our merchants will find a very large market in the United States for good quality cloth, fine linens,[13] chintz, taffetas, cotton goods, mirrors, glass, cambric, beige, lace, umbrellas, etc.[14] But before they export these goods I advise them to read the revelant articles in our work *De la France et des Etats-Unis.* I have heard Americans subscribe wholeheartedly to the points made in this book and express astonishment that French merchants have not followed its wise advice. On the whole, Americans are not happy that so little familiarity with the market and

[12] [Etienne] Clavière, *Opinions d'un créancier de l'état.* [Paris, 1789.]

[13] It is, however, quite certain that in Philadelphia much less linen and English cloth was sold this year (1788) than in the past. This drop is attributed to the increase of local manufactures.

[14] Mr. Swan has estimated that France could export to America goods amounting to over 40,000,000 [livres].

so little good faith goes into the choice of the goods French merchants send them.

It is indeed shocking to see the kind of goods French merchants are shipping to America. When asked for the best powder, they send bran mixed with flour; instead of excellent claret, they ship a sour Graves or a mediocre Provençal wine; instead of good heavy cloth, they send flimsy material.

It is not, however, sufficient that the merchants, at last rising to the noble attitudes of free men, deal with Americans as brothers. The French government must support them and remove the obstacles that are hindering the establishment and development of the ties between the two peoples which seem to be dictated by nature. The French government must unify the system of weights and measures; [15] it must simplify our commercial law; it must support and encourage the building of warehouses in various ports as places of deposit for imported American goods and as places where orders of French merchandise can be assembled for export; above all, it must establish and maintain a regular packet service [16] which is not rotten with irregularities and corruption like the

[15] So long as the multiple systems of weights and measures exist in France they will constitute a considerable obstacle to trade. An American merchant interested in trading with France on a speculative venture wishes to know what he stands to gain, but if he is not familiar with the thousand and one standards of measurement in use there and cannot tell how much his bushel of wheat will be worth, he becomes afraid of being tricked and refuses to trade. The National Assembly has already taken up this important problem and pursuant to a report from the Academy of Sciences has adopted a single basis for weights and measures. It now only remains to apply this system to the practical uses of commerce.

[16] The French packet service has been suspended since April 1788. I have already noted the bad consequences for commerce that have resulted [pp. 65–66]. It has since been restored, but the uncertainty of the sailings is not likely to inspire confidence. Moreover, the Revolution has caused the service to be irregular. It is to be hoped that the new legislature will find a better plan, and that they will eliminate even the breath of suspicion that the secrecy of letters is violated. It was generally believed in America that the former French government indulged in this perfidious practice, and consequently members of both Congress and the Executive Branch used roundabout ways to forward their correspondence. Since the purpose of re-establishing a packet service to America is to open an important channel of communication, and since this undertaking will at first be expensive, it is necessary that the government subsidize the entire cost and that it do not entrust this enterprise to private companies whose self-interest would conflict with the object in view. The nation must make a sacrifice, as does the English government, which sends each month a packet to America. It leases these ships at £2,000 per voyage, or about £50,000 a year. These ships have, or are supposed to have, a crew of thirty men. The one on which I returned to Falmouth, a 300-ton ship and an excellent sailer, had a crew of only twenty-three. The English maintain four packets to America, four to Lisbon, and twelve to the West Indies, and the ships take turns making the trips. The sailors are paid thirty shillings and the captain forty.

previous one,[17] for without such packets it is impossible to establish a durable foundation for extensive trade with America.

[17] The worst sort of peculation occurred in the maintenance of the French packets. I have seen the report of the first trip to America of Packet No. 1, built at Saint Malo at a cost of nearly 150,000 livres. This report was signed by the captain, M. Souville. It states that the worst possible timber had been used in the construction of the ship; that most of the planks pulled out, leaving open seams; that even the passengers' cabin was almost always full of water; that the sails were of inferior canvas, and all of them tore so that not a single one was whole when they reached New York; that the rudder was made of such poor wood that it broke; that instead of 2,600-pound anchors, the ship had only 1,600-pound ones; that instead of competent sailors he had been given a crew of country bumpkins, who were paid twenty-one livres a month and admitted they had never been to sea before; that he had been forced to sign on as carpenter, at eighteen livres a month, a man who knew nothing about his trade; that the passengers complained of the poor food, of the terrible accommodations, and of being without mattresses, blankets, or curtains. It appears that this ship was too unseaworthy to make a second trip. The people of New York could not believe that such a miserable, badly constructed ship could have been built in France. Such are the results of despotic government. Enterprises of the greatest importance to the public are abandoned to favoritism and intrigue. No one is responsible for anything, the most scandalous waste goes unpunished, and the industry of the people, slandered and discredited abroad, finds that all the doors to foreign trade are closing.

AMERICAN EXPORTS

If anything can indicate the great prosperity toward which these federated republics are making rapid strides, it is the picture presented by their ever-increasing exports. It is difficult even to enumerate all the manufactured goods now shipped abroad by Americans, almost half of which used to be unknown to them. Among the principal agricultural products and manufactured items forming part of this immense exportation we should especially mention ships, flour, rice, tobacco, woolens, linens, hemp, cotton goods, fish, oils,[1] various kinds of iron and steel goods, agricultural implements, nails, leather and numerous leather articles, paper and printing, cardboard, pasteboard, parchment, potash and pearlash, snuff and smoking tobacco, hats of all qualities, masts, spars, and other kinds of timbers,[2] woodwork and furniture, cordage and cables, carriages, cast iron, pewter, copper and lead ware, glassware, gunpowder, cheese, butter, calicoes, printed cloth, indigo, furs,[3] etc., etc.

Since space does not permit an exhaustive treatment of the subject, I shall here limit myself to the discussion of a few main items in order to give you an idea of the speed with which manufacturing in this country has been growing since the Revolution.

Shipbuilding is and will increasingly become one of the most

[1] It is difficult to conceive how anyone could be so shortsighted as to try to discourage this American export to France. It is undoubtedly wise to protect and encourage the Quaker establishment in Dunkirk, but we should not kill off those formed by other Americans in Le Havre and Rouen. Through competition we can hope to have fine whale oil at 60 to 65 livres a quintal. This oil can by certain processes be made superior to olive oil, which costs more than 100 livres a quintal. The duty on whale oil by the *Arrêt du Conseil* of 1784 was only 7 livres 10 sous per barrel of 520 pounds; it is now 6 livres per quintal.

[2] Almost all European states which have navies will someday have to depend on the United States. Good masts and spars from northern Europe are becoming scarce and expensive. The Russians, it is known, keep for their own use the best masts, give the English those of second quality, and the other nations get the rejected ones.

[3] The fur trade will bring Americans great profits for some time, when they gain control of the forts [near the Canadian border], at least if we are to judge by the profits the English made. The total sales in London in 1777 amounted to £133,941 sterling.

lucrative American industries, as we noted in our book on the United States.[4] There was shipbuilding previously under the English government, but Americans did not then manufacture the equipment for rigging and outfitting their vessels. Sailcloth, for example, is now manufactured in the United States. Mr. Shaw's fine eight-hundred-ton ship, the *Massachusetts*, built for the East India trade, was equipped with sails, cordage, and cables manufactured in Boston. Three other ships, sailing in the same trade, have been rigged with products of this country. The sailcloth mills of Boston can produce 2,000 yards a week.

The number of beer breweries here is increasing prodigiously, and they are replacing the deadly liquor distilleries. In Philadelphia alone there are fourteen breweries. This growth has led farmers to raise more barley and hops, which are of the finest quality.

Although woolen mills are still in their infancy, the quality of the goods they are producing gives high hopes for the future. The mill in Hartford produced over 5,000 yards between September 1, 1788, and September 1, 1789. Some of the cloth was of very good quality and sold for as much as $5 (26 livres 5 sols) a yard. Mr. Faulkner's woolen mill in Watertown, Massachusetts, is very promising and is encouraging farmers to raise more sheep.

The growing of hemp and flax[5] has increased prodigiously everywhere, and the crops are sufficient not only to satisfy the needs of the ropewalks and textile mills of the country but also to provide large quantities for export. Linseed is also exported.

You know what great strides Ireland has made in the production of flax and linen since that country has partially regained its independence. In 1701, exports of linen amounted to about £50,000 sterling; by 1771, they had risen to £1,895,000 sterling. Americans hope, and with justification, that they will make even more rapid progress. Cotton spinning is equally successful, and Arkwright's machines are known and will serve as models.

We were correct when we stated that forges are a type of industry in which Free Americans are destined to succeed, for nature has been prodigal in providing them with wood, iron, and coal

[4] There is no port in Europe where ships can be built as cheaply. A good ship of live oak and cedar, of 200-tons burden by measurement, can be completely outfitted in Philadelphia for £14 a ton Pennsylvania currency. There is no port in Europe where to build and equip a similar ship, built entirely of oak, will cost less than £20 Pennsylvania currency, or £12 sterling, a ton.

[5] The state of New York alone exported in 1788 more than 200,000 bushels.

mines,[6] and in short with everything that is necessary for the successful operation of forges to produce all the tools needed for agriculture, shipbuilding, house building, etc. No other industry employs as many workers. The states of Pennsylvania, New Jersey, and Delaware alone produce annually about 350 tons of steel and 600 of iron, nails, iron rods, etc. America now exports nails and carding machines for wool and cotton. These cards are both cheaper and better in quality than those made by the English, who are now buying American machines.

In the same three states there are sixty-three paper mills, which produce paper to the value of $250,000. In addition, the state of Connecticut manufactured last year approximately 5,000 reams worth about $9,000. The paper industry will certainly continue to grow, for printing presses and newspapers are being established everywhere. Four different printers at the same time have undertaken editions of the Bible printed on American paper with type cast in America and engravings made by Americans.

The extraordinary consumption in the United States of glasses, bottles, and window glass is causing the construction of glassworks. The one on the Potomac, it is said, employs over 500 people. How this consumption will increase when the canals now being built along the large rivers have cut transportation costs! M. De Fer has calculated that in France, where the roads are in general well maintained, transportation by land is 150 times more expensive than by water.[7] What can the ratio be here, where the roads are not as well constructed and land transportation is even more expensive?

Americans are beginning to produce printed calicoes, cotton goods, and linen. Near Philadelphia, Messrs. Hewson and Taylor have a mill which has been quite successful.

Many workers are also employed in the production of gunpowder; in Pennsylvania alone there are 21 powder mills capable of manufacturing 625 tons of powder. It retails at $5 for 25 pounds, or $16 per hundredweight. It is estimated that the annual production amounts to $200,000. The best powder mill is that owned by Mr. Miller near Frankfort.

The number of sugar refineries is increasing just as rapidly. In

[6] Virginia coal is exported as ballast from Philadelphia.
[7] [François de Fer de La Noverre, *De la possibilité de faciliter l'établissement général de la navigation intérieure du royaume . . .* , Paris, 1786.]

an average year Pennsylvania imports 5,692,848 pounds of un-refined sugar and only 4,480 pounds of sugar loaves. Between March 1785 and March 1786 this state imported 8,406,000 pounds of unrefined sugar and re-exported 6,667,687 pounds [of refined sugar] to the other states. The latter, however, are beginning to do their own refining. In 1787, 67,752 pounds of sugar loaves were exported from Boston.

Wheat and flour constitute important items in American trade, and the following figures will give you an idea of the growth in volume of these commodities: In 1786, 150,000 barrels of flour were exported from Pennsylvania;[8] in 1787, the amount was 202,000; in 1788, 220,000; in 1789, 360,000. About 120,000 tons of shipping must have been needed for this trade.

In November 1788 there were two French ships on the Dela-ware loading flour for France. And only the previous year people in Paris were tempted to make fun of us when we declared that in order to have enough food the French would have to resort to the importation of American wheat!

I cannot devote any more space to these details, and I shall now give an outline of the broad changes which have taken place in American trade.

Exports from England to the colonies which now form the United States, over a period of eleven years from 1762 to 1773, averaged $10,792,906.66 annually. During the same period, the average yearly exports from America were $5,562,004.44. There was, therefore, an annual balance of trade unfavorable to America of $5,230,902.22.

Now here is the other side of the picture, which must make Americans congratulate themselves on having won their independ-ence. During the debates in the House of Representatives on May 15, 1790, Mr. Madison, with whose excellent judgment and exactitude in questions of fact you are familiar, established that,

[8] Four hundred ships carried this cargo to the following ports:

English ports	51,053	barrels
French "	1,829	"
Spanish "	17,805	"
Dutch "	18,800	"
Danish "	7,466	"
Portuguese "	7,645	"
Hamburg	595	"
Bremen	30	"
Various U.S. ports	48,245	"

at the lowest estimate, the total annual imports into America were as follows:

From Europe	$13,506,666 ⅔
From the West Indies	4,121,946 ⅔
Total	$17,628,613 ⅓

On the other hand, Mr. Madison established that American exports amounted to annually:

To Europe	$14,233,101 ⅓
To the West Indies	4,184,675 ½
Total	$18,417,776
Balance of trade favorable to the United States	$789,163

Even if we take the figures given by English writers, who do not estimate the prewar balance of trade favorable to England at as high a figure as the one given above, and claim that the average was only $2,210,837, and if we add to this sum the $789,163 of the present balance favorable to the United States, we find that Americans have increased their [export] trade by over $3,000,000 since the Revolution. Note that this increase is in raw materials produced in America and in goods manufactured in America. Thus increase in trade produces here an increase in agriculture and population.

I could cite many more facts which would prove the prodigious growth in American trade.[9] Here is one chosen from a hundred similar examples:

Exports from Philadelphia to Europe in 1769 were	£272,391	16 s.
In 1773 were	£212,155	7 s.
From August 1 to December 31, 1789, that is, five months, the total exports from Philadelphia were	£1,113,239	
The imports were	£841,068	

[9] Several very well informed Americans have published various pamphlets on the growth of trade and manufacturing in the United States which are well worth reading. See in particular Tench Coxe, *An Enquiry Into the Principles on Which a Commercial System for the United States Should Be Founded* (Philadelphia, 1787); [William] Bingham, *A Letter from an American......on Lord Sheffield's Pamphlet on the Commerce of the American States* [London, 1784]; [James] Swan, *National Arithmetic* [Boston, 1786]. We have already mentioned another excellent work by Mr. Swan.

Another Example

Records of taxes on tonnage in Philadelphia
    from October 1, 1787 to October 1788 give   72,079 tons
From 1788 to 1789   86,969 tons
In 1789, ships built in Philadelphia   3,991 tons
In February 1790, ships totaling 4,400 tons were on order.

Finally, it is estimated that ships entering the port of Philadelphia total nearly 116,000 tons. If this constitutes only one fifth of the shipping in American ports then the total for the whole country is nearly 600,000 tons, more than half of which is American, the rest foreign. About two thirds of the foreign shipping is English.

You will remember, my friend, that Lord Sheffield estimated American exports at close to £4,000,000 sterling. We can be sure on the basis of the increase in tonnage, of customs records, and of the figures of well-informed merchants and financiers, that these exports now amount to approximately £5,200,000 sterling.

The increase in trade has necessarily increased the prices of foodstuffs, especially of articles for which the demand has increased considerably and suddenly. You will see this from the following table, which compares prices for two dates separated by a long interval:

PRICES OF VARIOUS ITEMS IN PHILADELPHIA, MAY 15, 1767
AND MAY 15, 1790

	May 15, 1767		May 15, 1790	
	s.	d.	s.	d.
Flour, barrel or quintal	16	6	34	6
Tobacco	15 to 30	6	16 to 60	
Rice	17		22	
Wheat, bushel	6		13	
Linseed	6		4	6
Beef, barrel	55		45 to 60	
Pork	75		55 to 67	
Pitch	16		22	6
Tar	12		13	6
Refined sugar, quintal	50		57 to 70	
Ship's bread, quintal	16	6	26	

You will note that the prices of only two articles on this comparative table have dropped, linseed and salt beef. These reductions are due to the great amount of flax now grown and to the increased number of plants for salting meat.

THE EAST INDIES TRADE—AMERICAN
FOREIGN TRADE IN GENERAL

It is in the East Indies trade, my friend, that you may see the best example of American enterprise. The original motive for embarking on this commerce was the hope of buying more cheaply from the East Indies merchandise which formerly had been imported indirectly through England. The saving is tremendous, if we may judge by the large consumption of tea in America and the high price of this commodity in England. In 1761, the English colonies in America paid Great Britain a remittance in Spanish dollars of £85,000 sterling for tea alone, and the consumption has tripled since.

But another motive which has induced so many American ships to sail to the China Sea and the Bay of Bengal has been the plan to flood with goods from the Indies South America, the Spanish West Indies,[1] the other West Indian colonies, and in general all the European countries, and to seize control of these markets by selling the merchandise at lower prices. This is not a hopeless ambition. By the nature of things Americans are destined to become the greatest "maritime carriers" in the world. They build ships at two-thirds less than Europeans; they sail with fewer men and at a lower cost,[2] though their sailors are well fed; they navigate

---

[1] Spain by a regulation of 1778 opened to foreign trade twenty-four ports distributed among her colonies excepting Mexico. But although she has reduced to a great extent the former obstacles to foreign trade, she still offers incentives to smuggling by the restrictions she has let stand, for instance the exclusion of foreign wines, oils, brandies, silk stockings, cotton goods, etc.—all items in great demand in her colonies. Americans are in the best position to supply them with these goods.

[2] The following is the pay list of a ship sailing from Boston in 1786:

Ship's Articles of a Brigantine out of Boston of 150 Tons Burden

	Dollars	Livres tournois	
The captain, at £4 a month	13½	70	
He also receives 5% on the sale of the cargo and 2½% on the purchase of the return cargo. He has a 5% privilege on board, that is, of 100 hogsheads of tobacco carried as cargo he can own 5.			
The lieutenant receives, per month	9	47	5 sous
He eats at the captain's table and has a 3% privilege on the cargo; that is, of 150 hogsheads carried as cargo he can own 4.			

with greater safety; their ships are cleaner; and they are more intelligent seamen, for the spirit of equality which reigns in America reigns also aboard their ships. Nothing can make better sailors than the hope of becoming captain, and no promise of a bonus is a more powerful stimulus.

Still other circumstances favor the East India trade and American shipping. Americans carry ginseng to China, and planks, ship's timbers, flour, and salt meat to the Cape of Good Hope, to Bourbon [Réunion] Island, and the Ile de France [Mauritius]. Therefore they do not have to take to the Indies as much money as do Europeans who have colonies there,[3] nor are they obliged like the Europeans to maintain at great expense troops, governors, intendants, clerks, all of those more or less useless trappings whose enormous expense in the end raises the price of Indian goods and places a burden on trade.

No sea is closed to the skill of American seamen, and their flag now flies everywhere. They are continually exploring all the

	Dollars	Livres tournois	
The cabin boy, who also serves as cook, per month	3	15	15 sous
Six sailors at $7 a month each	42	220	10 sous
About one sixth is deducted from the sailors' pay, but they have the privilege of loading aboard fourteen hundredweights of merchandise.			
The total monthly pay	67½	353	10 sous

The freight is 40 s. sterling per ton, or 34 *livres tournois.*

Every morning the sailors have either tea or chocolate or coffee; twice a day brandy with water; and as much bread and meat as they want.

The pay and all the provisions for the crew, plus port taxes, pilotage, and fresh provisions, are estimated at £40 sterling a month, or 880 *livres tournois.*

Americans sail very fast, spend little time in port, and are enterprising and alert. A ship will leave Boston for the West Indies with a cargo of cod, barrel staves, planks, etc.; with the proceeds of the cargo, it buys sugar and rum; then it sails to Charleston, where the cargo is exchanged for rice; hence to Cadiz, where the rice is sold for salt, wine, grapes, lemons, soap, brandies, Barcelona handkerchiefs, etc. All this is done in six months. "I have known of several ships," the merchant who provided me with this note told me, "that took only twenty-one days to reach the West Indies from Boston, sixteen days to go from there to the Carolinas, forty-two days from there to Cadiz, and thirty-five days from Cadiz to Boston."

[3] The money carried by an American ship is equal to the value of about one fifth of the cargo. The *Alliance,* which returned in 1788 from China with a large cargo valued at £75,000 sterling, had taken only £16,000 to £17,000 sterling. This return cargo consisted of: 1,725 cases of Bohea tea; 710 cases of Hyson tea; 384 cases of Souchong tea; 35 cases of silk; 15 of nankeen; 321 of porcelain. The whole cargo belonged to Mr. Morris. He is not the only American to undertake such a big venture without a partner. Mr. [Elias] Darby of Salem has done the same several times. There is reported only one man in London, Mr. Macaulay, who is the sole owner of a ship trading in the East Indies.

islands, studying the local needs, and going back later to satisfy them. They carry from Boston, and even from the Piscataqua and Kennebec rivers, planks, masts, and foodstuffs to the Cape of Good Hope, and they do not think this voyage any longer or less worthwhile than a trip to the West Indies.

Our languishing colony in Cayenne would have perished ten times over from lack of food supplies if it had relied on regular shipments from the mother country, but it has been supplied by Americans who have thus remedied the criminal mismanagement of the European monopoly which controls the colony. Mr. Prince, a captain from New York, makes this voyage every year.

A sixty-ton sloop from Albany with a crew of eleven men made a daring voyage to China. When the Chinese saw her arrive, they took her for the cutter of some large vessel and asked where the great ship was. "We are the great ship," they told the awestruck Chinese.

Our papers boast of the magnificent achievements of European states which make discoveries in the course of long voyages around the world. The Americans do the same, but they do not boast so blatantly of their exploits. In September 1790 the ship *Columbia*, Captain Gray, sailed on its second trip around the world with the intent of exploring the northwestern part of America.[4] The brig *Hope* had already sailed with the same objective.[5]

Wherever Americans open new routes they take with them enlightenment and bring back useful objects. They take their newspapers, and bring back new species of animals and unknown plants and grains, which they then grow in their own country.

Our papers resound with the quarrels between the English and the Spaniards over trade in Nootka Sound on the coast of Kamchatka.[6] Americans quarrel with nobody, but they have already established on that coast a trade in furs and pelts. Several vessels from Boston were there in July 1789, and they got along very well with the English. During the same year, forty-four ships sailed from Boston, as many to the northwest coast of America as to the East Indies and China. But the Americans have still higher hopes and are looking forward to the day when a more direct route will be established to Nootka Sound. It seems likely that this region is

[4] [Robert Gray (1755–1806), master of the *Columbia*, made the first American circumnavigation of the globe (1787–1790) and in 1791 revisited the Northwest and explored the Columbia River, naming it after his ship.]

[5] [The *Hope*, James Magee master, sailed from New York.]

[6] [Actually Vancouver Island.]

not very far from the northwestern branches of the Mississippi, which Americans will surely someday navigate to its source when they begin to settle Louisiana and spread out into the interior of Mexico.

This will be one of the most fortunate moments in the history of the human race. For the third time, a prodigious change in the routes of maritime trade will occur, and it is quite possible that the Cape of Good Hope will lose its importance as a focal point for commerce, just as the Mediterranean did. Free Americans are destined to open a canal linking the Atlantic and the Pacific. The exact route is not yet known but it will be easy to determine, and it will pass through Lake Nicaragua.[7] Geography favors this route, which would shorten prodigiously the distance to the East Indies. The only obstacle is the character of the men who control that area. Spaniards wish to grab everything and hoard it for their own use, but Americans wish to conquer only for the advantage of the great family of the human race.

If you would know the enterprising, daring, indefatigable spirit of Americans as it was embodied in one man, listen to the story of the famous traveler [John] Ledyard of Connecticut.[8] This tale will provide a refreshing interlude.

From his childhood, Ledyard was dominated by the desire to see with his own eyes all the parts of the world which had not yet been discovered or completely explored by other travelers. This was to be his career, and to make a success of it he did his apprenticeship by spending several years with the Indians and learning how to endure hardship and live close to nature.

A single incident will give you an idea of his courage. Forced, because he was not rich, to leave Dartmouth College, he decided to go to Hartford but he did not have a shilling in his pocket for the trip. So he built himself a canoe fifty feet long and three feet wide, took a few pieces of venison and for blankets some skins given him by the townspeople, and set out. After traveling 140 miles in an open boat down a swift river with which he was not familiar, he arrived in Hartford. Somewhat later, a chance opportunity took him to England.

[7] This plan does exist, but I cannot describe it here for lack of space. Americans expect to build this canal someday.

[8] [John Ledyard (1751–1789), born in Groton, Conn., spent less than a year at Dartmouth and sailed with Captain Cook in 1776. The account of his life given by Brissot is substantially correct. See Jared Sparks, *Life of John Ledyard, the American Traveler*, Boston, 1847.]

The unfortunate [Captain] Cook was at that time preparing for his third voyage around the world, and Ledyard found a chance to satisfy his insatiable appetite for travel by sailing with him as a corporal. Upon his return he conceived the plan of exploring by land the northwest coast of America, parts of which Cook had visited, and then making his way overland across the vast continent from the Pacific to the Atlantic. Prevented by a rapacious customs officer from embarking on a merchant ship sailing for Nootka Sound, on the west coast of North America, he decided to go by land to Kamchatka, from where it would be a very short passage to the western shores of America. With only ten guineas in his pocket he went to Ostend and from there to Stockholm. It was the middle of winter, and he tried to reach Kamchatka by the most direct route by walking across the Gulf of Bothnia on the ice. But after crossing about halfway he was forced to turn back because the ice was not strong enough to hold him. Back in Stockholm, he headed north to the Arctic Circle, and rounding the tip of the Gulf descended along the eastern coast to Saint Petersburg.

He already had the reputation of being an extraordinary man. Without shoes and stockings and without the money to buy any, he accepted an invitation to dinner from the Ambassador of Portugal, to whom he described his plan and his inability to carry it out in his present state of utter destitution. The ambassador lent him twenty guineas, for which Ledyard gave him a draft drawn on Sir [Joseph] Banks.[9] Ledyard admitted that he had no right to draw such a draft, but hoped that Sir Joseph would pay it in view of the importance of his enterprise and his past achievements. How small and mean this ambassador seems to us! With all his decorations, how contemptible he appears by comparison with this man, barefoot and dressed in rags! To be petty enough not to give his twenty guineas freely to this extraordinary man, who was gratuitously devoting his life to the service of the human race!

At the time the empress was sending a detachment of men to Yakutsk. You know this place and how cold it is there. Ledyard accompanied the detachment and covered six thousand miles across Siberia, eventually reaching Yakutsk. There he found an Englishman, a Mr. Billings, whom he had known on Captain Cook's expedition, and who had just been sent by the empress to explore

[9] [Sir Joseph Banks (1743–1820), a botanist, was president of the Royal Society and had accompanied Cook on his explorations.]

the northern regions. From Yakutsk, Ledyard went to Oczackow [Okhotsk?] on the coast of the Sea of Kamchatka [Okhotsk], intending to cross the peninsula [of Kamchatka] and embark on one of the Russian vessels which trade on the western coasts of America; but finding that no ships could sail because of the ice, he returned to Yakutsk to await the end of winter.

This was the situation when, suspected of he knew not what, he was arrested in the name of the empress. Despots are always suspicious and they are frightened by enterprising and independent men, and Ledyard was both. They fear discoveries which can shake the world and thereby shake their thrones. Two Russian soldiers placed Ledyard on a sleigh and in the depths of winter hauled him across the steppes of Northern Tatary and finally dropped him on the Polish frontier, telling him that if he returned to Russia he would be hanged, but that if he chose to go back to England they wished him *bon voyage*.

Utterly destitute, covered with rags, overwhelmed by his misfortunes, exhausted by illness, without friends and without credit, bereft of any resources, still Ledyard did not lose heart. He made his way to Königsberg, where he had the luck to meet a person kind enough to lend him five guineas on a draft drawn on the president of the Royal Society [Banks]. With this help, he arrived in England and went to see Sir Joseph Banks. This worthy man had not awaited Ledyard's arrival to respond to the latter's trust in him and had already paid the drafts.

After Sir Joseph had heard Ledyard's tale he suggested to him a new venture, the exploration of the interior of Africa. A society had just been formed to encourage discoveries in that part of the world. Ledyard accepted. "When will you be ready to leave?" Sir Joseph asked him.

"Tomorrow. Show me my route."

Whereupon Sir Joseph unrolled a map of Africa, drew a line from Cairo to Sennar [in the Sudan], and thence westward in the supposed direction of the Niger. That was the route along which the society proposed to conduct the exploration of Africa.

Nature had fitted Ledyard for the career he was called to follow. Of herculean strength, intrepid, energetic, fearless, indifferent to public opinion and to the luxuries or even the simple necessities of life, confident in his own strength and in the natural goodness of savages, Ledyard feared no more the African jungle and its dusky inhabitants than he had the American forest and its Indians. He had learned while living among the latter that natural man always trusts and welcomes strangers, and the open friendliness of Ledyard, who always traveled unarmed, dispelled any suspicion.

Africa was to be the end of the labors and travels of this insatiable explorer. After having traveled through a part of the territory he had promised to investigate, and after having forwarded to the society a large quantity of important information, he met his death in Cairo, thus depriving Europe of many curious and important discoveries.

Ledyard's astonishing travels may be compared to those of two other Americans, Peter Pond and James [Alexander] Henry, who have spent fifteen years exploring all the northwestern part of the interior of North America and who have discovered that the Lake of the Woods does not empty into the Mississippi, but flows into Hudson Bay.[10]

I must repeat, if any people deserve Horace's epithet, "Audax Japeti genus," it is the Free Americans. It is to this nation, therefore, that we French should bind ourselves.

The type of men America breeds is also exemplified by the daring Captain Read, who in 1787 was in command of the *Alliance,* bound for the East Indies. He sailed at an unfavorable time of year when the monsoon would give him head winds on his course to Macao. Scorning the established practice of navigators, he steered a new course and sailed south until he found between the seventh and ninth degrees [south latitude] southwest [southeast] winds which carried him to Macao. His arrival caused great astonishment among European seamen, who considered such a voyage impossible during that season.

Americans have such an advantageous position in the East Indies trade that I cannot understand why no French banker or merchant has thought either of establishing companies here to import Indian goods for resale in Europe, or of associating themselves with the companies in Boston, New York, and Philadelphia now successfully engaged in this trade. By doing so they would effect tremen-

---

[10] See Crèvecoeur, *Lettres d'un Cultivateur américain* [Paris, 1787], III, 524. This chapter [xvi, pp. 495–570] contains many interesting facts and gives a good idea of developments in America. [Peter Pond (1740–1787), soldier, fur trader, and explorer of the American and Canadian Northwest. Brissot picked this whole paragraph up from Crèvecoeur, including the incorrect reference to James Henry. Pond did accompany an Alexander Henry on a trip west.]

dous savings in the costs of ships,[11] in crew pay, in outfitting, and on the return voyage.

Everything leads Americans to hope that they will someday surpass their European rivals in this trade. The need to carry specie to India, which could have stopped them, becomes daily less of a problem, because of the restoration of public credit, which will soon permit the circulation of government stocks as a medium of exchange, and also because of the increase in the number of banks, whose notes can replace money for domestic purposes.

The first bank in the United States, called the Bank of North America, was founded by Mr. [Robert] Morris in Philadelphia in 1781. Congress, realizing how useful this bank could be to the government at a time when its paper money was completely discredited and specie was excessively scarce, granted it a charter. Congress was not deceived in its expectations and was able to draw on the resources of this institution to meet indispensable expenditures which had to be made in specie. Thanks to the talents, energy, and zeal of Mr. Morris, who was then Superintendent of Finance, the operations of the bank were so successful that in its third year of existence, that is, between January 1, 1784, and Jan-

[11] The following details will give an indication of the cost of a ship constructed for the China trade:

Dimensions, quality of wood, number of tons of the ship America, *built for the China trade, completed in New York October 7, 1788.*

Length of keel on a right line	102	feet
Rake of stem	20	"
Rake of sternpost	3	"
Rise of floor timbers amidships	24	inches
Beam	32½	feet
Depth of hold	13½	"
Between-decks	4½	"
Boat deck	5½	"
Height of poop deck	6½	"

All the cant frames and floor timbers are of the best white oak, as are the beams and the knees above the waterline. The first and second futtocks are of live oak, red cedar, and locust.

The builder provided and placed in position the masts, the spars, the topmasts, the figurehead, the bowsprit, the capstan, the head, and the quarter gallery at a price of £7 2½ s. per ton, New York currency, or $12,585.50, or 66,073 livres, 17 sous, 6 deniers *tournois*. Tonnage: 706 58⁄96 tons burden.

It is estimated that rigged and ready to sail the ship will have cost nearly £14,000. It should be noted that Americans spend a lot of money on finishing the interior of their vessels, on paneling, varnished woodwork, wall coverings, etc.

They have loaded masts in the hold of this vessel. These are much in demand in Ile de France and Bourbon Island, and in general in the East Indies.

uary 1, 1785, its cash assets rose to close to $60,000,000, or over 300,000,000 *livres tournois*. Later the bank caused resentment. Another bank was established in competition, which led to litigation, but the two banks merged. Then there was other trouble, and finally the monopoly it had been granted was revoked. Nevertheless, the bank vigorously continues its activities and enjoys excellent credit.[12]

There are now three large banks in the United States in Philadelphia, New York, and Boston. They discount only bills of unquestionable security, and they do not risk large amounts of money for fear of new issues of paper money. For the same reason they transact little business among themselves. As a result, the latest dividend of the Philadelphia bank was small, and its shares are below par. They sell at a discount of six to seven per cent, although there is no lack of confidence in them, and the bank's notes circulate at face value, perhaps because merchants find the use of them very convenient. The bank has suffered some losses in a number of bankruptcies.

Considerations of the advantages offered by banks ought to lead to the establishment of many more in the United States. The first effect of banks is to increase the amount of specie in circulation in countries which have little or which need more. Both these cases apply to the United States; there is a shortage of specie, and as population increases the need for specie grows in proportion. A second effect of banks is to make possible an expansion of foreign trade. Specie, no longer needed for circulation within the country, seeks employment abroad. For the same reason, and this is the third advantage, employment in the country increases, for the abundance of fictitious money causes a drop in the rate of interest and consequently is favorable to commercial enterprises, the settling of new land, etc.

It is not necessary to dwell any longer on the advantages of banks to domestic and foreign trade, for they are well known here and there is no doubt that banks will multiply in the future.

[12] The history of this bank is well treated in the American work [by Pelatiah Webster], *An Essay on Credit* (Philadelphia: Oswald, 1786), in which the doctrine of banking is examined, with remarks on the present condition of the Bank of North America.

THE NEW EMPIRE
OF THE WEST

I wish, my friend, I had the time to describe those new western territories that settlers enthusiastically call the Empire of the West. Although this empire is at present completely unknown to Europeans, by the very nature of things it will someday come to deserve its title, and there is no doubt that in less than a century the industrial and trading nations of Europe will be eager to establish commercial and political ties with this area. Since space is limited, I shall describe to you these astonishing settlements only in broad lines, and I shall leave for another time both the details and the broad conclusions that a speculative philosopher can draw from them.

The United States, which cover the eastern region along the Atlantic seaboard, constitute only one third of the vast area that now belongs to the Free Americans, while the immense Western Territory constitutes the other two thirds.[1]

From the foot of the Alleghenies, whose summits do not threaten the heavens as do those of the Andes and the Alps, spreads an immense plain, intersected by gently sloping hills and covered with topsoil three to seven feet deep. It is a fertile land with few

---

[1] The territory along the Ohio River, between the Alleghenies, Lakes Ontario and Erie, and the Mississippi and Illinois rivers, comprises 233,200 square miles, that is, a territory almost equal to that of France and Great Britain together, which is 235,257 square miles. — 233,200 sq. miles

The territory between the Illinois River, Lake Huron and Lake Superior, and the Mississippi River to the Falls of Saint Anthony comprises 129,030 square miles, a territory almost equal to that of Great Britain and Ireland combined, which is 131,800 square miles. — 129,030 " "

The territory from the Falls of Saint Anthony to the southern border and from the Lake of the Woods to the source of the Mississippi comprises 50,000 square miles, that is, more than Holland, Flanders and Ireland, which together contain only 47,908 square miles. — 50,000 " "

The thirteen United States comprise 207,050 square miles, that is, a territory almost as large as that of Germany, Flanders, Holland, and Switzerland, which together have 207,483 square miles. — 207,050 " "

619,280 " "

or no stones, quite different from that on this side of the Alleghenies, and suitable for every kind of crop, including tobacco, hemp, and Indian corn. These voracious plants grow to prodigious size, and cattle multiply rapidly and require almost no attention.

It is here that have been established a number of prosperous settlements which are attracting many emigrants—Kentucky, Franklin, Cumberland, Holston, Muskingum, and Scioto.

The oldest and most beautiful is Kentucky. You have read in M. Parraud's [Farrand's] translation the interesting story of its founder.[2] In spite of the atrocities suffered by the first settlers at the hands of the Indians, its population has grown rapidly. Kentucky began to be settled only in 1775; by 1782, it had seven to eight thousand inhabitants; by 1787, fifty thousand; and by 1790, seventy thousand. This territory will be shortly declared a free and independent state.

Cumberland, situated near Kentucky and just coming into statehood, counts eight thousand inhabitants. Holston has five thousand, and Franklin twenty-five thousand. Cumberland will shortly become a separate state. Franklin used to be a state, but could not raise sufficient revenue to subsist on its own and merged with Virginia.[3]

In the history of the creation of these settlements is manifested the stubbornly enterprising character of Americans. The following story is typical:

[Richard] Henderson was born in North Carolina of poor parents and received very little schooling, but, having an inclination for study, he stubbornly worked to improve himself. He became an accomplished speaker, was appointed Chief [Associate] Justice [of the Superior Court] of his state at a high salary, and made himself loved and respected.[4] But he had the ambition to be a legislator.

[2] [John Filson, *Histoire de Kentucke . . . traduite de l'anglais . . . par M. Farrand*, Paris, 1785, contains an account of the exploits of Daniel Boone. This is a translation of Filson's well-known *The Discovery, Settlement and Present State of Kentucke*, Wilmington, 1784.]

[3] [Holston was a settlement in what is now northeastern Tennessee, and Muskingum and Scioto were settlements in southern Ohio. Franklin was the name selected for the eastern half of Tennessee, which almost became a state in the period 1784–1789. The Transylvania Company established settlements, beginning in 1775, in the Cumberland Valley in north central Tennessee.]

[4] [Richard Henderson (1735–1795) was the leading promoter of the Transylvania Company, which in 1775 purchased from the Cherokees an immense tract in the northern half of middle Tennessee and a large part of Kentucky. In 1779 he founded Nashville and with James Robertson drew up the Cumberland Compact for the Cumberland River area.]

He bought a huge tract of land from the Cherokee Indians, left his birthplace, his position, his friends, in short gave up everything, and started out one day with two wagons of belongings to found a colony between the Kentucky, Cherokee, and Ohio rivers, where he established his own legislature. Under the leadership of such a remarkable man this settlement has been prospering.

When you behold the speed with which men settle new territories, and when you compare this speed with the slow development of colonies founded by despots, how grand the idea of liberty appears! Liberty can accomplish everything; what she wills is done. Liberty need but command, and forests are cleared, mountains are leveled, rich farms arise to provide havens for numberless generations. Whereas the proud city of Palmyra perished forgotten with the haughty woman who founded it, its ruins attesting that nothing endures save that which is free and remains free.

It seems that Kentucky will always have an advantage over the neighboring areas, for its territory is larger, its soil more fertile, its inhabitants more numerous, and it is situated on the Ohio, navigable in almost all seasons. This latter advantage is shared by two other settlements which I shall describe later.

The following toasts, given on the Fourth of July 1788 in Lexington, Kentucky, will give you an idea of the spirit of the settlers in this part of America:

"To the Western World—perpetual union based on the principle of equality, or else friendly separation."

"Free navigation on the Mississippi, at any price, except the price of liberty."

"Harmony with Spain and reciprocity of good offices."

"To our brothers in Muskingum—may their settlement prosper."

"May the Indians, enemies of America, be chastised by the force of arms!"

"May the Atlantic coast be just, the Western Territory be free, and both be happy!"

"A strong government based on federal principles."

"To the republic of Kentucky, the fourteenth star in the American constellation."

The colony of Muskingum, located on the river of the same name in the western part of Ohio, was settled by emigrants from Massachusetts and Rhode Island.

The Ohio Company at its meeting on July 2, 1788, gave to the town built at the confluence of the Muskingum and the Ohio the name of Marietta, combining the beginning and the end of the name of the Queen of France, Marie Antoinette. Such a gallant token of gratitude coming from half savages must surprise you, but this strange idea was due to General Varnum,[5] who displayed even more bizarre taste when he imposed such names as *Via Sacra* and *Campus Martius* on the streets of the town. Varnum is an enthusiastic lover of antiquity and such an enemy of the English that he urged that the English language be abandoned in the United States and replaced by Greek. M. Crèvecoeur had suggested that the town be named Castripolis, for the entrenched camp that was found there. This strange monument unquestionably proves that this continent was once inhabited by a civilized people.

The speech made by General Harmar [6] and Varnum's reply were clothed in a pompous style which caused a great deal of amusement among those in the United States who call themselves "gentlemen."

A man has published an account of making the trip from Pittsburgh to the Muskingum in 1788, floating down the river in forty-eight hours without the aid of oars or sails. He reports that the countryside is superb, that there were already many settlers' tents to be seen, and that everything grows very quickly there.

Within the Ohio Company has been formed another group which is much better known in France, the Scioto Company.[7] It

[5] [James M. Varnum (1748–1789), a director of the Ohio Company and U.S. judge for the Northwest Territory.]

[6] [Josiah Harmar (1753–1813), commander of the army stationed on the Ohio frontier.]

[7] There has been a great outcry against this company, which has been accused of selling lands that did not belong to it, of giving exaggerated reports of their fertility, of cheating emigrants, and of depleting France of its citizens to send them to be butchered by Indians. This company's title to the land is, however, incontestable and most of its American shareholders are important and respected men. The description they have given of the lands they are selling came from the published reports of an American geographer of repute, [Thomas] Hutchins (See his *Topographical Description* [London, 1778]). No one can deny that the area is prodigiously fertile; Indian corn, for instance, grows fifteen feet high. Certainly the French aristocrats who have had the mad idea of emigrating there to found a monarchy will be cruelly disappointed. They are running away from the French government because it is establishing equality of rights, and they will fall into a society where this equality is consecrated by the very nature of things, and where all the circumstances and the ease with which a man can satisfy his needs form constant invitations to independence. They are fleeing to preserve their titles, honors, and rights to special deference, and they will find a new society where titles conceived by pride and acquired by chance are spurned, or even are unknown,

takes its name from the Scioto River which flows into the Ohio
after traversing the two million acres which this company owns.
The Scioto colony can soon achieve great prosperity if the emigrants from France and other foreign countries are more carefully
selected, and if all precautions are taken to make the voyage less

---

and where respect is paid to scarcely anything but physical strength. Life in the
Scioto is the life of the wilderness, one step removed from the state of nature. To
live there one must give up pleasures, expensive tastes, epicurean habits, and the
prejudices of Europe. Not that happiness cannot be found under the humble roof
of the Scioto frontiersman, but it is not the kind of happiness that our European
aristocrats seek, for it consists in the freedom of all men from almost all the needs
and prejudices of civilized society. Our aristocrats have a thousand needs, a thousand extravagant appetites. The Scioto is a good place for unhappy Europeans who
have neither property nor employment, but who, strong in body, are ready and
able to work. They will find in the Scioto, and in general in all the frontier settlements, enough to satisfy their needs. The land will yield all the food they need
in exchange for a little work; the animals of the forest will provide meat for their
tables until the time when they can raise livestock on their farms. The Scioto
Company, therefore, by providing a haven and giving land to those who had been
deprived of their livelihood by the Revolution was offering a real service to these
unhappy people. But, it will be objected, the poor can find all these advantages in
France where there still is unused land. That is true, but are the owners of such
land willing to give it away? Are they willing to loan money? Will food be as cheap
in France as in the Scioto?—No—Then why rant against an emigration which was
useful to France, to the individuals concerned, and to the United States, an emigration which could lead to the establishment of a colony which someday might
prove very useful for the development of commercial relations between France
and the Western Territory? There are now thirty thousand beggars who are being
maintained in idleness on the outskirts of Paris, as much out of fear as out of
humanity. It is my firm belief that the man who could find a way to transport
them into the American wilderness, with their consent and at not too great expense,
would deserve an altar, for he would at the same time have cured our capital of a
leprous plague and also have restored thirty thousand unfortunate men to happiness and moral health. For beggary has no morals, but life in the wilderness can
teach morals.

[The Scioto Company was organized in 1787 by a group of American speculators headed by William Duer and Andrew Craigie, Brissot's business associates, for
the purpose of selling land to French emigrants. They sent Joel Barlow, the first
translator of these *Travels*, to Paris in June 1788 as their agent, and he, together
with an English adventurer named William Playfair, organized the French Com-
pagnie du Scioto in August 1789, one month after the fall of the Bastille. In the
current atmosphere of violence, uncertainty, and insecurity the glowing picture
these promoters painted in their prospectuses seemed to many French men and
women a miraculous solution to all their fears and problems. A veritable mania
swept Paris, and citizens of all classes and professions rushed to buy Scioto lands
before they were all sold. During the summer of 1790 about 1,000 emigrants bound
for the Scioto sailed on a number of different ships. On arrival they learned to
their dismay that the company could not give clear title to the lands it had sold
since it held only a pre-emption on the tract from the Ohio Company; that the
lands were a long, hard journey from the coast; that travel down the Ohio was
unsafe because of an Indian war; that no provisions had been made, in spite of
specific promises, for the transportation of the emigrants or their shelter during

distressing and their adjustment to a different kind of life less painful.

Fear of the Indians will undoubtedly keep many Europeans away from these parts for a long time, but it does not stop Americans, who merely build their houses closer together. As the settlements increase, new settlers push forward and force the Indians to withdraw.

I must here describe to you these American frontiersmen, who are undoubtedly destined to change the face of this part of the world. The frontiersman likes hunting and prefers it to farming. He raises only what he needs for his own use or to pay for his pleasures. Detesting work and any sort of ties and with no attachment to the place he inhabits, he loves adventure and is easily enticed by descriptions of better opportunities and finer country somewhere else. He enjoys fighting and is ready and willing to go off to war in Canada or Louisiana, but he will not enroll for more than a year, for he is also a husband and father and he likes some home life at least for a part of the year.

The frontiersman is courageous, daring, unafraid of death, and contemptuous of the Indians. He can sleep as soundly in the middle of a forest as he would surrounded by neighbors. When a sudden Indian raid alarms a settlement and a family is murdered, people within a range of two or three miles may worry, but no one else is concerned. The Indians almost never attack except in small parties, and as soon as the alarm is given all the Americans in the area get together and go off to hunt these unhappy savages, whom they are slowly decimating, for the Indians are miserably bad fighters and they are always defeated in the end.[8]

the approaching winter; and finally that the company was on the edge of bankruptcy, for the misnamed Playfair had absconded with the Paris funds. The situation was made even more tragicomic by the character of the would-be settlers, a heterogeneous crowd of conservative aristocrats, adventurers, and ne'er-do-wells. Naturally there were loud repercussions in France, and the affair took on a political character. The leaders of the emigrants were conservative aristocrats, and the democrats were loudest in their denunciations, arguing that it would be better for Frenchmen to demonstrate their faith in the new regime by staying at home and helping to develop the country than to go off to hide in the American wilderness. The extent of Brissot's connections with the affair is not clear, but it is obvious that he was closely involved, if only by association. Writing here at the height of the controversy in 1791, he was caught between, on the one hand, his loyalty to his business associates and his record of enthusiasm for such schemes, and on the other the increasingly difficult political implications of the affair. His embarrassment is clear from the tone of both this note and the addendum to this chapter.]

[8] Americans have trained English purebred dogs to hunt the Indians. This is the only way to flush them out of their ambushes.

The Indians most to be feared are those along the shores of Lake Erie, the Creeks, the Cherokees, the Chahtas and the Chickasaws. They have recently been waging a cruel war against the inhabitants of Georgia and Cumberland.

If you wish a description of the Indians, read Penn's, which is still quite accurate: [9]

Strong, well built, agile, their skins dark from the paint they put on themselves, they have small black eyes like the Jews.[10] They rub grease on their bodies to protect themselves from the heat and cold. They eat venison, corn, beans, etc. Their language is lofty and concise. They love their children. They are generous, brave, honorable, and hospitable, but irascible and cruel when offended. They are accused of being cunning, shrewd, suspicious, thieving, gluttonous, and excessively vindictive. Their numbers are constantly diminishing because of wars, smallpox, liquor, abortions, and the hardships of their nomadic life.

It cannot be denied that the majority of their faults are the result of their contact with Europeans, who have taught them dishonesty. Never would the tomahawk have killed so cruelly had all the American frontiersmen been as peaceable and as honorable as the Quakers. The following story is but one example of the deceit practiced by Europeans. In one of the states an agreement was signed with the Indians according to which they would sell for a given sum of money as much land as a man could cover from sunrise to sunset. The English sent for a man reputed the fastest runner in America, who managed to cover three times as much ground as an ordinary man could have done. The Indians were furious at being tricked and immediately began a war.

The Indians' affection for the French is touching and indicative of their virtues and of the gratitude of which they are capable. A Frenchman can travel among them from Canada to Illinois without weapons and in complete security. The Indians can tell by his appearance, by his skin, and by his speech to what nation he belongs, and they entertain him as a brother. But if they find him in the company of Americans, he suffers the same cruelty as the Americans, whom they detest.

This hatred, which seems almost ineradicable, permits no hope

[9] See his *Letters to His Friends*, VI, 48. [This is an example of Brissot's casual documentation. *The American Museum* 7 (1790), 255–259 contains a piece by Penn on the Indians headed "Letter from W. Penn to his friends in London. Continued from vol. VI, page 48 [of the *American Museum*]." Brissot's quotation is actually a much condensed paraphrase of Penn's observations.]

[10] Penn believed that the Indians were descendants of the Jews.

that a lasting harmony will ever prevail between the two peoples. Congress is taking, however, wise precautions to put an end to fighting and war. Henceforth no private individual and no state may buy land from the Indians. Laws have been passed severely punishing Americans who hunt on Indian territory. Various treaties have been signed with the largest and most respected Indian tribes, such as the Creeks, who are commanded by the famous McGillivray.[11] Congress, under the leadership of Washington, has undertaken to pay them an annual subsidy of $1,500 for the land they have lost by the new treaty. You will also be pleased to hear that in order to encourage agriculture among the Indians Congress has promised to give them seeds, cattle, tools, and commissioners to instruct them.

These steps have been taken in the hope of slowly inducing the Indians to be peaceable but not with any expectation of leading them to adopt the ways of European civilization. Many examples discourage any such attempt. There have been cases of Indians who have been taken from their tribes in childhood, educated in schools, and raised among Europeans until they reached the age of twenty, who at their first visit to their own people took off their European dress and reverted to the independent Indian way of life, despite all efforts to stop them.

While making every effort to assure peace, Congress has not failed to take wise precautions to prevent Indian raids. Fort Franklin defends the frontiers of Pennsylvania and the Ohio is dotted with forts: Fort Harmar at the mouth of the Muskingum, Fort Steuben at the rapids of the Ohio, Post Vincennes on the Wabash, etc. All these posts contain well-trained troops, consisting of young volunteers who enlist for three years and who at the end of this time settle on lands in the area that are given to them, thus guaranteeing the security of the territory and at the same time contributing to its prosperity.

This change in policy by the American government will undoubtedly benefit the Indians, for the government is essentially peaceable by nature. It will, however, cause an upsurge in the Indian population, and then either the Indians will become civ-

---

[11] [Alexander McGillivray (c. 1759–1793), a half-breed leader of the Creeks who exercised considerable power. He sided with the British during the Revolution and later received subsidies from Spain in support of his efforts to establish a southern Indian confederation to block American expansion westward.]

ilized and be assimilated by the Americans or else a thousand causes will bring about their annihilation.

There is therefore no need to fear that the danger of the Indians will check the drive of the Americans in their mass progress toward the south. Everyone hopes that once navigation on the Mississippi becomes free, enormous markets will become available for the products which Americans produce in abundance and which are needed by the Spanish colonies. Will the Spaniards open this navigation willingly? Will the Americans have to force them to do so? This is the question. Negotiations are in progress, but they have been dragging on for four years. The suspicion exists that certain American states, fearing an emigration which would leave them stripped of population, are secretly backing the Spaniards. It is this covert support of the Spanish position which has given birth to the proposal that navigation on the Mississippi be closed for twenty-five years on condition that Americans have free trade with Spain. Virginia and Maryland, although they have the most to fear from western competition, have opposed this proposal on the ground that it is derogatory to the honor of the United States, and the majority of the other states have concurred.

The suspicions that Westerners have of the real intentions of the American government and of Congress are construed by some people as a sign that the Union will not last long and that there will be secession, particularly since the English of Canada are trying to persuade the Westerners to unite with them.

But I believe, for many reasons, that the Union will endure. The largest part of the land in the West belongs to men who live in the East; the continuous migrations from state to state keep the ties strong; and, finally, as it is in the interest of both Eastern and Western states to establish trade on a large scale with South America and to expand across the Mississippi, they must and will remain united in order to achieve these objectives.

Westerners are convinced that navigation on the Mississippi cannot remain closed for long. They are determined to get it, either amicably or by force; they will succeed, even if they have to preach a crusade to do so. Even Congress will not be able to check their will. Americans who have won their liberty and who are masters of the Ohio and of the Mississippi cannot conceive the insolence of a handful of hidalgos who are trying to deny to 80,000 Americans the freedom of the rivers and the seas. These ideas, which are fermenting in everyone's head, as well as the enormous profits made by those who smuggle goods into New Orleans and the nearby settlements, or get them in on a passport, are drawing crowds of immigrants into the area.[12] A small quarrel will be enough to inflame men's minds, and if ever the Americans march on New Orleans, it will fall before them.

Spain is afraid of just such an eventuality and is trying to postpone it, but the time of decision is at hand. She should open up the Mississippi, and then New Orleans would become a flourishing mart for the products of both the Spanish colonies and territories to the north. But Spain will not do this; the shortsighted and superstitious policy she follows is opposed to any such move. Spain fears above all the propagation of this idea of liberty which Americans carry with them wherever they go and whose success they preach by example. But this communication of ideas has already been made possible by a shabby trick the Spaniards have imagined in an effort to check the enterprising spirit of Free Americans. They are inducing Americans to settle on the western bank of the Mississippi in Louisiana by promising them the exclusive privilege of trading with New Orleans.[13] This colony will become the center of a most flourishing and successful smuggling operation, and it represents the first step toward the conquest of Louisiana and the peaceful civilization of Mexico and Peru.

May this come to pass soon, for the good of the human race! Consider how necessary it is, how possible it is, and what tremendous advantages will result for the whole world. For the men who settle here and plant the seeds of civilization will thereby increase the prosperity and population of all the industrial nations of Europe.

The French inhabitants of the five little Illinois villages tread scornfully upon the richest soil in the world. The French and the Spaniards living in the territories of the Natchez, on land which will grow any sort of crop, have not cleared a single acre in a hundred years. The Americans who have just settled there have

[12] Major Dohm, who traded there [in New Orleans] in 1788, told me that tobacco sold for ten dollars a quintal, while it costs only three or four in Virginia; that indigo was a dollar a pound and butter half a dollar. He estimated that a cargo worth $6,000 would sell for more than $30,000. Note that almost all trading is in cash. It is a fact that the Spanish government sends each year from Havana to New Orleans a million dollars to cover government expenses. Most of this money ends up in American pockets.

[13] This settlement was established by Colonel [George] Morgan [(1743–1810), land speculator and Indian agent, at New Madrid in 1789].

today more than three thousand farms of four hundred acres each, which are supplying the major part of the food consumed in New Orleans. O Liberty! Liberty! How great is your power! Out of your womb is born industry, which brings the dead to life.

Some distance from the Mississippi and along its navigable tributaries the Natchitoches, the Opelousas, and the Atakapas are languishing, their numbers not increasing, on a great plain 150 miles wide and 600 miles long containing vast natural meadows, forests, and arable land whose riches are equal to those of the most fertile countries in the world. Transport into these wonderful valleys the hardworking citizens of Massachusetts or the orderly and sober Quakers, and what immense riches will they draw from the bosom of this bountiful land! They will produce wealth which, overflowing into the rest of the world, will make basic foodstuffs less expensive, increase employment, and reduce the number of paupers. The indolence and ignorance which condemn so beautiful a country to be an empty wasteland are digging the graves of unborn generations.

I sometimes imagine myself living a hundred years from now, and I see these wild forests replaced, not by cities, but by scattered farms stretching without interruption from New Hampshire to Quito.[14] I see happiness and labor hand in hand. I see beauty adorning the daughters of nature, liberty and virtue rendering government and laws almost unnecessary, sweet tolerance replacing the cruel Inquisition. I see a festival in which Peruvians, Mexicans, Free Americans, and Frenchmen embrace one another as brothers, anathematizing tyranny and blessing the reign of liberty which brings all men into universal harmony. But what will become of the mines and the slaves? The mines will be shut. The slaves will be the brothers of their masters, and they will deserve to be their equals by sharing their knowledge and their way of life. But what will men do without gold, that cynosure of universal greed? It is not right for a free people to seek it if they must use the hands of slaves to wrest it from the earth. Will a free people ever be without some token by which they can exchange their goods? Gold has served despotism better than it has liberty, and freedom can always find a less dangerous medium of exchange.

[14] There will never be in America great cities like London or Paris in which all wealth and power are concentrated. Money will be more equally distributed over the whole nation, the population will be larger and less subject to corruption, employment will be more general, and happiness more universal.

Our speculators are far from understanding that two revolutions are being prepared in the New World, revolutions which will change completely the commercial theories and practices of Europe. These will be the opening of a canal between the Atlantic and the Pacific and the abandonment of the mines of Peru.

Forgive me, my friend, if I do not dwell on all the many other changes which must be the inevitable consequences of American ideas, American enterprise, and the American character.

What is the American character? The following lines from *Tristram Shandy* define it rather well:

Nature, like a good mother, has shown the same kindness to them all. She has observed such an equal tenor in the distribution of her favors, as to bring nearly all the inhabitants to a level with each other; so that you will meet with few instances here of great genius, but you will find in all the inhabitants and in all classes good sense, understanding, and knowledge of all that concerns domestic happiness and the rights of man. Everybody has a share of this understanding, which is right. With us English, the case is quite different; we are all ups and downs. You are a great genius, or 'tis fifty to one you are a dunce. The extremes are more common than the mean.[15]

General prosperity can be found only in this mean. There can be no slavery where all men are equally enlightened. It is difficult for despotism to creep in when all men's eyes are opened and watching, when *each man* is free and has his own principles. What has restored despotism almost everywhere? These very two "extremes" of which Sterne speaks—the men of power or genius who use the ignorant populace as a weapon with which to destroy the enlightened but aristocratic middle order. Here in America there are no men of great power, no men of genius, no aristocratic middle order, no populace.

[15] [We have rendered into English Brissot's French version of this passage, but to do justice to Sterne and to enlighten those of Sterne's readers who may be bewildered, we give these lines in their pristine form:

"Nature was neither very lavish, nor was she very stingy in her gifts of genius and capacity to its [Denmark's] inhabitants;—but, like a discreet parent, was moderately kind to them all; observing such an equal tenor in the distribution of her favors, as to bring them, in those points, pretty near to a level with each other; so that you will meet with few instances in that kingdom of refined parts; but a great deal of good plain household understanding amongst all ranks of people, of which everybody has a share; which is, I think, very right.

"With us, you see, the case is quite different:—we are all ups and downs in this matter;—you are a great genius;—or 'tis fifty to one, Sir, you are a great dunce and a blockhead;—not that there is total want of intermediate steps,—no,—we are not so irregular as that comes to;—but the two extremes are more common, and in a greater degree in this unsettled island . . ." *Tristram Shandy*, I, xi. (*Complete Works*, ed. W. L. Cross [New York, 1899], I, 41–42.)]

THE NEW EMPIRE OF THE WEST

NOTE ON THE SCIOTO COLONY

I believe I ought to reprint here an article I find in the *Moniteur* of April 16, 1791. It confirms what I have said about the Scioto Colony on pages 416 and 417. It seems to me that these facts indicate that for both political and humanitarian reasons we should continue to support this project which, I repeat, will certainly be useful both to France and to the unhappy people who are to be resettled there. A sacrifice of several hundred thousand livres could buy the happiness of many millions of men.

The latest news received here from the French colony on the Scioto has been most satisfactory. The company heading this enterprise has felt obliged to make sacrifices in order to encourage the new settlement. First it assisted the emigrants in finding means to make the trip; then after their arrival it distributed considerable quantities of bread, meat, brandy, and other provisions, which made it possible for the settlers to await their first harvest. It is also employing, at its own expense, fifty hunters whose only duty is to provide venison for the settlers. Finally, it has sent a large number of American workers to help cut wood and build houses.

Supported by all this assistance, the settlers have started work enthusiastically and already have good reason to look forward to the best of success. The fertility of the land is even greater than what they had been led to expect; vegetables are, in general, of the best quality, and sugar maples are so plentiful that they will not need to import sugar from the Antilles and in fact are considering the possibility of exporting their own surplus.

Some of the French have already married Kentucky women. The colony contains about seven hundred settlers, all of whom seem very happy with their lot except for those who, having some money, expected to enjoy a greater degree of consideration and have found themselves deceived in their expectations. In spite of their elegant furniture and the fine food they serve they receive no special marks of respect and no one comes to call on them. The farmers are the ones who enjoy the greatest esteem, for here public respect is usually proportionate to the usefulness of a man's occupation.

The largest of the French settlements, Gallipolis, is no more than a fifteen-day journey from New York and is located on the northern bank of the Ohio, opposite the mouth of the Great Kanawha River, which facilitates travel to Virginia. Another settlement, which is just starting, will be called Aiglelys.[16]

There is, as yet, no government properly speaking, but it is easy to see already a general tendency toward democratic government. Until the time comes when they can establish laws, the settlers have designated from among themselves several persons of recognized ability and prudence to settle any disagreements that may arise.

[16] [(Eagle-lily.) There was, so far as is known, no such permanent settlement.]

INDEX

Abbeville, Le Havre trade, 71, 74

Abingdon, Md., 341n

Abolition, *see* Antislavery societies; Emancipation; Negroes; Slave trade; Slavery

Académie des Sciences, 396n

Académie Française, 309n

Accounting, by states, 54–55

Adams, John, xvi, 11, 86n, 101–103, 125; *Defence of the Constitutions of the United States*, 228n

Adams, Samuel, 104

Adeline, French dancer, 374n

Adresse à l'Assemblée Nationale par la Société des Amis des Noirs, 252n

Adultery, 86, 257

Africa, 65, 68–73, 93, 116, 146n, 149, 217, 250–252, 409–410

Agricultural societies, 197–198

Agriculture, in France, 61, 207n; in U.S., 34–35, 56, 197–198, 223–224, 246–248, 259, 326, 395, 398–399, 401–403: Connecticut, 116–117, 197–198, 237; Georgia, 350n; Maryland, 230–231, 237, 339, 346–347, 351n, 353; Massachusetts, 91, 102, 363; Mississippi Valley, 237, 353, 355; New Hampshire, 120, 363, 368; New Jersey, 161; New York, 142–143, 248; Ohio Valley, 215, 237, 355, 416n, 425n; Pennsylvania, 162–163, 197–199, 203–211, 213, 237, 247–248, 264–273, 276, 358–361, 401; Virginia, 207n, 231, 237, 342–343, 346–348, 350–353, 358–359; the Western Territories, 422–423

Aiglelys, Ohio, 425n

Ajan, Africa, 217n

Albany, N.Y., 138–139, 262, 281; foreign trade, 406; population, 262

Albany Congress (1754), 188

Alcibiades, 5

Alembert, J. L., d', article "Genève" in *Encyclopédie*, 90

Alexandria, Va., xxi, 341–342, 345–346, 352, 356, 359

Algiers, 243

Allegheny Mts., 357, 413

Allen, Ethan, *Reason the Only Oracle of Man*, French translation, 97n

Allen, James, 97n

Alliance (ship), 405n, 410

Almshouses, in Boston, 99; Quaker, 326

Altamaha R., Ga., 223n

Ameland, Miss (Quaker), 167

Ameland, Samuel, 194

American Academy of Arts and Sciences, 95, 97, 287, 290; *Memoirs*, 95, 97, 285

American Museum, 98, 189n, 192n, 193n, 198n, 234n, 235n, 236n, 259, 274n, 291n, 419n

American Philosophical Society, 186

Americanism, xviii–xix, 298n

Americans in France, xii, xix, xxvi, xx, 80, 328n, 398n

Amiens, products, 74; trade with Le Havre, 71

Amsterdam, foreign trade, 73

Anabaptists, 88

Anaxagoras, 320

Andover, Mass., 285–286, 369–370

André (preacher), 135n

Ann Street, Boston, 84n

Annuities, 284

Anti-Federalists, 125n, 148

Antislavery societies, xx, 64–65, 146n, 168, 219, 222, 224, 226, 228–231, 234n, 238–244, 246–247, 325

Anti-Trinitarians, 322

Apthorp, Frances Theodora (Fanny), 86n, 118n

Apthorp, James, 86n

Archaeology, *see* Prehistory

Architecture, 202, 234n, 255; *see also* Houses

Arkwright's spinning jenny, 399

Aristocratic spirit, 10, 298n

Aristocrats, French, xxiv–xxv, 298n, 317, 416–417n, 418n

Army, American, 268, 420

Army, French, in U.S., 310, 337–338

Arrêt du conseil of 1784 on French import duties, 398n

Arts and sciences, xxv, 44, 85, 98–99, 126, 253, 257–258

Assemblées primaires, France, 10n

Assemblies, state, *see* individual states

Assignats, 127n

Asylums, in France, 174, 178, 180; *see also* Bettering house; Hospitals

Atakapa Indians, 423

Atlantic Neptune, 367n

INDEX

Austrian Flanders, 61–62, 129, 133, 346n; products, 68n, 69; trade with Le Havre, 71

Aveland, Mrs. (innkeeper), 126

Babat (French minister), 331

Bache, B. F., 189, 337

Bache, Richard, 193

Bailey (American doctor), 282

Balance of trade, 389; of U.S., 401–402

Balch, Mr. (hatter), 105n

Baltimore, Md., 260–261, 339–341, 358

Bank of North America, 268, 411–412

Bank of the State of New York, 151

Banks, 54, 151, 268, 411–412

Banks, Joseph, 408–409

Barbados, 219–220

Barbeu Dubourg, Jacques, 337n

Barcelona, products, 405n; trade with Le Havre, 74

Barclay, Robert, *Apologie*, 321n

Barlow, Joel, 417n; translator of *New Travels*, xxvi–xxvii, 264n

Barrell, Colborn, 252n

Barrett, Samuel, 105, 362

Bassett, Fanny, 343–344

Bayonne, coasting trade, 72

Beauce, 61

Beaumarchais, 373–374n; *Requête à MM. les Représentants de la Commune de Paris*, 373n

Beauvais, products, 68, 73

Bedford, Dr. (of Pittsburgh), 276

Belknap, Jeremy, *The History of New Hampshire*, 97n, 287

Benevolent Institution, Philadelphia, 262

Benezet, Anthony, 166, 194, 203, 218–219, 222, 230, 318; *Observations sur l'origine des Quakers*, 321n

Bengal, Bay of, 404

Bergasse, Nicolas, xviii, 201

Bernardin de Saint Pierre, *Etudes de la nature*, 180

Bettering House, Philadelphia, 173–178; *see also* Hospitals; Prisons; Workhouses

Beverly, Mass., 363

Bhagavad-Gita, 306n

Billings, Mr. (Englishman in Russia), 408

Bingham, William, 314; *Letter from an American on Lord Sheffield's Pamphlet*, 402n

Birth rate, in Philadelphia, 292–293; *see also* Life expectancy

Bladensburg, Md., 341

Blair, Hugh, *Lectures on Rhetoric and Belles Lettres*, 77–78

Blaskowitz, Charles, *Topographical Map of New Hampshire*, 367n

Block Island, 136

Blue Mountains, 356

Bolbec, Normandy, 62

Bordeaux, 63; coasting trade, 72; products, 73, 163; trade with U.S., 92n

Boston, xi, xx–xxi, 82–106, 129, 362, 365; Almshouse, 99; banks, 412; Church of the Holy Cross, 88n; coffeehouse, 91; fire of 1787, 149; fishing, 81; foreign trade, 405n, 406, 410; Humane Society, 99; manufacturing, 399, 401; market, 129; merchant marine, 106, 404–405; streets, 84; Workhouse, 100

Boston Harbor, 82–83

Bothnia, Gulf of, 408

Bottes, Normandy, 62

Boudinot, Elias, 244

Bourbon I., 92; imports from U.S., 405, 411n

Bourgoing, J. F., *Nouveau voyage en Espagne*, 81n, 354–355

Bourgoyne's invasion, 367

Bowdoin, James, 86n, 91, 93n, 95–96, 105

Braintree, Mass., 102

Brandenburg, Germany, 289

Brandywine, Del., 336–337

Brazil, foreign trade, 355

Breck (Break), Samuel, 91, 105

Bremen, imports from U.S., 401n; trade with Le Havre, 73–74

Breslau, Germany, 285, 289

Bridges, 94, 115, 152, 362–363

Brissot de Warville, J. P., his Americanism, xviii–xix, 298n; and antislavery movement, xv–xvii, xx–xxii; and aristocracy, xvii, xxiv–xxv; and democracy, xvii; ideology, xxii–xxvi; name, xi, 25; Quakers, interest in, xiv–xvii, xx–xxi, xxiii–xxv; as thinker, xxi–xxii;

life, ix, xi–xxi; founds Lycée de Londres, xii, xiv; in Bastille, xii, 77; interest in U.S., xii–xx, 67; founds Société des Amis des Noirs, xviii; business ventures, xviii–xix, xxi; itinerary of travels in U.S., xx–xxi; elected to New York Manumission Society, xx, 164n, 239–240; elected to Pennsylvania Society for Promoting the Abolition of Slavery, 239–240; signs contract with Craigie and Duer, xxi; relations with Scioto Company, 418n;

INDEX

INDEX

INDEX

INDEX

INDEX

433

INDEX

Franklin, Benjamin (*continued*)
character, 182–185, 189, 191–192; death, 182, 190–193; eulogies of, 182n, 183n, 184n, 190–191; as journalist, 185; rules for Junto, 187; letters, 188n, 189; president of Pennsylvania Society for Promoting the Abolition of Slavery, 185n; *An Address to the Public*, 241; *Autobiography*, 183n, 193; *Historical Review of the Constitution and Government of Pennsylvania*, 330n; *Plan for Improving the Condition of Free Blacks*, 242n; *Poor Richard's Almanack*, 186; *La Science du Bonhomme Richard*, 186n; "Way to Wealth," 186n
Franklin, John, 189
Franklin, Temple, 160–161, 188n
Franklin, W. T., 193
Franklin, William, 193
Franklin, William, *Observations Made on a Tour from Bengal to Persia*, 193n
Franklin, Fort, 420
Franklin, state of, 414
Free America and Free Americans, 29n
Free trade, 392
French, in the United States, xix–xx, 21, 58, 162n, 203–216, 240n, 273, 276, 295, 337–339, 341, 346, 366, 394, 416–419, 422–423, 425; merchants, 259–260, 314
French and Indian War, 328
French language in U.S., 394
French West Indies, 66, 246; exports to U.S., 390, 392
Friends, Society of, *see* Quakers
Front St., Philadelphia, 255
Frontier life, 215–216, 251, 264–269, 417n, 418–419
Frossard, Benjamin S., *La Cause des esclaves nègres*, 64n
Fuller, Thomas, 235–236
Fur trade, 139, 383, 398, 406

Gallinas R., Africa, 70n
Gallipolis, Ohio, 212n, 425n
Gallois, J. A. G., 154n
Galvez, José de, 212
Gambia R., Africa, 70n
Gates, Horatio, 241
Gay, Ebenezer, 287
Geneva, xii, 90
Geography, 356–357, 413–414
George, Lake, 139
Georgetown, Md., 341, 359
Georgia, 419; agriculture and prices, 350n; immigration to, 350n; legisla-

tion on slave trade, 223, 225; Negro slavery, 223n, 225; Quakers, 319, 323
Gérard, Michel, 10
German Society for Encouraging Immigration from Germany, 262
Germans in U.S., 204–206, 262, 271–272, 359
Germany, life expectancy in, 285–286, 289; products, 69; trade with Le Havre, 71
Gerry, Elbridge, 244
Gilbert, N. J. L., 257
Gilpin, Mr. (paper mill owner), 337
Girondin party, ix
Good Hope, Cape of, 407; imports from U.S., 92, 405–406
Gore, Christopher, 105
Gorée, Africa, 70
Gorham, Nathaniel, 106
Gothenburg, 92
Government, city, 254; employment in, 100; international, 13; and liberty, 14–15;
state, 53, constitutions, 31, finance, 54–55, 150–151, law, 297, legislation on slave trade, 101, 223–229, 294, legislation on slavery, 227–230, 240, 242–243, police ordinances, 53, 200; salaries of officials, 100–101;
United States, 29–33, 52–53, 150, civil legislation, 53, Congress, 38–41, 140, 147, 215, 223–225, 243–245, 332, 371–382, 384, 386–388, 393, 411, 420–421, credit, 49, 147, 373, 378, 380–384, 387–388, 411, criminal law, 53, debt (*see* Debt, national), expenditures, 375–378, House of Representatives, 401, Indian treaties, 420, laws, 161, leaders, 18, 20, legislation on slavery and slave trade, 224–226, 243–245, loans, 373, 377–381, 387, monetary system, 53–54, Post Office Department, 377, restrictions on, 14, 33, revenue, 376–377, 382–383, 387, 393; salaries of officials, 375–376; taxes and duties, 376–377, 393–394
See also individual states and cities; Constitutions
Grand Turk (ship), 93n
Grant, Daniel, 340
Grant, James, *Topographical Map of New Hampshire*, 367n
Grant's Tavern, Baltimore, 340
Granville, trade, 71
Gras (Paris bookseller), 321n
Gravesend, England, 316

INDEX

INDEX

INDEX

La Rochelle, coasting trade, 72
Lauzun's Legion, 337–338
Law, 8, 9, 15 297; criminal, 53; English, 100, 297; and liberty, 14
Laws, 161; Maryland, 339; Pennsylvania, 265, 268
Lawyers, 100–101; in New York City, 144
Lay, Benjamin, 220; *All Slave Keepers That Keep the Innocent in Bondage, Apostates,* 219n, 220n
Leaders of U.S., 18, 20
Ledyard, John, 407–410
Le Gaux, M. (French farmer in Pa.), 203–211, 276
Legislation, civil, 53. *See also* Government, state and U.S.; individual states
Le Havre, xx, 61–74, 364, 398n; commerce, 68–74
Le Mans, products, 74
Les Oualos, Africa, 70
Les Poules, Africa, 70
Létombe, Philippe, 21n
Letters of Publius, The, 52
Lettres de la Société des Amis des Noirs à M. Necker, 252n
Lettsom, J. C., 325n
Le Veillard, Louis, 183n
Lexington, Ky., 415
Liberty, xi–xii, xv–xvi, xviii, xx, xxiii–xxiv, 22–23, 30–31, 67, 75, 84, 145, 157, 267, 272, 280, 284, 367, 371n, 415, 422–424; defined, 3; depends on moral principles and reason, 3–8, 13–16; effects of, 13; in England, 263n; in France, xi, 10, 12, 23, 102, 334–335; liberty and government, 14–15; liberty and law, 14; liberty and rural life, 9
Library Company of Philadelphia, 197–198, 255
Liége, 129, 133; products, 68n, 69
Life expectancy, tables, xxiv, 288–291; in countries of Europe, 285, 286, 288–289, 291, 292; in U.S., 283–294; in Connecticut, 285, 291n; of Harvard graduates, 286–288; of Lutherans, 292–293; in Massachusetts, 283, 285–288, 291–293; in New England, 286, 288; in New Hampshire, 285, 287–288, 291n; in New Jersey, New York, 291n; in Pennsylvania, 275, 277–278, 291n, 292–293; of Quakers, 301
Life insurance companies, 11, 292
Lille, products, 74
Linguet, Simon, xxi
Lisbon, Conn., 291n

Lisbon, Portugal, 396n
Literature, xxv, 17; in U.S., 253, 257–258, 394
Livingston, H. B., 153–154, 156, 257
Livingston, Nancy Shippen, 257
Livingston, William, 153–154, 228
Locke, John, xxi
London, England, xxi, 354; life expectancy in, 288, 291
Londonderry, N.H., 363
Long Island, 136, 139, 143
Longevity, *see* Life expectancy
Lorraine, trade, 71
Louis XIV, 125, 218
Louisiana, xxiii, 216, 355, 357, 407, 418, 422
Louviers, products, 74
Lowell, John, 101
Loyalists, 263, 366
Lübeck, Le Havre trade, 73–74
Ludlow, Edmund, 15, 103n
Ludlow, Vt., 103n
Lutherans, 171, 292–293
Luxury, xxv, 7, 142, 301–303, 307, 342, 347, 349, 359
Lycée de Londres, xii, xiv, 299–300
Lynn, Mass., 362
Lynn St., Boston, 84n
Lyons, trade, 71, 73–74

Macao, 410
Macaulay, Mr. (of London), 405n
Macaulay, Catherine, 311
Madeira, exports to U.S., 395
Madison, James, 146–148, 244, 401–402; *The Federalist,* 52n, 148
Magee, James, 406n
Malden, Mass., 362
Malden R., Mass., 94
Mail, *see* Postal systems
Maine, 103, 406
Maintenon, Mme de, 218
Maistre, Joseph de, ix–x
Manchester Literary and Philosophical Society, *Memoirs,* 264n
Manners, 57, 109, 279, 301, 395: in Connecticut, 118; in Massachusetts, 85–86, 90–91, 363, 368; in New Hampshire, 368; in New York City, 141–142, 145, 150; in North Carolina, 353; in Pennsylvania, 162, 199–201, 205, 208, 254, 256, 265, 267, 269, 280; in South Carolina, 353; in Virginia, 347–348, 353. *See also* Character; Morals

INDEX

INDEX

INDEX

INDEX

York, 151, 412; in North Carolina, 147; in Pennsylvania, 174, 259, 263, 412; in Rhode Island, xxiii, 127–132, 227, 293

Parcieux, Antoine de, *Essai sur les probabilités de la durée de la vie humaine*, 286, 289

Paris, 417n; fire insurance companies, 263; hospital, 178; life expectancy in, 292; products, 74; trade with Le Havre, 71

Parker, Daniel, xix

Parlements, France, xvii

Parliament, English, compensations, 263, 366

Parnell, James, 88n

Parraud (translator), 306n, 414

Patapsco R., Md., 340

Patriote français, Le, ix, 25n, 190

Patriotism, 6–7, 132

Paulus Hook, N.J., 152

Pauw, Corneille de, xxiii; *Recherches philosophiques sur les Américains*, 283; *Défense des Recherches philosophiques*, 283; "Amérique," *Supplément à l'Encyclopédie*, 283

Peale, C. W., 198n

Peale's Museum, 198n

Pease, Mr. (stage owner), 107–108

Peekskill, N.Y., 122n

Peking, China, 276

Pemberton, James, 168, 305, 334

Penn, William, xiv, 15, 37, 159, 184n, 253–256, 263, 269, 301, 330, 336; *Exposition des Quakers*, 321n; letters, 419; *Some Fruits of Solitude*, 300, 302, 304; *Works*, 321n

Penn family, 188, 263, 330

Pennington, Edward, 247

Pennsylvania, 14, 58, 93, 113, 115, 158–159, 161–164, 319, 325, 336, 356, 366, 378, 400, 420; agriculture, 162–163, 197–199, 203–211, 213, 237, 247–248, 264–273, 276, 358–361, 401; Catholics, 334; climate, 210–211, 213, 261, 274–278, 291, 360; diseases in, 274–275, 277–278; economic conditions, 256, 259–261, 358, 391; emigration to the South, 269–270, 357; Executive Council, 197, 203, 297, 332; foreign trade, 261, 358, 390–392, 401–402, 410; General Assembly, 174, 202–203, 209, 228–230, 255, 297, 305; government, 164; houses, 163, 203, 254–255, 264–269; laws, 265, 268; legislation on slavery and slave trade, 226, 228–230, 240, 242–243; life expectancy in, 275, 277–278, 291n; manners and morals, 162, 185, 199–205, 208, 254, 256–262, 265–271, 280, 295, 359, 392; manufacturing, 188, 199, 260–261, 395n, 399–401, 403; medicine, 282; Negroes, 237; paper money, 174, 259, 263, 412; Penn family, 263; prices, 113, 178, 199, 201, 203–204, 205n, 207–210, 215, 261–262, 268, 271–273, 349, 358–359, 361, 399; Quakers, 319, 323, 327, 329–334; settlements in, 261, 264–273, 319, 359–360; slave trade, 240; state debt, 385n; Swedes in, 159; taxes, 206–207, 265, 268, 272; travel in, 159, 216, 254–255

Pennsylvania Hospital for the Insane, 179–181

Pennsylvania Journal, 334

Pennsylvania Society for Promoting the Abolition of Slavery, 64, 168n, 228–230, 234n, 238–244, 325; *An Address to the Public*, 241

Percival, Thomas, 264n

Peru, 422–424

Philadelphia, xxi, 98, 159–160, 208–209, 212–214, 216–218, 220, 226, 246, 305, 315, 325, 331–332, 336, 340, 359; banks, 411–412; Benevolent Institution, 262; Bettering House, 173–178; birth and death rates, 292–293; Christ Church Hospital, 234n; climate, 274, 276–277; Dispensary, 262; doctors, 180–181, 233n, 234n, 235, 282; economic conditions, 256, 259–261; fire insurance companies, 263; foreign trade, 261, 377, 402, 410; government, 254; Hibernian Club, 262; Library, 197–198, 255; Lutherans, 292–293; manners and morals, 199–201, 254, 256–257, 280; manufacturing, 260–261, 399–400, 403; market, 129, 199–200; militia, 333; police ordinances, 200; population, 262; Presbyterians, 331; prices, 199, 201, 205n, 358, 403; prison, 295; prostitution, 173, 177; shipbuilding, 403; Society for Alleviating the Miseries of Publc Persons, 262; State House, 202, 234, 255; streets, 255; women, 279–280

Philadelphia Contributionship for the Insurance of Houses Against Fire, 263

Philadelphia Society for Promoting Agriculture, 197–198

Phillips, James, 321n

441

INDEX

INDEX

Quakers and government, 14, 200, 254, 295, 328; hospitals, 145–146, 326; Irish, 323, 326; life expectancy of, 301; meetings, 160, 168–172, 228, 253, 279, 300–301, 303, 307, 319, 322–325, 332–333; ministers, 169–171; morals, 162, 199–200, 254, 256, 260–262, 300; political principles, pacifism, 327–335; religious principles and practices, 162, 224, 256, 262, 302, 321–326; school for Negroes in Philadelphia, 198, 217–219; Shaking Quakers, 370; Wet Quakers, 301; whalers in Dunkirk, 80, 328n, 398n; women, 279–280, 283, 301–302, 305, 323; writings on, 321;

in Delaware, 230, 319, 337; in Georgia, 319, 323; in Maryland, 230–231, 319, 323, 341; in Massachusetts, 87–88, 319, 362; in Nantucket, 80, 316n, 328n, 398n; in New England, 323; in New Hampshire, 319; in New Jersey, 319, 323; in New York, 138, 142, 145–146, 319, 323, 333; in North Carolina, 319, 323; in Pennsylvania, 319, 323, 327, 329–334; in Rhode Island, 130, 132, 227; in South Carolina, 319, 323; in Virginia, 319, 323, 329, 333

Quarries, 203

Racine, 95; cited, 130n
Raguet (French traveler), 213
Rates of exchange, 100, 107, 143n, 161, 201, 358n, 399, 411n
Raynal, Abbé, xxiii, 311; *Histoire philosophique et politique*, 202, 255, 320n
Ré, I., France, 286
Read (ship captain), 410
Read, Deborah, 185
Reading, Mass., 362
Red Stone, Pa., 319
Reed, Joseph, 332
Regimentation, 33
Reims, products, 74
Religion, 13, 31, 57, 86–90, 135, 184n, 266–267, 369. See also Catholics, Quakers, etc.
Representative government, 23–24n, 133
Representatives, House of, 401
Republicanism, 15–16, 41, 116, 133, 150, 157–158, 223. See also Democracy
Réunion I., see Bourbon I.
Revenue, of federal government, 376–377, 382–383, 387, 393; of states, 54: New York, 150–151

Revolution, American, xii, xv, xix, xxiii, 20–21, 32–33, 140, 203, 226, 268, 270, 292, 305, 316, 328, 331–332, 346, 366–367, 371n, 398, 402
Revolution, French, ix–xi, xvii, xxvii, 3, 8, 10n, 15n, 17, 22, 212n, 345, 356, 396n, 417n; leaders of, 4–7, 9
Rhode Island, 127–136, 200n, 310, 369; climate, 369; economic conditions and paper money, xxiii, 127–132, 227, 293; emigration to the West, 133, 415; government, 129, 132–133; morals, xxiii, 130–133, 227, 257; population, 293; prices, 128, 130, 136; Quakers, 130, 132, 227; slavery, 128n, 227; travel in, 127–128, 134, 136
Richardson, Mr. (of Middletown, Pa.), 162–163, 248
Richmond, Va., 349, 351, 353, 358
Rittenhouse, David, 272
Roads, 108, 110, 113–114, 126–127, 152–153, 155, 158–159, 339, 341–342, 362, 366; in France, 400
Roberts, John, 331–332
Robertson, James, 414n
Robin, Abbé C. C., 299n; *Nouveau voyage dans l'Amérique Septentrionale*, 283
Robinson, Mrs. (of Salem, Mass.), 363
Robinson, William, 87n
Rockport, Mass., 370
Rohan, Henri, Duc de, *Mémoires*, 330–331
Roland de La Platière, J. R., xviii, 247n
Roland, Mme, 247n, 298n
Rotch, Benjamin, 80n, 316
Rotch, William, 80n, 316
Rouen, 62, 398n; products, 68–69, 73–74, 163; trade with Le Havre, 71–72
Rousseau, J. J., xiii–xiv, xvii xxi, 57, 184; *Contrat social*, xiv; *Nouvelle Héloïse*, xiv
Rousselot de Surgy, *Histoire naturelle et politique de la Pensylvanie*, 246n
Royal Society, London, 408n, 409–410
Rumsey, James, 194
Rural life, 8–9, 112
Rush, Benjamin, 180–181, 233n, 234n, 235, 247, 274–278, 282, 297; *Account of the Climate of Pennsylvania*, 274n; *An Account of the Progress of Population, Agriculture, Manners and Government in Pennsylvania*, 264–271; *Essays, Literary, Moral and Philosophical*, 264n

INDEX

INDEX

INDEX

447

THE JOHN HARVARD LIBRARY

*The intent of
Waldron Phoenix Belknap, Jr.,
as expressed in an early will, was for
Harvard College to use the income from a
permanent trust fund he set up, for "editing and
publishing rare, inaccessible, or hitherto unpublished
source material of interest in connection with the
history, literature, art (including minor and useful
art), commerce, customs, and manners or way of
life of the Colonial and Federal Periods of the United
States . . . In all cases the emphasis shall be on the
presentation of the basic material." A later testament
broadened this statement, but Mr. Belknap's interests remained constant until his death.*

*In linking the name of the first benefactor of
Harvard College with the purpose of this later,
generous-minded believer in American culture the
John Harvard Library seeks to emphasize the importance of Mr. Belknap's purpose. The John Harvard
Library of the Belknap Press of Harvard University
Press exists to make books and documents
about the American past more readily
available to scholars and the
general reader.*